W9-DIT-089

James Barbour,
A Jeffersonian Republican

An oil painting of James Barbour, c. 1827,
by Chester Harding.
Courtesy of the Virginia Museum.

James Barbour,
A
Jeffersonian
Republican

CHARLES D. LOWERY

THE UNIVERSITY OF ALABAMA PRESS

HOUSTON PUBLIC LIBRARY

RO156080969
SSC

Copyright © 1984 by
The University of Alabama Press
University, Alabama 35486
All rights reserved
Manufactured in the United States of America

Library of Congress Cataloging in Publication Data

Lowery, Charles D., 1937–
    James Barbour, a Jeffersonian Republican.

    Bibliography: p.
    Includes index.
    1. Barbour, James, 1775–1842. 2. Virginia—Politics
and government—1775–1865. 3. United States—Politics
and government—1817–1825. 4. United States—Foreign
relations—1825–1829. 5. Statesmen—United States—
Biography. 6. Virginia—Governors—Biography.
I. Title.
E340.B23L85 1984   985.5'03'0924 [B]   83-3453
ISBN 0-8173-0175-5

For Susie,

Tom, Trent, and Dan

Contents

Illustrations

Preface

This biography describes a little-known but important Virginian of the Jeffersonian period who is remembered today, when he is remembered at all, for his central role in the Missouri Compromises. His obscurity is undeserved. An eminent agriculturalist and an outspoken social reformer, he was also a prominent political leader whose active participation in state and national affairs during the formative first four decades of the nineteenth century exerted a positive influence upon the country's history.

Barbour's life provides an interesting and unusual portrait of a Jeffersonian Republican whose interpretation of republicanism differed significantly from that of his contemporaries. If we exclude the principal party leaders Jefferson, Madison, and Monroe, he stands in a category apart from other Virginia Republican leaders of his generation. Of all his many able and politically active contemporaries—John Taylor, Spencer Roane, John Randolph, Philip Pendleton Barbour, Thomas Ritchie, William B. Giles, and John Tyler—he alone embraced the progressive spirit and liberal political faith of the Jeffersonian age and avoided the pitfall of regional particularism into which the rest ultimately fell. His contemporaries treated the Jeffersonian political philosophy as fixed dogma, as static principles which they relentlessly tried to impose upon the national government to restrain its power. He viewed the same philosophy as organic doctrine which, to remain viable, must evolve and change with the times. He was, in short, the exception to the political rule in Virginia—a practical-minded political moderate who grafted onto the dominant political philosophy of his day those elements of the nationalist creed that were necessary for governing a dynamic, changing nation.

In addition to chronicling the life and times of a man who has long warranted a biography, this book attempts to understand Barbour in the context of his culture. His career dramatizes in interesting ways many of the problems and contradictions of his culture and details his personal struggle to cope with important changes occurring in the patterns of American life and thought. His life provides a window through which his age can be viewed. It also affords another and somewhat different vantage point for viewing party politics, both in Virginia and the nation, and for assessing the impact that individuals like him exerted on political affairs; for understanding how the Virginia Republican party functioned, who its leaders were, and how they acquired and exercised leadership; and for discerning the relative importance of the diverse economic, social, and political forces that shaped the collective political mind of Virginia during the Jeffersonian period and placed the state, ultimately, on a sectionalist course. The present volume sheds new light on many of the political issues in which Barbour was involved—the development of nationalism, the Missouri Controversy, Indian affairs, foreign relations, and the emergence of the Whig party. Furthermore, it traces the life of an important Jeffersonian who participated in exciting events that shaped the nation's future and details the difficulties that he, a southern nationalist, encountered in relating to an increasingly reactionary political constituency.

Barbour has had no biographer. The sketch of him by Dumas Malone in the *Dictionary of American Biography,* a short biographical essay by William S. Long in the *John P. Branch Historical Papers of Randolph-Macon College,* and my own essay on Barbour and agricultural reform in *America: The Middle Period; Essays in Honor of Bernard Mayo,* edited by John B. Boles, represent all the published material. The tardiness of this biography may be attributed largely to the paucity of personal material in Barbour's papers at the New York Public Library. That collection, which consists mainly of political correspondence in the 1820s and 1830s, was until recently the only source of materials available to scholars. The lifting of restrictions on Barbour's major collection of papers at the University of Virginia Library in recent years has made it possible to explore his life more fully. The latter collection, extensive as it is, has large omissions, especially where personal correspondence is concerned. By making a thorough search of major research libraries throughout the country, I was able to find additional letters which fill some but not all of the gaps.

I am indebted to many people who have shared in the work of preparing this biography. Bernard Mayo of the University of Virginia, who directed the dissertation on which this biography is based, provided perceptive insights and scholarly judgments, from which I benefited immeasurably. My colleagues at Mississippi State University who read various drafts or sections of the manuscript, and offered valuable suggestions for which I am grateful, included Glover Moore, Lyell C. Behr, John Marszalek, E. Stanley Godbold, and William Parrish. Howard Ball, at the University of Utah, gave more than he knows. To all of these people, who have saved me from mistakes and errors of judgment, I am heavily indebted. The failings of the book are my own.

Manuscript librarians at the repositories listed in the bibliography were most helpful and generous in offering assistance. Those at the University of Virginia Library, at the Virginia State Library, at the Manuscript Division of the Library of Congress, and the New York Public Library, have my special thanks. For permission to use the chapter on Barbour and Virginia agriculture, reproduced in revised form from John B. Boles, ed., *America:*

The Middle Period; Essays in Honor of Bernard Mayo (Charlottesville: University Press of Virginia, 1973), I am indebted to the University Press of Virginia. I am also grateful to Duke University, the University of Virginia, the Virginia Historical Society, the Virginia State Library, the Library of Congress, the New York Public Library, the Massachusetts Historical Society, the Alabama Department of Archives and History, and the Maine Historical Society for permission to quote from unpublished letters housed in the manuscript divisions of their libraries. The Virginia Museum, the Virginia State Library, and the University of Virginia graciously permitted me to reproduce portraits of James Barbour and pictures of Barboursville. Nancy Christian Yates of Charlottesville, Virginia, and Frank Christian of Richmond, Virginia, descendents of Barbour, generously shared with me family papers in their possession. Frank and Ruby Schumaker of Palmyra, Virginia, offered me not only bed and board when I was working at the University of Virginia Library but also their friendship, for which I am deeply grateful. My parents, R. F. and Frances Lowery, and mother-in-law, Estelle M. Bradford, offered support in countless ways.

For their work in typing various sections and drafts of the manuscript, I wish to thank Cindy Horton, Janet Lightsey, and Pat Wannamaker. I can never repay Linda Hilton, whose faithful help and superior work I will always remember with gratitude.

Finally, I acknowledge my large debt to Tom, Trent, and Dan, each of whom contributed in his own individual way, and to Susie, whose love and friendship kept me in touch during the nights and weekends when this labor separated me from the family. Her support and affection are written into every line and page of this volume.

James Barbour,
A Jeffersonian Republican

1

The Virginia Heritage

*O*ne late October day in 1829 a travel-weary party returning home from more than a year's sojourn in Europe, topped a crest on the deeply rutted red clay road that led to Barboursville, a quiet hamlet located in the central Virginia Piedmont's Orange County. In the group were former U. S. minister to England James Barbour, his wife, Lucy, and their youngest daughter, Cornelia. A spectacular panorama stretched before them. The brilliant scarlets, yellows, and russets of the surrounding hills contrasted sharply with the muted hues of the distant Blue Ridge Mountains, whose atmospheric magic, even at this colorful season of the year, imparted a bluish cast to the higher elevations. Nearby were Barbour's own terraced fields and fertile bottomlands watered by the meandering Blue Run. Just beyond his view was his large neoclassical country seat, where a happy family reunion awaited him.

On countless occasions during the past thirty years, during three decades of an active public life that carried him frequently to Richmond or Washington and required long separations from the family and land he loved, Barbour had passed this way and had surveyed this familiar landscape. But this time was different. He was retiring from public life. He would not be traveling the same way again, as he had regularly for most of his adult life, to and from the seats of political power. The orbit of his life was contracting. Henceforth his time would be measured not by the ebb and flow of politics but rather by the pulse and rhythm of life on a busy Virginia plantation: by the cycling of the seasons, by the planting and harvesting that had engaged farmers in this country for more than a century. For an agrarian whose attachment to the land had not diminished during his long years in public life, it was not an unhappy prospect. He was returning to the familiar land of his birthplace, not to await old age nor to be haunted by the implacable judgments of posterity, but to draw fresh strength and new life from the soil that had nurtured him and generations of Barbours before him.

It was in this land, not more than a few miles from the very crest on which he now stood, that James Barbour had been born more than half a century earlier, on June 10, 1775. The second son of Thomas and Mary Thomas Barbour, he was born to comfortable circumstances. His father was a well-to-do planter and leading citizen of Orange County—vestryman, gentleman justice, county sheriff, militia colonel, and member of the Virginia House of Burgesses. His mother, Mary Pendleton Thomas, came from a respectable Spotsylvania County family and was related to John Taylor and Edmund Pendleton of Caroline County, both of whom were prominent in Virginia political life.[1] Thus his family connections, though not impressive when compared with those of the proud and powerful ruling Virginia gentry, were strong enough to afford some advantages in an age when family ties continued to be of importance to individuals aspiring to public office.

The Barbour name was an old and respected one in the county. James Barbour's paternal grandfather, also named James, was one of the first settlers in the region and was apparently the first in Orange. He moved there from King and Queen County in about 1720. Although he was without property at the time, this typical Virginia yeoman through hard work and good fortune rose quickly into the ranks of the gentry. In 1731 the freeholders of St. Mark's Parish elected him to a position on the parish vestry. Three years later, when Orange was carved from Spotsylvania County, he was appointed county justice, certain evidence that by this time he had established himself as a member of the local ruling class.[2] That gentry included such men as Thomas Chew, Henry Willis, Benjamin Cave, James Wood, John Mercer, James Taylor and, until his death in 1732, Ambrose Madison, whose grandson was to become the fourth president of the United States.[3] For almost a century the descendents of these early Orange pioneers, bound ever closer with each passing generation by ties of consanguinity and friendship, constituted the social stratum from which most of the political leaders of the county were drawn.

Thomas Barbour, the third son of the first James Barbour, was born in 1735 at the family home near the Rapidan River, some eight miles northwest of the site where James Madison, Sr., was later to build Montpelier.[4] On this Virginia frontier, where the possibility of Indian attack was the normal condition of life until after the French and Indian War, he grew up, participating in the struggle to bring civilization to the backcountry. By 1775, when the second James Barbour was born, Thomas had become the master of a large estate, which during the years of James's boyhood fluctuated in size between 2,000 and 3,000 acres of land and had thirty to forty slaves.[5]

At the same time that he was establishing himself as a substantial planter, Thomas Barbour became involved in local government. In 1765 he was elected to the parish vestry and was appointed justice of the peace.[6] Both offices, especially the latter, were politically important in eighteenth-century Virginia. Their significance owed much to a tradition in which citizens of the colony looked to the local gentry as the leaders of the countryside. Long habit had made it natural for a rural populace to turn to men of property and social stature for guidance in local affairs. As both a large landowner and an agent of governmental authority, Barbour was in a position to influence and to direct the society around him. In his capacity as justice he served on the most important body of local government, the county court, which performed legislative, executive, electoral, and judicial functions. He took his duties seriously, devoting many hours to the political, religious, and economic affairs of the county. In attending to public business he must have demonstrated those same administrative abilities that he had shown in private affairs, for in 1768 the Orange electorate rewarded him with the highest elective office in the colony—a seat in the House of Burgesses.[7]

From May 1769 to June 1775, Thomas Barbour served continuously in the House of Burgesses, where he participated in the memorable debates and events of those years. He signed most of Virginia's special protests and nonimportation agreements and stood consistently with other Virginia patriots on all matters affecting colonial rights.[8] Although he was over-shadowed in the larger revolutionary arena by such men as Patrick Henry and Thomas Jefferson, he was, as Richard Henry Lee observed, a principal actor on the local stage.[9] Following the assembly's dissolution in June 1775, Thomas Barbour returned to Orange. There, with James Madison, Sr., and a few others, he assumed control of local affairs and worked hard to ready the county for war.

Although no seedbed of radical activity, Orange County was quick to fall in with the revolutionary movement once it began. Most of its citizens were willing revolutionaries, removed though they were from the major theaters of conflict. Thomas Barbour supported independence for the colonies and used his public offices to unite the county fully behind the war effort. As a member of the Orange Committee of Public Safety, he joined with a small group of other leading citizens to censure the slight loyalist sentiment in the county and propagandized energetically for the patriot cause.[10]

Some of James Barbour's earliest childhood recollections may well have concerned his father's activities in the Revolution. As county lieutenant, Thomas Barbour was responsible for supplying and drilling the Orange militia, and his young son undoubtedly witnessed some of those frequent musters. During the war years, the colorful Orange militia showed a rare seriousness of purpose as they drilled, marched, and practiced marksmanship. Armed with a miscellany of fowling pieces and squirrel rifles, they paraded proudly in brown linen hunting shirts across the front of which was emblazoned in bold white letters the motto "Liberty or Death." A bucktail hung from each hat, and from wide leather belts across their shoulders were suspended tomahawks and scalping knives, marking the wearers unmistakably as denizens of the backcountry. They were superb marksmen who rarely missed a mark the size of a man's head at the distance of 100 yards. Perhaps it was the confidence the riflemen inspired that moved the frail, scholarly James Madison to shoulder a weapon and join the ranks. In so doing, he showed greater courage than the local wag who said he would enlist only if the militia's motto were changed to "Liberty or Be Crippled."[11]

The trauma of revolution must have seemed minimal to the inhabitants of a country where civilization, because of its newness, still retained an unsettled and uncertain quality. Orange was a spacious country only a step or two removed from the frontier, and its life was still somewhat dispersed and fluid, at least for its 550 white families, who made up a little more than half of the county's population of 10,000 people.[12] Wealth was less concentrated here than in some of the older and more heavily populated Tidewater counties. Of its approximately 1,100 white adult male inhabitants, half were landowners, and of this number only nine owned fewer than fifty acres of land. While the average landholding was roughly 375 acres, the typical farm was between 200 and 300 acres in size. One-third of the adult white males owned slaves, but only seventeen planters in the entire county owned more than twenty, and slightly more than half of all slaveholders had five or fewer. The wealthiest man in the county in the mid-1780s, both in land and slaves, owned only eighty-five slaves and 7,000 acres of land. The James Madisons, father and son, together owned only 3,000 acres and eighty-one slaves. Compared with the great Tidewater planters, Orange's wealthiest planters, who typically owned 2,000 to 3,000 acres of land and thirty to forty slaves, were not very rich.[13]

It is noteworthy that the social structure of Orange, while beginning to assume the form of the older Tidewater society from which it sprang, had not yet become rigid. It was still a place of small farmers and moderate-sized plantations, where even the ruling gentry were wealthy by local standards only. Lines of social demarcation, especially between the upper and middle classes, were not nearly as sharp as in the older settled areas, a difference apparent from the fact that political office in Orange was not the exclusive domain of the wealthiest planters. Positions on the county court and other public offices were not infrequently held by men from the large middle class.[14] Society generally, though certainly less fluid than our own, was far from static. Opportunities for its energetic and ambitious sons to improve their station in life, to acquire property and exercise political power, were readily available.

In this open and generous society James Barbour grew up. Nothing is known of his childhood home except that it was called Bloomingdale and was adjacent to Madison's Montpelier on the west. Because of his father's social status, however, and because of the electorate's reluctance to reward with political office anyone who gave no outward or visible signs of success, we may safely assume that the plantation house was typical of those maintained by the successful Piedmont gentry. In all probability it was a large frame structure, more functional than aesthetic in design, situated on some knoll or prominence affording a sweeping view of the surrounding acres and buildings. The main dwelling was flanked in 1783 by twenty-one other buildings—slave quarters, horse stables, tobacco-curing barns, and numerous small buildings which, as a whole, gave the plantation the appearance of a small village.[15] Stretching along the western horizon some thirty miles away loomed the brooding Blue Ridge Mountains which, like a giant backbone, separate the Piedmont from the Shenandoah Valley. Visible from almost every part of the Barbour plantation, they became an inseparable part of James's consciousness. Growing up in their shadow, he developed an attachment to them which he never outgrew.

In addition to the good fortune of spending his formative years amid the verdant hills and mountains of Orange County, James Barbour enjoyed most of the advantages that comfortable circumstances provided sons of the Virginia gentry. It is true that during the Revolution his father was away from home much of the time attending county business, but it is unlikely that the observant and inquisitive young boy minded being left to his own resourcefulness for amusement and information. When Thomas Barbour was home, he sometimes took his son with him as he made his rounds of the plantation. And from that social and economic microcosm the youth learned about life. From his earliest recollections slavery was a part of his daily environment. The subjection borne by the slaves at Bloomingdale, and the constraints under which they lived, could only have infected him with prejudgments of their inferiority. The psychological implications of unrestrained power and the latent sense of guilt accompanying slavery would in time work their leaven on Barbour no less than on many other of his fellow Southerners; but to a youth innocently observing the slaves as they went about their daily tasks of planting and harvesting tobacco and grain, the system must have seemed perfectly natural and innocuous.

When the young Barbour was not watching Ben, Sampson, and other hands as they prized and cured tobacco or engaged in the more arduous labor of clearing forests to provide new tobacco land, he might go down to the family mill.[16] There, if he was lucky, he might find children of neighboring planters who had brought their grain to be ground. He must have delighted in the fresh cool air of the foothills laden in spring with the ubiquitous fragrance of honeysuckles, in marvelous summer days when the heart-lifting grandeur of the Piedmont countryside made the world seem boundless in prospect, in the sight of gently swelling hills blanketed with ripening grain in the fall; above all, in the winter excitement of rolling the giant hogsheads of tobacco over the rough road to market at Fredericksburg. From his boyhood rambles through deep woods of chestnut, oak, and hickory, and across fields jeweled with dew gleaming in the rays of the early morning sun, he developed a deep love for nature. He came to know and love the feel of damp, freshly plowed land underfoot and acquired a friendly dependence on the rich Piedmont soil, which in later years brought him into the company of Thomas Jefferson and James Madison in cooperative endeavors to develop improved varieties of plants and trees and to find ways of retaining soil fertility.

James was not the only child at Bloomingdale during the years of the Revolution. The first child of Mary and Thomas Barbour was a son, born in 1773, but he died in infancy, perhaps of the same "dysenteric irruption" generally incident to the country which in the summer of 1775 carried off a younger brother and sister of James Madison, Jr.[17] His death made James the oldest child in the Barbour household. Other children followed in rapid succession. Thomas, who also died in infancy, was born in 1777, and three years later the first daughter, Lucy Todd, was born. Philip Pendleton, who with James was to attain political prominence in the years to come, was the fifth child, born in 1783. During the next ten years the family continued to grow, as three daughters, Nelly, Polly, and Sally, were born.[18] In a home filled with the clamor and activities of five brothers and sisters, who were joined frequently by a host of visiting cousins and other relatives, there was plenty to keep James occupied.

These were carefree years for the developing youth. Since all the major tasks were performed by slaves, there was plenty of time for boyish pursuits, in which he engaged with his brothers, cousins, and the children of neighboring planters. The fields and woods abounded with game, affording opportunities for the more solitary sport of hunting, while the well-stocked stables of Bloomingdale provided him with a wide choice of blooded horses. In time he became an expert horseman; he developed during his early years a fondness for horses and horse racing which he never outgrew. As he grew older he joined the men in the ever-popular pastimes of foxhunting and cockfighting. Perhaps he also joined the men of the neighborhood in the periodic wolf hunts conducted to destroy those predators, which continued throughout the eighteenth century to be a problem in the county. It may have been on one of these hunts, or possibly at one of the monthly militia musters, which he began to attend at age sixteen, that he had his first taste of persimmon beer, a popular drink among the people of Orange.[19]

Although they lived in a rural environment, the Barbours were not socially isolated. Surrounded by an extensive family and by neighbors like the Madisons, the large Moore and Taylor clans, the Benjamin Johnsons, the Catlett Conways, the Andrew Shepherds, and several branches of the Gordon and Taliaferro families, all of whom were tied closely by bonds of either affection or kinship, they participated in an active and varied social life. A particularly warm relationship existed between the Barbours and Madisons—a relationship based on many years of living together in close proximity and association. A mutual dependence, especially pronounced in business, social, and religious matters, bound the families together, making them something more than casual neighbors.[20]

The first families of the county constituted a fairly homogeneous and tightly knit society. Community life among them was marked by day-long excursions and overnight visits that sometimes stretched into weeks. Dozens of relatives and friends often filled the Barbour home. People stayed for days, visiting and enjoying the busy round of dances and barbecues so popular among the gentry during the summer and fall months. The Barbour children shared in the excitement these occasions afforded. Even more appealing would have been the week-long visits to the mountain resort springs, which the family, sometimes accompanied by the Madisons or other neighbors, made annually when the late summer heat of the Piedmont became oppressive.[21] It is unlikely that James Barbour understood or appreciated the significance of the complex of family and friends that provided the nurturing environment of his youth. But in the years to come, his connections would assure him of easy access to a seat in the Virginia General Assembly, where he was to begin his long political career.

Although the home was the hub of social life during James's boyhood, the church was also important. Throughout the year, except when weather made travel impossible, the big event of the week was Sunday worship. Along with most of their immediate neighbors, the Barbours were active communicants of the Episcopal Brick Church, located near Orange Courthouse on the road to Fredericksburg. Thomas Barbour was one of the church's mainstays. As a vestryman, he participated for many years in the various legal and religious functions of St. Thomas's Parish, attending to the needs of the widows and orphans, appointing overseers of the poor, and enforcing the social codes and mores of the community. During the postrevolutionary years, when the parish was without a minister, he served regularly as lay reader and represented the parish in various church councils.[22] The entire Barbour family, of course, attended the services of the church. They were joined by members of the extended family and by neighbors—the Madisons, Taylors, Caves, Moores, Shepherds, Pendletons, Taliaferros, Bells, and others—who assembled weekly, perhaps as much to socialize as for religious purposes. It was customary for five or six families to meet at one of the homes for dinner after worship.[23] These gatherings afforded the men a chance to discuss the latest political developments or the prospects for the tobacco crop, while the women engaged in domestic conversation and the children played.

Such social events were an important part of the enculturation process in Virginia. Here the provincial country tenets so important to all Virginia gentry, the cultural values of the agrarian society, were transmitted to James Barbour and to others of the rising generation. James's politics had their roots in the traditions in which he was reared. Although they would leave him ill prepared for the America he encountered as an adult, he accepted the dominant concerns and conventions of his society as unexamined articles of faith. His political life was decisively influenced by his *patria,* by the aristocratic, republican, conservative English country traditions that found their strongest sanctuary in Virginia.

Orange planters, like most of the Virginia gentry, were carefully schooled in the oppositional ideology of the eighteenth-century English "Old Whig," or "Country," party. In the country view, power was the nemesis of liberty. Because power always corrupts, political power was inherently suspect. Hence governments must be carefully watched, their powers precisely circumscribed. Landowners were the only proper and safe foundation of society because they alone possessed the material independence to resist corrupting power. Independent, property-holding citizens constituted a natural order that was the bulwark of liberty. Farmers made the best citizens because they were the most vigorous, the most independent, and the most virtuous. The values of rural life, where the happy yeoman tilled his own acres far removed from the city's moneyed politics and corrupting influences, were widely and repeatedly extolled. Moneyed men—bankers, traders, stockjobbers—and their financial innovations represented the largest threat to the natural landed order, especially when they were closely tied by favor to the government. The greatest blessing a government could bestow upon its citizens was to leave them alone. Wealth should be distributed by work alone, and the goods produced by society should be allowed to find their own best markets without governmental intervention. All other political particulars enunciated by the Virginia gentry followed from these basic assumptions.[24]

The transmittal of rural values and country thinking constituted an important if informal element of James Barbour's early education. The opportunities for formal education, at least during the years of the Revolution, were more limited. Not until after the war was he afforded a chance to study under a regular tutor and to acquire the equivalent of an elementary education.[25] Until that time he studied at home, probably under his mother's tutelage, where he mastered the rudiments of learning. His earliest schooling apparently amounted to nothing more than instruction in reading, writing, and arithmetic. He probably learned some history, geography, and politics from the long discussions his father had with other men of the community when social occasions brought them together. In addition, he spent many hours following his father about the estate, studying the practical business of operating a plantation and learning the skills required by the farm, mill, and shop, all of which were practiced at Bloomingdale. Equally important was the practical schooling he received from his father in local government and politics.

Throughout James's formative years Thomas Barbour remained active in local government. In addition to his duties as justice of the peace and commander in chief of the county militia, he served for many years as county sheriff, in which capacity he collected taxes, maintained law and order, and presided over county elections. All of these duties made heavy demands on his time, but the most time consuming of all his offices was that of magistrate on the county court. For almost forty years he was a principal figure on the Orange court, serving a longer tenure and attending its sessions with greater regularity than any of his associates except James Madison, Sr. Because these two men were the most faithful members of the court, they bore a disproportionate share of the administrative burden of running the county: probating wills and deeds and registering powers of attorney, listening to legal pleadings, compiling tax lists and setting local tax rates, and appointing guardians and overseers of the poor.[26] Their public services during and after the Revolution set an admirable standard of character, of disinterested patriotism, and of responsible political stewardship for the following generation to emulate.

As soon as he was old enough to do so, James began to accompany his father on occasional trips to attend county business—to "view" a road, to assess the damage from the ever-flooding Rapidan River, to locate a new mill site, or to preside over a local election.[27] These outings, which carried him throughout the county and sometimes to neighboring towns, provided James with his first formative contacts with the world beyond Bloomingdale and constituted the beginning of his close schooling in local government and practical political leadership. Some of his most valuable and enduring lessons he learned outside the classroom.

If James Barbour's formal education had followed the pattern common in Virginia, he would have begun attending a plantation or field school at the age of six or seven. These schools, not unlike the one-room schools found throughout rural areas of the United States until well into the twentieth century, were normally taught by a minister. But St. Thomas's Parish was without a minister during most of the Revolution, and not until 1785, when he was ten years old, did the youth have an opportunity to enroll in such a school. In that year a new Presbyterian minister, James Waddell, who occasionally conducted services at the Brick Church, established residence near Gordonsville, some ten miles from the Barbour plantation. James Barbour, probably with Meriwether Lewis, went to study under him.[28]

Waddell, a native of Ireland who had spent his formative years in Virginia studying under that notable Presbyterian revivalist and spellbinder Samuel Davies, was heralded throughout the state for his eloquence. His loss of sight about the time he settled in Orange seemed only to enhance his effectiveness, and many Virginians thought he rivaled Patrick Henry in oratory.[29] The strong character and forceful eloquence of this blind backwoods orator-preacher-teacher left an indelible mark on the impressionable mind of the young Barbour. Continuing under his guidance for several years, he studied Greek, Latin, arithmetic, history, geography, and a little natural philosophy. Whether James excelled as a student or, indeed, even showed much aptitude for these subjects is a matter for conjecture, but he did demonstrate a love and talent for rhetoric that must have pleased his teacher. At an early age he learned to think and speak on his feet and began to practice the art that was the stepping-stone to a political career in Virginia.[30]

During the years when Barbour was studying Latin and Greek under Waddell, events of national interest were taking place that undoubtedly attracted his attention. In 1787 the Constitution was framed in Philadelphia, and the country quickly became absorbed in the struggle for ratification. Around their firesides that long winter of 1787–1788 and over their mugs at the local taverns, men throughout the country heatedly debated the proposed system of government. Sentiment in Virginia was sharply divided. The Antifederalists, who in the opinion of Henry Lee would have opposed any national system of government even if it were "sent from heaven," were a large and determined group led by Patrick

Henry and Richard Henry Lee. At the opposite end of the political spectrum were the Federalists, who favored the Constitution and, again according to Henry Lee, would have supported "any federal system, sooner than risk the dissolution of the confederacy." An intermediate group, led by George Mason, disliked the proposed government and wished to see it amended, but they too would have adopted the Constitution rather than see the union jeopardized.[31]

In Orange County little public opinion initially opposed the proposed government. For a while it appeared that the Federalists would easily carry the county. Thomas Barbour was one of the Constitution's few early critics. Objecting strenuously to its omission of a bill of rights and of any specific guarantee of religious liberty, he traveled throughout the county winning others to his point of view and rallying the opposition. He was very successful with the Baptists, particularly those in the Reverend John Leland's flock living along the Pamunkey River, who shared his concern with religious liberty. Others in the county, including some of the substantial planters, began to gravitate to his side, causing growing concern among the Federalists. James Gordon, James Madison, Sr., and others began to write to the younger Madison, who was still in New York collaborating with Alexander Hamilton and John Jay on *The Federalist*, warning him of the deteriorating situation and urging him to return home and assure the citizens that ratification was in their best interest.[32]

In February and March Thomas Barbour continued his campaign, and interest in the contest quickened. Rarely in a gathering of any sort, whether of the militia, the county court, or a religious or social group, did conversation not turn to the Constitution. Opinion became sharply divided. Despite the view held by some that only the Baptists and the ignorant part of the populace opposed the Constitution, men of social and political prominence could be found on both sides of the question. There seems to have been no important economic, political, or social differences between the two sides where the county was concerned.[33] The day before the election, the younger Madison returned home and, conducting a last-minute campaign, succeeded in winning a majority to his views. He defeated Barbour by the overwhelming vote of 202 to 56. James Gordon, the other candidate who favored ratification, was also elected, polling 187 votes. After the election results were announced, Madison, hoping to reconcile the Antifederalists and to assuage any remaining fears about the Constitution, addressed the people, who listened attentively despite a cold, piercing wind which carried occasional flurries of snow.[34] Though the crowd found Madison's remarks reassuring, Thomas Barbour continued to hold grave reservations, which were not laid to rest until the state ratifying convention in July accompanied its approval of the Constitution with recommendations for amendments of the sort he thought necessary.

What affected James Barbour more immediately than the Orange County tempest over ratification was his father's financial reverses of the late 1780s. Like other Virginia tobacco planters, Thomas Barbour suffered financially from the loss of markets and the general disruption of commerce during the Revolution. Although there was a brief period of economic recovery immediately after the war, it soon became apparent that tobacco was never again to hold the place in Virginia's economy that it had once occupied. Rapid decline in its price caused economic distress among farmers throughout the state, and in the summer of 1787 a severe drought followed by a bad winter hit Orange planters particularly hard.[35] Thomas Barbour suffered severely. Pressed by various creditors, especially a Fredericksburg firm of merchants which regularly handled his tobacco consignments, he was forced to sell more than a thousand acres of land during the period 1787–1792. For a brief period he tried his hand at trade, but he met with little success. His difficulties continued, and for more than a decade he struggled with money problems.[36]

Because of his father's financial plight, James Barbour never acquired a higher education. While many of the gifted sons of the gentry were at the College of William and Mary being exposed to the ideas of the Enlightenment and imbibing the abstract principles of natural rights under the guiding hand of Bishop James Madison, the less fortunate Barbour was at home in Orange pursuing an independent course of study. He continued his readings in the classics, being especially attracted to the writings of Cicero and Aristotle, whose rhetorical theories and ideas about the importance of oratory to society and the state coincided with those he had learned from Waddell. Both his philosophy and style of public address were influenced by his careful reading of Cicero's *De Oratore* and Aristotle's *Rhetoric*. But he also studied Hugh Blair's *Lectures on Rhetoric and Belles-Lettres,* which had become a standard guide to composition and the major manual of oratory in Virginia since its publication in 1783.[37] While he may have preferred the principles of public address expressed in the classics, the oratorical style that he developed, with its strained imagery and sententious arguments heavily ornamented with historical, classical, and metaphorical allusions, bore a much stronger resemblance to the spread-eagle oratory lauded by Blair and practiced by several generations of Americans in the first half of the nineteenth century than to anything of the ancients.

In addition to the classics, Barbour studied history and government and read some of the economic and general philosophies of Adam Smith, David Hume, and the Scottish Common Sense School. Although he showed considerable dedication and desire for learning, he did not obtain the solid foundation in the arts and sciences that such contemporaries as Dabney Carr and Francis Walker Gilmer acquired studying under closer supervision. Only in the study and practice of rhetoric and oratory can it be said that he was as well prepared as they. While he would continue to read in the various branches of knowledge as he grew older, his education lacked both breadth and depth, a limitation he would feel throughout life.[38]

Sometime about 1791 Barbour began actively to prepare for a career in law, a profession whose lure proved as irresistible to him as it had to countless other talented and ambitious Virginia youth. While the study of law was generally considered to be the road to opportunity and distinction, in Virginia no less than elsewhere, it was also, according to John Adams, a "dreary ramble." Few law textbooks or compilations existed to make the process of learning less laborious. A young man aspiring to become a lawyer in Virginia at this time had several courses open to him. He might serve as a copyist or assistant in the clerk's office of some inferior or higher court and glean such information as he could from his work and reading; he might apprentice himself to a leading member of the bar and work under his direction; or he might study the statutes and commentaries on his own, as Patrick Henry did, and stand for admission to the bar. James Barbour adopted a combination of the last two courses. For a short period he read law under a Richmond lawyer and then studied on his own in Orange.[39]

In his role as apprentice in Richmond, Barbour had access to all of his preceptor's law books, abstracts, statutes, and notes of cases. These he was expected to study and assimilate. His introduction to the systematic reading of law probably was Lord Coke's *Commentary on Littleton,* the formidable legal primer on feudal tenures which law students, as a matter of course, were expected to surmount. Barbour left no record of his struggle with Coke, but probably he, like Justice Joseph Story, found the dry, technical old jurist intricate, crabbed, and obsolete. Blackstone's *Commentaries* were not as prohibitive. Appearing in the first American edition in 1771–1772, the *Commentaries* had proved a great boon to law students, becoming to the postrevolutionary generation of lawyers what Coke had been to the prerevolutionary generation.[40] In addition to studying Coke, Blackstone, and the Virginia statutes, Barbour may have studied Brownlow's *Entries,* Plowden's *Commentaries,* and any other law books available in his senior's office. Like all law students at the time, he would have been expected to assist his mentor in preparing briefs and also to observe active courtroom argument and procedure.

Apparently Barbour worked hard at his studies. Before long he had completed his apprenticeship and by 1792 was back in Orange serving as deputy sheriff, an appointment his father was instrumental in securing for him.[41] This first venture into public life, which carried him throughout the county delivering various writs and summonses and performing other minor jobs for the county court, did not divert him from his legal studies, however. In September 1793 he presented to the Orange County Court of Quarter Sessions a license from the Virginia General Court authorizing him to practice in the inferior and superior courts of the Commonwealth.[42]

Family influence and connections provided a nurturing environment for Barbour's studies and ambitions and would in the future prove important in launching his political career, but the extraordinary accomplishment of gaining admission to the bar at the age of eighteen, unusual even in eighteenth-century Virginia, was his own. It was characteristic of Barbour always to be in a hurry. Hard driving and impatient by temperament, he tried to compress time and accelerate processes, sometimes without proper regard for consequences. This tendency enabled him to accomplish a great deal, but at times it hurt him. Certainly where his legal education was concerned, a less hurried approach that allowed time for broader and more systematic study during a period of years rather than months would have been far more valuable.

Because of his youth and inexperience Barbour's practice was at first very limited, dealing mainly with debt and trespass cases.[43] Potential clients were understandably reluctant to entrust their affairs to one so young. To some extent Barbour's physical appearance may have offset the liability of his age. He looked older than he was. Just under six feet in height, he had a large frame which, though lithe and angular now, would become more portly in later life. He had dark brown hair, unusually heavy eyebrows, and intelligent, piercing brown eyes.[44] He was affable and instinctively gregarious, qualities which served him well in his chosen profession. No less important to his advancement was his capacity for hard work, accompanied by a dedication and seriousness of purpose essential for success. Although he must certainly have exhibited the self-conscious awkwardness of youth in his early appearances before the bench, he was not long in gaining self-assurance. As he acquired poise and experience, he extended his practice beyond Orange—to Albemarle in 1794, to Louisa in 1795, and to Fluvanna in 1796.[45]

A lawyer's life in late eighteenth-century Virginia had aspects of both drudgery and gaiety. Office work was often long and tedious, for everything—wills, pleadings, depositions, and other papers—had to be written out in longhand. Many arduous hours also had to be spent in the fields and swamps following the surveyors and chain bearers as they determined the lines in boundary disputes, an especially profitable source of litigation. Less burdensome were the hours spent in pleading cases before the county courts. For Barbour, with his love of oratory, these courts provided his first real audience for public speaking, and he welcomed the opportunities they afforded him to test his forensic skills in his declamations, pleadings, and summations.[46]

Much of a lawyer's time was spent in traveling from county to county in attendance at the local courts. While riding the circuit, which for Barbour included most of the central Piedmont and upper Tidewater counties of the state, lawyers enjoyed a convivial life. Unbounded hospitality was extended to them by the gentlemen of the country. The contests of the bar often served as "provocatives to that indulgence which found free scope when evening brought all together, under one roof, to rehearse their pleasant adventure, and to set flowing the currents of mirth and good-humor . . . kept merry by the stimulants of good cheer."[47] In these travels from court to court, "when gentlemen of the bar, booted and spurred, rode forth more like huntsmen than learned clerks," lawyers usually rode together in groups of two or three. Barbour's companions on many such occasions were William Wirt and Jefferson's nephew Dabney Carr, with whom he developed lasting friendships.[48]

During the years he was riding the circuit and building the foundation for what would soon become a moderately successful legal practice, Barbour began to court Lucy Johnson. Lucy's mother was Thomas Barbour's sister, and her father, Benjamin, a leading Orange citizen, had for many years been a prominent planter and member of the county court. That she and James were first cousins was no obstacle to marriage, for unions among cousins were common practice. The ties between the Barbour and Johnson families were strong. Since early childhood James and Lucy had been thrown together at the frequent family gatherings. As they grew older, they saw one another at the many social events which provided diversions for the local gentry—the annual visits to the mountain spas and sulphur springs, the round of barbecues held every fall, and the dances and dinner parties which leading families gave throughout the year. On October 20, 1795, amid a great deal of lively festivity occasioned by the large turnout of family and friends, they were married.[49]

The young couple began their married life comfortably but modestly. For a few years they apparently resided at Bloomingdale until they were able to build a house of their own. At the time of his marriage, however, Barbour owned 150 acres of land in Orange along the Blue Run, which he soon began to develop. In January 1797 he asked the county court to appoint a magistrate to view a road that would make the land accessible, apparently with the intention of building a house. For a wedding gift his father gave him 5,000 acres of choice land bordering Panther Creek in Kentucky, and shortly thereafter he purchased another small tract in Mercer County, Kentucky. During the next few years he acquired additional acreage in Orange to form the nucleus of what would become in time a large plantation. He also began to acquire the furniture necessary to set up housekeeping.[50]

During the years immediately following his marriage Barbour divided his time between his legal practice and farming. In 1796 he qualified as captain in the Orange militia, and by 1798 he had acquired ten slaves and an equal number of horses, which suggest that his career as a planter was well launched.[51] As he rode the circuit and directed the operations of his farm, his thoughts turned more and more to politics, which had an irresistible attraction for him. Ambitious, impatient with the monotony of the legal practice in which he was competent to engage, and anxious to involve himself in the political life of Virginia, he entered upon the road that was to lead to a long and successful, though at times unhappy, public career.

Early in 1798 Barbour declared himself a candidate for the Virginia House of Delegates. Isaac Davis, Jr., a well-to-do planter who had represented the county the previous year, had decided not to stand for reelection. John Spottswood, a planter of moderate wealth, opposed Barbour. It was not customary in Orange for political candidates to campaign openly for office, but they were expected to observe such time-honored practices as circulating among the voters on election day and treating them to alcoholic refreshments. To ignore this custom, as James Madison, Jr., had done in 1777, was to invite certain defeat. If Barbour, like Madison, objected to the practice, we have no record of it. Apparently he, along with the other candidates, provided his share of treats. It is unlikely, however, that he attempted to buy the election, as his neighbor Charles Porter had done a few years earlier, by overindulging the electorate with "spirituous liquors." Indeed, he was always careful to avoid any activity that might be construed as a direct solicitation of votes, which as in previous generations was considered an ungentlemanly practice. But like gentlemen of the earlier age he knew how to go among the people and to present himself for their political consideration with such a delicacy of phrase as to avoid any appearance of campaigning.[52]

Although election days, like court days, were social as well as political occasions when freeholders throughout the county could gather at the courthouse to transact business and to engage in convivial exchanges, only about a third of the electorate turned out for the election in April 1798. A 50 percent voter turnout was normal for the county.[53] In any election, of course, the number of freeholders who voted depended on many variables—the weather, personal convenience, and the importance of the issues. It is probable that the poor turnout in 1798 reflected the absence of any political issues important enough to generate much interest. Whatever

the case, Barbour outpolled Spottswood by almost 100 votes of the approximately 200 cast.[54]

Barbour's victory was attributable in no small part to his family's good
name and extensive connections throughout the county. His father's personal reputation and popularity with the electorate helped him immeasurably in defeating an older and more experienced man. The voters must
have seen ability and promise in him, however, or they would not have
chosen a man so young to represent them. That he attained such a high
office before he was yet twenty-three, and before he had served the
traditional apprenticeship in county government, was more than a personal tribute: it suggested that changes, however subtle, were operating to
alter the character of the old political order. Barbour did not take lightly
the faith the electorate showed in him. His conduct in the years ahead
revealed that it was a trust well placed.

2

In Defense of
Republicanism

During the months following Barbour's election to the House of Dele-gates, a dramatic change occurred in Virginia's political climate. Party feeling in the Old Dominion, which had been mounting since John Adams's election to the presidency, reached unprecedented heights as a result of Federalist political successes in Congress. Capitalizing on the anti-French sentiment and on the war hysteria that swept the United States following the XYZ Affair, the Federalist-dominated Fifth Congress passed in the summer of 1798 the repressive Alien and Sedition Acts, designed to restrict Republican opposition and to extend Federalist control of the national government. These laws, along with the military and tax measures accompanying them, provoked a loud outcry from Virginia Republicans,[1] among whom James Barbour was one of the most vocal. His loud denun-ciation of the partisan laws, both before and during the Virginia assembly's session, placed him in the political limelight and gave him a visibility that novice legislators rarely attain.

Barbour was not the first Virginian to sound the alarm, nor did he take the lead in opposing the objectionable measures. That initiative was taken by Thomas Jefferson. As presiding officer of the Senate during the debates on the bills, Jefferson observed firsthand the ominous mood and temper of Congress. When it became apparent that neither he nor the distinctly beaten Republican congressional minority could arrest the course of events, he left Philadelphia and returned home. Stopping en route for an overnight visit at Montpelier, the distraught vice-president consulted with James Madison on ways to terminate "the reign of witches" and restore the government to its "true principles."[2] Both men agreed that decisive action was required. It was imperative that Republicans raise constitutional objec-tions and reaffirm the basic freedoms of speech and press. Resolutions of protest issuing from state legislatures seemed to promise the greatest success. Accordingly, Jefferson went into seclusion at Monticello and penned the Kentucky Resolutions, while Madison soon thereafter began to work on a set of resolves for the Virginia assembly.[3]

While Jefferson and Madison worked covertly to marshal the opposition, Barbour and other lesser Republican figures throughout the state proceeded more openly. Unaware of the steps being taken by the principal party leaders, they held public rallies and county meetings, where they drafted memorials and petitions to the state legislature, to Congress, and occasionally to the president himself, denouncing not only the Alien and Sedition Acts but the entire Federalist program as well. Meetings of this sort were held in Spotsylvania, Albemarle, Goochland, Madison, Louisa, Prince Edward, Caroline, Hanover, Essex, Buckingham, Powhatan, and Orange.[4] These protest assemblies played an important role in rallying Republican opposition and in setting the stage for the political contest that would take place when the Virginia assembly met in December.

Like Republican leaders throughout the state, Barbour saw the Alien and Sedition Acts as incontrovertible proof of country beliefs that power corrupts and that governments must be closely watched and restricted to prevent abuses. Republics, he believed, because of their dependence on public opinion, were inherently fragile. Laws like the Sedition Act, limiting freedom of speech and press, would destroy the foundation on which liberty rested, which was an enlightened, well-informed citizenry. The Federalist program, he exclaimed, was the handiwork of extremists and liberticides who, in their "political villainy," would not rest until they had ruthlessly sacrificed every "friend of American liberty" on the altar of their own "vice and ambition." With Jefferson and Madison he believed that Republicans must act decisively to defend basic freedoms and to "raise a rampart against the inroads of usurpation."[5]

Most of Barbour's Orange neighbors, though less vocal than he, shared his dislike of the Federalist program. Francis Taylor, whose home near the Barbour plantation was a frequent gathering place for the county gentry, spoke with considerable understatement when he observed that "the people do not appear pleased with political matters."[6] To give voice to public opinion, James Barbour and other Orange political leaders decided to hold a countywide meeting in September. Although Madison played no prominent role in this meeting, Barbour, who was its principal organizer, almost certainly conferred with him and undoubtedly was guided by his counsel in the proceedings. Now and afterward, Barbour looked upon Madison as a mentor whose opinions and extensive experience in government provided reliable guideposts for his own political course.[7]

Barbour opened the meeting, held September 14 at Orange Courthouse, by reading to the large gathering of citizens a memorial to the legislature he had drafted earlier. Taking the form of a remonstrance based unequivocally on country assumptions, the memorial forcefully articulated republican fears of arbitrary power and governmental tyranny. It condemned the Federalist press and administration for intentionally fostering war hysteria, which they in turn had employed as justification for raising an army and navy "more likely to awe the people than face an enemy." Federalists wanted war against France in order to better pursue their antirepublican plans at home. War would give the administration a free hand to restrain personal liberty and to impose repressive measures on a people who, under other circumstances, would surely revolt. But the people were alert to the danger: "To make an expected attack from abroad a pretext for attacking the principles of liberty at home has drawn aside the curtain and clearly illuminated for all who are willing to see," Barbour said.

The memorial then detailed some of the constitutional objections to the Alien and Sedition Acts. The Alien Acts subverted the Constitution by giving the president unauthorized powers over aliens. They represented the logical culmination of the Federalist tendency to bend the Constitution in the direction of unlimited executive power. The Sedition Act was even more frightening because it threatened the very foundations of representative government: the constitutional guarantees of freedom of speech and press. It was a blatantly partisan measure designed to muzzle the Republican press and to coerce conformity of opinion. Under its provisions political opinions hostile to the administration were to be construed as criminal assaults on the government. Republican government was impossible without the right freely to examine the conduct and actions of elected officials, a right dependent upon a free press. The memorial concluded with a defense of the people's right to assemble peacefully for the purpose of expressing political opinions, which should always guide public figures in their conduct of public affairs. After Barbour finished his presentation, other citizens spoke on behalf of the memorial, which was approved overwhelmingly and was forwarded to the legislature.[8]

At the Orange County meeting, as at most of the other protest gatherings, belief in the sovereignty of the people was evident. The right of the people to instruct their representatives and to hold them to a strict accounting was emphatically affirmed. The toast offered by a Richmond Republican on an earlier occasion typified the prevailing sentiment: "To the Constitution—may all those appointed under it, ever bear in remembrance that it was made by the people for the guidance of their servants, and that the sovereign people will be obeyed."[9] Equally unequivocal was the language used by the citizens of Powhatan in their resolutions: "The people are the foundation of power and authority, the original seat of majesty, the author of laws, and the creators of officers to execute them."[10]

Not all Virginians felt this way, of course. In Federalist strongholds such as Richmond and Norfolk, as well as in the Valley and Eastern Shore counties, there was considerable support for the Alien and Sedition Acts. Elsewhere in the state there were pockets of support where Federalists, if they did not defend the laws specifically, did uphold the Adams administration and endorsed the Federalist program as a whole. In many areas, particularly in the towns, rivalry between Federalists and Republicans became extremely intense. In Fredericksburg John Marshall, after having been honored at a dinner sponsored by Federalist friends, was insulted by Republicans in the town's theater, from which he was all but driven to the tune of the "Rogue's March." In Charlottesville a dinner sponsored by Republicans to honor Jefferson brought a prompt response from Albemarle Federalists, who presented Marshall with an address congratulating him for his conduct abroad during the XYZ Affair. In Williamsburg, students at the College of William and Mary denounced President Adams by parading through the streets of the town an effigy portraying him as a monarch. And so it went, throughout the summer and fall. Winter brought no diminution of party feeling. By the time the legislature convened in early December, Barbour, along with other public figures, had become alarmed by the widespread rumors of disunion.[11]

It was in this suspicious, highly charged atmosphere that Barbour set out for Richmond in early December 1798 to represent Orange in the House of Delegates. Greatly lacking in education and experience and keenly aware of the importance of the legislative contest that lay ahead, he probably suffered from feelings of uncertainty and inadequacy that could hardly be considered unusual for a twenty-three-year-old legislator of untried mettle. But as events were soon to prove, his firm attachment to republican principles and his skill in defending them in debate would do much to compensate for inexperience.

Arriving in Richmond on a wintry day, Barbour made his way over the quagmire that was Main Street. Recent rains had swollen the little stream that ran diagonally across the street, making passage difficult. The other main thoroughfare, Broad Street, cut by gullies and deep wagon ruts, was in even worse condition. Barbour was no stranger to the thriving little metropolis of almost 6,000 inhabitants, where he was to spend a large portion of his time during the next fifteen years. Some years earlier he had studied law here, and on numerous subsequent occasions he had visited on routine business affairs. But his familiarity with the town did not compensate for its harsh aspects. Despite the fact that it was the social and intellectual center of the cultured planter aristocracy of Virginia, its physical appearance was drab and unprepossessing. The whole city was rough and very much in need of improvement. Streets were crude, and the stores and shops, grouped in clusters along Broad and Main streets, were simple, colorless frame structures. With few exceptions, the homes, concentrated at the lower end of Main Street, were modest one-story dwellings. The most imposing building in the city, the capitol, was still in an unfinished state; and Capitol Square, grown up in weeds, was cut by deep ravines. Near the statehouse Barbour secured comfortable lodgings which he would share the following year with James Madison.[12]

Before the legislature sat, a group of eighteen Republican legislators, including Barbour, met in secret caucus to plan their strategy for the session. The leader of the group was John Taylor of Caroline. An inveterate foe of governmental consolidation who during the fall had maintained close contact with Jefferson and other party leaders, Taylor presented to the caucus what was to be the major weapon in the Republican arsenal— the resolutions that Madison had drafted earlier at Jefferson's urging. The caucus edited the resolutions and selected six men to serve as their chief advocates in the assembly. Barbour was among those chosen. Initially he resisted accepting, saying that the party's interests would be served better by an older and more experienced man. But his objections were overruled. He accepted the role proffered him by colleagues who may have been influenced in their choice by Madison: he quite possibly suggested to Taylor that Barbour would be an effective advocate for the resolutions.[13]

On December 3 Barbour assembled in the capitol with 169 other representatives for the opening session of the assembly. Federalists and Republicans took their seats in an atmosphere heavily charged with suspicion and distrust. Former friends, separated now by party barriers, refused to speak to one another and dared not stop at the same tavern. Though outnumbered by Republicans, Federalists had increased their strength in the past election and were now a strong minority. In George Keith Taylor of Prince George, who was soon to marry John Marshall's daughter, and Henry Lee of Westmoreland, Robert E. Lee's father, they had able leaders as they prepared to combat the Republican majority.[14]

That a major battle was to take place there could be no doubt. The *Philadelphia Aurora* had reported as early as August 6 that Republicans in the Virginia assembly were preparing to act in defense of freedom of speech. About the same time the Republican-dominated Council of State had made an unsuccessful preemptive move to call the legislature into early session, which would have made it difficult for Federalist legislators living in distant western Virginia to attend.[15] Federalists thus had adequate warning that their opponents in the assembly were planning a direct frontal assault on the national government. What they did not anticipate was just how intense and partisan that attack would be.

On the opening day Republicans launched their offensive by trying to replace Federalist Speaker of the House John Wise with Jefferson's lieutenant and political confidant from Albemarle, Wilson Cary Nicholas. Heretofore the speakership had never been subject to party considerations. The move to oust Wise failed, mainly because many Republicans were unwilling to carry partisanship to the extent of rejecting the experienced and respected Speaker, but the fact that the effort was made served notice of the Republican mood. After the speakership question had been settled, Republicans dispensed quickly with the other necessary preliminaries and turned their attention to the main business at hand—challenging the Alien and Sedition Acts. Resolutions and memorials drafted and submitted by public meetings condemning the acts were read, after which committees were appointed to draft bills relating to the preservation of the broad range of civil liberties guaranteed by the first ten amendments to the Constitution.[16]

On December 10 John Taylor introduced the Virginia Resolutions. Those resolves, along with the companion resolutions passed a month earlier by the Kentucky legislature, were to precipitate a controversy perhaps as fierce and certainly more enduring than that aroused by the detested laws against which they were aimed. Madison's resolutions opened with an expression of attachment to the Constitution and then proceeded immediately to a defense of the compact theory of the Union. The Union was founded on a compact among the states, which were "duty bound to interpose for arresting the progress" of the federal government when it assumed the "deliberate, palpable, and dangerous" exercise of powers not granted it. The lamentable tendency of the federal government to enlarge its powers by forced construction of the Constitution could only lead to the gradual consolidation of the states into a single sovereignty, the inevitable result of which would be the transformation of the "present republican system of the United States into an absolute, or at best, mixed monarchy." The Alien and Sedition Acts were examples of what the country might expect under such a government. The Sedition Act, the "very essence of arbitrary power," was especially offensive because it was "leveled against the right of freely examining public characters and measures, and of free communication among the people thereon, which has ever been justly deemed the only effectual guardian of every other right." The other laws were objectionable because they involved the exercise of powers not delegated to the federal government. By combining the legislative and judicial powers with those of the executive, they subverted the "general principles of free government." Finally, the resolutions appealed to the other states to join with Virginia in declaring the acts "unconstitutional and not law, but utterly null, void, and of no effect."[17]

This last phrase had not been a part of Madison's original draft. Without his friend's knowledge, Jefferson had suggested that the phrase be added, and Taylor, Barbour, and the other members of the Republican caucus which edited the resolutions had adopted the recommendation. Madison had been more cautious than Jefferson. He did not believe that a state legislature could render an act of Congress null and void merely by saying so. Perceiving that his friend's doctrine, lacking express qualifications or procedural safeguards, could totally paralyze the general government if carried to its logical conclusion, Madison had avoided the extreme position and had used very guarded language. He was thus able to assert later that the Virginia Resolutions were intended to be an expression of opinion only.[18]

The first few days of debate were dominated by the principal Republican and Federalist leaders, John Taylor and George K. Taylor, respectively. The Republican Taylor vigorously attacked the Alien and Sedition Acts and defended the resolutions as an appropriate response for a people whose "most essential human rights," their political and civil liberties, were imperiled by an arbitrary and ruthless government. The Federalist Taylor was no less aggressive in defending his party's program and in denouncing the resolutions as incendiary measures designed to encourage open resistance to federal authority. During the course of his impassioned speech he made a demagogic play on Virginians' ever-present fear of slave revolt. He succeeded in moving some delegates to tears with his lurid depiction of the rape and murder that might accompany such an insurrection, but he did not manage to shift the focus of debate away from the central concern with the Alien and Sedition Acts.[19]

The arguments postulated by the Taylors on the first two days of debate were representative of the Republican and Federalist positions. For almost two weeks, during which time patience wore thin and tempers occasionally flared, representatives explored every conceivable facet of the question and frequently manifested a concern for party matters which seemed to outweigh constitutional concerns. Although party considerations, especially the politics of the approaching presidential election, influenced much of the course of the discussion, the focus of the debate was actually rather sharp: were the Alien and Sedition Acts constitutional, and could a state nullify or declare unconstitutional an act of Congress?

On December 17 Barbour addressed the house for the first time. The youngest member of the assembly, he had not expected when he left Orange to make a major speech in his maiden legislative appearance. His selection by the Republican caucus as one of the principal advocates of the resolutions had altered matters, however, and he had used the intervening two weeks to prepare what proved to be one of the strongest indictments of the Federalist program made during the session.[20]

Barbour began his speech with a brief exposition of the nature of the Constitution. His views reflected a solid grounding in traditional republican doctrine and a strict adherence to the compact theory of the Union. The Constitution, he contended, created a national government of specifically enumerated powers. Nowhere in that document could he find an explicit grant of authority empowering Congress to pass laws such as those recently enacted. Nor could the general welfare and necessary and proper clauses be so construed. The latter clause, despite George K. Taylor's interpretation, was designed not to create new powers but rather to enable the government to implement the specific ones granted. The Tenth Amendment, he continued, left no doubt that at the time the Constitution was adopted, the American people had intended all powers not specifically granted to the federal government to be retained by the states. He could not accept the Federalist doctrine of implied powers because it was destructive of those very principles upon which the republic was founded.

Thereafter Barbour turned to a more specific examination of the Alien Acts in relation to the Constitution. Like other Republicans, he objected more to the Sedition Act than to the Alien Acts, but because John Taylor had already spoken on the former, he focused on the latter. These laws, he claimed, violated portions of the Sixth, Seventh, and Eighth amendments. In direct contradiction to the Sixth Amendment, they allowed the president, "without probable cause, without an oath, and merely ... upon suspicion," to apprehend aliens. In violation of the Seventh and Eighth amendments, they empowered the president to banish aliens without the formality of an indictment or a public trial by jury. Finally, the laws were contrary to the spirit of the Constitution in that they destroyed the "main pillar upon which all free governments stand, namely, a separation in the three great elements of government." Echoing Madison's resolutions, he noted that the laws invested the president with legislative, executive, and judicial powers, a usurpation defined by Montesquieu as "the essence of despotism."

Barbour then turned to a minute dissection of the statements George K. Taylor had made earlier in defense of the Alien and Sedition Acts. Resolved to follow that Federalist's arguments through all their "meanders and twistings" until he had exposed fully their "fallacy and dangers," he presented a devastating commentary on his opponent's constitutional views, showing a temerity that the older man must have regarded as brash. Citing the same authorities as Taylor but interpreting them differently, he challenged the former's view that aliens, because they were not a party to the Constitution, were excluded from its protection. Quoting from Emmerich de Vattel's *The Law of Nations,* he argued that aliens coming to the United States tacitly agreed to uphold the Constitution and to abide by the laws of the country. For them to be bound by those laws but to be excluded from their protection was an "appalling travesty" of both the Constitution and basic human rights. He dismissed as absurd Taylor's argument that the federal government, in the absence of any authority to expel aliens, would be powerless to prevent Virginia or any other state that might choose to do so from admitting foreign troops to American soil. If no other reason could be advanced in favor of the obnoxious laws than "an idea so wild as the danger of admitting Bonaparte and his army," he said, Federalists "must be in pitiful distress." To anticipate danger of this kind was to attribute to the state not only criminality "of the blackest kind, but [also] stupidity bordering on idiocy." It was preposterous to think that a free people would invite into their midst a powerful foe capable of destroying their liberty. The whole notion was the fanciful fabrication of "a mind laboring to but little purpose" to find some justification for unconstitutional laws.

But Barbour's attack focused on the doctrine of implication and on a closely related argument of expedience which had been central to George K. Taylor's presentation. Taylor had said that Congress, if it lacked the express or implied power to pass a law, might employ expedience as justification. This was a "monstrous doctrine," Barbour said, the mere mention of which caused him to tremble. Expedience was invariably the pretext of tyranny. If the time should ever come when that doctrine prevailed, "we might date it as the era of the downfall of American freedom. From that moment, let the votaries of liberty be shrouded in sackcloth, and with ashes upon their heads, deplore the departure of their protecting genius." In concluding his critique of Taylor's speech, Barbour chided that Federalist for resorting to the shabby and desperate tactic of trying to divert the assembly by raising the specter of servile insurrection. Such efforts, he said, "calculated only to inflame the passions at the expense of reason," would never sway intelligent and reasonable men.

It remained for Barbour to address the question of whether a state could declare federal law unconstitutional and, if it could, to specify the proper state agent for doing so. Jefferson and Madison had opposing views on the question. In the set of resolutions he drafted, Jefferson had claimed for the states the right to judge infractions of the original compact and to determine an appropriate method of redress. Taking a more extreme position than the Kentucky legislature was willing to endorse, he had said that the Alien and Sedition Acts were "unauthoritative, void, and of no force" and that the individual states should take whatever steps were necessary to prevent them from being enforced within their respective territories. He implied, although he did not explicitly say so, that the proper state agent for declaring a federal law unconstitutional was the state legislature.[21] Madison, on the other hand, had been much more cautious. He did not believe that a state, acting through its state legislature rather than through a special convention of the people, which had been the original mechanism for ratifying the Constitution, could nullify a federal law. Fearing the centrifugal tendencies of Jefferson's categorical resolves, he had eschewed the critical phrase "unauthoritative, void, and of no force." Madison had intended the Virginia Resolutions to be an expression of opinion only, not an attempt to invalidate federal law.[22]

In some respects Barbour's position was closer to Jefferson's; in others it was nearer to Madison's. Like the vice-president he maintained that the states possessed the right to pass judgment on federal laws, but only when those laws exceeded the powers specifically authorized in the Constitution. Once it is admitted, he said, "that states have no check against the encroachment of the general government," ferocious despotism "will stalk with impunity amongst us . . . , until those great rights, which are guaranteed by nature and the Constitution . . . [are] destroyed one by one, and a monarchy erected upon the ruins thereof." If the federal government assumed unauthorized powers, it was "guilty of usurpation, and all usurpation, being founded in wrong, must be void." Moving from abstractions to specifics, he asserted that the Alien and Sedition Acts, in addition to violating the spirit of the Constitution, were contrary to certain of its specific provisions, which meant that they had no force as law and were not binding on the people.

As to the proper state agent for judging infractions of the Constitution, Barbour rejected Madison's notion that only the people, acting through the medium of special conventions, could make such determinations. State legislatures, he asserted, possessed a right concurrent with that of the people to make such judgments. While conventions were one mechanism for the public to express its will, they were rarely the quickest and not necessarily the best way for doing so. He believed that legislatures, chosen by the electorate to represent their interests, were the most effective voice the people had. As such, they were duty bound to "sound the tocsin of alarm" whenever those interests and rights were imperiled, as now they were.

But Barbour would go no further. At this time, at least, he was unwilling to take the next critical step with Jefferson, which would have been to give teeth to the nullification doctrine by developing a procedure for preventing enforcement of the unconstitutional laws within the states. In his speech he carefully avoided any reference to the nullification clause that he and other caucus members had added to Madison's original draft of the resolutions. He prudently backed away from the position he had taken at the beginning of the session. The resolutions, he now maintained, were nothing more than a "pacific protest" inviting sister states to join with Virginia in arresting the "tendency and effect of unconstitutional laws." He hoped that simultaneous protest from the states would "overawe tyranny, which in the embryo is timid," and would cause Congress to repeal the objectionable laws. This, he said, was the real intent of the protest.

The resolutions, Barbour continued, were not an invitation to the people to resist federal authority openly. Such a response would be insurrection. He deprecated "intestine commotion, civil war, and bloodshed, as the most direful evils which could befall a country," except for the loss of liberty. Present circumstances did not warrant insurrection. Still, he was not willing to forswear the right of rebellion. Freedom and government by consent, he said, must be preserved at all costs. If all else failed, an appeal to arms would be justifiable as "the last resort of an oppressed and injured nation" when public servants "convert themselves by usurpation into masters and destroy rights once participated."

Following Barbour's presentation, which lasted several hours, other prominent Republicans spoke, reaffirming many of the arguments Barbour had advanced so effectively. William B. Giles of Amelia County and Wilson Cary Nicholas of Albemarle broadened the Republican attack by assailing the entire Federalist program and philosophy—the increase in taxes, the military appropriation bills, and the national bank. Federalists defended their party's leaders and policies and attempted whenever possible to put Republicans on the defensive by attacking them at some vulnerable point.[23] Federalist Archibald Magill of Frederick County challenged Republicans to show how the Sedition Act differed from a similar statute enacted by the Virginia assembly in 1792 entitled "An Act against Divulgers of False News." The Virginia law, he said, was more severe than the federal law, because under it a person accused of spreading defamatory propaganda could not offer in his defense proof that the statement was true, which he could do where the federal law was concerned.[24]

Barbour, Taylor, and several other Republicans were quick to argue the impropriety of citing state laws to justify congressional laws, saying that "it would be as just to say that a state could pass laws for raising fleets and armies, because Congress had done so, as that Congress could infringe the liberty of speech because the states had done so. The states are expressly forbid to do the one, and Congress the other." Both Barbour and Taylor rejected the Federalist claim that the federal courts already had common-law jurisdiction over seditious libel. They also denounced as absurd the

Federalist argument that the Sedition Act was an amelioration of the existing laws regulating seditious libel.[25]

Many Republican representatives, though supportive of the resolutions in general, were disturbed by the phrase declaring the Alien and Sedition Acts "null, void, and of no effect." Agreeing with Henry Lee that those words "inspired hostility and squinted at disunion," and fearful of the precedent they would be setting, they joined with Federalists and removed the offending phrase.[26] In the absence of a division on the vote, it is impossible to say how Barbour voted. Although he had been a member of the caucus that had added the nullification clause, he never once alluded to it in his speech. That he made no attempt whatever to defend or to justify so controversial a measure suggests strongly that he had changed his mind about the advisability of including it in the resolutions. His public assertion, both during the debates and afterward, that the resolutions were intended to be only an expression of opinion, and not an attempt to nullify federal laws, provides an additional reason for thinking that he probably voted with the majority to delete the phrase. After this change was made, the resolutions passed the house on December 21 by a strict party vote of 100 to 63.[27]

Federalist representatives criticized Barbour's defense of the resolutions, especially his argument that states could judge infractions of the Constitution. That power, Archibald Magill claimed, belonged exclusively to the federal judiciary.[28] Under normal circumstances Barbour would not have claimed such powers for the legislature. He did not believe that the people, in electing representatives to accomplish the routine purposes of legislation, also conferred upon them ordinary judicial authority with respect to laws that they or other legislative bodies passed. That power, he ever afterward maintained, rightly belonged to the judiciary. But these were not normal times. The country had not faced so grave a crisis, he said, since the new government was launched. He was convinced that the Alien and Sedition Acts constituted a threat to basic rights and liberty that went beyond the question of free speech and press, for to violate the constitutional amendment guaranteeing those rights was to destroy the sanctuary protecting every other right.

First principles were at stake. The great achievement of the Revolution— establishing the sovereignty of the people and free government as their instrument—was in jeopardy. Barbour was fully committed to the ideals and promise of the Revolution, but he was uncertain about their durability. The republic was vulnerable. Federalist tyranny was corrupting original principles. He would not now trust the liberty and future happiness of all Americans to federal judges, who were too much under Federalist sway to act independently and impartially. The voice of the people, speaking through their elected representatives in the legislature, should be heard. Inasmuch as most of the federal judges had already unofficially expressed opinions that the Alien and Sedition Acts were constitutional, legislatures were, in his opinion, the only effective voice and recourse the people had.[29]

In his attack on the Alien and Sedition Acts and in his advocacy of the resolutions, Barbour exhibited the zeal of an embattled partisan. But in view of his belief, shared by many others, that the "already overgrown power" of the federal government darkened the political horizon and threatened to destroy, finally and irrevocably, the rights of a free people, his response is understandable. The danger he and other Republican colleagues saw in Federalist actions was real: they firmly believed that Federalists intended to destroy the natural order and to transform the republic into "an absolute, or at best, a mixed monarchy." The Alien and Sedition Acts were not merely arbitrary and illiberal, not simply a violation of the Constitution: they were the principal Federalist devices for subverting republican government. Country thinkers had long prophesied the dangers that had now come to pass. Barbour, Taylor, and other Virginia Republicans were simply engaging the enemy on the only ground they could. Not to have done so would have seemed treasonous to them.[30]

The acrimonious debate accompanying the passage of the Virginia Resolutions was but one manifestation of the intense party spirit which dominated deliberations of the assembly on the eve of the national election of 1800. Not long after the resolutions were passed, Barbour and other Republican strategists secured passage of a long campaign statement entitled *Address to Congress from the General Assembly*. Drafted by Madison, it was a partisan political document attacking Federalist policies and philosophy on a broad front. Its real intent was to provide an unofficial party platform for the approaching presidential contest.[31] Federalists responded with a partisan document of their own, entitled *Address from the Minority*, which defended the Federalist program. Perhaps the most significant aspect of this document was that Virginia Federalists, who in the past had not been very vocal in supporting such Federalist measures as Hamilton's financial program, were now actively and unequivocally defending the most unpopular and repressive of all their party's measures—the Alien and Sedition Acts.[32]

The house continued in session until the end of January, but to Barbour and his colleagues the routine business that remained after the resolutions were passed must have seemed anticlimactic. As a freshman legislator Barbour had much to learn, and he was a willing student. In many respects the house had changed very little since his father had sat as a burgess

during the early 1770s. The committee structure and the operating procedures were essentially the same. Most of the business was conducted by
four standing committees, the largest and most important of which was the
Committee on Propositions and Grievances. This committee dealt with a
host of local petitions and citizens' complaints and prepared most of the
bills, both public and private, passed by the assembly. The Committee of
Claims, responsible for reviewing citizens' claims against the state, spent
most of its time acting on petitions for relief from disabled veterans of the
revolutionary war and their widows. The Committee of Courts of Justice
ruled on matters concerning county courts and determined whether
claims and petitions should be considered by the house or should be
referred to another state agency. The Committee of Privileges and Elections ruled on disputed elections, sometimes unseating one of its fellow
members, and certified election returns.

Barbour was appointed to all these committees except Privileges and
Elections.[33] His position was unusual, for normally a new member was
assigned to only one of the committees and was given additional assignments only after he had gained the necessary experience or had demonstrated unusual talents. Committee chairmen usually served on more than
one committee, but apart from the Speaker, they were the most influential
members of the house and were expected to serve in several capacities.

In the absence of reliable evidence, we are left to wonder how Barbour
came to play such a large role during his first year in the house. If he had
been a member of one of Virginia's first families with powerful political
connections, the reason would be plain. But the name Barbour, while
solid and respected, was hardly the political or social equivalent of Carter
or Lee. One strong possibility is that Madison, who knew Barbour better
than did any other prominent Virginia Republican leader, promoted him
informally with influential members of the legislature. His participation in
the Republican caucus at the beginning of the session and his selection as
one of the principal advocates of the resolutions certainly support such an
explanation. Another possibility is that the structure of the assembly was
more fluid than it had been in earlier years, affording greater opportunities for men of talent to play politically important roles without first
serving a long apprenticeship.[34] Barbour's activities in Orange during the
summer and fall of 1798 also provide at least a partial explanation. His
efforts at that time to oppose the Alien and Sedition Acts and his memorial
to the legislature attracted attention beyond Orange. Thus he was not
altogether a political unknown when he began his legislative career. His
political principles seem to have been well known, at least among many of
his Republican colleagues, as a result of which he apparently enjoyed
greater stature than most freshman legislators.[35]

Having been given the chance initially to act in a responsible role, Barbour demonstrated abilities which gained for him the respect of his associates and, in time, a principal role of leadership. In this session he proved himself worthy of the larger trust. His speech opposing the Alien and Sedition Acts was generally regarded as one of the most effective and fluent delivered during the long debate. Even some of his Federalist opponents (Archibald Magill, for example), acknowledged that his eloquence and talents were impressive. While John Taylor was unquestionably the major legislative party leader at the time, Barbour, by accurately representing the Republican position in his powerful, sweeping indictment of the Federalist program, and by skillfully answering the objections raised by George K. Taylor and other Federalists to the resolutions, served his party in an important way. His performance apparently did not go unnoticed by Jefferson, who began to send pamphlets and treatises of various kinds to cultivate the young Republican.[36]

When the assembly adjourned in late January, Barbour returned to the quieter pursuits of his farm and law practice in Orange. But his thoughts were never far from politics, and throughout the spring and summer he watched political developments closely, showing particular interest in the reaction of the other states to the resolutions. He was disappointed that none of the state legislatures, not even those from the sister states to the south, supported Virginia and Kentucky in their protest. He undoubtedly expected that Federalist-dominated legislatures in the northern and eastern states would react negatively, as indeed they did, and that Federalists such as Fisher Ames could be counted on to denounce "crazy Taylor" and other Virginia Republicans for their part in securing passage of resolutions which reduced the Constitution to a "mere cypher," but he did not anticipate the vehement reaction of some of his fellow Virginians.[37] In the Shenandoah Valley, the Staunton court, upon receiving copies of the resolutions, contemptuously tore them to pieces and trampled them under foot. And at Mount Vernon, George Washington, convinced that Republicans in the assembly were bent on destroying "everything dear and valuable to us," wrote to Patrick Henry, urging him to return to the legislature and to resist the "torrent that carries others away."[38] There was a feeling among many citizens throughout the state, Federalists and non-Federalists alike, that the resolutions went too far, and this feeling greatly benefited Virginia Federalists, who entered the elections of 1799 with a strength and confidence that caused Barbour and other Republicans concern.[39]

Such concern was not unwarranted. No longer compelled to maintain the defensive posture that the Alien and Sedition Acts had necessitated, Federalists happily took the offensive by focusing public debate and attention on the resolutions, which they depicted as evidence of the disloyalty of their Republican adversaries. This strategy was successful, at least where the congressional elections were concerned. Federalists captured eight of the state's nineteen seats in Congress, a gain of four over the previous session. They retained their strength in the Valley, the Norfolk area, and the Eastern Shore and increased their strength in the Richmond area, the southern Tidewater, the Northern Neck, and the southern Piedmont.[40]

The success of the Federalists in the congressional elections did not extend to the General Assembly. There the Republicans retained firm control, which they knew was essential if they were to renew the arguments of the previous year, as they felt they must. Upon learning that Patrick Henry had been persuaded by Federalists to seek a seat in the legislature, a group of Republican legislators, with Barbour as their spokesman, asked Madison to lead them in the forthcoming session. Madison consented.[41] On April 14, at their customary Sunday afternoon gathering, a group of leading Orange County families, which included the Barbours, Taylors, Moores, and Madisons, met at William Moore's farm and made plans for the election. It was agreed that Barbour would join Madison on the county ticket. Ten days later the two were elected without opposition.[42] John Taylor and William B. Giles also won their elections; in Jefferson's opinion, Republicans had never had a more able legislature than the one which met in December 1799.[43] In the end the Republicans were never required to engage their full strength in that session, for Patrick Henry died in June 1799.

In late November, Barbour and Madison set out for Richmond to attend the opening session scheduled for December 2. Staying at the same quarters that he had had the previous year, but now sharing them with Madison, who was debilitated by a "dysenteric attack" for the better part of a month, Barbour prepared to join with other Republicans in defending the "Principles of '98."[44] But before they could take up that important matter, there were pressing house-cleaning tasks that required attention, tasks which this legislature, with its greater measure of party discipline, did not shun. The Republican majority systematically removed Federalists from state offices, beginning with the clerk of the house, John Stuart. William Wirt, a young Richmond lawyer who was beginning to play a prominent role in Republican party councils, was his replacement. John Wise, Speaker of the House, was next. This time moderate Republicans were unmoved by Federalist pleas to consider Wise's distinguished record of leadership, and he was replaced by Republican Larkin Smith of King and Queen County. Shortly afterward they appointed Wilson Cary Nicholas to the U.S. Senate and elected James Monroe governor over Federalist candidate James Breckinridge.[45]

Early in the session Madison was appointed chairman of a committee to draft a reply to the various states that had criticized the resolutions. Several months earlier Madison, Jefferson, and Monroe had met at Monticello and had agreed that the principles advanced by Virginia and Kentucky in 1798 were not to be "yielded in silence" and that Madison, with his surer grasp of the constitutional issues, should draft a Republican manifesto to present at the next legislative session. It was December before Madison managed to draft his famous *Virginia Report of 1800*. Unable to consult with Jefferson during the time he was actually composing the document, he worked essentially alone, though he did confer with several Republican members of the legislature, including Barbour. It appears, indeed, that he took Barbour completely into his confidence at this time, discussing fully with him the problems and objectives of the *Report* and perhaps listening to his young friend's opinions and suggestions.[46]

In January 1800 the *Report* was considered by the House of Delegates. A meticulously reasoned and carefully worded exposition of the nature of the compact between the state and national governments, it reaffirmed the basic position taken by the General Assembly in 1798 and defended, one by one, the resolutions passed that year. Its basic philosophy was the same as that which had underlain Barbour's speech of the previous year. It emphasized the fact that the Constitution was a compact binding its members only to the extent that its terms were honored. The states, acting in their sovereign capacity as parties to the compact, were obligated to "interpose to arrest the deliberate, palpable, and dangerous exercise of powers not granted" to the general government when the violation "deeply and essentially affect[ed] the vital principles" of the political system. The *Report* then indicted the Federalist administration for its centralizing measures and forced construction of the Constitution, as exemplified in the national bank and the carriage tax as well as in the Alien and Sedition Acts. In the final section Madison asserted that the Virginia Resolutions were not an interposition by the state adjudging the Alien and Sedition Acts unconstitutional but merely an expression of opinion on the subject.[47]

The debate on the *Report* was not recorded. It may safely be assumed, however, that Federalist opposition was comparable to that expressed to the resolutions during the previous year. Again led by George Keith Taylor, Federalists challenged the right of a state legislature to interfere in any manner with measures of the federal government. The Republicans enjoyed a substantial majority, however, and under the leadership of Madison they effectively countered Federalist objections. Barbour was appointed to a select committee designated to confer with the upper house in explaining the *Report* and in working for its adoption. In the lower house he, along with John Taylor, William B. Giles, and other Republicans, ably defended it and consistently opposed all Federalist efforts to weaken or amend it. After a brief struggle the house approved it by a vote of 100 to 60, which was almost identical to the vote on the resolutions. The senate concurred a few days later.[48]

While the Virginia and Kentucky Resolutions and the *Report of 1800* were intended primarily as a defense of civil liberties and an exposition of the compact theory of the Union, they were also electioneering documents whose importance in Republican party strategy should not be overlooked. As a political attack on the Adams administration on the eve of the election of 1800, they served as a rallying point for Republicans and prompted Jefferson, Madison, and other leaders to improve party discipline and organization. A hardening of party lines and a greater sense of rigor were very much in evidence in the Virginia legislature during this session. Illustrating this trend was the change which Republican leaders—Madison, Barbour, Giles, and John Taylor—secured in the state's presidential electoral law. Before 1800, when there was no uniform method for selecting presidential electors from the various states, electors in Virginia were chosen by districts. Although Jefferson had received all but one of Virginia's electoral votes in 1796, the approaching election was viewed as a critical one in which every vote was expected to be of unusual importance. Responding to the challenge, Republican leaders in January 1800 managed to change the electoral law. Electors were now to be chosen on a general statewide ticket, which meant that the victorious party would receive the state's entire electoral vote.[49]

The new electoral law, which narrowly passed the assembly, met with more opposition than Republican leaders had expected. Federalists were joined by some Republicans in denouncing it as a partisan measure which excluded a large number of citizens from a voice in national elections.[50] Faced with significant opposition and with an apparent increase in Federalist strength, Republican strategists decided to take two additional steps to assure Republican victory: they launched a publicity campaign defending the general ticket, and they instituted formal party machinery for nominating electors and for conducting a coordinated statewide election campaign.[51]

On January 21, 1800, ninety-three Republican members of the legislature and a number of prominent citizens met in special caucus in Richmond to nominate electors. After agreeing upon a slate that included such venerable patriots as Edmund Pendleton, George Wythe, and Madison, the caucus appointed five persons to prepare a plan of organization for conducting the election campaign. Barbour was chosen chairman of the committee.[52] He had probably not yet acquired the political stature in party affairs that would logically explain his selection for this important task, and it is likely that Madison had a hand in the choice. Surrounded as he was by men with greater political experience, Barbour must have accepted the job with some diffidence, though he could not have failed to appreciate the expression of confidence it represented.

On January 23, after two days of lengthy committee sessions, Barbour presented to the caucus an organizational plan which resulted in the formalization of Republican party structure in Virginia. A general standing committee of five persons was created with headquarters in Richmond. Charged with responsibility for directing the overall campaign and headed by Philip Norborne Nicholas, it was to act as a general committee of correspondence. County committees of correspondence were created with instructions to work with the general standing committee in ways that would best promote the Republican ticket. The general committee was expected to send information and instructions to the county committees, to inform the electoral candidates of their nomination and to determine whether or not they would support the Republican ticket, and to maintain a close vigilance over developing events in general. The county committees were expected to communicate to the people pertinent information regarding the election, to keep the general committee informed of the local situation and of any changing opinion, and to promote the ticket in every way possible.[53]

In implementing the recommendations of Barbour's committee, Virginia Republicans entered a new political era. They began to turn away from the old, informal mode of conducting elections, in which political candidates relied primarily upon family connections and personal prestige among the electorate to secure elective office, and embraced a more structured system in which the party, with its central committee and county committees across the state, would play a much greater role.[54]

In the election that followed, Barbour worked hard for Republican success. As a member of the Orange County Committee of Correspondence, he spent many hours acquainting the voters with the new electoral procedure, distributing ballots among the freeholders, and keeping the central committee in Richmond posted on developments in the county.[55] The campaign which he and the other members of the county committee conducted during the summer and autumn of 1800 was quite effective. In November Adams received only 7 of a total of 344 votes cast in Orange. Although the Federalists succeeded in carrying several districts elsewhere, the general Republican ticket prevailed, and Jefferson received Virginia's entire electoral vote. Barbour rejoiced in Jefferson's victory and gladly awaited the republican fruits of his administration.[56]

The crisis in freedom which Barbour encountered during the impressionable first years of his public life deeply influenced his politics. State sovereignty and strict construction of the Constitution, which John Marshall said were the creed of every politician who hoped to rise in Virginia, assumed an importance for him they almost certainly would not have had under different circumstances.[57] In the Alien and Sedition Acts he and his colleagues saw all the elements of incipient tyranny. Those measures served as a stark and fearful reminder, both then and afterward, that the American republic was fragile. Their action in elevating the "Principles of '98" to the status of holy writ, by which they hoped to protect the nation from social and political degradation, can be understood only within the context of the country ideology that shaped their outlook. Conditioned to distrust governmental power and always to be on guard against political usurpation, they magnified the Federalist threat to personal freedoms and self-government. The contest of 1798–1800 simply confirmed their tendency to see in every particular conflict an ultimate challenge to republican institutions. Their reaction to the Federalist program was more than a mere protest against obnoxious and repressive laws: it was a crusade to return the country to the original principles which they believed Federalist tyranny had corrupted.

Although Barbour participated in this crusade as wholeheartedly as the most doctrinaire Republicans, there were indications that he was not irrevocably and permanently committed to principles of states' rights. During his house speech opposing the Alien and Sedition Acts, he implied a willingness, once the Federalists had been removed from power and the danger to personal freedoms had passed, to apply to the Constitution the liberal construction which a "benign philosophy" sensitive to "the welfare of the thousands" required.[58] A change in political leadership and policy, not a change in the structure of government, was all that he thought necessary to redeem the country. He made no apology for interpreting the Constitution one way when Federalists controlled the government and another when Republicans were ascendent. The methods and motives of the two parties were radically different. Once the "Federalist conspirators" had been deposed, the Republican friends of liberty could be trusted to use political power responsibly to promote the general welfare without imperiling individual rights.

Barbour's goal was not to restrict the national government to the narrowest of bounds but to protect basic freedoms and to keep government responsible to the people. For him, no less than for Jefferson and Madison, state sovereignty and strict construction were practical means to more essential ends. The means were taken seriously, to be sure, but they were not absolutes. It was not his intention to offer a cure more dangerous than the disease. Measures that had been proper and needful in 1798 might be inappropriate in 1801. He accepted this basic political reality. His own political stance, unlike that of some of his Republican colleagues, was not frozen in time. He was amenable to new and different influences as his political and social environment changed.

3

An Expanding World

Following the legislature's adjournment in late January 1800, Barbour
returned home to Orange, where family and personal business claimed
his attention. The weeks before the busy spring planting season passed
quickly, filled with family, friends, and farming. As he made his rounds of the
plantation, perhaps as he planned for the clearing of new bottomland along
the Rapidan River and watched the newly blossomed willows along the bank
dip their switchy branches into the swollen stream, he found time for
reflection and assessment. He could justifiably be proud of the political
distinction he had gained in his few brief years of adulthood. Rarely did
anyone enjoy comparable political stature at so young an age. Older party
leaders viewed him as a promising legislator of firm republican convictions
who, having been tested in the heat of political conflict, could reasonably
anticipate a promising future in Virginia and national politics. Moreover, his
law practice was growing, and his farm was beginning to return profits that
would enable him to invest in additional land and slaves. From his vantage
point the future looked bright. He stood at the beginning of the new century
open to life—expectant, hopeful, confident.

The decade was a busy one for Barbour. His law practice, farm, and
political career required long hours of work. In addition, a growing family
made increasing demands on his time. He and Lucy Barbour had two
children—Lucy Maria, who was three years old in 1800, and James, who
was two. During the next three years another daughter, Frances Cornelia,
and a second son, Benjamin Johnson, named for his maternal grandfather,
were born.[1] Although the time Barbour spent with the children during
their formative years was limited by his frequent and sometimes extended
absences from home, he was an attentive father. His concern for their
personal development was especially apparent in his efforts to ensure that
all of them, daughters as well as sons, were well educated. When he was
home he periodically reviewed their educational progress with them, and

when he was away he left detailed instructions for their studies with their schoolmaster, James Waddell. These he supplemented from time to time with letters admonishing them to study hard in order to acquire the solid foundation of learning he considered essential to their future happiness. He was equally concerned about their character development. His letters stressed the importance of personal discipline, diligence, sober attitudes, and good moral habits.[2]

During this decade Barbour began to develop long-range plans for a country seat, which in time would become one of the largest and most prosperous plantations in the Virginia Piedmont. With its carefully maintained fields and fences, its rich green pastures kept closely cropped by merino sheep, its handsome buildings thoughtfully designed and laid out to command a panoramic view of the distant Blue Ridge Mountains, Barboursville was widely heralded in the 1820s and 1830s, not only for its good management, but for its beauty and hospitality as well.[3] The estate had its genesis in the efforts Barbour made to consolidate into several large tracts the many small parcels of land he was able to acquire in the early 1800s. The property eventually included some 5,000 acres. His first acquisition was 150 acres situated along the Blue Run, a stream that originates in the Southwest Mountains and meanders along the Orange-Albemarle county line. Soon after his return from Richmond in January 1800, he purchased two additional tracts in the same area, one of 214 acres and the other of 600. The next year his father-in-law, Benjamin Johnson, died, and Lucy Barbour inherited an adjacent tract of 1,352 acres, which more than doubled the estate. During the next ten years he purchased a total of 2,108 acres in Orange County and 3,263 in neighboring Albemarle. Those parcels which could not be incorporated into one of his two working plantations were sold, traded, or held for speculation.[4]

The plantation system was a form of agrarian capitalism that intensively exploited both land and labor. Without a source of cheap labor, the land itself was of little value to the plantation owner. The very abundance of land precluded southern planters like Barbour from commanding the services of a white laboring class and left them dependent upon chattel slavery. With no apparent misgivings about the morality of the institution, Barbour acquired his first slave in 1795 and added steadily to the number thereafter. Between 1800 and 1810 his holdings increased from eight adults and two children to thirty-two adults and fourteen children.[5]

In the nineteenth century no less than in the eighteenth, successful southern planters built their fortunes on slave labor. Certain economic trends of the age suggested slavery's obsolescence, and the social philosophy even of Jeffersonian Virginia strongly opposed it, but the fact remains that slavery not only endured but also expanded during the period. That expansion, as Barbour's experience clearly confirms, was not entirely dependent upon the new slave markets created by the cotton kingdom nor, for that matter, upon a single-crop economy. In his lifetime he demonstrated the profitability of slavery. His success at employing his hands in a variety of sophisticated and productive endeavors—diversified farming, small-scale manufacturing, the artisan and building trades—offers convincing evidence that slaves could be adapted to pursuits other than monoculture and, more important, that slavery itself was not necessarily inefficient.[6]

True to the liberal impulse of the Jeffersonian age, Barbour denounced slavery, in the abstract, as an evil. It was, he said in the 1820s, a blight on the nation's free character, an institution as degrading to the master as to the slave. But his denunciation had a hollow ring; it lacked conviction. His public lamentations were unaccompanied by any positive effort to eliminate slavery. In the end he always defended it as a necessary evil. It was, he said, a legacy from the past which, curse though it was, could not be changed without "dire consequences" to the present and future.[7] Unwilling to reason from the fundamental principle of the Negro's rights as a human being, and equally unwilling to ignore the property rights of the slaveowner, he defended the status quo. Neither he nor anyone else could conjure up a magic formula that would free the slaves without destroying the economic base of southern life, which he was committed to preserving. The cost of emancipation—and without emancipation there could be no mitigation of the Negro's condition—was more than he was willing to pay. Compared with contemporary Virginians, he was a benevolent master, but there can be no humanity in slavery. The tragedy was a double one: his slaves were condemned to bondage, and he, by holding property in man, was unfaithful to the ideals of human freedom he espoused.

Barbour devoted a great deal of time during the early 1800s to farming, taking a progressive, scientific approach that distinguished him from most planters of his day. Historians have duly noted the agricultural reform efforts of such men as George Washington, John Taylor, and Edmund Ruffin but have largely overlooked the equally important contributions of men like Barbour. Barbour was one of Virginia's foremost agriculturalists. As he farmed and addressed the problems facing southern agriculture in the early 1800s, he embodied the best of the progressive spirit. By precept and example he advocated new methods when the general tendency was to continue the same exploitative practices that had been followed for generations. His interest in agricultural reform brought him into close association with a small group of progressive Virginians whose research, experiments, and exchange of ideas eventually did much to restore fertility and prosperity to the depressed agricultural regions of the state. His commitment to scientific farming increased rather than diminished when he became active in national politics. At heart a Virginia planter whose lands were an inseparable part of his existence, he did everything within his power to make farming the profitable and intellectually satisfying occupation that republican social philosophy required it to be.[8]

In devoting so much time and energy during this period to farming and politics, Barbour compromised his chances of gaining distinction as a lawyer. Law was a demanding profession. It required little enough of country advocates who were content to earn a modest living filing writs and arguing cases before county courts, but the fulfillment of higher aspirations called for long and unremitting hours, indeed years, of hard study. With so much of his time given over to farming and to his political career, Barbour found that not enough remained for the persistent and close study of the legal commentaries, statutes, and chancery case reports that was essential to success at the bar. While he possessed much of the same capacity for analytical and logical thought that distinguished his younger brother, Philip Pendleton, who sat on the Supreme Court during the 1830s, he never developed his potential to the same extent.

The Virginia bar at the turn of the century was crowded with talented men. It was, in the opinion of several justices of the U.S. Supreme Court, the "most enlightened and able on the continent."[9] Many young lawyers of Barbour's generation, viewing skeptically the competitive situation in their native state, left Virginia for the newly developing states of the lower South and West—Kentucky, Tennessee, Ohio, and the Mississippi Territory. Henry Clay left Hanover County in the late 1790s to set up practice in Kentucky, and Philip Pendleton Barbour, after studying law under St. George Tucker at the College of William and Mary, moved there in 1801 and practiced for a year before deciding to return to take his chances in Virginia. William Wirt, James Barbour's colleague and traveling companion on the Virginia circuit, in 1802 and 1803 seriously considered moving to Kentucky, where he believed opportunities for rapid advancement were greater and prospects good for securing the much-coveted independence that would allow him to retire to literary pursuits. He abandoned the idea upon learning that lawyers in Kentucky, because money was scarce, routinely accepted horses and other livestock in payment for their services.[10]

Perhaps Barbour, viewing the prospects before him in 1800, also felt the lure of the West. There he might reasonably have expected his practice to grow not by small increments, a client at a time, but by leaps and bounds. But if he did, he resisted the temptation and remained behind to compete with the crowded field at home. He had already established a promising practice in the late 1790s, and the prominence he was gaining in the

Virginia assembly did much to increase his business. For the next decade—indeed, until he became governor of the state in 1812—his practice
flourished. His ledger indicates that, during these years, he handled as
many as 150 cases annually before the courts of Orange, Albemarle,
Fluvanna, and surrounding counties, sometimes representing Jefferson or
Madison while they were in Washington. He tried some criminal cases, but
the largest portion of his practice involved civil matters—the collection of
debts, battery and trespass, assumpsit, and land litigations. While he demonstrated ability as a lawyer and commanded the respect of his colleagues,
drawing occasional praise from Madison or from some other respected
legal authority for his arguments before the court, he never made law his
primary profession. Like so many of his contemporaries, he used it as a
convenient avenue for political advancement. When the higher objective
was attained, as in 1812 when he became governor, he willingly turned
over his practice to his apprentice and cousin from Culpeper County, John
Strode Barbour.[11]

Barbour devoted a great deal of time during these years to intellectual
improvement. Rising in midsummer with the dawn to begin his rounds of
the plantation, he returned to the house by mid-morning, breakfasted, and
retired to his study to spend three or four hours with his books. If he was
traveling the circuit, he tucked into his saddlebags enough volumes to
occupy his evening hours in the comfortless inns, where he could forget
the tedium of the assault, theft, and trespass cases he had argued during
the day by reading Gibbon, Defoe, and Hume. His hunger for knowledge,
fed by a sharp awareness of his inadequate formal education, set him to
devouring books and treatises of every description—novels, history, natural philosophy, literary criticism, political economy, and poetry. He preferred the classics. He derived particular pleasure from the restraint,
dignity, and cultural discipline of such Greek and Latin writers as Homer,
Horace, Plutarch, and Virgil. He was also attracted to the eighteenth-
century neoclassical writers, especially Alexander Pope, of whose restrained and sonorous heroic couplets he seemed never to tire. He often
carried one of Pope's volumes—*Rape of the Lock, Essay on Man,* or *Essay
on Criticism*—with him when he traveled. He was greatly influenced in
both his writing and speaking by the classical forms, and his public
speeches—highly polished in form, elegant in expression, and sprinkled
with Latin phrases and classical allusions—amply attest to this influence.[12]

Barbour read widely in other areas as well. In 1805 his library contained
some three hundred volumes, including the legal works of Coke, Bacon,
and Blackstone; a heavy concentration of histories, not only the Greek and
Roman, but also Gibbon, Goldsmith, Voltaire, and Hume; a miscellany of
politico-economic studies such as Adam Smith's *Wealth of Nations* and

Jefferson's *Notes on the State of Virginia*; the writings of Rousseau, Locke, Montesquieu, Vattel, Burlamaqui, and Adam Ferguson; thirty volumes of Buffon, Priestley's *Lectures,* and various scientific treatises, such as James Keir's *The First Part of a Dictionary of Chemistry,* which had practical application to agriculture; various collections of poetry by Milton, Dryden, Shakespeare, Addison, and others; and many volumes of biography, philosophy, religion, geography, and oratory.[13] That he read widely and intensively in these fields is apparent from his familiarity with the major authors and from his natural and easy reference to them in both public and private life.

Barbour did not neglect his political career during these years. His legal practice and farm required much of his time, to be sure, but they also provided him with opportunities to mingle with family and neighbors in a social setting, where he could promote himself politically in various subtle and indirect ways. His travels as a lawyer, carrying him throughout the county and district on court days, enabled him to maintain close ties with an extensive family complex—uncles, cousins, and other relatives throughout Orange and neighboring counties whose support at the polls was important. Influential family connections continued to be important to Virginians in public life, but by 1800 the number of men with ties to the first families had become so large that family alone no longer provided a guarantee of political success. The authority of the aristocracy and its political control of society were unmistakably weakening, as Barbour knew. While he, like the Randolphs and Taylors and Harrisons, employed family to good political advantage, he did not ignore the electorate or remain aloof from it. Instead he sought to build a solid political base in the county by keeping the people informed of what was happening in the assembly. He communicated with them in personal letters, in occasional circulars, and by "going among the people" on court and election days to establish the kind of rapport likely to gain their support. He succeeded to a remarkable degree. During thirty-odd years of public life, only once, when he made a bid from retirement in 1830 to regain his old seat in the House of Delegates, did he fail to win an overwhelming majority of the vote.[14]

During the period 1800–1812, except for three years when private business required his attention, Barbour was a regular member of the General Assembly. More than any other branch of the government, the legislature, and the House of Delegates in particular, was the locus of political power in Virginia. It selected the governor, U.S. senators, state judges, members of the Council of State, and a host of lesser state officials. As a delegate, Barbour was in a position to influence the actions and the policies of the government. Building upon the solid beginning he had made in 1798, and profiting no doubt from the counsel of his father, whose political experiences of a lifetime he had telescoped into a few short years, he rose rapidly to a position of leadership in the house. It is easy enough to document his rise to prominence by studying the legislative journals and assessing the significance of the number and variety of committees he worked on or chaired, but it is less easy to say why he succeeded to a greater extent than others. His political or family connections were certainly not better than those of his colleagues in the house. Many men had stronger ties than he. Nor can it be argued that his success was due to wealth. For while he had become one of the wealthiest members of the body by 1810, he was still very much a planter on the make early in the decade when he emerged as one of the principal legislative leaders.[15] Family connections, social status, and friendships were all undoubtedly significant, but talent, intellect, ambition, and perhaps other qualities that defy analysis were more important in explaining his rise to political prominence.

Barbour's experience in many ways reflects the political and social changes that were taking place in Virginia. Virginia was in a state of flux in the early 1800s. Some of the time-honored political customs were beginning to break down. In the eighteenth century, for example, it was extremely rare for a man to be elected to the House of Burgesses without first serving a political apprenticeship at the county level. The office of justice of the peace, which carried membership on the important county court, was the normal first upward step in a political career and was often accompanied by appointment to the vestry and frequently by a term as county sheriff. Barbour short-circuited this process, gaining the highest political office the county could award without ever serving the traditional apprenticeship. Indeed, he was not accorded the rank of gentleman justice by the Orange court until 1822. His case was probably not unique. Experience in county government, while still valuable, was no longer the prerequisite for higher office.[16]

The old oligarchic system of government was also beginning to break down. That system, dominated by a few wealthy and influential men who in turn were maintained by an extensive network of family connections, may have stood firm against the shocks of revolution, but it was unable to withstand the steadily mounting pressures for change in the new century.[17] The authority of the planter aristocracy and its political control of society, which had been largely a matter of unchallenged social habit before 1800, were being called into question now by an increasingly vocal populace no longer willing to acquiesce in a government in which they had little voice and by a rising generation of political hopefuls from the professional ranks—lawyers mainly, but some ministers, physicians, newspaper editors, and merchants—whose status in the community did not depend on the amount of land or number of slaves they owned.

The results of the challenge to the political leadership of the old aristocracy are nowhere more apparent than in the changed composition of the House of Delegates during the years when Barbour was a member. Traditionally composed of the richest men in the state and dominated by a few powerful families, the house came increasingly under the control of less wealthy men who were somewhat below the highest stratum of Virginia society. In the period 1788–1800, for example, twenty-seven men as chairmen of the various standing and select committees dominated the affairs of the House of Delegates.[18] Of this number eighteen were from the first families of Virginia, including three Lees, two Taylors, two Harrisons, and two Cabells, and nine were among the one hundred wealthiest men in the state, with landholdings in their home county, representing in many instances only a small fraction of their total holdings, of as much as 15,000 acres.[19] With each member of the group possessing an average of fifty-one slaves and 2,870 acres of land, at least two-thirds were among the ten wealthiest men in their respective counties. Only seven, or roughly one-fourth of the group, owned fewer than a thousand acres, while only nine, or one-third, had fewer than twenty slaves, and most of these were professional men whose wealth probably consisted of nontaxable property. Of those who engaged principally in agriculture, only two could be called small planters.[20]

No comparable group of men dominated the house so completely during the period 1800–1815. During these years leadership was more dispersed than earlier, and fewer men held power for extended periods of time. The twenty-five who, by virtue of serving at least two terms as Speaker or as chairman of one of the standing house committees, can be identified as the most influential in house affairs during the period were not nearly as wealthy nor as prominent socially as their predecessors. While they were by no means impoverished, they owned on the average only 1,083 acres of land and fifteen slaves—less than half the average wealth of the earlier group, a rather dramatic decline for so brief a period of time.[21] Only two men from the post–1800 group possessed as much land as the average held by the pre–1800 group, and only Edmund Harrison of Amelia County and, toward the end of the decade, Barbour, approached in overall taxable wealth the earlier average. With Larkin Smith of King and Queen County, they were the only house leaders whose holdings in land and slaves placed them among the ten wealthiest men in their respective counties.[22] Thus only about 15 percent of the later group stood at the apex of the social pyramid at the county level, versus 65–70 percent for the earlier group. Moreover, only half of them possessed a thousand or more acres of land and only one-fourth owned more than twenty slaves, a rather unimpressive index of wealth when we recall that at least 2,000 planters in all of Virginia in 1788 owned as much property.[23]

Slightly more than one-third of the post–1800 group owned fewer than 600 acres of land, a fact which suggests a sharp decline from the earlier period in the number of legislative leaders whose primary income was derived from farming. It is likely, indeed, that not more than one-third of the twenty-five men, and probably fewer, depended on farming as their principal source of income. Half of the group were professionals who, if they farmed at all, did so on a very limited basis. The remainder were men who combined farming with a profession—law, the ministry, teaching, the judiciary, and trade or commerce—and depended to an important degree on both for income.[24]

The decline of the old aristocracy is readily apparent in its diminished visibility in the house during the period 1800–1815. It was represented during these years by only two men, Edmund Harrison of Amelia and Hugh Nelson of Albemarle, who alone among the first families played an active and continuing role of leadership in the house. Many of the other leaders of this period had, or claimed to have, close ties to the old aristocracy, and at every legislative session there were Carters, Cabells, Lees, Randolphs, Fitzhughs, or other representatives of the old ruling elite in attendance. But they did not sit for any length of time, nor did they monopolize the positions of power on the important standing committees, where the major business of the house was transacted, as they once had. In the late colonial period, for example, the six standing committees in the House of Burgesses were normally chaired by a Randolph, a Harrison, or some other member of the ruling oligarchy, who typically served until retirement, death, or some other appointment prevented him from continuing as chairman. With their lengthy tenure, these men were able to monopolize political appointments and completely dominated house affairs.[25]

Although this pattern continued into the postrevolutionary years, it did not persist into the nineteenth century. During the 1800–1815 period the five standing house committees were chaired by no fewer than thirty-six different men, who collectively had an average tenure of only two years. The longest tenure of any chairman was four years, a claim shared by three different men, only one of whom was from the old aristocracy. Fourteen different individuals served two-year chairmanships, and the rest served only one year. Only four of the thirty-six men—Joseph Cabell, Edmund Harrison, John Page, and Peter Randolph—were immediately associated with the families who had dominated politics in the earlier period.[26]

A similar situation existed where the most important legislative office, the house speakership, was concerned. In the colonial and, to a somewhat

lesser extent, the postrevolutionary period, the office was typically occupied by a wealthy planter who served an uninterrupted tenure of many
years. For example, during the thirty-eight year period from 1738 to 1776,
only two men, John Robinson and Peyton Randolph, filled the Speaker's
chair in the House of Burgesses, while during the years 1786–1799 two
men, both Federalists, monopolized the position.[27] But during the first
fifteen years of the nineteenth century, no fewer than seven different men
held the office. The longest tenure was held by Barbour, who was elected
four times. Only two of the seven men, Edmund Harrison and Hugh Nelson,
who served a total of three years between them, were a part of the old
aristocracy.[28] It is significant not only that a new breed of politician, best
typified perhaps by the Richmond lawyer Andrew Stevenson, was replacing
the planter aristocrat as Speaker, but also that the office itself was becoming
more political in nature. After 1799 a legislator, in addition to the requisite
political experience, needed the right party credentials. It is significant, too,
that during the period 1800–1815 every Speaker but one appointed the
person who had nominated him for the office to the chairmanship of a
standing committee. In many instances this action involved demoting an
incumbent chairman to make a place for the new appointee.[29] Old
traditions were yielding to new political realities.

As the old aristocracy's political power was declining in the House of
Delegates, the center of power was shifting westward in the state. In the
period 1788–1800, 58 percent of the house leaders lived in the coastal, or
Tidewater, counties, 33 percent in the Piedmont, and 9 percent in the
western counties. In the period 1800–1815, only 29 percent resided in the
Tidewater. The Piedmont counties, where 46 percent of the leaders now
lived, had replaced the Tidewater in importance, and the counties west of
the Blue Ridge Mountains were now the home of 25 percent of the political
leaders.[30] Possibly the increased political power of the Piedmont and
western counties resulted initially from the fact that many of the powerful
Tidewater families had themselves moved westward, where they continued
to be active politically, but the long-range effect was a gradual democratiza-
tion of the state's political structure. The diffusion of power led inevitably to
a greater political diversity based on the different regional interests of a
large and populous state. That diversity was destructive of the political
homogeneity which had characterized the lower house throughout most of
the eighteenth century. Moreover, the physical proximity of the legislators
to their constituents ensured that they, whatever their own personal pre-
dilections, must in the final analysis be responsive to the public will or be
prepared to give up their seats in the assembly.

A number of factors, many of them economic in nature, help to explain
the political decline of Virginia's great landowners. The economic difficul-

ties arising out of the Revolution, especially the disruption of trade and the loss of markets for tobacco and other agricultural staples, created hardships from which many planters never recovered. Then, too, the declining productivity of Tidewater lands and the unprofitability of slavery during the uncertain 1780s accelerated the trend, evident by the last quarter of the century, toward smaller land units.[31]

In addition to the Revolution, of course, certain inexorable forces were working with time to break up the large estates. The absence of operative laws of primogeniture and entail meant that eventually the land would be divided and subdivided with each new generation. As the population increased, the demand for agricultural land quite predictably mounted, making it difficult for large landowners to retain their holdings and even harder, given the rising value of land and the lack of capital that always plagued planters, for a rising generation of gentlemen farmers to assemble estates as large as those of the earlier age. Among the hundred wealthiest men in Virginia in the 1780s, only a handful were nouveaux riches.[32] Barbour, who fell into this category himself, managed by 1820 to create an estate which, a generation earlier, would have gained for him a place among the One Hundred. But it should be noted that during the early years of his political career, when he was rising to a position of political leadership, he was not among the wealthiest members of the house.[33] With the breakup of estates like those of the Carters, Burwells, Harrisons, Cockes, and Byrds, the economic and political hegemony of the old aristocracy inevitably declined.

The diminished role of the old aristocratic oligarchy in the assembly may be explained in part by the fact that some of the ruling elite after 1789 exchanged their positions in the state government for places in one of the branches of the national government. The number of such offices was hardly sufficient, however, to provide berths for all the old leaders, nor for that matter were all the national offices filled with men from that rank.[34] Quite simply, the character of Virginia's political leadership, as Barbour himself observed some years later, was changing. Indeed, the declining importance of planters and the rising prominence of lawyers was one of the most pronounced trends of the period. During the years 1778–1800 only 20 percent of the political leaders in the Virginia House of Delegates were lawyers, but during the years 1800–1815 the number increased to more than 50 percent.[35] The same trend was apparent in Congress. In the 1790s, for example, Virginia's delegates to the House of Representatives were about equally divided between lawyers and planters. During the next twenty years lawyers came to dominate to such an extent that during the decade 1820–1830 they outnumbered planters almost five to one.[36] The overwhelming majority of Virginia's U.S. senators during the period were also lawyers, but like Barbour they were generally wealthy planters as well.

The rise of the legal profession and the decline of the old aristocracy in Virginia did not go unnoticed nor, for that matter, unlamented. John Randolph, for one, expressed a decided preference for the political leadership of the "good old Virginia gentlemen" who, with their "coaches and sixes" and their "forty bowls of rack punches, and madeira, and claret," were far superior to the "knot of deputy sheriffs and hack attorneys" who now sat in the Virginia assembly with "cruets of whiskey" before them and "puddles of tobacco spittle" at their feet.[37] There is, of course, nostalgic exaggeration and distortion in Randolph's comments, but he was an astute, if caustic, observer of the Virginia scene. The old aristocracy, which he in thought and action epitomized, was disappearing. Wealth and family influence were still important ingredients of political power, to be sure, but not nearly as important in the first two decades of the nineteenth century as they once had been. The way was opening for talented and ambitious men of moderate financial means, especially those trained in the law, to play important political roles in Jeffersonian Virginia.

Virginians like John Randolph who desired to preserve the old oligarchic system of government based on wealth and personal influence found themselves at the turn of the century engaged in a two-front struggle: with the federal government on the one hand, which threatened to destroy state autonomy and with it their own power base; and on the other with growing popular pressure within the state for greater political democracy.[38] That struggle, along with a closely related effort of some of the state's political leaders to reconcile the old system to the competing and often contradictory demands of the newly emerging system of party politics, constitutes a major political theme in Virginia during the years Barbour was active in the legislature.

Pressure to broaden the base of political power by extending suffrage and reforming the system of representation began to increase in Virginia soon after Jefferson's inauguration in 1801. Newspapers like the *Virginia Argus* and the *Examiner* of Richmond joined with various citizen groups to urge the legislature to call a constitutional reform convention. Barbour favored the move. He was, according to one western legislator, a "very zealous advocate" of reform. During the first decade of the century the assembly desultorily debated the question but refused to act. In 1810, when he was Speaker, Barbour worked hard behind the scenes to secure a bill authorizing the convention. He was unsuccessful, however, and it was not until 1829 that one finally convened.[39]

In supporting political reform, Barbour did not advocate universal white male suffrage. Always sensitive to the rights of property, he subscribed to the view common among Virginia agrarians that distinctive moral and intellectual endowments attached to land ownership. He believed that citizens, to be responsible, must have a stake in society. But that stake should be small enough to ensure that the industrious members of all classes and professions, urban as well as rural, could acquire the franchise after a few years of work. Throughout his political career he sought to extend economic opportunity and advocated popular rule based on just representation. A principal function of government, he believed, was to promote policies that would provide maximum social, political, and economic opportunity for the people. Failing to obtain changes that would have given Virginians living in the western part of the state a voice in government proportionate to their numbers, he tried, as Speaker, to compensate for this inequity by giving their delegates important committee assignments and calling upon them to play a larger role in government than they had before. And while he embraced the widely held political assumption that property and persons were distinct types of interest, he was at least responsive to that democratic impulse which, although still feeble, was operating to make Virginia government and society more open.[40]

Significantly, the changes taking place in Virginia's old political order helped make possible Barbour's rapid rise to a position of leadership in the House of Delegates. He served a remarkably brief political apprenticeship in that body. During his first five terms of service, 1798–1804, he served on three of the standing committees and chaired a large number of select ones. In the latter capacity he drafted and reported bills on a wide variety of matters. In addition, he served as the house's liaison with the senate. In 1804 he was appointed chairman of the standing Committee of Privileges and Elections and also of the important Finance Committee. The latter, which did not become a standing committee until 1806, was small by house standards, but it was usually composed of the most powerful men in the legislature. In 1807, for example, seven of its twelve members were or recently had been chairman of one of the other standing committees. Thus after only five years of legislative experience he was elevated to a major position of house leadership—a position shared with perhaps a half-dozen other men, to be sure, but nevertheless one which involved him in a substantive way in conducting legislative business and in implementing party policy. Within a short time he would also assume the position of Speaker.[41]

While experience was essential to advancement in the house, important committee assignments and chairmanships did not come with length of service alone. Men such as Barbour who showed exceptional ability could advance rapidly to leadership positions, bypassing members with greater seniority but less talent. Thomas Jefferson's rise to the chairmanship of the Committee of Propositions and Grievances in the 1770s after only six years in the House of Burgesses was considered unusual. Barbour's rise, which resulted in part from the ability he demonstrated, reflected also a dearth of political talent in the assembly comparable to that of the revolutionary generation. There were able men in the assembly during the early 1800s, but few of them rivaled Jefferson, Madison, Edmund Pendleton, and others of the earlier age.

Barbour's political role in the legislature was closely linked to his role in the Virginia Republican party. Although he was never a member of the party's controlling central committee, he had close connections with that group and was usually a key figure in the party's political caucuses. In addition, he was closely associated with the party's national leaders, especially Madison, and sometimes served as the administration's liaison and spokesman in the assembly. On occasions Madison, acting on his own or Jefferson's behalf, called on Barbour to secure the assembly's support of some administration measure. His loyal support of Jefferson and Madison and his able advocacy of their measures undoubtedly contributed to his own political strength in Virginia.[42]

Barbour's party loyalty did not include blind adherence to the party line regardless of the issue. When he differed with other party leaders, he was not afraid to take an independent stand. In 1804, for example, Republican leaders in the assembly attempted to remove the Federalist state auditor, William Shepherd, from office. It was a partisan move, for Shepherd was a competent public official. Barbour eloquently and successfully defended the Federalist, arguing that merit rather than party labels should be the chief criterion for office. While his independence on this and other issues evoked criticism from some party regulars, it won him favor with others, including some Federalists, whose political support Barbour sometimes enjoyed.[43]

Barbour's oratorical skills on such occasions were highly regarded by many of his colleagues. His effectiveness in debate helps explain his rise to prominence. Although it was not essential to political success in Virginia, fluency in debate was no less an asset in Barbour's day than in Patrick Henry's. William Wirt, who as house clerk heard Barbour speak on many occasions, thought that his speeches were "the highest specimens of the solidity and dignity of parliamentary debate" that he had ever heard or read. He went on to express regrets that Barbour's talents were not as fully appreciated in the house as they would be in a body composed of more talented and sophisticated men.[44]

Barbour's service in the house was interrupted on two separate occasions, first in 1803–1804 and then in 1805–1807. The first interruption resulted from the death in late August 1802 of Frances Cornelia, then fourteen months old. Some of the parents' sorrow was dispelled by the birth two months later of their second son, Benjamin Johnson. But Lucy was slow in regaining her strength, and Barbour was reluctant to leave her when the legislature convened in early December 1802. He left the session early and returned home. Finding Lucy still weak and depressed, he announced in January 1803 that he would not stand for reelection. In addition to the 1803 – 1804 session, he did not attend the 1805 – 1807 sessions, again because of pressing private affairs. Thereafter he attended the sessions without interruption until he was elected governor in 1812.[45]

During the years 1805 – 1806 Barbour gave some thought to running for Congress, but private affairs were so demanding that he dropped the idea.[46] Much of his time during this period was spent in building a house for his growing family, an undertaking which the vagaries of the weather made particularly vexing. Torrential rains in the spring and summer of 1807 delayed progress by making the transportation of building materials he had ordered through Richmond and Fredericksburg next to impossible. The country's roads, poor at their best, became mudslides and quagmires. In one instance a team of nine horses was unable to budge a wagon stuck in front of the Orange courthouse. Twelve inches of rain falling on a single June day swept away bridges and mills and flooded lowlands, destroying much of his tobacco crop along the Rapidan and Blue Run. He had to delegate some of the construction workers to repair the damage. Despite these and other nettlesome delays, the house was finally completed in late 1807. A spacious if undistinguished structure, it housed the family until 1819, when a larger and much handsomer two-story neoclassical residence designed by Jefferson was built.[47]

In May 1807 Barbour took time off from domestic pursuits to serve on the grand jury which indicted Aaron Burr. While those proceedings were under way, an incident occurred off the Virginia capes which electrified the county. On June 22 the H.M.S. *Leopard* bombarded the American frigate *Chesapeake,* killing three of its crew and wounding many others. The British then impressed four sailors, one of whom they later executed as a deserter. In humiliation and disgrace, the crippled *Chesapeake,* her masts and rigging in tattered shambles, and shipping almost four feet of water, returned to Norfolk.[48]

While the impressment issue was by no means new, this was the first time the British had imperiously violated American sovereignty by firing on the flag and destroying American life and property. The response of the country to the British attack was immediate and vociferous. Citizens of Hampton, enraged by the sight of dead and wounded seamen being unloaded from the *Chesapeake,* destroyed several hundred casks of water about to be shipped to the thirsty British squadron anchored in nearby Lynnhaven Bay. Residents of Norfolk and Portsmouth on June 24 decreed an immediate embargo against the British fleet and created committees of correspondence, reminiscent of the Revolution, to promote unity of action.[49] News of the

North front of the Barbour residence,
built c. 1807.
Courtesy of the University of Virginia Library.

Chesapeake-Leopard incident reached Richmond simultaneously with the grand jury's presentments against Burr and his associates on June 24. The impact of those indictments was almost lost in the wave of anger that swept the city. Barbour lingered in the city for several days after the grand jury completed its work to await developments. He read with indignation the full account of the "unexampled outrage" that appeared in the *Richmond Enquirer* on June 27, in which Ritchie wrote that "the honor and independence of our nation [have been] insulted beyond the possibility of further forbearance." When he departed the city shortly thereafter, the populace was astir as the Richmond Light Infantry Blues and other uniformed militia companies in the vicinity, responding to the call of Gov. William H. Cabell, assembled and tendered their services.[50]

Barbour carried news of the British attack back to Orange. At a mass meeting of its citizens in mid-July, which he had been instrumental in convening, he delivered a bellicose but "eloquent and impressive speech" reviewing the many indignities the country had endured at the hands of Great Britain. He challenged those present to join with others throughout the nation in avenging the country's honor. He then offered a set of resolutions, which he had drafted with the help of his brother Philip Pendleton and several others, expressing the county's indignation at the outrage "perpetrated on their national honor." The resolutions went on to pledge Orange's firm support of President Jefferson in whatever retributive action he might choose to take, including war, which "with all its infamy" was preferable to "submission to such treatment and dishonor at the hands of Great Britain." The citizens overwhelmingly endorsed the resolutions.[51]

Ignoring these and other similarly angry resolutions, Jefferson chose peace, not war. When Congress convened in late October, the president proposed a program of economic sanctions against Great Britain. The response of the nation to his embargo was divided. Many members of the Virginia assembly, which met on December 7, were unhappy with it. When the embargo went into effect in late December, the Virginia Federalists and merchant class protested in the strongest possible terms. Speaker Hugh Nelson appointed Barbour, who was once again a member of the legislature after a two-year absence, chairman of a select committee to study the embargo and report back. In the deliberations of the committee, Barbour, whose ardor for war had now cooled, urged acceptance of the president's policy of peaceable coercion. He drafted a report supportive of the embargo and, after securing the committee's endorsement, presented it to the house in early January.[52]

A sharp debate followed. Several delegates, fearing a reduced market for agricultural commodities, opposed the report and called for revocation of the embargo. Federalists denounced both the embargo and the Republican administration's entire conduct of national affairs. Barbour was the administration's principal defender. He upheld the embargo as a "great national measure," praised the president's handling of the national crisis, and rebuked his colleagues for their selfish concern with agricultural prices. After much discussion, the report was approved by the Republican majority.[53]

If the assembly's Federalist minority was angered by the embargo, the Republican majority was angry for other reasons. Aaron Burr's acquittal in September 1807, following a long and widely publicized trial, provoked a loud cry of protest from many Republicans throughout the country. Republicans in the Virginia assembly, disturbed by what they believed was the "unwholesome supremacy" of the federal judiciary over other branches of the government, passed a resolution early in 1808 advocating a constitutional amendment that would limit the tenure of federal judges to a specified term and would provide for their removal upon the address of two-thirds of both houses of Congress. Barbour opposed the move. He argued that the independence of the judiciary and stable tenure for federal judges must be preserved at all costs. Such "great and settled principles," sanctioned by the Founding Fathers and confirmed by experience, should not be precipitately abandoned or affected by "ephemeral agitations of the day." His forceful appeal, though endorsed by the Federalist minority, did not deter the Republican majority. The resolution was forwarded to Virginia's senators in Washington to be presented to Congress.[54]

In opposing the dominant Republican mood on this and other occasions, Barbour acted with an independence that placed him somewhat outside the rhetorical extremism and partisanship that characterized Virginia politics during the early nineteenth century. He was sometimes criticized by his colleagues for disrupting that "unanimity which ought to prevail among Republicans."[55] But he was no political maverick. His support of James Madison for president in 1808 attests to this fact. Early in that year the struggle between possible successors to Jefferson intensified. For the first time the Republican party was not united on its choice of a nominee. There were three rivals—George Clinton, James Monroe, and James Madison. Clinton had the support of his powerful New York machine and the benefit of a widespread sentiment that Virginia had furnished enough presidents. Monroe was supported by John Randolph and his followers and also by the high priest of Federalism, Timothy Pickering, whose bankrupt party could only support the least objectionable Republican. Madison was supported by Jefferson who, despite his professed neutrality, left no doubts as to his choice of a successor.

In Virginia the rival candidacies of Monroe and Madison had been developing for several years. As early as the summer of 1806 John Randolph, disaffected with both Jefferson and Madison, had begun to work and intrigue for Monroe, whose political views he believed to be more compatible with his own conservative philosophy and the "Principles of '98" than were Madison's. Many Virginians distrusted Madison's republicanism and thought he was "too much of a federalist." Although Monroe represented no real threat to Madison nationally, his challenge did create tactical problems for Madison's campaign managers. In Virginia, where Monroe had a significant following, it posed a serious threat to party unity.[56]

Barbour was one of Madison's principal Virginia managers. Disturbed by the Monroe movement, which he feared would split the Republican party in Virginia, he and other Madison backers attempted to quash it by emphasizing the fact that Madison was simply too strong nationally to resist. Without waiting for the results of the congressional caucus which William B. Giles and Wilson Cary Nicholas were organizing in Washington, they moved quickly to head off the challenge. To avoid a floor fight in the assembly between supporters of the two men, Barbour and his colleagues decided not to hold the customary open legislative caucus. Instead they quietly issued invitations to Madison's friends in the legislature to attend a private caucus on the evening of January 21 at Richmond's Bell Tavern. Monroe's friends in the assembly learned of the move and attempted unsuccessfully to pass a house resolution calling for a general legislative caucus on the same day.[57]

At the caucus that evening, which was attended by 123 regular Republicans, Barbour played the leading role in organizing the meeting and, once Madison had been unanimously endorsed, in forming the strongest electoral ticket possible. After appointing a central corresponding committee and similar committees for each county, the caucus, which had been characterized throughout by a rare "concord, unanimity, good order and good humor," adjourned. It was clear that most of the influential legislators were in the Madison camp. Thus preempted, the Monroe faction had no recourse but to hold a caucus of its own. This they did, though theirs was not as well attended or as well organized as that of the regular Republicans. They met three times before finishing the business of nominating Monroe and establishing the necessary machinery for conducting his campaign.[58]

The presidential contest, especially in its early stages, focused mainly on peripheral issues. Neither the Madison nor the Monroe faction seemed anxious to discuss the embargo, foreign relations, or other basic issues which might have widened the split in the party. Both sides, for the most part, exercised considerable restraint in referring to opposing candidates, making a deliberate effort to avoid statements which might be injurious to either man. As the summer drew to a close, regular Republicans flooded the public print with futile appeals urging Monroe to withdraw in the interest of party unity. The results of the election in November came as a surprise to few. The Madison ticket won by the overwhelming vote of 14,665 to 3,408.[59]

Barbour's efforts on Madison's behalf, while certainly not crucial to his election, contributed to his landslide victory in Virginia. His predictable choice of Madison over Monroe was based on personal as well as political considerations, but the former, stemming from their long association as neighbors and friends, was unquestionably paramount. In the years ahead, however, Barbour would become closely associated with Monroe and in the presidential election of 1816 would champion Monroe's cause as enthusiastically as he had championed Madison's in 1808.

Despite the efforts of Barbour and others to prevent a party rupture, the election contest of 1808 had serious repercussions for the party in Virginia. Following the election, regular Republicans, led by Thomas Ritchie, whose *Enquirer* was the primary vehicle of attack, undertook reprisals against many of those who had supported Monroe. Monroe himself escaped without censure and, indeed, would soon be elected governor. But others did not fare so well. In 1809 the assembly removed two Monroe men from the Council of State. Two of Monroe's most important Old Republican supporters, John Randolph and John Taylor, came under heavy attack which culminated finally in the former's defeat in his bid for reelection to Congress in 1813. Taylor, who had been the chief party theorist and mainstay in the legislature during the 1790s, was shunted aside by party regulars and was not restored to a place of honor in party councils until the revival of states' rights doctrines after the Missouri Controversy.[60]

Not long after Madison's victory at the polls in November, Barbour set out for Richmond to attend what was to be a rather uneventful session of the assembly. Continuing as chairman of the Finance Committee, he served on several other standing and select committees. On February 8, 1809, Speaker Hugh Nelson of Albemarle resigned his position to accept a judicial appointment. To fill the vacancy thus created, William Wirt nominated Barbour. Opposed by James Semple of Williamsburg, who had been a member of the legislature since 1797 and, like himself, had served as chairman of the committee of Privileges and Elections and the Finance Committee, Barbour won the election and immediately assumed the chair.[61]

Because it was not customary to record the vote in contests for the speakership, it is difficult to comment on the political significance of Barbour's election or to determine the sources and extent of his support. The office itself, the most important and powerful of any in the legislature, was awarded only to men who consistently demonstrated leadership ability and commanded the respect of their colleagues. An additional qualification, operative since 1799, was membership and stature in the majority party. The position was not one which candidates openly sought or campaigned for.

Rather, an individual was advanced by his friends for the office. Since 1800 names had usually been submitted quietly, either by correspondence among the candidate's friends or during an informal party caucus held in Richmond shortly before the legislative session began.[62] In Barbour's case, because the unexpected resignation created the vacancy, there was little opportunity for consultation in advance. His nomination may have been impromptu, or it may have resulted from a caucus hastily convened by Wirt and other supporters. Whatever the case, his election was confirmation of the leadership role he played in state politics.

In his capacity as Speaker, Barbour made no major changes in the way business was conducted. Most of the work was done by one of the five standing committees or by ad hoc committees appointed by the chair, a practice whose long tradition militated against change. The system worked well enough, and Barbour saw no reason to alter it. The heaviest burden of drafting legislation and making reports was borne by the chairmen of the various committees, a relatively small group of men who influenced house affairs strongly. Barbour broadened the base of political participation by appointing many veteran legislators who had not previously served in such positions to head the important committees. Of the twelve standing committee chairmen he appointed during his three-year tenure, for example, nine had not served in such roles before. He made a conscious effort also to include more western delegates in his appointments, as chairmen of both the standing and select committees. In the eleven years since he had first attended the assembly in 1798, only four delegates from the western counties had served in the former capacity. Among the first five chairmen of standing committees he appointed were two western representatives.[63]

In addition to being able through his appointive power to ameliorate inequities in the distribution of political power, Barbour was in a position as Speaker to give legislative priority to measures he deemed important. One such item was a bill for public education. His concern with self-improvement sparked an interest in public improvement. He optimistically believed that society, no less than the individual, was capable of improvement through conscious effort and that it was the role of government to promote measures like public education that would raise the moral and intellectual level of society. Education would accomplish the dual objective of unleashing individual potential and creating the literate, well-informed, disciplined populace essential for the proper functioning of democratic government. In December 1809, he appointed a special house committee which he asked to study the education question. Shortly thereafter it reported back a bill that he himself had personally prepared. It provided for the creation of a Literary Fund to consist of all escheats, nonmilitary fines, confiscations, penalties, forfeitures, and delinquent property rights. The revenue from the fund thus created was to be used solely for the benefit of schools to be maintained in each county of the state. The bill passed the assembly on February 2, 1810.[64]

During the 1809–1810 session of the assembly, another measure concerned with redeeming individuals and raising the moral level of society, also sponsored by Barbour, passed—the antidueling law. Barbour had long been an outspoken critic of dueling. Its increase during the early nineteenth century was a matter of growing concern to him and others. That concern culminated in the passage of the Anti-Duelling Act of January 26, 1810. The law disqualified from all public offices any person who had engaged in dueling and prohibited him from initiating legal action of any kind in courts of the state.[65] While the law did not end the practice, it did cause a noticeable decline. Barbour's desire to arrest the evil continued throughout his life.

In December 1811 Barbour became a gubernatorial candidate. A number of prominent politicians had privately supported him for that position the previous year, when James Monroe had been a candidate. They preferred him to Monroe because of the divisive effect exerted on the party by the latter's presidential candidacy in 1808. But Monroe had managed to explain away past differences with the administration and, after assuring regular Republicans of his readiness to support administration measures, including its foreign policy, had been elected governor. Barbour had not accepted the candidacy at that time, and Monroe had easily defeated his opponent, George William Smith, who had accepted the position of lieutenant governor. But Monroe, after serving only three months, had resigned to become President Madison's secretary of state, and Smith had been elevated to the governor's chair. Barbour thus opposed an incumbent who had served only nine months. The reluctance of the legislature to turn out someone who was performing the duties of office satisfactorily and who had not served the customary three terms was probably the decisive factor in Barbour's defeat. Even so the vote was extremely close—100 to 97.[66]

Having been assured by friends that his election was certain, Barbour had been confident of victory. His defeat came as a hard blow and caused him to consider retiring from public life. Richard M. Johnson, his kinsman and political confidant from Kentucky, upon learning of his defeat and discouragement wrote from Washington urging him not to retire: "You have . . . advanced rapidly up the steps of fame, as well as in the affections of the people." Reminding Barbour that his political principles had led him frequently to take positions that were not the most popular, Johnson tried to reassure him, predicting, accurately, that "opportunity will soon be provided for your success."[67] The opportunity came in a way that Barbour could hardly have wished for.

On the evening of December 26, 1811, some 600 people packed the Richmond Theatre to enjoy a new drama, *Father, or Family Feuds,* and a pantomine called *The Bleeding Nun.* During the pantomine the scenery on stage caught fire and the entire building was soon ablaze. In the conflagration and panic that followed, seventy-two persons, including Governor Smith and a number of other prominent citizens, perished. On January 3, the assembly, having observed an appropriate period of mourning, proceeded to elect a new chief magistrate. Apparently Barbour was the consensus candidate. Neither the newspapers nor the house journals indicate that he was opposed. By secret ballot in joint session both houses elected him governor. Barbour responded in a brief speech expressing appreciation for the confidence placed in him and formally resigned his position as Speaker.[68] He immediately assumed the executive responsibility and prepared as best he could for the new trials that awaited him.

4

"War's

Wild Alarm"

*W*ith war approaching, the challenge Barbour faced was the formidable one of finding some way, within the limits of a state constitution that severely restricted executive power, to exercise effective leadership. The governor of Virginia, though he enjoyed considerable prestige, had little authority. Elected annually by the legislature and limited to a maximum of three one-year terms, he had no veto power. He could recommend legislation, make minor appointments, act as commander in chief of the militia when it was embodied, and convene the Council of State, a body of eight men chosen by the legislature. In all executive action he was required to have the approval of a majority of the council, four members of which constituted a quorum.[1]

Such limits on executive power during wartime, Barbour realized, could be disastrous. He turned to Thomas Jefferson for advice. The retired president, who had served as governor of Virginia during the Revolution, gave him no reason for optimism. The governor, he wrote, was the creature of the legislature. Strictly speaking he was not even a member of the Council of State. He presided at council meetings, where he could express opinions but could not vote. Only in the case of a tie, or in an emergency where there was no vote at all, could he act on his own authority. It was a situation, Jefferson noted, that had once prompted Gov. Benjamin Harrison to remark wryly that the executive branch consisted of "eight governors and one councillor."[2]

The limits on executive authority were to frustrate Barbour as much as they had Jefferson a generation earlier. The office did provide a platform which the governor could use to shape public opinion and influence legislation. It also afforded him an opportunity to determine executive action in council meetings if he could be personally persuasive. Although Barbour thought the constitution excessively restrictive, he scrupulously adhered to it. The fundamental law was not so sacred that it should not be changed, but in the meantime it stood as the expression of the public will which all elected officials were obliged to obey. Although he refused to assume powers not rightly his, he did not hesitate to try to change the law. Throughout his tenure he indefatigably sought to persuade the legislature to broaden executive power and to make other changes required by the war. The few prerogatives he did enjoy he used to full advantage. He went before the people frequently in an effort to influence public opinion and skillfully managed the Council of State, which responded in most instances with prompt executive action.

In experience and temperament, Barbour was well prepared to deal with those problems which inevitably accompany war. The years he had spent as a captain in the Orange militia had disabused him of the notion that an inspired yeomanry was the best defense of a free people in time of war. He clearly recognized the inadequacies of the militia system as it then existed—its lack of organization, its poor discipline and lack of proper training, its problems of leadership and supply. His experience as a legislator had given him a realistic awareness of the jealousies of an assembly always quick to defend its prerogatives against executive encroachment. More important, he brought to office those attributes of character most needed in the impending conflict: confidence, persistence, and energy. These were essential in a wartime executive. Jefferson, warning Barbour that the trials which lay ahead would not be easy, expressed confidence in his ability to deal with them: "I fear the station you have accepted . . . will be a laborious and disquieting one in the trials of war now coming upon us. But it is happy for us that the moment finds at the helm of our state one who will not sleep at his work."[3] The events of the next three years, as Jefferson predicted, would indeed test the quality of Barbour's leadership.

In time Barbour would become totally immersed in the problems of war, but in January 1812 he was occupied with more mundane matters. Apart from routine but necessary adjustments to the new office, he had to move his family to Richmond, a city which had changed greatly since his first winter there in 1798. Its population, which had doubled in fourteen years, numbered slightly more than 10,000, and the limits of the town had expanded significantly in every direction except to the south, where it was bounded by the James River. Richmond was the teeming commercial center of the state, with an ever increasing number of flour mills, small manufacturies, banks, and mercantile establishments. More and more it was beginning to take on a cosmopolitan air as planters, legislators, merchants, mechanics, and sailors from ports around the world went about their daily business. Coastwise schooners and square-riggers crowded the docks along the river. Singing Negro stevedores and roustabouts loaded giant hogsheads of tobacco and flour for shipment to distant markets and unloaded vessels laden with aromatic cargoes of Brazilian coffee and wood, East Indian spices, and French perfumes and wines. Rowdy seamen confined for months aboard cramped ships thronged the city's numerous taverns, where their boisterous behavior occasionally landed them in jail.[4]

The wooden structures which Barbour had found when he first came to the town were being replaced now by brick buildings. Brick Row, the principal business section on Main Street, was an impressive new addition, and a number of fine brick and stone residences near Capitol Square and along Fifth Street had recently been built. The city now enjoyed daily stage connections to Hampton in the east and to Staunton in the west. It also had a public library, chartered by the assembly in 1806, and several theatrical groups, which continued to perform despite the disastrous 1811 fire at the Brick Theatre. On the site of that tragedy a memorial in the form of Monumental Episcopal Church was under construction. A major horse-racing center, the city had several racetracks which were crowded with spectators in season, a festive time much enlivened by the Richmond Jockey Club's gala balls. Other entertainment was available at the famous Haymarket Gardens, the Dancing House, and the Musical Gallery, where visitors could amuse themselves with all sorts of diversions—riding machines and flying gigs, cockfights and bearbaiting, quoits and bowling, musical performances, or quiet walks in terraced gardens.[5]

Despite the increasing signs of affluence, Richmond still lacked many of the amenities of urban life. The streets, which had only recently been given names, were not yet paved and were impassable much of the time except on foot. Intersected by ruts and gullies that worsened with every rain, they were made all the more hazardous by the absence of lighting. An attempt in 1802 to provide gas illumination had been unsuccessful. Capital Square itself, the showpiece of the city, was cut by ravines and covered with weeds which provided meager forage for the goats and cows which seemingly roamed at will. The classic lines of the capitol were marred by two unsightly exterior lateral staircases, and shabby wooden barracks occupied by members of the Public Guard and their families stood nearby. The governor's residence, located just to the northeast of the statehouse, added nothing of architectural distinction to the square.[6]

Into this house, pretentiously called the Palace, the Barbours moved in January 1812. A plain two-story frame-and-brick structure, it was dilapidated and poorly furnished. Two years earlier Gov. John Tyler, father of the future president, had complained that the place was "fast going to destruction."[7] It was barely fit for human habitation. Fortunately, the Barbours' residence there was brief. The assembly appropriated funds for a new mansion, and a short time later the governor and his family moved to temporary quarters. The old structure was razed to make room for a new dwelling, which was completed in 1813. The new residence was an impressive two-story Georgian structure with four large rooms on each floor. On the upper level were spacious bedrooms commanding excellent views of the surrounding grounds and city, while the lower level consisted of a large entrance hall, a library, which Barbour used for his study and office, a drawing room, a parlor, and a dining room. All were handsomely finished.[8]

Under normal circumstances the governor's residence was the center of the gay social life of Richmond, especially when the legislature was sitting. It was customary for the governor to keep a five-gallon silver punch bowl filled with drink for the benefit of thirsty solons who might wish to drop by in the afternoon or early evening. Balls and dinner parties, either at the governor's house or at one of the fashionable homes on nearby Shockoe Hill, were held frequently. Despite the advent of war, the wealthy Richmond merchant Thomas Rutherfoord thought the city had never witnessed a more festive winter than the one of 1812–1813. But the festive spirit did not continue long. After the spring of 1813, when the danger of British invasion increased, the city's social life suffered greatly. There was little time and even less inclination for social levity. Many of the families, at least the women and children, left Richmond and sought refuge with relatives and friends living in less exposed areas. Barbour sent his own family—increased now with the birth on March 22, 1812, of Frances Cornelia—back to Orange, where they remained much of the time during the war. Detained by the demands of office and unwilling to expose his family unnecessarily to danger, he dwelt alone in the large but almost empty mansion. It was not a happy experience.[9]

The demands on Barbour's time and energy were great throughout his governorship, but at no time did they seem greater than during the months immediately after he took office. From the outset he was swamped with paperwork, council meetings, interviews with legislators and private citizens, the appointment of justices of the peace and militia officers, and a seemingly endless list of duties. At first he devoted considerable time to the mere task of mastering the cumbersome executive machinery, which threatened to overwhelm him. But he was not too busy to follow the deliberations of Congress.

In November 1811, just two months before he became governor, the Twelfth Congress assembled in a belligerent mood. Federalists in that body were a decided minority, conservative Republicans were without unity or effective leadership, and War Hawks—aggressive, contemptuous of the mild Jeffersonian policy of peaceable coercion, and anxious to avenge the nation's injured honor—were firmly in control. Henry Clay, Speaker of the House and leader of the War Hawks, appointed John C. Calhoun, Felix Grundy, Peter B. Porter, and other war advocates to all the important congressional committees. The war party prodded the nation along the tortuous road to war.

While Congress debated and made menacing gestures, Barbour worked untiringly to accomplish what he considered his most urgent task—to prepare Virginia for war. Though war had not yet been declared, he believed it was inevitable. Indeed, he welcomed it. Since the *Chesapeake-Leopard* affair of 1807 he had privately favored it, but loyalty to Jefferson and Madison had restrained him from openly espousing a cause inconsistent with national policy.[10] In the early months of 1812, however, he made no effort to conceal his true feelings. By both words and actions he advocated war. Too long, he believed, the United States had borne the insults of "perfidious Albion"; too long the country had tolerated British encroachments on national sovereignty. The time had come to vindicate national honor, he told the assembly in March 1812. "It is time that we . . . shake off the supineness which paralyzes every manly effort. . . . It seems that no alternative is left but an appeal to arms or ignominious submission. . . . How long shall we sit with our arms folded together, and still hope for the continuance of peace, when by a long series of acts, such hope is proved to be illusory?"[11] These were strong words. They might have been spoken by Calhoun or by some other member of Henry Clay's War Mess in Washington. If he was slower than the congressional War Hawks in calling for war, he was, nevertheless, a War Hawk—though perhaps the tardiest of the group.

In late January 1812 Barbour asked the assembly for a special grant of emergency powers. Hoping to avoid a situation like that of 1780–1781 when Governor Jefferson, because of constitutional restrictions, had been powerless to respond adequately to British invasion, he sought to broaden the powers of the office. He urged the legislature to grant him greater authority over the militia and, in the event of war, power to act upon his own authority as military exigencies demanded. To leave the hands of the executive bound by constitutional shackles with war approaching, he warned, could prove disastrous. He urged the legislature to place the state on a better defensive footing. Contrary to popular belief, in the event of hostilities, Virginia could not rely upon the national government to defend her against invasion. She must assume this responsibility herself. Many things were needed. The supply of military stores, which was dangerously low, should be substantially increased, and the antiquated and cumbersome militia system needed general overhaul. Barbour's appeal fell on deaf ears, however, for the legislature, apparently thinking that his requests were either premature or extravagant, elected to do nothing except to pass a law authorizing him to purchase and distribute eight tons of lead and two tons of gunpowder.[12]

Undaunted, though quietly chafing at what correspondent Robert Quarles called the "invincible torpor" of the assembly, Barbour continued his efforts to put Virginia on a stronger military footing. At the end of March he placed the militia of the Tidewater counties most vulnerable to attack virtually on a war footing and two weeks later ordered up 12,000 troops, the state's quota of the 100,000 called for by President Madison. In addition, he conducted tours of inspection, drew up plans for improving harbor defenses, and secured such additions to the supply of arms and ammunition as limited funds permitted. He asked militia commanders to hold special musters to drill their troops and instructed the regiments to be ready for action on a moment's notice.[13]

In these actions, of course, Barbour acted upon the advice and with the consent of his eight councillors, who met with him regularly—sometimes daily when circumstances required it. For the most part he enjoyed a good working relationship with them, both individually and collectively, but he was no mere tool for implementing their votes. He was, instead, the dominant figure on the council. He gave energy and direction to the executive, and councillors followed his lead. "We go on smoothly in the Executive," wrote one councillor, whose initial skepticism of Barbour's administrative qualities quickly disappeared. "Barbour takes it *rough, roll and tumble*.... He is quick as lightning, to use a common figure, and is willing to do everything in his power, I believe, for the country."[14] His capacity for decisive action, and his ability to lead the council and present a united executive front, gave the office an authority it lacked under less vigorous leaders.

In the deliberations of the council, rising young lawyers were beginning to play an increasingly important role, replacing the older and politically more experienced men who had traditionally dominated it. Two such individuals who were particularly active during Barbour's governorship, both elected to the council before they were thirty years old, were Edmund Randolph's son Peyton and Peter V. Daniel. The majority of the councillors were relatively inexperienced, at least as far as executive matters were concerned, having served on the council for a year or less. Only James Wood, a crusty and somewhat disagreeable former governor, had significant administrative experience. A member who was very supportive of Barbour was Charles K. Mallory of Elizabeth City, a newcomer to the council but an associate of Barbour's in the House of Delegates for almost ten years. The willingness of the councillors to follow Barbour's lead may have been owing, in part at least, to the fact that he had greater political experience in state government than any of them except Wood, and that Daniel, Mallory, and John Campbell of Washington County had served political apprenticeships in the house under his leadership.[15]

On April 21 Barbour embarked upon a three-week inspection tour of the eastern part of the state. Reviewing the defenses of the maritime frontier, he studied possible routes of enemy invasion and noted the best sites for the erection of additional defenses. On April 23 and 24 he toured the Jamestown-Yorktown-Williamsburg area and then traveled to Norfolk, where he was warmly received despite the opposition of town merchants to war. Upon studying the defenses of the area, he noted the strategic location of Craney Island, a small island several miles below Norfolk near the left bank of the James River, which commanded the channel. For more than a week he remained in the Norfolk area interviewing militia officers, receiving local visitors, reviewing troops, and inspecting arms. He was particularly concerned by the revelation that guns produced by the Richmond armory, operating under state auspices, were inferior and unreliable. The locks malfunctioned and the poorly welded barrels sometimes exploded, so that militiamen refused to fire the weapons for fear of injury. On May 5, after making a final survey of sites for the erection of communication towers along the major rivers, he traveled to Petersburg, where he was warmly acclaimed by citizens at a public dinner. He used this occasion, as he had an earlier one at Norfolk, to address the people, appealing to their patriotism and urging them to prepare for war.[16]

Upon his return to Richmond, Barbour convened the council. Calling attention once again to the state's lack of preparedness, he stressed the need to improve existing forts and to build new ones at strategic points. Craney Island, because of its excellent location and command of the river channel, should be fortified, and a chain of communication towers should be erected from Cape Henry to Norfolk to give advance warning of an approaching enemy fleet. Finally, the Richmond armory should be reorganized and the quality of muskets produced there improved. A few days later he informed Secretary of War William Eustis of his tour and made additional recommendations for strengthening Virginia militarily. Admitting the value of Barbour's suggestions, Eustis commended him on behalf of the president for his "prompt and energetic action," but he failed to act upon his recommendations.[17]

During the weeks after his return from the tour, Barbour remained active. In numerous public addresses and communiqués to militia regiments he sought to prepare the people for the impending war. While it is difficult to assess the reaction of all Virginians to his efforts, the response of the citizens of Richmond is a matter of record. On May 30 a large number of people from the capital and vicinity assembled in a public meeting over which he presided. After listening to several spirited anti-British speeches, they adopted resolutions calling for war: "Though peace is very, very dear, the rights and honor of the country are still dearer.... It is time, therefore, to fly to arms." Barbour must have been gratified, but he could hardly have been surprised, for he had been careful to appoint Thomas Ritchie, Andrew Stevenson, and other war advocates to the committee which drafted the resolutions.[18] What credit is due him for uniting Virginia behind the war is impossible to say, but this much is clear: he worked tirelessly to arouse a war spirit among the citizens, and when war came an overwhelming majority of Virginians favored and supported it. If it would be a mistake to attribute this wholly to his efforts, it would be no less a mistake to deny their importance.

On June 1, 1812, Congress went into secret session to consider President Madison's war message. Two weeks later it declared war. Rarely has a nation been so poorly prepared for war—militarily, financially, or psychologically. The regular army, despite an authorized strength of 35,000 troops, had fewer than 12,000. Almost half were raw recruits; and the ranking officers were, for the most part, old and incompetent or young and inexperienced. The navy consisted of only six forty-four-gun frigates and a few smaller vessels, along with a fleet of useless gunboats, to engage the mammoth British navy of some 800 ships. The national treasury, depleted by years of embargo and nonintercourse, was practically empty. Congress had adjourned without financing the war it had declared, and Secretary of the Treasury Albert Gallatin faced the difficult task of trying to borrow $20 million to cover the anticipated budget deficit. In addition to these problems, the nation entered war disunited. New England objected strenuously to a Virginia-dominated policy which first disrupted her commerce with embargo and nonintercourse and now threatened to ruin it completely with war. Die-hard Federalists like Timothy Pickering, who viewed the contest as a wicked and foolish war against "the world's best hope, Britain's fast-anchored isle," openly yearned for a separate New England republic. For the duration of the conflict, cacophanous sounds of disloyalty and disunity, which proved in the final analysis to be the death throes of Federalism, emanated from the Northeast.[19]

Sectionalism, a depleted treasury, and a woeful state of military preparedness were an ominous portent. But many of the national leaders seemed undisturbed. To the more ardent War Hawks, drunk perhaps on dreams of Canada, Florida, and a new United States avenging old wrongs with its righteous sword, the braggadocio of that "Kentucky Hotspur" Henry Clay—who believed the militia of his adopted state capable of single-handedly capturing Canada—must have seemed unexceptional. But the delusion that if war were declared victory would inevitably follow was short lived.

Barbour had taken a more realistic view of the demands war would make than had many of the congressional War Hawks. He had done all he could to put Virginia in a position of readiness. Thus the declaration of war prompted no change in his policies. He sent additional militia regiments to the exposed maritime frontier and renewed his plea to the secretary of war that the national government repair and strengthen key Virginia forts. But little could be expected of the incompetent Eustis.[20] Even had he been competent, it is doubtful that he could have done much to aid Virginia, for the War Department suffered from shortages of every sort—money, troops, arms, and military supplies.

Barbour was not too occupied with problems in Virginia to follow national developments. The military campaign undertaken against Upper Canada was of particular interest. He was appalled by the news he received in August that Gen. William Hull, an aging revolutionary veteran, had ignominiously surrendered the entire Northwestern Army at Detroit without firing a shot. Overcoming his initial shock and indignation, he responded positively to that disaster by offering the administration Virginia's full cooperation in another invasion. To Secretary of State Monroe he wrote that Virginians anxiously awaited an opportunity to "recoup the honor of the United States so ingloriously lost at Detroit." Deprecating the spirit of disunity which prevailed in the Northeast and the opposition of that region to the war, he gave the administration repeated assurances of Virginia's loyalty and support. As evidence, he called for 1,500 volunteers in early September, outfitted and equipped them at the state's expense, and dispatched them to the western frontier of Ohio, where they were to join the Northwestern Army.[21]

Following General Hull's defeat, the United States attacked at other points along the Canadian frontier, but all of the land campaigns of 1812 were humiliating failures. If the close of the year found the nation dispirited by defeat in the field and division at home, Virginia seemed more buoyant and optimistic. Despite the administration's bungling of the war effort, Virginia had not become cynical. The state was united in its support of the national government and remained firm in its resolve to push the war to a successful conclusion. For this stance Barbour deserves much credit. But he was supported in his efforts by the highly vocal Ritchie, who used the columns of the *Enquirer* to arouse his countrymen, and by other prominent political figures such as Spencer Roane, William Wirt, and Andrew Stevenson. The result of their collective efforts was that opposition from the Federalist- and Quid-dominated[22] areas of the state virtually disappeared. The maverick Quid leader John Randolph and his associate Edwin Gray of Portsmouth were defeated in their bid for reelection to Congress in 1813, leaving Virginia without any Quids in the Thirteenth Congress. James M. Garnett of Essex County, who had represented the middle Tidewater district in Congress during Jefferson's administration, continued to voice opposition to the war in the columns of the *Spirit of Seventy-Six,* but even that lone voice became silent when the Quid organ folded in the spring of 1814 for lack of subscribers.[23]

The course which Barbour pursued during his first year in office was not always applauded. Occasionally he was charged with seeking too much power for the executive branch or with advocating defensive measures too extravagant for the limited financial resources of the state. But for the most part he enjoyed the support of both the people and the politicians. Not infrequently citizens held mass meetings and adopted resolutions expressing approval of his policies and congratulating him for his effective leadership.[24] The legislature, when it convened in late November 1812, indicated its approval by reelecting him governor without opposition. The committee appointed to inform him of the fact expressed its confidence by declaring: "The ability with which you have heretofore discharged the duties of this office furnishes the surest pledge that the continuance of your services will redound to the honor and prosperity of our common country."[25]

On the opening day of the session, Barbour presented a lengthy message recapitulating the grievances against Great Britain which had led to war and summarizing executive actions during the preceding year. But most of the message was devoted to another appeal to adopt military measures which he considered essential to the state's defense. Military supplies, dangerously inadequate, should be increased. More pressing was the problem of the militia, whose organization and discipline were deplorable. To correct this deficiency he proposed that the regiments be assembled at some central spot and drilled in camp until the necessary skills and discipline had been obtained. Training handbooks should be written and distributed to all the troops. In the interest of uniformity and efficiency, the offices of adjutant general and inspector general should be combined and the salary of the position increased so as to enable the state to secure the services of an able officer.[26] While the changes he proposed were hardly revolutionary, they did run counter to the attitude of complacency that had so long prevailed where the militia was concerned, and the assembly was loath to do anything.

In early February 1813, while the legislature was still sitting, a British squadron under the command of Adm. Sir George Cockburn moved into the Chesapeake to enforce the blockade proclaimed by the British government several months earlier. The appearance of the British vessels caused panic throughout Virginia's entire eastern frontier. Hundreds of terror-stricken citizens abandoned their homes and fled, while those who remained flooded the governor's office with calls for aid.[27] The situation gave immediacy to the assembly's consideration of the defensive measures Barbour had been urging since the day he took office. On February 15 the body passed a bill providing for additional troops and supplies and appropriated a rather meager $350,000 for defense purposes, but it declined to pass other desperately needed measures such as militia reform. Shortly before it adjourned at the end of the month, a select committee reported that "radical reform, at this time, in the present militia system, would be dangerous and highly inexpedient."[28] It seemed clear that however great the danger, the legislature was simply unwilling to enact measures which would impose an additional financial burden on the state or would modify a military structure that had behind it the weight of tradition. It continued to cling to the militia as the sheet anchor of its faith that free people were the only defense of liberty and that a regular army would jeopardize the very liberties it was called upon to protect.

On February 5, the day following the appearance of the British fleet, Barbour ordered 3,000 additional militia to report without delay to Norfolk. He then hastily departed for the town himself. After conferring with Brig. Gen. Robert Taylor, whom he had placed in command, he reviewed the militia units as they arrived, delivering to each a stirring speech. Having satisfied himself that the situation was well in hand, he returned to Richmond. There he summoned the Council of State and prepared a plan of defense, which he immediately sent to Washington for approval. Secretary of State Monroe, assuming functions of the War Department, responded a few days later, assuring him that the necessary steps for defending the state were being taken.[29] There was nothing to do now but wait.

The next few weeks were relatively quiet, but soon there were further alarms. In March another British squadron, under Adm. John B. Warren, sailed into the Chesapeake. Enjoying undisputed control of the bay, the enemy sent out marauding parties which attacked and raided isolated farms and villages and spread terror throughout the region. Barbour expected a major attack on Norfolk and called out 2,000 additional militia, ordering them to the beleaguered town. He kept in close contact with General Taylor, whom he advised to fortify Craney Island with redoubts and artillery. In addition, he issued a proclamation on April 1 calling the assembly back into a special session. He had been disappointed by that body's refusal earlier to provide adequately for just such an emergency, and he refused now to abide the consequences of its inaction.[30] In mid-May the legislature convened. In an opening address, Barbour detailed the crisis confronting the state and recounted the defensive steps he had taken. A committee including his brother, Philip Pendleton, was appointed to consider the problems he presented. During its ten-day session the legislature belatedly enacted several limited measures giving the executive greater powers and allocating additional funds for military purposes.[31]

They were not as much as the governor had hoped for, but they were better than nothing.

In early June additional warships and transports, filled with some 4,000 marines and soldiers, joined the British fleet in the Chesapeake and prepared to attack Norfolk. Opposing them was a small force of some 700 American volunteers on Craney Island, which commanded the approach to the town. Confident of success, the seasoned British regulars attacked Craney Island on June 22 only to be repulsed by the devastating fire of the Virginia riflemen. Following a second attack more disastrous than the first, the British retreated to the safety of the fleet. Humiliated by what must have been, along with the Battle of New Orleans, one of their most discomfiting defeats during the war, the British then attacked the sleepy little hamlet of Hampton. There they wreaked their vengeance, raping, plundering, and killing several civilians. Barbour wrote Admiral Cockburn protesting vigorously against the barbaric conduct of the occupying army.[32]

After several days the British quit Hampton and spread their work of destruction throughout the Chesapeake, making landings on the Eastern Shore, at Smithfield, where they were repulsed by the local militia, and at Williamsburg and Yorktown. When part of the fleet entered the mouth of the James and proceeded upriver, the citizens of Richmond, certain that their city was the British objective, panicked. The bell on Capitol Square, which served as the tocsin for the city until the close of the Civil War, rang out, alarm guns were fired, and before an hour had passed the public square teemed with men of all ages and ranks, armed and ready to take the field. The city's Nineteenth Regiment had never seen such a turnout. Within hours a new company of Flying Artillery with William Wirt as captain was organized. But this quick response seemingly did little to quiet the fears of the people. Exaggerated reports of British atrocities and the imminence of attack circulated widely, creating consternation among the women and children and the infirm, while bank officials prepared to remove their specie to safer regions.[33]

Barbour responded to the crisis with characteristic vigor. He delivered several spirited speeches to the militia and citizens, after which he met with the Richmond Vigilance Committee, made up of John Marshall, Thomas Ritchie, William Wirt, Philip N. Nicholas, and nine other prominent citizens, to consider appropriate defensive steps. They decided, in effect, to place the city under martial law. The troops were drilled morning and evening in excessive heat that hovered for weeks at 100 degrees.[34] But the expected attack never materialized. Instead, the British moved to the Potomac, where they continued their raids. Barbour responded by ordering to that area a detachment of cavalry and mounted riflemen under Lt.

Col. James McDowell, which managed to check the depredations of the enemy on the Virginia side of the river. On July 21 the British dropped down the Potomac.[35] After this, the fleet, with the exception of a small squadron which remained in Lynnhaven Bay, quit the Chesapeake.

With the immediate threat of invasion past, and unable financially to maintain a large force in the field, Barbour disbanded most of the militia. He then dispatched General Taylor to Washington to press for adoption of a permanent state defense plan he and the general had drawn up. It called for the placement of a permanent force of 7,600 regulars at Norfolk and the formation of "flying camps" composed of cavalry, light artillery, and mounted riflemen. It was hoped that the latter would afford the mobility necessary to counter the thrusts of a mobile, seaborne enemy which could attack at random any portion of the exposed maritime frontier. Secretary of State Monroe, speaking for the War Department, considered the plan but reduced the permanent force proposed for Norfolk to 5,000 men and unwisely disallowed the flying camps.[36]

Barbour was disappointed in the changes, especially in the rejection of the flying camps. While he recognized the limitations of such a body, he was correct in his opinion that a mobile force could more effectively check British depredations than the unwieldy militia. Why the War Department refused to endorse the plan is unknown. It is, however, a matter of record that the department, poorly organized and inadequately staffed, headed first by the notably incompetent William Eustis and then by the equally inadequate John Armstrong, was often more hindrance than help to Virginia in the formulation and enactment of defensive measures. In addition to rejecting sound proposals which would have increased the state's ability to repel invasion, the department made promises of military aid which, realistically, it could not hope to fulfill. Time and again Eustis, Armstrong, and Monroe assured Barbour that adequate military assistance would be extended when it was needed, but invariably that aid came either too late or not at all.[37]

To elicit a response from the War Department required, it must have seemed to Barbour, Herculean effort. In the months before the British first attacked Norfolk and Hampton, he had repeatedly urged Secretary Eustis either to repair the dilapidated federal forts on the Chesapeake or to authorize the state to do so. More than a year later, and then only after he had written to President Madison himself, belated action was taken.[38] When the promised aid was not forthcoming and Barbour, at state expense, undertook the necessary defensive measures, the War Department was slow to acknowledge the legitimacy of reimbursement claims. Aware that the national government was unable to meet the financial demands made of it, Barbour did not press for payment. Instead, he turned to the state banks to borrow the funds necessary to continue the war effort. When the state's credit was exhausted, he borrowed $200,000 on a pledge of personal security to carry the state through the summer crisis of 1814. When Virginia's war debt mounted to more than $2 million in 1814, a group of Barbour's critics charged him with executive extravagance, saying that his war measures were excessive. To that criticism he turned a deaf ear. To do less than he had done, he said, would be to abdicate executive responsibility and to invite military disaster.[39]

Despite the difficulties he encountered in his dealings with the War Department, Barbour refrained from criticism. Instead, he minimized the problems. Appalled by New England's antiwar stand, he did all he could to unite Virginia solidly behind the war effort. In early December 1813, following a short vacation at Barboursville, he urged the assembly to demonstrate its loyalty to the administration by paying without delay the state's quota of the direct tax levied by Congress the preceding August. Aware of the significance of the struggle in which the country was engaged, and recognizing the need for national unity, he appealed to the delegates:

> The period, fellow citizens, in which we are called to act, is among the most eventful in the annals of the world. Both hemispheres are bleeding under the dreadful scourge of war. And, from the prodigious efforts which are made in the old [world], the present crisis seems to be in travail with the destinies of half mankind. . . . It behooves us to be sensibly alive to the magnitude of the occasion and to prepare for any result. Let us practice forbearance and moderation . . . , cherish concord and brotherly love, draw close to the cord of Union, and thereby give full and undivided scope to the energies of our country.[40]

The assembly approved Barbour's request, but before it did so, it took up the annual business of choosing a governor. In the previous year Barbour had been reelected without opposition. This year his enemies organized to oppose him. Chief among them was a group of disgruntled militia officers who were upset because he had placed Gen. Robert Taylor, the youngest of twenty-one militia brigadier generals, in command of the forces at Norfolk. Barbour's choice of Taylor, who surpassed the others in energy and ability, had been an act of political courage, for he had known that in passing over the senior officers he would arouse strong opposition. The opposition had not been long in appearing. Some of the aggrieved officers, who exerted political influence, together with a few of Randolph's Quid followers and a scattering of antiwar dissidents, attacked him bitterly for calling up the militia and for putting the state on a war footing in the summer of 1813. While he was trying to provide protection for the exposed

Chesapeake towns and villages, his enemies were accusing him of reck-lessly spending state funds for unnecessary defensive measures.[41] "The Governor," wrote one councillor in July 1813, "is the daily subject of the most vile and infamous calumnies."[42] His critics attempted now to unseat him.

The disgruntled faction first approached Francis Preston, a brigadier general himself whose brother John Preston was treasurer of the Com-monwealth, to see if he would consent to become a gubernatorial candi-date. The Prestons were an old and influential Virginia family, and Francis Preston was politically ambitious. But he refused to oppose Barbour. "Governor Barbour," he explained, "has acted honestly, energetically, and correctly for the good of our country."[43] It would be an act of ingratitude, he continued, for him to stand against an incumbent with so distinguished a record. The dissidents then turned to James Pleasants, Jr., clerk of the House of Delegates from 1802 to 1811, who agreed to run. But Barbour's friends stood behind him in the balloting, and he defeated his challenger by the vote of 133 to 53.[44]

With the political challenge behind him, Barbour turned his attention to other matters. Throughout the winter of 1813–1814, he kept a watchful eye on international developments. After Napoleon Bonaparte's defeat in Oc-tober 1813 in the Battle of Nations at Leipzig, Great Britain was free to prosecute her war with the United States with greater energy. Although peace overtures were made early in 1814, Barbour doubted that the war would end quickly. Expecting England to step up her military activities in America, he sent additional troops to Norfolk and held twenty-four reg-iments of state militia in readiness. By summer the peace negotiations, as Barbour anticipated, had broken down, and on July 21 the British fleet again entered the Chesapeake in force. For the next several weeks raiding parties attacked exposed or weakly defended settlements, plundered farms, seized slaves, and once again spread terror throughout the region.[45]

In August an army of 4,000 British regulars, led by Gen. Robert Ross, sailed up the Patuxent River and marched the short distance overland to Bladensburg, on the outskirts of the District of Columbia. There they routed the American forces and marched to Washington, where they put the government to flight and burned all the important public buildings. News of the sack of Washington caused widespread alarm in Virginia. Expecting Richmond to be attacked next, Barbour immediately ordered out 10,000 militia for the defense of the capital, the Northern Neck, and the surrounding country. On August 26 he issued an additional proclamation calling all able-bodied Virginians to arms and instructing the recruits to proceed immediately to Richmond. Excited volunteers poured into the city by the thousands. William Wirt's Flying Artillery prepared to take the field, mounted riflemen from west of the Blue Ridge organized themselves into a company, and the Junior Blues of Richmond, a group of twenty-five boys under the age of fifteen, tendered their services. The overwhelming response made it necessary for him to issue a second proclamation halting the influx. At the height of the alarm some of his friends, recalling the example of Jefferson and other members of the government during the Revolution, urged him to flee to the protection of the interior. He spurned their pleas and remained in Richmond to supervise its defense.[46]

After taking the immediate precaution of ordering that additional breastworks and cannons be placed on the peninsula along the York River, which seemed the most likely route of attack should the British move against Richmond, Barbour summoned the legislature to another special session. When the delegates assembled on October 10, he informed them that the war, "no longer waged at a distance but brought into the bosom of our country," demanded their immediate attention. Once again he pressed for a complete reorganization of the militia, the erection of state arsenals at strategic points throughout the state, and the appropriation of funds for other defensive measures.[47] For months the assembly dawdled and frittered indecisively with the recommendations. It was not until mid-January 1815, a month before news of the Treaty of Ghent arrived, that it acted, and even then it approved only part of the governor's requests. But it did finally acknowledge the cogency of his arguments concerning the militia. It authorized the enlistment of a regular force of 10,000 troops, to be placed under federal authority, as a replacement for the cumbersome militia.[48] If this measure had been taken earlier in the war when Barbour first requested it, Virginia would have been better able to defend itself against British depredations. But the concession came too late. The invasion of Richmond, which was really of no strategic importance, never materialized, and hostilities ended after the signing of peace on Christmas Eve, 1814.

Like most other Americans, Barbour greeted the peace with a sigh of relief. Even though the treaty left unresolved the issues that had led to war, he was satisfied. If the United States had not emerged from the conflict laden with the laurels of victory, at least the nation had fought with honor. The important thing was that it had fought. For Barbour and others, the war had been a psychological necessity—a rite of passage which marked the nation's coming of age. Above all else, it had been a war for national honor.[49] Events would soon prove that this second war for independence was, in some ways, more successful than the first. In the years ahead Barbour and other nationalists would commit themselves to achieving for the United States what Great Britain had denied them after the Revolution—their rightful place among the family of sovereign nations.

No one in Virginia acted more responsibly than Barbour in waging that war. Upon assuming office in 1812, he took a more realistic view of the approaching crisis than most leaders and wisely set out at once to prepare the state. Consequently, when war did come, Virginia was better prepared, psychologically if not otherwise, than the rest of the country. During the two and one-half years of hostilities, he conducted the government with confidence, demonstrating a rare ability to attend to details without losing overall perspective. His war measures, for the most part, were well conceived and, when approved by the assembly, were effectively administered. While acknowledging that the state was performing functions belonging to the national government, he recognized the plight of the latter and refused to criticize it. Instead, he urged the citizens to make whatever sacrifices were necessary for victory. "This is not the time," he said, "to be guided by a calculating policy which is content with drawing an abstract line, marking with scrupulous nicety the limits where the duty of one government terminates, and that of the other begins."[50]

For his effective leadership during the war, Barbour was commended by President Madison, Secretary of State Monroe, Spencer Roane, and others. One member of the Richmond Junto wrote at the time of the threatened invasion in July 1814 that Barbour had energetically "taken the field, and pitched his tent in camp. . . . By his vigilant and able conduct of affairs he has nobly maintained the honor of Virginia."[51] A member of the Council of State, John Campbell, initially a critic of Barbour, had high praise for his conduct as governor: "His ardor and attention in business has elevated him far above my expectations. He is spoken of as the best governor we have ever had."[52] The *Virginia Argus* praised him effusively and the *Baltimore American* exclaimed that his decisive conduct contrasted boldly with the "inaction of the Maryland Executive, who did nothing but make pitiful supplications to Washington while enemy forces were robbing and destroying all along the Bay!"[53] But perhaps the most gratifying commendation came from the people themselves. The resolutions drafted by the citizens of Patrick County were typical:

> Resolved, that the firm and dignified conduct of our worthy chief magistrate is calculated in a super-eminent degree to insure the confidence of the people, and is entitled to the enthusiastic gratitude of every lover of liberty and free Government.
>
> Resolved, that the activity and vigilance displayed by the Chief Magistrate of this Commonwealth in personally visiting the most exposed and vulnerable points bordering on our coast and making the necessary arrangements for its protection and safety, entitles him to the warmest thanks and unfeigned assurance of our confidence and support; and we are happy to add that the sentiments expressed by this meeting pervade the country generally.[54]

Although Barbour was occupied during his governorship primarily with the problem of war, he did devote time to other matters, especially to internal improvements. To the assembly which convened in December 1812 he expressed regret that the state had done so little in the area of turnpike and canal construction. The growing importance of the West, he declared, made a program of internal improvements highly desirable. The connection by canal of the James and Rappahannock rivers with western rivers and the construction of turnpikes throughout the state would stimulate trade, would increase wealth, and would strengthen the bonds of union between East and West. Such a program of internal transportation would, he contended, connect Virginia "with those vast and fertile regions destined to become in the progress of time the emporium of wealth, a portion of which, as from a never failing fountain, will constantly pour into our lap."[55]

During his administration Barbour encouraged the formation of private corporations devoted to river improvement, canal building, and road construction, and urged existing companies to increase the scope and pace of their work. He persuaded the directors of the Dismal Swamp Company, which had been formed in 1787 to connect the waters of the Elizabeth River with those of Albemarle Sound, to revive and accelerate their lagging efforts. In June 1814, when the shipping of the state had virtually ceased because of the British blockade, the canal was finally opened, and communication with the North Carolina sounds was greatly facilitated. Numerous charters were granted to turnpike and canal companies for the construction of roads and canals and for the improvement of waterways, all of which would, it was hoped, promote economic growth by connecting the interior and western portions of the state with the coast.[56] Thus his domestic program, despite the demands of war, was not one of retrenchment but one of expansion and development. The foundation for an ambitious program of internal improvements, financed by state and private funds, was laid during his administration. After the war Virginians would enthusiastically endorse various improvement projects, though that enthusiasm would be greatly dampened by the Panic of 1819.

In addition to his attention to internal improvements, Barbour demonstrated a continuing interest in public education. As governor he was chairman of the board which controlled the Literary Fund, and in that capacity he acted with care to see that its monies, limited though they were, were employed wisely to promote and advance public education. In December 1812, he urged the legislature to consider establishing a state university which would correspond in magnitude with the "extent, population, and resources of the state."[57] Although the legislature took no action at this time, his interest in public education continued unabated and served, perhaps, as a stimulus for later action.

That Barbour managed as war governor to provide effective leadership despite constitutional restrictions was owing in part to the influential place he occupied in Virginia's political power structure. That structure, formerly dominated by a planter aristocracy possessing extensive and powerful family connections, had been in a state of metamorphosis for more than a decade. While the old political leadership continued to be important, it was yielding to a new and less homogeneous leadership which combined in itself a greater diversity of social, economic, and political interests. This trend had been apparent during the years Barbour was a member of the assembly. No single group or combination of groups during that period, except those who called themselves Republicans, and they certainly were not of a single mind or doctrine, was able to fill the political void left by the decline of the old aristocracy. Political and social crosscurrents created eddies that made it difficult for anyone or any group to provide consistent and integrated direction to the political life of the state. Thus a condition existed in which a number of men like Barbour, who were newcomers to the political scene in the sense that they had few or no direct ties to the old ruling aristocracy, were able to achieve political prominence. And like Barbour they tended to look to Jefferson and Madison, at least until the end of the War of 1812, for political direction in state matters. During these years local concerns and issues, for Barbour no less than for most of his political associates, were clearly secondary to national issues.

The group which came the closest to providing cohesiveness and direction to the state's political life during these years was the Richmond Junto. Composed of about twenty men whose activities centered in Richmond, the Junto was very influential politically. Prominent members included Thomas Ritchie, editor of the *Enquirer* and almost perpetually the public printer; Dr. John Brockenbrough, president of the Bank of Virginia; Philip Norborne Nicholas, president of the Farmer's Bank, and his brother Wilson Cary Nicholas, who was president of the Richmond branch of the Bank of the United States; John Hay, James Monroe's son-in-law; Peter V. Daniel, member of the Council of State; Spencer Roane, senior judge of the Virginia Court of Appeals; William H. Cabell, former governor of the state; Andrew Stevenson, who succeeded Barbour as Speaker of the House; Benjamin Watkins Leigh, a successful Petersburg lawyer; and William Wirt.[58]

The Junto, in which membership seems to have been determined at least in part by family relationships, operated secretly and informally in its efforts to control the state's political processes and governmental machinery. For many years it was able to dominate the Republican party's central committee, a body whose creation had resulted from recommendations Barbour made to the legislative caucus of 1800 for formalizing party structure. Although the Junto possessed a large measure of homogeneity and was able to influence political matters significantly, it did not control the legislature, the most powerful political body in the state. Nor, for that matter, was it always of one mind on issues affecting the party and state. In 1808, for example, it split on the question of Jefferson's successor, with a substantial number of the group supporting Monroe over the majority candidate, Madison. Not until after the war, with Virginia's reaction to nationalism and the concomitant growth of the states' rights movement, did it enjoy sufficient power and unity to control political elections or to determine who would hold office.[59]

Barbour's own experience in Virginia politics serves as a good case in point. He rose to a position of political prominence largely on the strength of his performance and record of achievement as a legislator, not as a result of his friendship or affiliation with the Junto. It is true that he, like his brother, Philip Pendleton, had influence with the group and was on close personal terms with such individual members as Ritchie, Wirt, Stevenson, Leigh, Roane, and William Fitzhugh Gordon.[60] But some of these friendships, for example, those with Wirt, Leigh, Gordon, and perhaps others, grew out of associations predating or independent of the Junto. After the war he would develop stronger ties to the group as a whole, though he was never to become an actual member; but before the war his association with it was essentially casual. And while he was supported by some of its individual members for governor in 1811 and apparently by most of them the following year, he was not their candidate for the U.S. Senate in 1814.[61]

Virginia's senators during the war, Richard Brent and William B. Giles, had both incurred the displeasure of Virginia in 1811 when they refused to defer to legislative instructions directing them to oppose recharter of the national bank. Giles, who opposed the bank, voted against recharter but refused to acknowledge the right of the legislature to send instructions, while Brent asserted his independence by voting for recharter. By ignoring the instructions, Brent killed whatever chances he may have had for reelection when his term of office expired in March 1815. The legislature had no intention of tolerating such conduct in its elected representatives.

The senatorial contest which took place in Richmond in November 1814 generated more interest than was normal, perhaps because of the anger that Giles and Brent had provoked among the legislators. Friends of the various candidates politicked and canvassed legislators for weeks before the election.[62] A number of men in addition to Barbour were mentioned as possible choices—Jefferson's son-in-law, John W. Eppes; the popular James Pleasants, who had abandoned his Quaker principles to become one of Virginia's War Hawks in the Twelfth Congress; and William Wirt, who at first resisted becoming a candidate because he did not want to oppose Barbour, whose conduct during the war entitled him, Wirt said, "to my respect and gratitude." For several weeks it seemed that Barbour would be opposed by either Eppes or Pleasants, both of whom had some support among members of the Junto. But when it appeared that neither of them could win, Joseph C. Cabell, who like his brother, William, was part of the Junto, approached Wirt. Cabell appealed to Wirt's sense of public duty, which the latter professed to be unable to resist, as well as to his obligation to the party, which Cabell said supported him rather than Barbour. In consenting to run, Wirt may have acted more from pecuniary than from altruistic motives. His legal practice had fallen off sharply during the war, and he was deeply concerned about how he would support his wife and seven children. He had somewhat reluctantly concluded earlier that "the business of law" was dead for the duration of the war and that unless he chose "to stay at home like a drone," he had no recourse but to enter public life. While a senator's salary was not large, it must have appeared rather attractive to him at the moment.

If Wirt, upon the withdrawal of Pleasants and Eppes, was the choice of the Junto, at least one of its members, Leigh, who by 1813 was about the only Randolphite left in the assembly, supported Barbour. An unexpected ally was John Randolph himself, with whom Barbour had had very little contact and with whom he had even less in common politically. Randolph, according to Wirt, acted as the governor's "topographical organizer" among the legislators. But Randolph had so completely alienated the Junto and the legislature by his antiwar, antiadministration stand in Congress, that his efforts on Barbour's behalf probably did more harm than good. Barbour's policies as governor and his politics in general could hardly have been popular with the embittered Quid leader; Randolph's activities at this time probably stemmed mainly from a desire to strike out at the Junto and at its candidate, Wirt.

Until the day of the balloting on November 14, the outcome of the contest was uncertain. Republicans in the legislature were fairly evenly divided between Barbour and Wirt. As a result the Federalists were in a position to decide the election. Charles F. Mercer, a Federalist legislator from Loudoun County, canvassed his party colleagues, urging them to vote for Barbour. With their support, Barbour won by the vote of 107 to 80.[63] It is likely that Federalists would have voted for him even without Mercer's intervention. Most of them represented western counties, whose delegates Barbour had favored with major committee assignments when he was Speaker of the House, and the importance he attached to internal improvements while he was governor was welcomed by western Virginia. More than anything else, though, Barbour's victory was the assembly's affirmation of his "patriotic and energetic" record of leadership during the war. Wirt himself acknowledged this tribute when he wrote, "It cannot, I imagine, be thought any great degradation to have made such a run *vs. the Governor of Virginia,* a Governor too who has rendered himself so popular both at home and abroad by the zeal with which he has defended the state." Even some of Wirt's warmest friends believed that Barbour's long and outstanding record of service to Virginia gave him an undeniable claim to the Senate seat.[64]

Barbour's senatorial career, as it turned out, began earlier than he had expected. In December Brent died and the legislature appointed Barbour to complete the three remaining months of his term.[65] Having served for some fifteen years in state government, Barbour now faced a new career in national politics, a career which would strain old political relationships and would test political creeds which were demonstrably inadequate for the nationalist era the country had entered.

5

The Lure of Nationalism

*I*n early January 1815, after a busy but happy few days at home in Orange, Barbour bade his family farewell and set out for Washington. Despite the military and financial crises then imperiling the nation—crises compounded by the recent Hartford Convention, which Barbour and other critics of New England's antiwar stand deprecated—he was optimistic about the future. He did not yet know that peace had already been signed at Ghent, of course, and it would not be until mid-February that he and his congressional colleagues heard the welcome news. But ever since the British defeat at Plattsburg in September 1814 he had looked forward to a speedy settlement. He was anxious now to see the country put behind it the frustrations and tribulations of the war years and engage the great postwar challenges which awaited; his mood was one of hopeful expectancy.

Traveling by horse rather than by the safer but slower stage, Barbour made his way over an unmarked and little-traveled road that Jefferson once called "the worst in the world."[1] North of Fredericksburg he took a wrong turn. At dusk of his second day's journey he found himself in an abandoned tobacco field, completely lost. For several hours he wandered aimlessly in the cold darkness, piqued but at the same time somewhat amused at his plight. "How strange," he thought, "and going to the *eternal city,* I expected to find a fine spacious road." At length he came upon a dilapidated structure that passed for an inn. Lounging at its door was the barefooted and shabbily dressed proprietor, who responded to Barbour's query. "No, you are not mistaken," he said. "This is a hotel, and I assure you that you will meet with few houses where you will find better *incommodation*! I have plenty for your hos' to eat, and my wife has some coffee, and I have good old brandy too."[2] After a comfortless night in the drafty, dirt-floored inn, he continued his journey and arrived the next day in the national capital.

The scene that greeted him as he rode down Pennsylvania Avenue was dispiriting. At its best, Washington was a raw, bleak, sprawling cluster of villages and vast empty spaces. Having been invaded and burned by the British a few months earlier, it presented a depressing spectacle. Before him stood the gutted, smoke-stained hulk of the president's house, flanked on both sides by charred heaps of brick and rubble, all that was left of what had formerly housed the Treasury and War departments. A mile to the east loomed the stark shell of the once imposing but uncompleted Capitol, its beautiful Corinthian columns cracked and broken and its white walls blackened. Midway between the two buildings stood the Post and Patent Office, the only public building spared the British torch. Some of the private buildings and residences, huddled in little groups along the main avenue, had also been burned, while others had been damaged or destroyed by a recent tornado. Though Barbour was overwhelmed by the sight, his initial despair quickly gave way to patriotism. What the British had destroyed, the United States would rebuild. To that he was firmly committed. A new and grander capital would rise from the ashes of the old, just as a proud new nation, which he would help lead, would emerge from the terrible ordeal of war.[3]

On the morning of January 11 Barbour went to Congress's temporary quarters at the Post and Patent Office and presented his credentials.[4] There a distinguished assembly somberly considered the fate of the nation. The most prominent of the group were Cong. Daniel Webster of New Hampshire, Congs. John C. Calhoun and William Lowndes of South Carolina, and Sen. Rufus King of New York, all of whom would play important roles in the political debates of the postwar years. A newcomer was Philip Pendleton Barbour, who would emerge as one of the most fluent spokesmen of conservative Republicans in the House at the same time his brother became the ablest leader of nationalist Republicans in the Senate.

Differences between the two brothers were not limited to political philosophy. Their physical appearance contrasted sharply also. Philip Pendleton, smaller and thinner than James, was a "decidedly ugly man," according to one contemporary. Senator Barbour, on the other hand, was generally thought to be strikingly handsome. A few years earlier a member of the Virginia assembly had written that he was "the handsomest, gayest, and most fluent man in speech" ever to preside over the legislature. Just under six feet in height, he was heavy framed—not corpulent, but not slender either. His large physique and sharply marked features, wrote one observer, created a singular impression of strength. He had an expressive face, a wide forehead, thick eyebrows, and dark piercing eyes which, in the opinion of some, gave him a look of ferocity. But most contemporaries thought his countenance conveyed intellectual intensity, not ferocity. Almost everyone agreed that his commanding physical presence, together with an eloquence in speaking that could be captivating, were major political assets. He never lost that presence. As late as 1840, just two years before his death, he still impressed a political opponent as a remarkably handsome man whose "striking face, long scraggy eyebrows . . . , silver flowing locks and majestic sonorous voice" were reminiscent of the "grandeur of a Roman citizen in the best days of the Republic."[5]

There were also marked differences in the personalities of the two Barbours. Philip Pendleton was reserved and somewhat taciturn socially. James was the very opposite—gregarious, genial, and loquacious. In private discourse he exhibited a warmth and sincerity which flowed, in the words of Librarian of Congress George Watterson, "from the heart rather than the head, delight[ing] all who have the pleasure of his acquaintance."[6] An excellent conversationalist with a quick wit and good sense of humor, he could and often did entertain listeners for hours. His large store of funny anecdotes, facile wit, and clever ripostes, said a colleague, could "make the dead laugh."[7] That grande dame of Washington society Margaret Bayard Smith was charmed by his "eloquent and amusing conversation" and thought that few equaled him in colloquial powers, an opinion her brother shared. Mrs. Anne Royall, a British traveler who toured the United States in 1824, found the tedium of a stage journey from Washington to Fredericksburg much relieved by "the wit and sprightliness of Gov. Barbour . . . , a gentleman of very agreeable manners as well as liberal sentiments . . . , [who] shone in his ability to entertain."[8] His engaging personality and social graces made him a welcome guest at the popular "squeezes" hosted by Dolley Madison and Margaret Bayard Smith or at the more sedate and sometimes Spartan dinner parties of Presidents Madison and Monroe.

The congressional session had been under way for almost four months when Barbour took the oath of office. A heavy pall had hung over Congress since it assembled in September 1814. Congressmen had returned to find their capital sacked and the country facing the likelihood of another British invasion by way of Lake Champlain, which the demoralized and understrength American army could hardly hope to prevent. In addition, the treasury was empty, and the country was on the brink of bankruptcy. If the government collapsed, as it certainly would unless the tangled strands of wartime finance were straightened out, military defeat and a humiliating peace would inevitably follow. Congressmen listened solemnly as Secretary of the Treasury Alexander J. Dallas bluntly told them in October that a national bank was the nation's only hope. Responding to this dire necessity, the party of Jefferson became the reluctant advocate of the institution it had so adamantly opposed in 1791 and which it had refused to recharter in 1811.[9]

Most Virginia Republicans, including Barbour, had opposed recharter in 1811. The Virginia legislature at that time had instructed the state's senators to vote against the renewal bill. But political opinion in Virginia had shifted somewhat since then, and some influential men like Barbour now favored a bank.[10] Even a few of the state's more doctrinaire Republicans, to whom a national bank, or for that matter any bank that issued paper currency, was anathema, privately conceded that it appeared to be the only alternative to military defeat. The ultraconservative Spencer Roane, for one, confided to Barbour that a bank seemed necessary "to avert disastrous and overwhelming consequences."[11] But that opinion was short lived among orthodox Republicans, who quickly changed their minds upon learning of the peace settlement. Barbour did not. He saw more clearly than they that peace did not alter the need for a stable currency and a sound banking system. Setting aside his constitutional reservations for what he believed was the compelling need of the country, he vigorously supported the national bank. Politically it was a risky move. But in view of the government's imminent collapse, it was one he willingly took.

The bank bill being considered by the Senate when Barbour arrived had followed a tortuous course since its introduction in the House in November. Its difficulties did not end once it passed that body. Barbour listened as his Senate colleagues debated and amended it in such a way as to make it unacceptable to the House. After several unsuccessful attempts at compromise, the two chambers reached an impasse. When it appeared that all would be lost, Barbour defended the bank in a speech which George Watterson said was "conceived and uttered in the very spirit of true eloquence." Pointing to the fearful dimensions of the fiscal crisis threatening the nation, he urged his colleagues to recede from their amendments and approve the House proposal. A few days later they did so. All was in vain, however, for Madison considered the bill unacceptable from the standpoint of the needs of the government and vetoed it on January 30.[12]

With bankruptcy looming, the administration hastily convened a caucus to devise a compromise. When this effort failed, Madison sought Barbour's assistance. Like Jefferson, his predecessor, Madison directed legislation during his presidency with the help of key congressional figures who acted as unofficial spokesmen for the executive. Because Barbour, whose personal ties to Madison had grown closer over the years, had frequently acted as the administration's liaison in the Virginia assembly, it was natural for the president to turn to him now. That he did so before the freshman senator had had an opportunity to establish any kind of power base in the

Senate suggests the confidence he placed in Barbour. Barbour met with the president and with Secretary of the Treasury Dallas and agreed to make another effort to secure a bill acceptable to the administration. Accordingly, he introduced a measure drawn up by Dallas and managed to pilot it through the Senate only to see it fail in the House in mid-February, when news of the peace settlement brought indefinite postponement.[13]

In early March 1815 Congress adjourned and Barbour returned home to Orange. His stint in Washington, though brief, had given him a different perspective on the country's problems and opportunities. And as so often happens, the responsibility that goes with power forced him to reexamine old political beliefs and assumptions. His experiences of the war years, during which the inadequacies of the old political creeds had been dramatically and very nearly tragically revealed, had affected him profoundly. As governor, he had known the frustrations of trying to govern under a restrictive constitution that was woefully inadequate for the times. And since the war he had glimpsed the difficulty of governing by country tenets an expanding nation whose economy was becoming more complex, whose expectations were rapidly increasing. It was patently clear to him and many others that the nation which had emerged from the War of 1812 was no longer the simple agrarian republic idealized by Jefferson. Agrarian primacy was being challenged now by a combination of interests which, in time, would bring about the economic modernization of America. The demands of modern capitalism, especially for banking, massed capital, roads and canals, protective tariffs, and the encouragement of commerce, were becoming insistent. How would Republicans respond to changing times? Would they cling to the old creeds and insist on applying static principles to dynamic events? Barbour, along with Henry Clay, John C. Calhoun, John Quincy Adams, and others who were becoming impatient with the Old Republican emphasis on agrarianism, states' rights, and constitutionalism, could see the need for a more dynamic and imaginative government—one that would encourage national growth and expansion in all areas, commerce and manufacturing as well as agriculture. Obvious utility, not blind adherence to rigid political principles, should be the real test of programs and institutions.

When Barbour first entered upon the political stage in 1798, the pressing need, as he saw it then, had been to restrain a Federalist-dominated government which threatened to destroy personal liberties. That situation no longer existed. The immediate danger to the republic had disappeared once the Federalists had been removed from public trust, and since 1801 the national Republican leadership had moved a long way from the doctrines enunciated in 1798. The War of 1812 had accelerated change and made it easier for Republicans to pursue a new course: first, by ensuring that the American republic would persist without becoming a satellite of any of the European powers; and second, by destroying the Federalist party and thereby ending the long contest over the shape of society and government. The republican nature and future of the country were firmly fixed, making it safe to pursue the great benefits of union without fearing that the nation's free character would be lost. Thus freed from the problems of the past, Republicans could turn their attention to the needs of the future.[14]

Barbour understood that Republicans, if they were to meet the challenge of the present and build for the future, must not look too much to the past. His actions in the first two postwar Congresses reveal that he had never made dogma of the restrictive dicta his party had fashioned while out of power in the 1790s. During the sessions of the Fourteenth and Fifteenth Congresses, indeed, he emerged as one of the foremost nationalists in the Senate. None of his colleagues in that chamber were more committed than he to a national bank, internal improvements, the encouragement of commerce, a stronger military establishment, and other nationalist measures which he thought postwar America required. His nationalism was not without limits, but for a Virginian schooled in the doctrines of 1798 it was certainly extraordinary.

Barbour was by no means the only Republican who embraced nationalist principles after the war. Jefferson himself acknowledged that an equilibrium between manufacturing, commerce, and agriculture might be a good thing. Madison went much further. In his seventh Annual Message to the Fourteenth Congress, which convened in early December of 1815, the president outlined a nationalist program that bore a strong resemblance to Federalist legislation of the 1790s. He recommended that a national bank, safely subordinated now to Republican ends, be chartered to establish a uniform national currency. In the interest of national defense, he advocated reorganization of the militia, the establishment of a small standing army, expansion of the navy, and enlargement of the Military Academy at West Point. The creation of a national university in the District of Columbia would prove a great blessing to the nation. A protective tariff, he believed, would provide a powerful impetus to manufacturing and domestic wealth. As a final means of advancing public interest, he suggested that a federally financed program of internal improvements, though it might require a constitutional amendment, would serve as both the cement of the Union and an avenue to national prosperity.[15]

If John Randolph and his small band of disciples ever required confirmation of their fear that the war would result in a strengthening of the federal government, they needed it no longer. Madison's message seemed to them an ominous presage of the future. Although Barbour praised it, calling it "one of the happiest efforts of Mr. Madison's mind," it raised for them the frightening specter of a national government of unlimited powers.[16] Randolph, back in Congress after a two-year absence, exclaimed on the House floor that Madison "out-Hamiltons Alexander Hamilton." Other Old Republicans who had supported the war but were now anxious to return the nation to its original republican purity were equally alarmed. For them to embrace the nationalist program proposed by Madison would be to abandon, finally and irrevocably, the "Principles of '98." Their ranks had been thinned considerably by the war, but conservative Republicans, led by Philip Pendleton Barbour, Nathaniel Macon, and Randolph, prepared to oppose the postwar nationalism of the Republican majority.[17]

In January 1816 John C. Calhoun submitted to the House a bill, essentially an administration measure, calling for the creation of the Second Bank of the United States. It was to be capitalized at $35 million, one-fifth of which was to be subscribed by the federal government in the form of coin or government stocks, while bank stock representing the remainder was to be offered for public sale. A clause permitting the president to appoint five of the twenty-five bank directors assured a close connection between bank and government. Still, the government was denied the right to suspend specie payment. It was to have an exclusive charter for twenty years, for which it would pay the Treasury a bonus of $1 million.[18]

In the debate on the bill in mid-March, Virginia's veteran congressman John Clopton raised the constitutional issue. But the majority of his colleagues no longer opposed a national bank as unconstitutional. They were impatient now with his objections. As soon as he sat down they loudly called for the question. The bill passed by a vote of 80 to 71, with John Randolph, Philip Pendleton Barbour, and a majority of the Virginia delegation voting in the negative. It was then forwarded to the Senate.[19]

In late March the Senate took up the bill. Debate focused not on the constitutional question but rather on details. Initial discussion concerned what proportion of bank stock subscribed by the government should be paid for in specie. Federalists Jeremiah Mason and Rufus King both wanted to double the specie payment recommended by the House. Anything less, they argued, would merely compound the nation's banking problems by creating a paper bank. They noted other defects in the bill and offered a number of amendments which, in their opinion, would strengthen the bank.[20]

Barbour responded to King and Mason by agreeing with them that the country required a specie rather than a paper bank. But he did not share their opinion that the specie payment stipulated in the bill was inadequate for that purpose. Nor did he accept as valid their objections to the government's right to appoint a fifth of the bank's directors. Federalists had not opposed such a connection between the government and the First Bank of the United States, which led him to conclude that their present objections stemmed simply from a desire to limit executive patronage. He went on to argue that because the bank would have a direct bearing on the nation's credit and financial transactions, public interest required that the government have some voice in its operation.

Barbour admitted that the bill had minor defects. But on balance he believed it would provide a satisfactory remedy to the nation's economic ills, perhaps the best that could be hoped for under the circumstances. The real issue, he said, was whether or not the bank should exist. He reminded his colleagues of the smallness of the House majority that had passed the bill and argued that the Senate could not insist upon amendments that might be unacceptable to the other chamber without imperiling its passage. If the bill failed, the country would be paralyzed. Immediate action was necessary.[21]

The Senate did not approve the bill without amendments. Mason's proposal to increase the government's specie payment failed, but other amendments were taken up, and a few minor ones were passed. Only one attempt, led by William H. Wells of Delaware, was made to kill or postpone the bill. That effort failed by the overwhelming vote of 29 to 6, which reflected fairly accurately the Senate's opinion on the bank's constitutionality. On April 3 the amended bill passed the Senate by a vote of 22 to 12. Having failed to gain approval of the amendments they desired, Mason and King, together with six other Federalists who opposed the bank primarily because it would be Republican controlled, voted against it. They were joined by four Republicans, including Nathaniel Macon, whom the North Carolina legislature had recently appointed to the Senate.[22]

Barbour played a major role in guiding the bank bill through the Senate with only minor changes. He was undoubtedly relieved when the House concurred in the changes and the president, shortly thereafter, signed the bill into law. This victory, his first major one in the Senate, was personally satisfying. But its fruits were to be disappointing. Time would prove that Mason and King, who had accurately predicted that the Second Bank would be an instrument of speculation, understood banking and public finance much better than Barbour. The larger specie payment for which they had fought would have helped to curb the speculative mania that brought on the Panic of 1819. Barbour was probably correct, however, in contending that the House would not support the amendment that Mason and King had wanted.

By serving as the bank's chief advocate in the Senate, Barbour reaffirmed the nationalist position he had taken in the previous Congress. Significantly, he was not troubled by the constitutional objections raised by Old Republican colleagues both in Congress and back home. Thomas Ritchie, reflecting the opinion of his father-in-law, Spencer Roane, and probably that of most Junto members, declared that he was not opposed to a national bank "established upon a Constitutional Grant. . . . [But] it is yet to be proved that the Constitution of the United States *does* give the power to establish a Bank." He went on to say that as long as state banks were allowed to suspend specie payments, the constitutional provision authorizing Congress to regulate the currency was meaningless. The solution, he thought, was to prohibit banks from suspending specie payment.[23]

Barbour shared Ritchie's opinion that Congress had not exercised its power to regulate the nation's currency. One of his principal arguments on behalf of the bank had been that the national government had surrendered that power to the states, with the predictably resulting financial chaos. It was the government's compelling duty, he said, to establish a stable and uniform currency "impressed with the seal of the nation." This argument, Ritchie and other Virginians conceded, was the strongest that could be made for the bank.[24] But Barbour, unlike Ritchie, was convinced that the only way to guarantee a stable, uniform circulating medium was to create a national bank. The constitutional question that bothered Ritchie and others he minimized. No less an authority than Madison had argued earlier that precedent and usage, accompanied by a concurrence of the general will of the nation, had settled the constitutional question. Barbour used a similar argument in his lengthy speech defending the bank. The opinion of the country on the question of constitutionality, he said, had been "audibly and distinctly expressed" and had been confirmed by the actions of the various branches of the government.[25] This affirmation, for the time at least, seemed sufficient for him to put the constitutional question to rest.

Soon after it had approved the bank bill, the Senate turned its attention to another nationalist measure—the tariff of 1816. Tariffs were not new to the nation's history. They had long provided an important source of revenue. The tariff of 1816 was different in that it was the first specifically designed to protect American industry. An administration measure, it was intended to shield from cutthroat British competition the fledgling industries that had sprung up in the country during the war. As compared with later tariffs, it was moderate: a duty of 25 percent on woollen and cotton textiles and 30 percent on such goods as hats, paper, cabinet wares, and carriages. Although the bill passed the House by a safe majority, John Randolph and an overwhelming majority of the Virginia delegation opposed it. Despite their opposition, however, the House debate and vote reveal that the principle of protection had not yet become a sectional issue. Representatives from the middle states voted almost without exception in its favor, while New Englanders and Southerners voted both for and against.[26]

In the Senate the tariff generated less debate than in the House. Barbour opposed it, not because he objected to the principle of protection, but because he thought the rates were too high. He admitted that protection was desirable. It was essential, he said, that domestic manufacturing be encouraged and that the United States not remain dependent on Great Britain for manufactured goods. Believing that the hostile spirit still pervading Anglo-American relations might result in another war, he said that industrial self-sufficiency was a legitimate and necessary measure of national defense.[27]

It can hardly be said, on the basis of this opinion, that Barbour opposed per se one of the major objectives of American postwar nationalism—the promotion of national self-sufficiency through the erection of a protective tariff system. But he was unquestionably playing politics, trying to balance the interests of his section against those of other regions. Protection would bring wealth to the manufacturing localities, he said, but it would impose a heavy burden on the nonindustrial areas—especially the agricultural South, which would receive no practical benefit from the tariff and would be forced to pay higher prices for its manufactured goods. Although it might be proper to sacrifice regional interests to national objectives, there should be a limit to the sacrifice required. In a matter that so materially affected the South, there was a point beyond which he was unwilling to go.[28]

Barbour did not support the effort made by Robert G. Harper of Maryland and Nathaniel Macon to kill the bill without discussion. But he did attempt to reduce the rates. Those on textiles, he believed, were excessive. Accordingly, he moved to reduce the rates on woolens from 25 to 20 percent, a level which the South could tolerate and which he would support. His motion was defeated 20 to 9, a division which clearly indicated a sectional alignment. All the senators present and voting from the southern states east of the mountains favored the lower rate, while Jonathan Roberts of Pennsylvania was the only northern senator voting with the minority. On the other hand, only one senator from the three southern states west of the mountains voted for the reduction.[29]

Having failed in his attempt, Barbour offered a second amendment to shorten from three years to one the time that the maximum duties on manufactured woolens would be imposed. That motion, by the same 20 to 9 vote, was lost. When the engrossed bill with minor amendments came up for a final vote in mid-April, he voted with the minority against it. Significantly, the sectional alignment apparent on earlier votes was missing in the final division, for only four southern senators, along with two New England Federalists, voted against it.[30] The tariff of 1816 proved too strong a test for Barbour's nationalism. Anxious though he was to promote economic self-sufficiency, he was unwilling to sacrifice southern interests to such an extent. Rather than vote for what he considered excessive protection, he voted for none at all.

During the debates on the bank and tariff bills, Barbour became involved in the politics of the presidential succession. He favored James Monroe. But the secretary of state did not have the unanimous backing of his party. William H. Crawford of Georgia, who enjoyed the support of many conservative Virginia Republicans, emerged early in 1816 as a serious contender for the nomination.[31] Barbour, the most important of Monroe's congressional managers, became concerned about the challenge. He conferred with other Monroe backers on an appropriate strategy for the approaching Republican congressional caucus, which would select the party's ticket. A group of them decided that they would boycott the caucus if it appeared that Monroe would not be nominated.[32] Barbour himself was prepared to denounce the caucus system altogether and to have state legislatures nominate candidates. To keep this option open, he appealed to a group of Republican friends in the Virginia assembly urging them to postpone the state caucus until after the congressional caucus had met. If Crawford were selected by the latter, Virginia would then be free to pursue an independent course.[33] But Thomas Ritchie, Spencer Roane, and other influential Old Republicans who had not forgiven Monroe for his "political errors" of the past were unwilling to postpone the state caucus. They met and nominated a slate of twenty-five uncommitted electors.[34]

Disappointed by Virginia's action, Barbour turned to the congressional scene. Though he was convinced by early March that Monroe would be nominated at the congressional caucus scheduled for the middle of the month, he was not happy about the prospects of a narrow victory. Consequently he met with Henry Clay and John W. Taylor of New York and developed a plan for thwarting caucus action. When the caucus met, Clay offered a resolution declaring that it was inexpedient to nominate candidates, and Taylor presented one condemning the caucus system. Both resolutions failed. Barbour and others felt they had no choice but to enter Monroe's name in competition with Crawford. The result was as Barbour had predicted: Monroe won by the close vote of 65 to 54.[35]

In the absence of a strong opposition party, nomination by the Republican caucus was tantamount to election. The Federalist party nominated Rufus King for president, but he posed no real threat to Monroe, who won the election easily. Despite their initial reluctance to endorse Monroe, most of the Richmond Junto and other influential state political leaders, including William B. Giles and Gov. Wilson Cary Nicholas, whom some had suspected earlier of conspiring with New Yorkers to form an anti-Monroe coalition, eventually supported him.[36] Barbour's efforts earned for him Monroe's gratitude and confidence. During his presidency he would frequently seek Barbour's political counsel.

Congress did not manage to consider in its first postwar session all the nationalist measures recommended by the president. It did not take up the matter of a national university, and it deferred the question of internal improvements until a later time. It did vote to retain some of the wartime taxes necessary for the government's recovery and maintained the army and navy at a higher level than before the war. Barbour supported these measures.[37] When Congress adjourned at the end of April 1816, he and other nationalists were satisfied with the knowledge that they had responded constructively to the pressing needs of postwar America.

It had been a long session, and Barbour was anxious to return home. The long months of separation from Lucy and the children could be very lonely at times, especially during the dreary winter months when senators and congressmen, exhausted from their labors of the day, gathered at their hotels and boardinghouses to pass the evening. Barbour's messmates at Mr. Dowson's, where he frequently stayed, were not always exciting company. One evening Barbour invited fellow Virginian William Cabell Rives to join him for dinner at his lodgings, which he was sharing with John C. Calhoun, Henry Clay, Charles Tait of Alabama, Nathaniel Macon, and Thomas Telfair of Georgia. Rives found the company boring. Calhoun was silent and unsociable, and Macon was coarse, blunt, and imperious. Never was he in a "company where the genius of dullness prevailed with more imperial sway. After dinner, three of the wise men (Tait, Calhoun and Telfair) actually fell asleep in their chairs and snored in 'horrible discord'. . . . The rest of the party seemed not to observe what was happening."[38] Barbour's messmates may not always have been such poor company, but even when they were feeling more sociable, they were no substitute for his family.

Barbour returned home to a family increased two weeks earlier by the birth of his and Lucy's sixth child, a son whom they named Philip Pendleton. Lucy had recovered quickly, but the infant was not strong. They cared for him lovingly during the next few months, but he died in August. The family was changing in other ways as well. Lucy Maria, their oldest child, had recently married John Taliaferro from a neighboring plantation, and the family circle would soon be extended by the Barbours' first grandchildren.[39] Their oldest son, James, was no longer living at home. He had left for Harvard College the previous year, where he was about to complete his first year of education. His performance there had been disappointing. Academically he was doing well enough, but he had been wasteful with money, had not written home as dutifully as he should, and was having difficulty getting along with some of his classmates. His suspension from school in November 1816 for assaulting a fellow student was a great disappointment to his parents.[40]

Having ceased his legal practice some years earlier, Barbour was able during the summer and fall, when Congress was not in session, to devote full attention to farming. In the course of years, despite the demands of public life, he had steadily increased the scope of his planting activities. On the two farms he operated at this time, totaling nearly 5,000 acres and worked by more than a hundred slaves, he grew tobacco, corn, wheat, and other grains and raised cattle, sheep, and horses. Wheat and tobacco were his chief money crops, but the sale of livestock, especially fine thoroughbred horses, significantly increased his farming income. The accumulation of wealth from staple crops alone could be a painstakingly slow and uncertain business. To hedge against the vagaries of the staples market and to increase the return on his large capital investment in land and slaves, Barbour engaged in collateral activities which, though agriculturally based, were primarily commercial in nature. He operated a large mill capable of handling not only his but also his neighbors' wheat crops and marketed the flour in Richmond and Fredericksburg. He produced wool, ran a tannery and distillery, and manufactured leather goods, plug tobacco, and liquor, which he sold in local markets. No one of these interests alone would have produced great wealth, but collectively they enabled Barbour to amass a sizable fortune.[41]

Barbour's farming operations had become too large and complex for him to manage them, as he had in the early years of his public life, without help. He now had the services of a capable overseer, something of a rarity in the antebellum South. Even so, many things required his personal attention. He had to decide where to plant the experimental fruit stock Jefferson had sent him and which fields were best suited for the new varieties of wheat seed with which he was experimenting. A number of farmbuildings—new stables for his growing herd of blooded horses, sheds for the new breeds of sheep he was importing, and new slave cabins—required his supervision. In addition, he was about to begin the construction of a larger house that Jefferson was designing. He had to locate suitable clay nearby and to build a kiln for firing the 300,000 bricks that would be needed.[42]

A more pressing concern, however, was the weather. The summer of 1816 was unseasonably cool—as cold, indeed, as a moderate winter. Killing frosts continued into late May. A severe drought that lasted throughout the summer, followed by another frost in August and torrential rains in September, had a devastating effect on the crops. Barbour wrote his son at Harvard, saying that "we shall not make half a crop." The $2,000 that he had spent thus far on James's college education was excessive. James would have to learn to be more frugal, for money would be scarce in the months ahead.[43]

The second session of the Fourteenth Congress convened on December 2, 1816. Congress had moved from the Patent Office, which was too small to accommodate both houses, to a plain brick structure nearer the Capitol, where temporary halls had been fitted out. The room in which the Senate met was large and comfortable, a big improvement over the cramped quarters of the Patent Office. It had two fireplaces and a carpet, along with a gallery which was open to visitors. Each of the thirty-eight senators had his own mahogany desk. Senate sessions, which were marked by an "utmost quietness and decorum" not found in the House, began each morning at 11:00 A.M. and ended at 4:00 P.M., leaving most of the morning and late afternoon for committees to do their work.[44]

One of the foremost items on the agenda of this Congress was the question of internal improvements, a subject that over the years had generated more debate than action. It was soon to become a bitterly divisive issue. On December 6 Barbour took the initiative in the Senate by moving that a standing committee on roads and canals be created. Several New England senators objected, saying that except for the Cumberland Road, the country had no roads or canals on which to legislate, and that the national government probably had no constitutional jurisdiction in the matter. Barbour replied that there was a universal sentiment in the country in favor of internal improvements. Their importance to the welfare and prosperity of the nation was so great, and the public sentiment favoring them so overwhelming, that he believed a standing committee should be created to recommend legislation designed to accomplish those "great objects of domestic improvement." Although the motion failed, Barbour left no doubts as to his opinion regarding the importance of internal improvements.[45]

The next move was made by Calhoun in the House. In mid-December he introduced his controversial Bonus Bill authorizing the government to apply the bonus it had received from the bank for its charter to internal improvements. The bill precipitated a heated debate in which Philip Pendleton Barbour carried the standard for conservative Republicans. He challenged the constitutional power of the government to authorize a national program of internal improvements. Joined by other Old Republicans like John Randolph, he came within two votes of killing the proposal. The sectional distribution of the final House vote is revealing. The West was heavily in favor; the Northeast, with the exception of New York and Pennsylvania, was generally opposed; and the South was fairly evenly divided. The Virginia delegation, with the exception of the representatives from the western part of the state, was overwhelmingly against it.[46] Significantly, many of the Virginia representatives who had earlier supported nationalist legislation voted against the Bonus Bill.

When the Bonus Bill was taken up in the Senate in mid-February, Barbour and Martin Hardin of Kentucky acted as its chief advocates. Challenging the particularistic arguments his brother and John Randolph had used against it in the House, Barbour argued that Congress possessed the power to appropriate funds for public improvements. That power, he said, derived from the constitutional provision authorizing the government to provide for the common defense and general welfare of the country. He also used again the precedent argument that he had employed earlier on behalf of the bank. Practice and usage, he said, as evidenced by the expenditure of federal funds for the Cumberland Road, sanctioned the national government's involvement in internal improvements. Yet the strength of his presentation rested not on constitutional but rather on practical arguments: internal improvements would advance the general welfare and would bind the Union. They would encourage trade and transportation, would facilitate the movement of troops in times of war, would tie the newly developing sections of the country to the older eastern states, and would pave the way for an era of unrivaled prosperity.[47]

Nathaniel Macon, David Daggett of Connecticut, and others spoke against the bill. Employing the same orthodox Republican arguments that Philip Pendleton Barbour had used in the House, Daggett observed that Jefferson himself, upon contemplating in 1806 the possibility of appropriating federal funds for objects of public improvement, had been able to find no authorization in the Constitution for doing so. Macon challenged Barbour's precedent argument by suggesting that if time and usage made an act constitutional, Congress could, with constitutional sanction, pass another sedition act, since the precedent existed.[48] But Barbour stood his ground and stoutly opposed all efforts to weaken the bill. Its passage in late February with only minor changes was owing in no small part to his efforts.

Those efforts came to nothing when the president, on his last day in office, vetoed the measure. The Constitution, Madison said, did not authorize Congress to construct roads and canals. In an opinion that paralleled the arguments of Philip Pendleton Barbour, he said that he could not sign the bill without applying to the Constitution an "inadmissible latitude of construction." To accept the general welfare and precedent arguments that Senator Barbour and others had used in its defense would have the effect of giving to Congress a general power of legislation that would leave future generations without adequate landmarks to the powers of the general government.[49] In rejecting the precedent argument, Madison seemingly ignored the fact that he himself had used it earlier on behalf of the bank. The president's veto caught Congress by surprise. If Barbour, like Clay and Calhoun, was stunned by the action, we have no record of it. But he must have been disappointed, for he firmly believed that internal improvements would provide invaluable benefits to the nation. He was not yet willing to give up the fight.

Although Barbour possessed a keen awareness of the limiting character of the Constitution, he believed its restraints were meant to secure personal freedoms and to provide a political context in which the social ideals of the Revolution could be achieved. The Constitution was a means for keeping government responsible to the people, to be sure, but it was, moreover, an instrument for promoting the public welfare through positive action. His constitutional arguments in support of internal improvements, a national bank, and other postwar nationalist measures were based squarely on the Hamiltonian doctrine of implied powers. Only the times and motives were different. The intent now was to implement the popular will, not to thwart it. In his enthusiasm for the new nationalism, seduced according to Thomas Ritchie by "splendid visions of public benefit," Barbour opposed the public will of Virginia, at least to the extent that it was represented by Ritchie, Randolph, Roane, Philip Pendleton Barbour, and other conservative Republicans who adhered faithfully to the old creeds.[50] The nationalist legislation Senator Barbour supported, and especially internal improvements, provoked a strong reaction in Virginia which led to a general revival of states' rights doctrines.

That bellwether of Virginia political opinion Thomas Ritchie, whose reaction to the bank and tariff had been rather temperate, signaled the new mood when he hailed Madison's veto of the Bonus Bill. The president's action, he exulted, had stayed "the proud waves of federal usurpation" that threatened to sweep away every right of the states. Had the Bonus Bill been enacted into law, there would have been no "impediment to save us from the gulph of consolidation." He then went on to express his opposition also to the bank, which had been "enacted in the teeth of the Constitution," and to other nationalist legislation enacted since the war.[51] The Bonus Bill became something of a rallying point for Old Republicans and for many of the large planters of eastern Virginia, who feared the economic consequences of internal improvements. They were not happy at the prospect of being taxed to pay for roads and canals which, by opening up fertile lands in the West, would enable western farmers to compete with them for eastern agricultural markets. Awakened to this danger, they began to speak out not only against internal improvements but against the entire nationalist program as well.[52]

Barbour was untroubled by their fears. When internal improvements were discussed at the next session of Congress, which met in December

1817, he still favored them. In his first Annual Message to Congress, President Monroe stressed the importance of roads and canals and urged the adoption of a constitutional amendment that would clearly give Congress authority in this area. On December 9 Barbour introduced an amendment designed to give Congress the power in question. It provided that Congress could pass laws appropriating money for constructing roads and canals and for improving water courses, provided that no action was taken without the consent of the states directly affected and provided that the money appropriated was distributed among the states in proportion to their representation in the lower house of Congress. Although he still believed that Congress possessed the authority, it was best, he stated, in all cases of doubt, to recur to the people— "the original and only legitimate fountain of power." His proposed amendment, he said, stemmed not so much from a desire to see the powers of the national government increased as from a wish to have it exercise control over projects which were clearly national in scope and which only it could implement.[53]

Before the Senate debated Barbour's proposal, the House listened to the report of a special committee that Speaker Henry Clay had appointed to study the internal improvements question. Its chairman was the former Virginia Quid Henry St. George Tucker, who had been a nationalist since the war. Tucker reported that the committee had carefully reviewed the constitutional issue and had concluded that Congress, provided it obtained the consent of the states affected, had the power to appropriate money for the repair of post roads and the construction of military roads and canals. The committee was confident that the republican virtue of the nation's leaders would lead them always to act in the public interest. This confidence inclined them to interpret the Constitution liberally. Accordingly, they recommended that the government's annual dividend from its bank stock be earmarked for internal improvements.[54]

Tucker's report provoked an angry response from Virginians. A pseudonymous writer in the *Enquirer*, seeing that "the Rubicon is passed," foresaw the commencement of a system of internal improvements "which is to end in the complete consolidation of our confederacy." There was, he said, no precedent for what Congress was contemplating. "They mean to amend the Constitution by legislative act. . . . If what Congress has done becomes Constitutional, it is only for Congress to do anything, and anything becomes a part of the Constitution." He did not share the committee's confidence in the virtues of the country's leaders, whom he would hold by a "well-bitted and short rein." To protect the Old Republican doctrines from this "last and greatest calamity," he urged the people to rise from their lethargy and "save their liberties from perdition."[55]

Virginia congressmen, led by Philip Pendleton Barbour, attempted to do just that. He, Archibald Austin, James Johnson, and other Virginians made lengthy speeches, occupying more than three days of the House's time, objecting to the committee's report. Finally a resolution was passed, 90–75, declaring that Congress had the power to appropriate money for the construction of roads and canals but leaving unanswered the question of whether Congress could actually construct such improvements. The Virginia delegation voted against the resolution 12 to 5. With the exception of Henry St. George Tucker, all the Virginians who supported the resolution were Federalists.[56]

It was late March before the Senate discussed Barbour's proposed amendment. Apparently unaffected by the special interests that had prompted such an angry reaction in the Virginia press, Barbour once again spoke of the great national benefits a federally sponsored system of roads and canals would provide. He urged his colleagues to settle the constitutional question once and for all by approving the proposed amendment. After a brief debate the amendment was rejected by a vote of 22 to 9. The majority of the senators, feeling that Congress already possessed the power in question, were unwilling to refer the question to the people for fear they might withhold the power. It is clear that among the Virginia Republicans in Congress, Barbour was part of a very small minority favoring internal improvements. His colleague in the Senate, John W. Eppes, who had replaced Armistead T. Mason in December 1817, voted against the amendment and stood firmly with Virginia's Republican congressmen on the larger question of internal improvements.[57]

With the defeat of the constitutional amendment Barbour, for the time being, at least, abandoned his efforts to secure legislation for roads and canals. When such bills came before the Senate during the next few years, he voted against them, not because he opposed them in principle, but because he doubted they would be approved. There was nothing to be gained politically from supporting legislation unpopular with his constituents when that legislation was certain to be vetoed by the president.

On several other postwar issues, Barbour assumed an unequivocally nationalist position. One such question concerned the much-discussed standing army. Following the Treaty of Ghent, there was considerable pressure in Congress to reduce or abolish the peacetime army, not only because it was expensive to maintain, but also because, in the minds of some, it was a potential threat to a democracy. In early 1817 Jeremiah Mason of New Hampshire, in a speech that must have warmed the hearts of conservative Republicans, moved to reduce the army from 10,000 to 5,000 men. Barbour, who had earlier been chairman of the Senate Military

Committee, opposed the move. He argued that a standing army, far from being a threat to a free people, was essential to their well-being. With Mason and others, he too cherished the republican principle that a well-ordered militia was the natural defense of free men. But he did not believe that the nation then had, nor was it likely to acquire, such a force. Bitter experience suggested that liberty and peace could never be secured by the militia alone. That body, he said, was too ponderous and too undisciplined to be relied upon. A standing army of moderate size, large enough to serve as the nucleus of an expanded force in time of war, was essential to the preservation of liberty.

He expressed surprise at Mason's concern about the sharp increase in military expenditures since 1789. The country had greatly altered since that time, both in size and wealth. Changing times called for changes in attitudes and policies. What had been adequate in 1789 was inadequate in 1817. "Then we were the infant Hercules, rocked in the cradle; now we are the full-grown man, successfully contending with the fifty-headed hydra." Understanding realpolitik better than most of his colleagues, he argued that "peace can be preserved only by being ready for war." He believed, moreover, that a strong defense was also essential to an effective foreign policy. "Is a disbanded army the instrument of negotiation, with which you mean to arm your Minister?" he asked. "Would Talleyrand ever have been dubbed a prince for his adroitness in diplomacy, if he had not been supported by fifty thousand bayonets?" He then moved that further consideration of the bill be postponed indefinitely. The motion carried by a vote of 24 to 11.[58]

Although he was momentarily successful at blocking the move to reduce the army, the issue itself was not dead. Conservative Republicans, including most of the Virginia congressmen, stood by the doctrine that the militia was just as reliable as a standing army and was far less dangerous. With the aid of northern Republicans concerned about the solvency of the national government and a group of Crawford supporters who wanted to embarrass Secretary of War Calhoun, they finally succeeded in 1821 in reducing the army to 6,000 men.[59]

Another postwar issue on which Barbour took a firm nationalist position was that of commercial relations with Great Britain. He had a strong interest in international trade and foreign affairs. Since its inception in 1816, he had been chairman of the powerful Senate Foreign Relations Committee, which included among its members Rufus King and Nathaniel Macon. In that capacity he consulted frequently with the president and with Secretary of State John Quincy Adams on foreign affairs and directly influenced the country's nationalistic postwar commercial policy.[60]

That Barbour, a Virginia planter, had so great an interest in protecting and encouraging American commerce is itself evidence that he acted from national rather than regional interests alone. He objected strenuously to British colonial regulations which discriminated against American shipping, especially where the West Indian trade was concerned. In April 1818 he submitted to the Senate a stringent navigation bill designed to force England to change her policy. He and Rufus King, who played a major role in drafting it, acted as its principal advocates.[61]

The Navigation Act of 1818 closed American ports to all British ships arriving from ports closed to U.S. vessels and required consignees of British ships carrying American goods to post bond that the cargo would go only to ports open to ships of the United States.[62] In a long speech Barbour defended the bill, which he justified on the grounds of "perfect reciprocity." The British navigation system had been extremely detrimental to American commercial interests. It was time for the country to respond in kind. Admitting that the market for American goods, especially agricultural, would initially be adversely affected by the bill's enactment, he argued that regional interests should be sacrificed to preserve the maritime rights, dignity, and self-respect of the nation.[63] His presentation received the acclaim of Madison and the censure of the London *Courier*, which declared that "the speech of Mr. Barbour . . . breathes an angry and vindictive feeling towards Great Britain."[64] He was followed and supported in his arguments by King, after which the bill passed by an overwhelming vote. On April 11 it passed the House, and a few days later was enacted into law by the president.[65]

Although the Navigation Act of 1818 led to a substantial reduction of British tonnage entering American ports, it did not succeed in forcing England to change her navigation system. In the years that followed, Barbour, John Quincy Adams, and others would make repeated efforts, culminating finally in the extraordinary Elsewhere Act of 1823, to secure reciprocity. Perhaps the act of 1818 was chiefly significant in that it not only revealed a growing American impatience with economic dependence on Great Britain but also (and more important) indicated that Barbour and other nationalists in Congress knew what had made England great and shared a vision of similar wealth and power for their own country.

During the years 1815–1819 Barbour played an important role in the political life of the nation. Because of his close ties to both Madison and Monroe, he frequently acted as the administration's spokesman in the Senate, a role he performed effectively. Monroe, especially, found him to be a valuable political adviser. Monroe consulted with him regularly on matters concerning foreign relations and trade; and when problems arose relating to Florida, the Yazoo land claims, and Indian affairs, or when Monroe had important appointments to make, such as justices of the Supreme Court, he sought Barbour's counsel.[66] Barbour also enjoyed the confidence of his colleagues in the Senate, who in 1819 elected him to the position of president pro tempore.[67] In Senate proceedings, whether in committee meetings or floor debate, Barbour wielded considerable influence.

Barbour's influence in the Senate rested primarily on two qualities: his capacity for hard work in committee, where he demonstrated both an understanding of complex issues and a willingness to engage in the give and take of practical politics, and his effectiveness in debate. Both he and his brother, Philip Pendleton, were generally recognized in Washington as fluent speakers. Their styles were often compared. The senator had greater personal magnetism, which made him more engaging in private circles, while the less personable Philip was probably a better, though not necessarily a more effective, public speaker.[68] The latter was a close reasoner, a subtle and acute logician who was at his best in grappling with complex constitutional questions. Though he spoke rapidly, the powers of his mind were such, and his logic so overpowering, that fellow congressmen were often transfixed by the lucidity and force of his speeches. "I felt my heart distend with all the pride of the 'old dominion,'" wrote James Pleasants, "when I observed the mark of profound and respectful attention with which ... [Philip Pendleton Barbour's] elegant and ingenious speech ... was received."[69] James Barbour, though capable of sustained logical reasoning, was generally more flamboyant and grandiloquent than Philip. He relied too often upon the power of words and personality to carry a point, as the congressional wag who penned the following couplet noted: "Two Barbours to shave our Congress long did try,/One shaves with froth; the other shaves dry."[70]

By modern standards, James Barbour's unrestrained style of speaking would unquestionably be judged inferior to his brother's. He loved the long roll and thunder of rhetoric, fashioned somewhat on the Burkean model. Possessing that dramatic instinct and romantic imagination common to the actor and the orator, he sought splendid imagery and classical allusions. His brother, Philip, observed that he could "clothe a beggarly idea in robes of royalty and call down the lightning of heaven to kill a gnat." Others, who sometimes referred to him as "The Thunderer," thought he was too theatrical, his language too "charged with guns, trumpets and blunderbuss."[71] But if his exaggerated rhetoric, his addiction to mock heroics and pseudo-Ciceronian speech, was not to the taste of some of his colleagues, nor to ours today, the same cannot be said for the majority of his contemporaries.

Most people had high regard for James Barbour's oratory. John P. Little, an Episcopalian minister and author who, during his long residence in Richmond, heard most of Virginia's public figures speak, believed that Barbour was one of the foremost orators Virginia produced during the Jeffersonian period. Barbour possessed, he said, "a pleasing flow of eloquence, and an energy and force of expression, accompanied by a gracefulness of gesture and dignity of manner," that were rarely seen in the Old Dominion.[72] William Wirt and other careful students of oratory also gave him high marks. In 1827 E. B. Williston included him, along with Wirt, Henry Clay, Patrick Henry, and others, in his compendium of *Eloquence of the United States*.[73] To many who heard him speak, Barbour was "a giant in language," an orator in the best tradition who, even in his old age, could speak extemporaneously for five hours and could deliver, by the admission of his opponent, "the ablest speech ever heard from the lips of any man."[74]

Not even his critics maintained that Barbour was ineffective as a speaker. George Watterson, who thought his speech too poetical and grandiose, admitted that he employed his "full flowing rhetorical style" with such skill in "setting off his arguments and . . . enforcing his reason" that few listeners could resist its persuasive effect. John Quincy Adams was sometimes critical of his rhetoric, but he too acknowledged that there were few speakers in Congress more effective than he.[75] And Henry Bradshaw Fearon, a British traveler who toured America in 1817, observed that although Barbour violated some of the rules of oratory, he possessed a physical presence and openness of manner which, his limitations notwithstanding, enabled him to win listeners to his point of view.

> [He] possesses an irresistible charm from his evident sincerity, and the manliness of his deportment, which, while it rivets the attention of his audience, compels them to love the object of their admiration. His countenance is one of that kind which, in a few minutes, enlists in its favour all the social affections, and you insensibly feel anxious and predisposed to take that side of the argument of which so apparently kind and able a man professes himself the advocate.[76]

When Barbour relied on ardor and enthusiasm, rather than careful preparation, to carry a point in debate, he was likely to become bombastic. Then the limitations of his formal education, or perhaps the lack of time to prepare properly for the question at hand, were glaringly apparent. When he brought the full powers of his intellect into sharp focus and spoke from the depths of profound knowledge, he could be eloquent. And on such occasions he could be very persuasive.

The keen intellect Barbour brought to the issues before the Senate, no less than his oratorical skills, was essential to his effectiveness in debate.

The most prominent characteristics of his mind, in the opinion of several contemporaries, were brilliancy and fervor.[77] He was not brilliant, at least not in the degree that Randolph or Calhoun was, but his mind was incisive and analytical. He could quickly grasp the complexities of a difficult problem and could lay bare its essential elements with a logic that rivaled his brother's. He was able to compete on equal terms with the best minds in the Senate. In 1820, at the height of the Missouri Controversy, John Quincy Adams despairingly wrote that "with the exception of Rufus King, there is not in either house of Congress a member from the free states able to cope in the powers of mind with . . . James Barbour."[78]

During the immediate postwar years, few political leaders of the North or the South showed a greater awareness than Barbour of the community of interest and purpose that bound people from all sections of the country to a common destiny. Like other nationalists, he was anxious to see the country put behind it the internal divisions of the war years and move as one people to capitalize on the extraordinary economic and political opportunities that awaited. His support of the national bank, internal improvements, a strong military establishment, and a nationalistic commercial policy intended to accomplish this end. Confronted with the imperatives of a world being transformed by social and economic forces of a fundamental order, forces which he understood imperfectly, he tried valiantly to transcend the limits of his rural Virginia culture and to respond positively to complex national needs.

Barbour's advocacy of nationalist legislation underscored a fundamental difference in political outlook that distinguished him from his conservative Virginia colleagues. John Taylor, John Randolph, and others of their political persuasion, all of whom were committed to preserving intact the eighteenth-century republican social ideal, believed that the very structure of society was at stake—its morals, manners, and values. The society of virtuous farmers, they believed, could not survive the corrupting influences of large-scale industry, urbanization, a professional standing army, and a polity committed to a mysterious and dangerous English-style finance. Banking, manufacturing, trade, entrepreneurial daring—these were the first stirrings of what they viewed as a frightening commercial age, tremors that were alarming because they augured quakes to come. As the defenders of some nostalgic halcyon age, more fondly remembered because it was past, they opposed American modernity. They were unable to accept change because, at heart, they distrusted the ways of the modern world and were repulsed by the responses necessary to adjust to it.[79]

By contrast, Barbour accepted change as natural and inevitable, a sine qua non for political and social progress. Though nurtured by the same rural culture as his conservative Republican colleagues, he, unlike them, moved from the particularism, the local patois, of country thinking to a larger view of the good society. He had not abandoned the agrarian ideal; he had simply expanded it. Farmers remained the backbone of the republic, but there was room also for mechanics and tradesmen, for manufacturing and banking and commerce along with agriculture. A commercial North and an agricultural South could coexist. His advocacy of nationalist legislation was not so much a corruption of the republican social ideal as an enlargement of it. Above all, it was a practical response to altered national realities. Like Madison, who acknowledged after the war that he "had been reconciled to certain measures and arrangements" that were as proper in 1816 as they had been "premature and suspicious when urged by the champions of Federalism" before 1800, he accepted the necessity of formulating national policies in response to changing needs.[80]

It was Barbour's willingness to compromise, his recognition that the demanding exercise of forging agreement was the regular business of politics, which more than anything else distinguished him from his doctrinaire Virginia colleagues. Where they were dogmatic, inflexible, apocalyptic, and at times even hysterical, he was a political realist. His empirical approach included a willingness to compromise conflicting principles when, by doing so, a larger good was served. "My disposition," he said in 1815, "is to meet by mutual concession those with whom I am in the habit of acting."[81] Pleading with his Senate colleagues during the bank debate to yield their constitutional objections to the bank and to acknowledge the compelling requirements of a changing nation, he said: "We must adapt our course to the suggestions of our best judgements, enlightened by a deliberate reflection, acting on existing circumstances."[82] Like Edmund Burke, he believed that reason, not abstractions, should be a man's guide. Blind adherence to political dogma was not a virtue.

Unlike his Old Republican colleagues, Barbour was willing to accept and, indeed, to advocate those changes which experience and reason dictated were necessary. It was in this context that he suggested an expansion of the power and role of the national government. But he was not completely comfortable with the Hamiltonian doctrine of implied powers that was the vehicle for expanded powers, and he stopped short of applying it uniformly to every postwar nationalist question. He could not completely overcome the influence of country ideology or of political opinions deeply entrenched in his native state. While he helped to launch the new nationalism, he did not completely cast off from his Jeffersonian moorings. He would draw close to them once again when the storm of the Missouri Controversy unleashed its fury in 1820.

6

A Dream Shattered

During the years following the Treaty of Ghent, many hopeful Americans saw in James Monroe's presidency the auspicious beginning of a new Era of Good Feelings. Barbour was more sanguine than most. He believed that "in the day now breaking upon us, the nation expects a new era in the annals of our country. A long and bright course to the sun that is rising will be the prayer of every Virginian."[1] He and other nationalists seemed confident that the political factionalism and sectional animosities of earlier years would soon yield completely to the expansive energies of a united people—a people whose common hopes, goals, and nationalist commitments would in time overshadow every combination of local interests. They envisioned an era of unrivaled prosperity and goodwill in which the United States, with its democratic institutions and seemingly unlimited economic opportunities, would establish itself as the foremost political power in the world. That rendezvous with greatness, apparently so close when the Panic of 1819 hit, was delayed and almost destroyed by the Missouri Controversy of 1819–1821, which struck the country with the unexpected suddenness and force of a tropical storm, rekindling sectional antagonisms and irrevocably destroying whatever good feelings may have existed during Monroe's early years as president.

Although few seemed to notice, there were repeated warnings throughout 1818 and early 1819 of the approaching storm. In April 1818 New Hampshire's freshman congressman, Arthur Livermore, tried unsuccessfully to persuade the House to endorse a constitutional amendment prohibiting slavery in all new states admitted to the Union. Following his futile effort, a group of northern congressmen, with no greater success, attempted to impose federal restrictions on the interstate movement of slaves.[2] Debates soon thereafter on the suppression of the African slave trade and on the fugitive slave law of 1793, though ignored by many, aroused deep fears in the minds of such ever-vigilant Virginians as Spencer

Roane, John Taylor, and Thomas Ritchie.[3] One prescient citizen of the Old Dominion, probably Roane, writing pseudonymously in the *Richmond Enquirer*, observed that the "political horizon seems again overcast with darkness and lowering clouds, and recent events appear to be fast dissipating that 'era of good feelings' so clamorously hailed by a certain party in our country."[4] But most Southerners apparently dismissed the numerous warnings as nothing more than straws in the wind.

Barbour was one who did not take the early warnings very seriously. He noticed the gathering clouds and commented on them in a letter to Ritchie in December 1818, but he was wholly unprepared for the fury with which the storm finally struck.[5] "Who would have thought," he asked during the height of the Missouri debates in 1820, "that the little speck scarcely visible above the horizon we saw . . . [last session] was to be swelled into the importance that it has now assumed, and that upon its decision depended the duration of the Union?"[6] The storm did not destroy the Union, but it did significantly alter its political contours.

The Missouri question first arose in February 1819, shortly before the historic Fifteenth Congress adjourned. At that time an enabling act to grant Missouri statehood was taken up in the House of Representatives. When the bill was considered by the Committee of the Whole on February 13, 1819, Cong. James Tallmadge, Jr., of New York promptly moved an amendment prohibiting the importation of additional slaves into the proposed state and freeing, at the age of twenty-five, all those born to slavery within its borders after its admission to the Union. On February 17 the Missouri bill with the Tallmadge Amendment passed the House and was forwarded to the Senate. Referred there to a select committee headed by Charles Tait, it was reported out a few days later with the recommendation that the clause restricting slavery be stricken. When the Senate voted on the bill a week later, the Tallmadge Amendment was rejected. The southern senators were unanimous in their opposition to the amendment and were supported by several senators from the free states, including Harrison Gray Otis of Massachusetts. On the day before Congress adjourned, the bill, as amended by the Senate, was again considered by the House. By the narrow margin of two votes the lower chamber refused to concur in the deletion of the antislavery amendment.[7] When the Senate declined to yield, Congress adjourned with the future of Missouri still in question.

No record of the first Senate debate on the Missouri bill was entered in the *Annals of Congress*. The reporter simply noted that there was a "long and animated" discussion. If Barbour participated in the discussion, which seems likely, he certainly would have opposed any effort to restrict slavery. He did not seem to be overly alarmed at this time, however, perhaps because he did not think that the Senate, dominated by proslavery senators, would ever approve such a restriction. While admitting that awful consequences might result from "this portentous question," he was not yet prepared to abandon that confident, nationalist mood he had carried with him to Washington in 1815. He continued to hope that the old party and sectional enmities which had been so destructive of national objectives during the recent war would remain dormant and that the nation might retain the unity of spirit that would enable it to "advance to that height of prosperity when all nations shall resort to us, whence to draw the oracles of political wisdom and the sublime truths of civil and religious liberty."[8]

During the summer and fall of 1819, Barbour's view of the Missouri question began to change. Late in the year antislavery groups throughout the North, their activities closely followed and reported by the *Enquirer*, held public meetings and launched a massive propaganda campaign to limit slavery expansion. Barbour could no longer ignore the growing threat those activities posed to slavery. Having refused until now to become alarmed, he began to fear that northern antislavery groups had ignited a spark which, "communicated to an immense mass of combustion, will produce an explosion that will shake this Union to its center."[9] By the time the Sixteenth Congress assembled in early December, the Missouri question had divided the country into opposing sectional blocs, each determined to yield nothing in the approaching contest. Barbour's own position by that time had hardened. His earlier optimism about the nation's future vanished as the specter of sectional conflict, precipitated by the politics of slavery, loomed threateningly.

Barbour played a conspicuous role in the Missouri Controversy. He entered that contest reluctantly and fearfully, knowing that no question was more intractable and insoluble, more fraught with danger, than that of Negro slavery, an evil that mocked the moral integrity of a nation resting on the Declaration of Independence and threatened the Union itself with disruption. He responded initially as a Southerner who, though admitting the immorality of slavery, was either unable or unwilling to wrestle honestly with the contradictory claims of conscience and self-interest. Like other Southerners, including Republican patriarchs Jefferson and Madison, he opposed restrictions on slavery in Missouri and adamantly insisted upon the right of slaveowners to carry their black chattels into the territories west of the Mississippi. But as the crisis mounted and disunion loomed, he subordinated sectional to national interests by championing compromise, which he firmly believed was the only way to avoid political disaster. In evolving the details of that compromise and securing its acceptance, he played a role that rivaled Henry Clay's in importance.

From the outset of the Missouri Controversy, Barbour, like President Monroe, was firmly resolved to oppose any measure that made the exclusion of slavery a condition for Missouri's statehood.[10] He emerged early in the debates as one of the most formidable and politically astute Senate opponents of restriction. He was joined by other southern senators—able men like the recently appointed Richard M. Johnson of Kentucky, the ultraconservative Nathaniel Macon of North Carolina, and William Pinkney of Maryland. But Barbour was clearly the most effective Senate leader of the antirestrictionists. His position as president pro tempore provided some advantage in this respect, but that office, which was not nearly as powerful as the House speakership held by Henry Clay, was less important than personal influence in guiding Senate actions. In informal conferences and private negotiations, where much of the real business of the upper house was conducted, personal influence and the power to persuade were all-important. To the extent that political power rested on these factors, Barbour was among the most powerful members of either house of Congress at this time, rivaled only by Federalist Rufus King in the Senate and by Clay in the House. Private persuasion was an important adjunct of public oratory, both of which Barbour and Clay used adroitly to lead the struggle to bring Missouri into the Union as a slave state.[11]

Barbour's initial strategy for thwarting the restrictionists involved joining a bill authorizing Missouri to draft a constitution to a bill admitting Maine to the Union as a free state. Maine's petition for statehood, presented to the House on December 8, resulted from an act passed by the Massachusetts General Court in June 1819 permitting the District of Maine, a Republican stronghold that had long identified itself as separate from the rest of Massachusetts, to become a separate state. Because Maine, unlike Missouri, had been part of another state, it could be admitted directly to the Union without first securing congressional approval to draft a constitution. Massachusetts, however, had attached an important proviso to its enabling act stipulating that Maine would revert to its former status unless Congress granted statehood before March 4, 1820.[12] Barbour saw in the Maine petition the leverage needed to secure Missouri's unrestricted admission. By linking the two bills, a move that offered the additional inducement of preserving the balance between the free and slave states, he hoped that Northerners, rather than sacrifice Maine, would admit Missouri with slavery.[13]

During December both the Senate and the House drafted bills for Maine's admission. The House took up its bill first. In the first debate on December 30, Speaker Clay warned that the South would not admit Maine unless the North agreed to accept Missouri without restrictions. He did not intend at that time to unite the two questions, he said, but "if you refuse to admit Missouri also free of conditions, we see no reason why you shall take to yourselves privileges which you deny to her."[14] While the house debated, Barbour announced his intention of joining the two. On January 3 he told his colleagues that he would, at the appropriate time, propose an amendment to the Senate bill admitting Maine that would allow Missouri to come into the Union on an equal footing with the original states. Before he could formally submit his motion, however, the Senate tabled its Maine bill in favor of a similar bill passed by the House on January 3. That bill was promptly referred to the Senate Judiciary Committee, chaired by William Smith of South Carolina and dominated by Southerners. A few days later the bill was reported out of committee with the amendment Barbour had suggested.[15]

It is not altogether clear whose idea it was to link Maine and Missouri. At this time Barbour was regularly in contact with both Monroe and Clay, and any one of them could have suggested it. There is reason, however, to believe that it was Barbour's idea and that Clay, in predicting that the bills would be joined, was simply alluding to the amendment that he knew the Virginian was about to propose. This conjecture is based on the fact that Barbour's announcement of January 3, following closely on the heels of Clay's prediction, was known in advance by some of his colleagues. Several days before he said anything publicly about his intentions, John Holmes of Massachusetts, a congressman who had earlier voted against the Tallmadge Amendment and who subsequently voted with the Southerners, told a constituent that Barbour would propose the merger.[16] Former senator Christopher Gore of Massachusetts apparently thought that Barbour rather than Clay was the originator of the scheme, as did the anonymous citizen of Maine who warned Barbour that "you will be remembered!!!" for "uniting Maine with the Negro State."[17] Whatever the case, it was an idea so obvious that embattled defenders of slavery, desperately needing additional political leverage in their contest with the House's restrictionist majority, could hardly have failed to see and to seize upon it.

The union of the two bills, denounced by citizens of Maine as a "miserable, unworthy, and unwarrantable course," caused a heated Senate debate that lasted for two days. Jonathan Roberts of Pennsylvania, Harrison Gray Otis of Massachusetts, Samuel Dana of Connecticut, and other northern senators protested strongly against the connection and moved to recommit the bill to committee, with instructions that the amendment pertaining to Missouri be deleted. It was, they argued, an unnatural union, a "perfect novelty," for which there was no precedent in the history of Congress. Dana observed that nine states had been admitted to the Union since the Constitution was adopted, and in no instance had two been combined in one bill.[18]

The northern strategy, of course, was to separate the two questions and to admit Maine before taking up the matter of Missouri. By way of justification, they argued that the two petitions bore no resemblance to one another. Missouri was asking for congressional permission to form a constitution preparatory to becoming a state, while Maine, having already drafted a constitution and having met every other condition of statehood, was asking to be admitted to the Union. An act for admission to statehood, they contended, was entirely distinct from all other objects of legislation; each was, by its very nature, an individual case. The two petitions should be discussed separately and should be decided on the basis of their individual merits. There would be time enough, once Maine's case was acted upon, to consider Missouri. Only David Morrill of New Hampshire honestly acknowledged the dilemma that joining the two posed for northern senators: "Now sir, you couple these two together, and on the final question you compel gentlemen to vote for both or neither."[19]

This was precisely the response that Barbour and those who supported the connection expected. In answering Morrill's objection, the Virginian said that he had proposed the combination of Maine and Missouri for the plainest of reasons: "You who ask justice for Maine shall be compelled to do it for Missouri. And shall we be called unreasonable who view the question in this light, if to preserve equality, which is but another name for justice, we unite them indissolubly together and subject them to a common fate?" The two questions were not unrelated, he said. The citizens of both Maine and Missouri had equal claims to statehood. The real issue was whether restrictions would be imposed on Missouri and not on Maine. The people of Missouri, he blusteringly warned, would not submit to restrictions that relegated them to inferior status. "Suffer not yourselves to be deceived. The same spirit which animated the heroes and patriots of the Revolution warms the bosoms of those hardy sons of the West; and when you, by your resolves, arrest the mighty flood of the Mississippi, then, and not till then, will you be able to repress this unconquerable spirit."[20]

Barbour was supported in his arguments by Nathaniel Macon, William Smith, and Edward Lloyd of Maryland. When the motion to recommit the bill to committee with instructions to delete the amendment relating to Missouri failed on January 14 by a vote of 25 to 18, it became apparent to all that a majority of the senators opposed restriction.[21] If Barbour and the other Southerners rejoiced in this victory, they acted prematurely. For this was but a skirmish. The real battle remained to be fought.

Throughout the months of January and February the Missouri debates raged in both houses of Congress. Spectators in unprecedented numbers—European diplomats, women, and many anxious blacks—crowded the galleries to hear orator after orator expound on the subject of slavery restriction.[22] Senators and congressmen tediously reiterated the arguments both for and against restriction. They argued about the boundaries of Louisiana and the meaning of the provision in the treaty of cession guaranteeing to the citizens of that territory "the enjoyment of all rights, advantages, and immunities of citizens of the United States," and they raised points of order or split constitutional hairs. As the debate intensified, congressional tempers flared and nerves became threadbare. "You can hardly conceive," wrote William Plumer, Jr., "of the rage and fury which prevail here on this subject."[23] Monroe observed despairingly, "All other business is suspended, and indeed so completely absorbed are all here in that great question, that you never hear mention made of Florida, or any other subject, however interesting."[24] The great debate was mounting, and for the next twelve months its discordant sounds would reverberate throughout the land.

On January 17 Sen. Jonathan Roberts again assumed the initiative for the North by introducing a proviso which, attached to the Maine bill amendment admitting Missouri, would have prohibited the transportation of additional slaves into the territory. For the next several weeks debate focused on his proposal. At the end of January, after the measure had been passionately and exhaustively debated by both sides, Barbour addressed the Senate. In a speech that lasted for three hours on January 31 and continued the next day, he adamantly opposed the antislavery proviso.[25]

Barbour based his defense of slavery on the narrowest of constitutional grounds. The moral issue, which had been the primary focus of northern arguments, he refused to discuss. He admitted that slavery was inherently evil, but he insisted that the only question to be debated was whether Congress possessed authority to impose conditions or restrictions on the admission of a state. He answered with a resounding "No!" The Constitution simply stated that "new states may be admitted by Congress into this union." Congress might admit or refuse to admit a state, but it could not impose restrictions. If admitted, Missouri was entitled to all those privileges enjoyed by the older states, including the right to fashion her government according to the wishes of her citizens. To prohibit slavery in Missouri was to deny the free inhabitants of that region a right guaranteed by the Constitution and confirmed in the treaty of cession, by which Louisianians were promised protection of their liberty, religion, and property.

Barbour was quick to remind his listeners that slaves were a species of property which, like every other legitimate form of property, deserved the government's full protection. The South's investment in slaves amounted to millions of dollars. That investment, he argued, was gravely jeopardized. To prohibit slaveowners from moving into new territories with their black chattels was to threaten the institution itself with destruction, for once it was conceded that Congress could control one aspect of slavery, there was nothing to prevent the national government from controlling every aspect, including its abolition in the states where it already existed.

Barbour's response was predictable. Like other Southerners whose elegant life-style depended on black labor, he easily deduced his section's common interest and adamantly defended it. "It is my property they seek to take," he protested. "It is my peace, my happiness, that are put to hazard." His intent in advancing the property argument was obvious: he hoped to subordinate any discussion of the slave's human rights to a consideration of the slaveholder's property rights. It is not surprising that he resorted to this argument. It was one of the most effective weapons in the southern arsenal. Even Rufus King, the Senate's foremost advocate of slavery restriction, conceded that slaves were a form of property.[26]

It would be difficult to distinguish Barbour's remarks on the slavery question from those of John Randolph or other conservative Republican critics of postwar nationalism—critics whose unending jeremiads against expanding federal authority, largely ignored until recently, were suddenly recognized for their prophetic truth. Barbour's speech certainly contrasted sharply with earlier ones in which he argued for loose construction and an expansion of the national government's powers. That earlier flush of optimism was gone now as he earnestly fought to preserve the South's distinctive institutions. Angered by what he thought was a bold northern play for power and a hypocritical charity that sought to gratify itself at southern expense, he turned instinctively, as did Henry Clay and others, to the old restrictionist arguments Republicans had used so effectively against Federalist aggrandizement in the 1790s.[27]

A few days after Barbour spoke, Sen. William Pinkney of Maryland, a superb but ostentatious orator, delivered a speech that many considered the ablest defense of slavery presented during the debates. Foppishly dressed in a splendid suit draped with gold and silver scarves, he electrified the Southerners with his rhetoric. Barbour joined with Thomas Hart Benton and others in applauding it as the "most gorgeous speech ever delivered in the Senate." Northerners were more critical, however. King called it "gaudy and captivating," and Otis likened it to the rays of a diamond that "sparkled, dazzled, and were gone."[28] Pinkney was followed by William Smith of South Carolina, who glorified slavery and, developing the argument that Southerners would articulate more fully in the years ahead, contended that it was a moral and positive good. There was no laboring class anywhere outside of the United States, he said, that was "better clothed, better fed, or . . . more cheerful" or that enjoyed "more liberty and indulgence."[29]

In the heat of controversy during the long, protracted debates, there was much talk in Congress of disunion. Cong. John Tyler wrote that his colleagues talked of "dissolution of the Union with perfect nonchalance and indifference." Henry Clay added that the words "disunion" and "civil war" were uttered almost without emotion. Harrison Gray Otis, having changed his position on restriction after consulting with constituents in Massachusetts, exclaimed that if Congress assented to allow the "sphere of human slavery and servitude" to expand "from the Mississippi to the setting sun . . . , it would have been happier for us if the Mississippi had been an eternal torrent of burning lava . . . , and the regions beyond it destined to be covered with brakes and jungles, and the impenetrable haunts of the wolf and panther."[30]

John Quincy Adams charged that in the "hottest paroxysm" of the debate, Barbour canvassed all the Senate's free state members on the advisability of calling a convention to dissolve the Union.[31] What truth there is to this allegation, based on information Adams obtained from Samuel Dana, is difficult to determine. One would think that such a move, if indeed it was made, would have attracted widespread attention. Such was not the case. No corroborative evidence, either in the press or in the letters of his contemporaries, can be found. Certainly Barbour was not at heart a disunionist. But if in the heat of the moment he did make such overtures, his conduct would not have been much different from that of his colleagues. Adams himself, convinced that it would be better to dissolve the Union than to allow the spread of slavery, thought that another convention might be necessary to "remedy the great imperfections" of the existing system of government. Clay blustered and threatened to go to Kentucky, where he would raise troops to defend the rights of Missouri. John Randolph, exclaiming that "God has given us the Missouri and the devil shall not take it from us," formulated a plan whereby all the southern delegation would leave Congress, presumably never to return. Sen. Walter Lowrie of Pennsylvania said that if the alternatives were "a dissolution of this Union, or the extension of slavery over this whole Western country, I, for one, will choose the former." Monroe was convinced that restrictionists, if they did not prevail, were prepared to split the Union at the Allegheny Mountains.[32]

During the controversy Barbour did warn that the patience of the South was limited. No section of the country, he said, had been more loyal to the Constitution or more supportive of the national government than his own. "To the Union we have looked, as the ark of our salvation and the resting place of our hopes. Is this your reward for our loyalty? Sir, there is a point where submission becomes a crime, and resistance a virtue. . . . Beware how you touch . . . [slavery]. The South . . . can endure anything but insult." These were threatening words, spoken in a tone little calculated to effect reconciliation. But they were the exaggerated rhetoric of momentary passion. In a calmer moment he expressed his deep desire to see the

Union endure. "When I finally contemplate the glory and happiness . . . [the Constitution] has produced, I will not now distrust that Providence which has been so pleased to dispense to us so many and such distinguished blessings. I will not permit myself to believe that this mighty scheme of political salvation, in which all nations are interested, will pass away like the grass of the field. I will rather continue to indulge the hope that we shall remain united and free."[33]

The second opinion was more characteristic of Barbour than the first. In the early stages of the contest he unquestionably overreacted. But as the debate raged and he perceived more clearly its seriousness, he dropped his own adamancy and adopted a more responsible posture. Anticipating that an impasse would soon be reached, he began to work quietly behind the scenes for a compromise, which he saw as the only possible constructive solution—not for resolving the larger slavery issue itself, but for saving the Union. He maintained close contact with key political leaders in Virginia, especially with Roane, Ritchie, and the principal leaders of the legislature then in session. He made a quick trip to Richmond to try to prepare them for a compromise, which they firmly opposed. In addition, he consulted regularly with Monroe and Clay and probably with Crawford and Calhoun.[34]

On February 2 Barbour conferred with Monroe about the advisability of separating the Maine and Missouri bills, a move that he thought might persuade Notherners, once Maine had been admitted, to reciprocate by admitting Missouri without restrictions. Though risky, he thought it was worth trying, especially since he was uncertain of a safe Senate majority for the combined bills. Monroe concurred and suggested that Barbour proceed with the plan, provided that he could obtain the consent of the other southern senators.[35]

Before Barbour had time to implement the new strategy, Sen. Jesse B. Thomas of Illinois on February 3 proposed an amendment to the Missouri portion of the Maine-Missouri bill which prohibited slavery in the unorganized Louisiana Purchase Territory north of the line 36°30'. This proposal, which ultimately became the basis for the Missouri Compromise of 1820, was withdrawn shortly thereafter, ostensibly to allow its author a chance to modify it, but actually to give Barbour and other southern and western moderates a chance to organize support for it among their colleagues. With this development, Barbour decided not to move to separate Maine and Missouri. Instead, he allowed the combined bills to remain before the body as a holding action until the necessary support for the compromise could be secured.[36]

In endorsing the Thomas Amendment and working for its adoption, Barbour did not support the constitutional arguments of the restrictionists. He continued to say that the regulation and control of slavery were vested solely in the states and that Congress had no right to legislate on the subject. Rather he supported the amendment for a combination of pragmatic and political reasons. In the first place, he saw it as a quid pro quo: slavery in Missouri in exchange for free territory north of it. In the contest before Congress, he said, "if either party completely triumphs, it is much to be feared that the other will not submit." Practical necessity required compromise.[37]

Second, Barbour was convinced that behind the attempt to restrict slavery in Missouri was a thinly veiled play for political power—perhaps an attempt by Federalists to revive their old party or even to forge a new one in which they, joined by northern antislavery groups and other dissident Republicans, would attempt to unseat Virginia from political control of the country.[38] John Holmes lent credibility to this notion in late January when he somewhat vaguely warned his House colleagues that a Federalist plot, led by New Yorkers, was responsible for the antislavery agitation.[39] Barbour apparently found that allegation believable. He suspected that Rufus King, who had visited Massachusetts during the previous summer, was somehow responsible for many of the antislavery protests emanating from that state. His suspicion seemed to be confirmed by the fact that King, after a long silence in the Senate, a silence that was "as mysterious as it . . . [was] unexpected," had suddenly emerged as the principal spokesman of the restrictionists. Barbour charged that the New York Federalist had been ingenious in his efforts to "delude and mislead our northern brethren . . . , to excite their prejudices, and to enlist their opposition to any and everything which even savored of compromise." What was King's purpose? His immediate objective, Barbour thought, was to suspend the Missouri question for another year—to let the yeast of conspiracy ferment, in order that "he may derive every possible advantage from the excitement . . . [the antislavery agitation] is so well calculated to produce." His ultimate objective, if not to revive the Federalist party or to create another, might well be to form a northern confederacy, of which he would be president.[40]

While there is no evidence to suggest that Federalist political ambitions were responsible for the move to limit slavery, Federalists were not oblivious to the fact that an alliance with dissident Republicans would greatly broaden their political base, which had become precariously narrow.[41] That many Federalists had been deeply involved in the northern antislavery movement seemed to Barbour evidence enough that the real issue was political power, not the morality of slavery. And he was not the only one who believed this. Jefferson, Madison, Monroe, Clay, and many other Republicans shared his conviction.[42] It was partly in the hopes of thwarting Federalist plans, especially of preventing a ruinous North-South sectional alignment of political parties, that Barbour pushed for an early resolution of the Missouri question.

Finally, Barbour favored the Thomas Amendment because he believed it would preserve the Union. "I am penetrated with the deepest regret and horror," he said, "at seeing that too many on both sides view disunion with so little repugnance."[43] Convinced as he was that northern restrictionists were prepared to ignore the consequences of their uncompromising stand, and that his own constituents, especially the inflexible members of the Richmond Junto, were determined to yield nothing, he saw a division of the unsettled territory west of the Mississippi as the only possible hope of saving the nation. While it would not be easy to induce either side to accept what both regarded as an unpalatable compromise, they would accede, he thought, choosing "a lesser evil than either dividing the union, or throwing it into confusion." This opinion he expressed freely in correspondence with Madison, with his old Senate colleague John J. Crittenden of Kentucky, and with certain members of the Junto.[44] It was in this same spirit that he told his senatorial colleagues, "The fact is, in all great national questions, where different views and different feelings prevail, it is indispensable to any practical result that we practice towards each other some degree of deference and concession."[45] In abandoning his initial intransigence for a conciliatory stance calculated to preserve the Union, Barbour acted with a political moderation that he knew would be criticized by his constituents. But he was not prepared for the severity of the criticism he received.

News of the impending compromise that would admit Missouri without restriction but would prohibit slavery north of the line 36°30′ struck Virginians like a thunderbolt. On the evening of February 9, a Republican caucus met in Richmond to nominate a slate of presidential electors. Shortly before it assembled, a group of Monroe's political enemies circulated the rumor that a compromise on Missouri, planned and advocated by the president, was about to take place in Washington. Included in the group were Ritchie and some twenty-five or thirty legislators, who hoped to embarrass Monroe by putting forth an unpledged slate of electors unfriendly or, at best, lukewarm to his reelection.[46] Charles Yancey of Louisa County, a member of the caucus, indiscreetly disclosed the contents of a confidential letter he had received the day before from Barbour saying that the Thomas Amendment would probably be approved. Barbour himself, Yancey divulged, favored the compromise, as did Monroe, cabinet members Calhoun and Crawford, and most of the southern senators. Members of the caucus were infuriated. One of the group, advanced in years, was reportedly so upset that he wept. In a prophetic utterance he exclaimed: "Would to God we had war with England, France, Spain, or any other nation, which would unite the people, rather than civil war with the Northern states, which must inevitably take place if any restriction is made on our right to hold slaves, and to transport them where we please." Distraught and angry, the caucus adjourned without acting.[47]

Political observers in Richmond said that they could not "recollect any occasion in which the feelings of the citizens and of the legislature were wrought up to a higher pitch. Indignation at the idea of such a compromise is the ruling sentiment." Ritchie was thrown into a frenzy: "A compromise! Who will compromise with the Constitution of his country and barter away its essential principles...? If we yield now, beware! They [restrictionists] will ride us forever.... We had rather wait the progress of events; leave Missouri to futurity; pursue what is right, 'with an eye that never winks'—and leave the rest to God."[48] Yancey informed Barbour that the legislature was adamantly opposed to any compromise. "If you wish to speak the voice of our present legislature," he said, "you must stand stubborn in opposition to the compromise.... Do not yield the 19th part of a hair." Henry St. George Tucker, who had abandoned his nationalism and had become a member of the Junto, wrote at greater length on February 11: "I declare to you that I am unable to describe the sensation in Richmond at the intelligence conveyed in your letter. A compromise which gives up the fairest and largest part of the Western territory and leaves to us a narrow strip intersected with mountains in one direction, destroyed by earthquakes in another, and interspersed in a third with swamps and bayous, and infested with mosquitoes, and bilious diseases, never can be grateful to us." Roane, Stevenson, and other influential members of the Junto wrote Barbour and Monroe denouncing the proposed compromise and vowing that Virginia would not abide by the laws of the country if their constitutional rights were subverted by slavery restriction.[49]

Following the caucus's adjournment, both Barbour and Monroe were deluged with letters from angry constituents reminding them of their duties as Virginians and as defenders of the Constitution. There was talk in Richmond of disunion and of abandoning Monroe for some other candidate. Henry St. George Tucker expressed the feelings of many Virginia politicos when he inquired if the purpose of the compromise was to secure the reelection of Monroe.

> What ... is the spirit that prompts this compromise? ... Is it for fear that the president may lose his Election? We are unwilling to purchase his service at such a price: still less willing to support him if *he* can with a view of his own Election thus surrender the valuable rights of the South. The caucus has adjourned accordingly. I trust in God if the president does sign a bill to that effect, the Southern people will be able to find some man who has not

committed himself to our foes; for such are, depend on it, the Northern Politicians.[50]

Roane was only slightly less emphatic when he wrote that Virginia would not "sign the instrument of her own degradation. She will say, with the revered patriots of 1776, 'we have counted the cost of this contest and find nothing so intolerable as *voluntary* slavery.'" He would rather have taken the South out of the Union than be "damned up in a land of slaves by the Eastern people."[51]

While Virginia hotspurs fumed and Congress debated, Barbour attempted to placate his angry constituents. In letters to Roane, Ritchie, Stevenson, and others, he explained his position, discussed aspects of the problem that had been generally overlooked, and urged moderation.[52] Gradually tempers cooled. Excitement subsided. On February 16 Yancey again wrote Barbour saying that distrust and anger were diminishing as the intricacies of the issue became better understood. On the following day he wrote: "The intelligent and honorable among us see how you were surrounded on all sides by difficulties which would have embarrassed Wisdom itself in making a choice. . . . The hostile feeling against you has all passed away and all idle clamor has ceased, reason has resumed her empire, and you again [enjoy] the former hold you had to our confidence and esteem."[53] William Fitzhugh Gordon, a personal friend of Barbour and a member of the Junto, admitted that he and his friends had not "perceived the whole ground, nor seen through all the mazes" of the difficult problem. Linn Banks, writing in the same vein, conceded that the information which prompted the Junto's response had been partial and imperfect.[54]

Barbour wrote many letters trying to appease Virginians. In addition, two of uncertain authorship appeared in the February 17 issue of the *Richmond Enquirer* addressed to "Friends in Richmond" and anonymously signed "A Gentleman in Washington." They were apparently written by Barbour and Monroe. Their style and content, as well as their timing (they were published on the day the Virginia legislative nominating caucus met), show traces of both men. Probably Barbour, after consulting with Monroe, drafted them and then passed them on to the president for revision.[55] The letters argued strongly for compromise of the Missouri question, not only to avert national catastrophe, but also to prevent Rufus King and his Federalist allies from carrying out their plan of reorganizing political parties along sectional lines. "In standing firm against compromise, you are playing into the hands of King and his friends, who are drawing highest advantage from the stand you are taking." Furthermore the South, because of the decided Senate majority favoring exclusion of slavery from the unsettled territory north of 36°30', ran the risk of having slavery excluded from all the Louisiana Purchase territory if the compromise was rejected.[56]

These letters, along with the others that Barbour and Monroe wrote individually to Virginia legislators and to members of the Junto, were crucial in winning over the state to an acceptance of the compromise, reluctant though it was. The legislative caucus reconvened on the evening of February 17 and nominated a slate of electors favorable to the incumbent president. The Junto was not enthusiastic about its action, but its members really had no other choice, for no other candidate was acceptable both to the anti-Missouri faction and to the Southerners.[57] If Monroe failed to win their support, he at least had their neutrality. Ritchie continued to deplore the betrayal of Republican principles, but he and others braced themselves for the acceptance of a compromise that seemed inevitable. When Congress did approve the Thomas Amendment in its final form in early March, Ritchie expressed the prevailing sentiment of most Virginia politicos when he wrote:

> The deed is done—the treaty is signed, sealed and delivered. The compromise which threw this city and commonwealth into a flame and suspended for a week the Electoral Caucus is consummated. We submit. It is the duty of good citizens to hold by the sheet anchor, the law of the land, so long as it remains law. We bow to it, though on no occasion with so poor a grace and so bitter a spirit. The South and West are wronged, they must be patient. The Union is too dear to us all to be torn asunder.[58]

No one was more instrumental than Barbour in winning Virginia over to this acceptance of compromise, grudging though it was.

Barbour weathered better than Monroe the political crisis that their support of the compromise caused. While most of the Junto, many of whose members had never trusted Monroe anyway, continued to blame the president for the "guilt of concurrence," they seem to have forgiven Barbour rather quickly for what Roane called his "error of judgment."[59] After the initial shock had subsided in Richmond and when calmer counsels prevailed, William Fitzhugh Gordon wrote Barbour that "unless it may be with those who never were your friends . . . , your standing in the legislature is not injured." Linn Banks similarly wrote that "for my part, I am confident that whatever . . . [you] may have done or hereafter do has been the result of pure and disinterested patriotism." And Roane, though he thought Barbour erred, assured him that he acted in "high character, according to your best convictions, and in a most trying crisis," adding that he still enjoyed the confidence of most Virginians.[60]

Barbour managed to retain the confidence of the legislature and Junto, at least in part, by a political move which seemed to indicate a complete lack of principle. He voted against the Thomas Amendment when it came before the Senate for action on February 17. In light of the fact that he had earlier endorsed it and, during the two-week period from the time it was first suggested until it was acted on, had worked untiringly to marshal support for it among his colleagues, his vote is difficult to explain.[61]

It is possible, of course, that he voted as he did because of the overwhelming opposition of the Junto and the Virginia assembly to compromise. If so, he did indeed demonstrate a lack of principle and political courage. One is then left to wonder why he was less courageous in this instance than on other occasions, both past and future, when he voted for such measures as the bank and internal improvements, which were almost as unpopular in Virginia as the slavery compromise. A more plausible explanation is that he voted against the amendment in order to argue more effectively, as one who had opposed restriction but lost, the need to compromise. By giving the appearance of having steadfastly resisted any sacrifice of southern principles, he maintained the support of Virginia politicos and, with that, the hope of being able to influence their conduct. Because he had carefully canvassed his colleagues and was assured of the amendment's passage, he could engage in this bit of deception without fear of affecting the final result. His conduct throughout the contest suggests that if the vote had been close or uncertain, he would have voted for the amendment. This interpretation is supported not only by his numerous letters to Virginia politicians urging acquiescence in the compromise, but also by his subsequent votes in favor of the combined Maine-Missouri bill with the attached antislavery amendment.[62]

The response of Virginia to the Thomas Amendment and the whole question of slavery restriction was far more militant than that of the rest of the South. In addition to the uncompromising stance of the Junto, Virginia's militance was expressed by inflammatory resolutions passed by the House of Delegates in January 1820 threatening a resort to interposition over the Missouri question. Indeed, there is reason to believe that if Virginia had had her way, the issue of slavery, instead of being postponed until 1861, would have been fought to a finish in 1820.[63] Of the other southern states, only Georgia reacted with a comparable belligerence. The Virginia delegation in the House of Representatives, for example, cast eighteen votes against the amendment and only four in its favor, while representatives from the remainder of the South supported it by a vote of 35 to 19. In the Senate only eight of a possible total of twenty-two southern votes were cast against it. Public opinion in most of the southern states ran in its favor. Sen. Charles Tait, writing from southern Alabama, declared that he had not heard a single word in opposition to it. The *Southern Patriot* of Charleston, South Carolina, expressed its approbation of the compromise measure, as did most of the newspapers of Mississippi and Alabama.[64]

How, then, does one explain Virginia's intransigence? At the time of the Missouri Controversy, the state was undergoing a particularistic reaction to the growing powers of the national government. Opposition to slavery restriction was but one facet of a campaign the state was conducting against federal aggrandizement and nationalism. Clay's American System and the nationalistic decisions of the Supreme Court were the specific targets of conservative Virginia Republicans.

Economic factors underlay Virginia's reaction. Following a brief period of wartime prosperity, the state's agriculture succumbed to a chronic depression, aggravated by western competition and by the Panic of 1819. Narrow agrarian particularists had little difficulty convincing Virginians that the national bank and tariff were major contributors to the economic malaise. The entire nationalist program, including internal improvements, which threatened to reduce even more the marginal utility of lands in eastern Virginia by opening up the virgin lands of the West, was denounced by a leadership centering in the Richmond Junto, which pushed the states' rights doctrine into a prominence it had not known since 1798.[65]

Recent decisions of the Supreme Court impressed upon Virginians a heightened awareness of the implications of the new nationalism and contributed to the reaction. They were particularly disturbed by the *Martin* vs. *Hunter's Lessee* (1816) and *McCulloch* vs. *Maryland* (1819) decisions, which they correctly interpreted as a serious threat to their cherished doctrine of state sovereignty. Roane, who as chief justice of Virginia's state supreme court was overly sensitive to the prerogatives of his own office, responded by publishing a series of legalistic, verbose essays maintaining that the federal compact was nothing more than a union among sovereign states in which only limited specific powers had been given to the national government.[66] Jefferson, Ritchie, John Taylor, John Randolph, and others joined Roane, and almost every issue of the *Richmond Enquirer* reflected the new spirit of Virginia reactionaries. The relative liberalism that characterized state leaders in earlier years was rapidly giving way to a dogmatic, strict constructionist, states' rights attitude.[67]

The Thomas Amendment had little chance in this hostile environment. The issue was too sensitive, the stakes too great, to be passed over lightly. Roane, Ritchie, and company were convinced that northern politicians were conspiring to destroy the economic and political strength of the South. Already painfully aware of Virginia's waning influence in national councils and determined to protect its prestige and prerogatives, they interpreted correctly the issue: prohibition of slavery north of the latitude 36°30′ would weaken the South politically. With the political balance between the sections destroyed, southern economic interests would inevitably suffer. They were little inclined to compromise on an issue that affected their future so vitally.

In reacting to the Senate's approval of the Thomas Amendment as if it represented a final disposition of the Missouri question, Virginians responded prematurely. The question was far from settled. On February 17 the Senate, having amended the original House Maine bill by attaching provisions enabling Missouri to form a constitution and state government without slavery restriction, passed the engrossed bill with the Thomas Amendment. The House rejected the amendments, however, and returned its original bill to the Senate. The upper house refused to recede from its amendments, and the lower refused again to accept them. A heated discussion then followed in the Senate. A number of senators insisted upon standing firmly by their amendments, while others favored yielding. Barbour moved that a joint House-Senate committee be appointed to find a way out of the impasse. On February 28 the recommendation was adopted, and Barbour, William Pinkney, and Jesse B. Thomas were chosen to represent the Senate. John Holmes and John Parker of Massachusetts, William Lowndes, John Taylor of New York, and Charles Kinsey of New Jersey were selected from the House.[68]

Before the joint committee could confer on the problem, however, the House passed its own Missouri bill prohibiting slavery. When the Senate took up the bill on March 2, Barbour moved that the section prohibiting slavery be removed. His motion carried overwhelmingly. Then, without a division, the Senate attached to the bill the Thomas Amendment and returned it to the House. On the same day the joint committee submitted its report. It recommended that the Senate withdraw its amendments to the House Maine bill; that the clause prohibiting slavery in the House Missouri bill be removed; and that the two houses add to the Missouri bill the Thomas Amendment prohibiting slavery in that part of the Louisiana Purchase lying north of the latitude 36°30' which was not included within the limits of the proposed state of Missouri.[69]

The historic Missouri Compromise of 1820 consisted of these three measures. That the compromise was accepted by the House was due largely to Clay's astute leadership. Had it been voted upon as a whole, it would undoubtedly have been defeated, but Clay adroitly steered it through the House by dividing it into sections and voting upon each separately. The House approved the compromise on March 2, and Clay, thwarting John Randolph's last-minute effort to kill it, passed it on to the Senate. There it encountered no difficulty. On March 3 the upper house, without a division, approved it, and with its passage the second Missouri debate came to a close.[70]

What role Barbour played in the deliberations of the joint conference committee that evolved the details of the compromise is unknown, but it was probably an important one. Like Clay, he was an eminently practical politician who recognized that compromise was the "indispensable tool" of democracy. Few excelled him in negotiating political differences in committee, where his pragmatism and his ability to cajole and persuade reluctant colleagues were unsurpassed. Since he had decided a month earlier that it would be politically expedient to separate Missouri from the Maine bill, he quite possibly persuaded the committee to divorce them in its report. The provision restricting slavery north of 36°30' he could hardly have accepted gladly, but as he interpreted the situation in 1820, it was the only way of securing a compromise to avert national catastrophe.

Barbour was aware of the implications of accepting the Thomas Amendment, which some have called the death warrant of slavery. He recognized that the states which in the future might be carved from the free territory would ultimately upset the balance between the sections, and he was greatly troubled. He could only defer the problem to posterity in the hopes that it would provide a solution. In practical terms, however, he thought the natural limits to the expansion of slavery minimized the actual southern loss.[71]

What he did not see, or was unwilling to admit, was that slavery itself was doomed and that the most statesmanship could do was to postpone its demise. Neither he nor his colleagues seemed to recognize or understand the strength of certain inexorable political and social forces working against slavery. Nor did he see that the Missouri discussion offered an excellent opportunity to attempt a permanent solution for the problem, applicable initially to the territories and in time to the slave states themselves. A policy of gradual emancipation, coupled with compensation to slaveowners, would have been one possible and ultimately far less expensive way of averting the terrible cost, both in money and blood, that many prescient observers foresaw. But none of the southern leaders was willing to accept the social and economic revolution that such a move would have wrought. Instead they chose to continue to live with the contradiction between the ideal of human liberty and the reality of slavery, defying Jefferson's expectation that the new generation, unwilling to tolerate such a contradiction, would take the side of morality and would eliminate this great blight on the American character. In voting against the possibility of gradual emancipation, they committed themselves and the South not merely to the existence of slavery, but to its permanence as well. It was perhaps the most momentous decision in the whole history of the slavery controversy.[72]

Although Barbour's response to the Missouri question was more moderate and conciliatory, and certainly more responsible, than that of his doctrinaire Virginia colleagues, the controversy put him on the defensive. For several years after 1820 he was more sensitive to the sectional implications of national legislation. Together with postwar mercantilism, the

Missouri struggle heightened southern awareness of the threat that centralized government posed to their cherished interests and institutions. Once the antislavery movement had been linked to nationalism, furthermore, it became increasingly difficult for defenders of slavery like Barbour to advocate loose construction and to support expansion of federal power. He did not take up the states' rights standard, but he did assume a more cautious nationalist posture, one that would allow him to defend the special interests of the South and at the same time to participate in some of the benefits which only nationalism offered.[73]

The first session of the Sixteenth Congress lasted until May 15, 1820. Weary from the length and trauma of the session, Barbour returned home to attend neglected personal affairs. Springtime was at full flood when he reached Barboursville. The planting season was already well advanced, and most of the crops were sprouting. The daily routine of the plantation, interspersed with short trips through a lovely countryside fragrant with the fresh smells of early summer, did much to heal his spirit and restore his morale. But the domestic tranquillity he found in such large measure at Barboursville was shattered in midsummer by the sudden death of seventeen-year-old Benjamin, his and Lucy's second son. In many ways Benjamin had been a greater joy to his parents, and certainly the cause of fewer heartaches, than had James. A studious lad who had shown considerable scholarly promise, he had also been the more dutiful and obedient of the two.[74] His loss came as a terrible blow. Earlier the Barbours had lost two children in infancy, but Benjamin's death, occurring as he stood on the threshold of manhood, was much more difficult to bear. His parents were a long time in recovering from the shock.

Barbour was still grieving when he returned to Washington in mid-November, 1820, for the second session of the Sixteenth Congress. Instead of lodging at one of the larger boardinghouses, as he customarily did, he shared a private residence with Sen. Richard M. Johnson of Kentucky, perhaps because he did not feel ready for the active social life that attended lodging at the crowded Indian Queen or at Mr. Dowson's.[75] Once the session had begun, Barbour immersed himself so completely in his work that there was little time for grief. His attention was quickly diverted from personal concerns by the magnitude of the crisis that once more imperiled the nation. From the outset it was abundantly clear that Congress and the nation must drink again from that "fountain of bitter waters" which he hoped had been "forever sealed" at the previous session.[76]

During the summer, Missourians, angered by the attempt to restrict slavery in their borders, had drafted a constitution which not only sanctioned slavery but also excluded free Negroes and mulattoes from the state and prohibited the legislature from emancipating slaves without the consent of their owners. This action had prompted an equally angry response from the antislavery press and free state legislatures. Denouncing the constitution in the strongest possible language, antislavery forces returned to Washington firmly resolved to block Missouri's admission until they could muster enough strength to bring the territory into the Union as a free state. They believed that if they could postpone the question for two more years, northern immigrants would overrun the territory and, in due time, would abolish slavery of their own accord. To achieve their immediate goal of rejecting the Missouri constitution and thus delaying her admission, they focused their attack not on the larger question of slavery but rather on the clause concerning free blacks and mulattoes, which northern opinion almost unanimously opposed.[77]

Most of the debate during the session centered in the House, where the real battle was fought. In the upper house a majority of senators from the beginning could be counted on to favor immediate admission: all of the southern members; three northwestern senators who had been born in the South (Ninian Edwards and Jesse B. Thomas of Illinois and Waller Taylor of Indiana); and Maine's two new senators, John Holmes and John Chandler, both of whom distrusted the motives of their Federalist antislavery neighbors and felt some moral obligation to honor the spirit of the Compromise of 1820.

The Senate acted first. In early December it took up a resolution admitting Missouri on an equal footing with the original states. John H. Eaton of Tennessee promptly moved to amend the resolution by stipulating that Congress, in granting statehood, did not assent to any provision of the Missouri constitution, "if such there be," which contravened the clause in the federal Constitution providing that "the citizens of each State shall be entitled to all privileges and immunities of citizens in the several States."[78] A sharp exchange followed. King and some of his antislavery colleagues opposed the amendment because it did not do enough to weaken the effect of the repugnant article excluding free blacks and mulattoes. An extended debate, accompanied by numerous postponements of the question, then followed. Barbour declined to participate. Concerned about the effects another protracted and acrimonious debate would have on the nation, he urged his associates to act without further delay. "The mind of every gentleman is fully made up on the subject," he said, and public tranquillity required that they decide the issue quickly and quietly.[79] After a week of debate the Eaton amendment was incorporated into the resolution admitting Missouri. By a vote of 26 to 18, Barbour voting with the majority, the engrossed bill passed to a third reading. The following day, December 12, it was passed on to the House without a division.[80]

In the House the resolution was heatedly debated. Passions rose as the antislavery and proslavery factions locked horns. Henry Clay, who had been detained earlier by personal business in Kentucky, appeared in the House in mid-January 1821 and attempted to extricate the body from its impasse. In a characteristically conciliatory gesture, he called upon both sides to reconcile their differences and to accept the Senate resolution. After days of futile wrangling, it was decided, upon Clay's suggestion, to refer the resolution to a special committee. On February 10, Clay reported the resolution back to the House, amended to admit Missouri upon the condition that the state pass no laws preventing citizens of other states from entering and settling there. By the close vote of 83 to 80 the committee's recommendation was rejected, and once again there was stalemate.[81]

The Missouri question affected almost every issue that came before Congress in January and February. In mid-February it threatened to disrupt the Electoral College canvass. There was no doubt of Monroe's reelection, but there was a question as to whether Missouri's three votes should be counted. The South was determined to count them, and the North was no less determined to exclude them. Fearing a deadlock that would result in no election, Barbour moved that a joint House-Senate committee be appointed to resolve the problem. As a member of the committee he was instrumental in devising a compromise, grudgingly accepted by both houses, that skirted the constitutional issue. The committee agreed to read two sets of returns, one including and the other excluding the Missouri vote. When Congress assembled jointly on February 14 to conduct the canvass, tumult and confusion followed. The Senate decorously withdrew until order was restored. Both sets of returns were subsequently read, and Monroe and Daniel Tompkins were proclaimed president and vice-president.[82]

The Barbour-Clay compromise, as it was called, may have assured a minimum of controversy in canvassing the electoral vote, but it had little bearing on the course of the Missouri debates. By the middle of February the deadlock seemed hopeless. While the House continued its interminable discussion and Clay looked desperately for some way out of the impasse, the Senate sought a compromise measure of its own. On February 16, Jonathan Roberts introduced a resolution admitting Missouri upon the stipulation that it repeal the clause in its constitution which excluded free Negroes and mulattoes. Barbour, speaking in opposition to those of his colleagues who felt they could take no further action on the matter until the House had acted, supported the measure. The Roberts resolution was defeated by a vote of 24 to 19, however, and a solution to the "ominous and ill-boding question" remained as elusive as ever.[83]

In a final effort to resolve the issue before the Sixteenth Congress adjourned, Clay on February 22 suggested that a joint committee be appointed to work out an acceptable plan for Missouri's admission. The House was amenable to Clay's proposal, but the Senate balked. When it appeared that opponents of the proposal might prevail, Barbour appealed to his associates to make one final effort to "untie the Gordian Knot." They finally agreed, and Barbour, along with Richard M. Johnson, Rufus King, and four other senators, was appointed to the committee, which consisted of a total of thirty members, including Philip Pendleton Barbour from the House.[84]

In the late afternoon of February 24, the thirty-member House-Senate committee met and agreed to a resolution suggested by Clay stipulating that Missouri would, by proclamation of the president, be admitted to the Union as a slave state on the condition that its constitution "never be construed to authorize the passage of any law . . . by which any citizen of either of the States in this Union shall be excluded from the enjoyment of any of the privileges and immunities to which such citizen is entitled under the Constitution of the United States."[85] This resolution constituted the basis of the second Missouri Compromise.

On February 26 Clay reported the compromise resolution to the House, which after a brief discussion passed it by the uncomfortably close margin of only six votes. The only southern representative to vote against it was John Randolph. The most unyielding proponent of states' rights in Congress, he would have opposed any measure that did not admit Missouri unconditionally. Most Southerners shared Hugh Nelson's opinion that it was "better to make some sacrifice to form, than to lose the substance."[86] Voting with the proslavery delegates were eighteen northern representatives, some of whom, as members of the joint committee of thirty, had apparently come under heavy pressure from Clay, Barbour, and other moderates to change their position and to support the compromise. John Quincy Adams was critical of the tactics the moderates used to detach enough votes from the House's antislavery majority to carry the compromise. "They have threatened and entreated, bullied and wheedled, until their more simple [restrictionist] adversaries have been half coaxed, half frightened into a surrender of their principles."[87] But the strategy worked.

When the compromise resolution was taken up by the Senate on the twenty-seventh, Barbour acted as its chief advocate. Speaking in opposition to Nathaniel Macon, who like Randolph was opposed to conditional admission and attempted to kill the compromise, he pleaded for harmony and concession. Compromise, he believed, was the only way out. When the final vote was taken the next day, the measure passed by a vote of 28 to 14.[88] Thereupon the second Missouri Compromise was accepted, and the third

Missouri debate came to an end. The great contest over slavery had, for the moment, ended.

On March 3, 1821, the Sixteenth Congress ended its stormy session and adjourned in time to participate in Monroe's second inaugural ceremonies. It had been a momentous Congress—the most dramatic and trying one, Barbour said, in which he had ever participated.[89] Pressed to the wall by the restrictionists, the South had demonstrated an unequivocal conviction that its destiny was inextricably bound to the future of slavery and the maintenance, at least in the Senate, of political equilibrium. The contest posed for Barbour an insoluble dilemma. As a Southerner and a slaveowner, he was committed to maintaining his section's political power and institutions. But he was also an American whose loyalties and interests were not bounded by region. He could see only one way of reconciling the two conflicting interests.

In 1820 and again in 1821, when the Missouri crisis was most threatening, Barbour turned to compromise because he thought it was the only way to save the country. He believed that compromise was the basic working tool of a republic; perpetuation of the Union depended on the continual adjustment of competing interests. As emotionally charged as the issue was, especially for slaveowners like himself, he acted responsibly to reconcile extremes and to secure practical political action. Admittedly, the compromise attempted to preserve the status quo for whites at the expense of indefinite postponement of freedom for blacks, but Barbour did not consider the price large. It was consistent, indeed, with his and his generation's ideal of progress—one of order and stability, balance and harmony.

During the Missouri Controversy, Barbour demonstrated qualities of statesmanship which, to some extent, at least, transcended sectional loyalties. In engineering compromises and working adroitly for their acceptance, he showed a mastery of congressional political processes equaled by few of his day. But he recognized the limits of what had been accomplished. There had been no happy termination of the contest, no permanent settlement of the issue itself. Congress had not legislated for posterity. The most it could do was legislate for its own time. At best the compromises merely postponed the question. "The spirit in which that contest originated," he sadly acknowledged, "is not dead."[90] The present was but preface to the future.

7

Between
Two Worlds

The Missouri Controversy shattered Barbour's illusion that the Era of Good Feelings had ushered in a new age in which political and sectional rivalry would cease to be important determinants of American life. It did not destroy his hopes for progress or permanently alter his politics, but it did force him to confront certain new political realities. The most compelling of these was that a militant, doctrinaire political mood was settling heavily on the Old Dominion and was imposing a rigid orthodoxy on the life of the state. The liberal spirit of Jeffersonian Republicanism was being transmuted by Old Republicans into a very different political creed. The new creed, narrowly restrictive, anachronistic, and denunciatory of anything modern, appealed to men's fears, whereas the Jeffersonian faith appealed to their hopes. As an elected representative, Barbour could not ignore this development.

The Old Republican doctrines of strict construction and state sovereignty, especially as expounded by John Taylor, had always had a strong theoretical emphasis. After the Missouri debates they lost that emphasis. They ceased to be abstract political principles and became the common southern grounds of political allegiance, the grounds on which the South would defend its cherished interests and institutions against the threats posed by a centralized and democratic national regime. For years Roane, Ritchie, Randolph, and other Old Republicans had been warning that constitutional latitudinarianism threatened to destroy the reserved rights of the states. The challenge to slavery simply imparted a new urgency to their message. By giving currency to the old doctrines of strict construction and state sovereignty, the twin pillars on which southern sectionalism rested, and by tying them to the defense of slavery, these men helped usher in a new political age. With Taylor providing the philosophy, Roane the judicial pronouncements, Ritchie the journalistic reiteration, and Randolph and Philip Pendleton Barbour, among others in Congress, the legislative articulation, Virginia prepared to move from the political mainstream that carried the nation forward into the troubled eddies of southern sectionalism, where the state would languish for decades.[1]

Signaling the new age in Virginia was the restoration to public favor of those twin apostates Randolph and Taylor, whose opposition earlier to certain Jeffersonian measures had resulted in their political eclipse. In 1821 Roane eulogized Taylor, saying, "This venerable patriot deserves great praise for his intrepid and unceasing efforts to preserve our beloved confederacy."[2] Ritchie also called upon the old agrarian: either he should return to public life or he should "illuminate our benighted citizens with some of the good old doctrines of '98." Taylor gratified Ritchie by doing both. Soon after he wrote *Construction Construed*, which Ritchie happily published in 1820, he accepted an appointment to the U.S. Senate.[3] Along with Taylor, John Randolph, whose unwavering attachment to the past and unending jeremiads against national consolidation had made him a political pariah, was now called upon by his countrymen to defend the old creeds against their many assailants. As a prophet long without honor, he must have felt vindicated when fellow Virginians, who a few short years before would have seen him "roasted almost as soon as drink...[his] health," turned to him in their hour of trial.[4]

Thomas Jefferson, growing more conservative with the years, was perhaps as much infected with this new contagion as was the rest of Virginia. The reinstatement of Taylor and Randolph and the elevation of their ideas moved him to boast that he had "as companions in sentiments, the Madisons, the Monroes, the Randolphs, the Macons, all good men and true, of primitive principles." He thought that Taylor's *Construction Construed* was the "most effectual retraction of our government to its original principles which has ever yet been sent by heaven to our aid."[5]

It was not easy for Barbour to adjust to Virginia's reactionary mood. The hostility of his constituents to every form of nationalism placed him in a tenuous position. For while he shared their deep concern about the future of slavery, he did not believe with them that every piece of nationalist legislation threatened the rights of the states. Although he pulled back from his earlier nationalist position, he did not retreat completely. He sought, instead, a middle ground—one that would enable him to support certain measures of unquestionable benefit to the Union without relinquishing altogether the old Virginia doctrines. Thus he supported certain nationalist measures which, to his mind, were essential to the welfare of the country. Those that he considered less crucial he opposed. But he chose his ground carefully, realizing that whenever he supported legislation opposed by his constituents, he must be able to explain and justify his actions to them.

The influence of the Richmond Junto was increased by the Missouri Controversy, and Barbour made a greater conscious effort to keep the channels of communication open to the group. During the next few years he corresponded with its members more frequently and visited them as often as he could.[6] By doing so he was able to allay some of their fears and to temper, however mildly, their reaction. On those occasions when he differed with the Junto on public policy questions, he argued that local interests must sometimes be subordinated to national ones, that it was his responsibility as a member of the U.S. Senate to legislate not just for a state or region but for the entire country.

For a while he was able to convince the Junto and other constituents that his ground, though perhaps different from theirs, was nonetheless solid, and that he acted from proper motives to promote the good of the country. In this way he was able to retain their confidence and to command broad popular support in the assembly without becoming the mere tool of those groups.[7]

Soon after the Missouri debates ended, Barbour voted against two nationalist measures, one for extending the Cumberland Road, the other for increasing the protective level of the tariff. The yeast of the slavery controversy had worked its leaven on others as well, however, for most Southerners who had supported the tariff of 1816, including William Lowndes, voted against it now.[8] But at the same time, Barbour took a strongly nationalist position on the question of protecting American commerce.

In the spring of 1820 he presented a new navigation bill designed to put additional pressure on Great Britain to open up her West Indian colonies to American shipping.[9] He defended the measure, which was more stringent than the act of 1818, on nationalist grounds. It was true, he said, that the commercial ship-owning section of the Northeast would profit most from a strong navigation policy, but the entire country would benefit from a flourishing trade and from a large merchant marine. The country should nurture its commerce and seapower as an avenue to national strength and prosperity. If such a policy advanced the interests of one section more than those of another, all would nevertheless benefit. The whole question afforded an excellent opportunity to assuage sectional feelings:

> We have heard during the present session the harsh and discordant sound of disunion; we have been told that there exist separate views, interests, and feelings. What a fine occasion does this present to silence these unhallowed insinuations! The South and the North, the East and the West, uniting in a great measure of policy—particularly, indeed, beneficial to one quarter of the union, but cheerfully submitted to by the others—in furtherance of

national benefit. We will not permit any occasion of this kind to pass by without disproving these sectional aspersions. We [the South] will cheerfully meet the sacrifice . . . , and find our indemnity in the proud reflection that the interests of the whole constitute the popularity of all our movements.[10]

The bill passed the Senate in mid-April without a division and encountered only moderate opposition in the House, which approved it in early May.[11] During Monroe's second administration, the navigation question, along with tariff and internal improvements, would be recurring issues of national policy. Where navigation was concerned, Barbour would continue to take a nationalist position. But as events of those years proved, it was not easy for a Virginia politician to be a nationalist in these reactionary times.

Following adjournment of the Sixteenth Congress on March 3, 1821, Barbour remained in Washington long enough to attend Monroe's second inauguration. He had more than a passing interest in the proceedings, for he had developed a close personal friendship with the man whom he had served as political adviser for four years. As soon as the festivities were over, however, he returned to Barboursville. He found his family well, though Lucy was confined by her seventh and last pregnancy. In June she gave birth to their fourth son, Benjamin Johnson, named for the son who had died the previous summer. Their oldest son, James, who had left Harvard without earning a degree, was now living at home, where he was assuming a large role in managing the farm. Their youngest daughter, Frances Cornelia, almost nine, was beginning to exhibit some of the social graces which in the years ahead would delight Margaret Bayard Smith, who found her charm captivating.[12]

Barbour had no difficulty, once home, in turning from politics to farming. It was by now a familiar cycle, one that had repeated itself almost annually since he first entered public life in 1798. He welcomed the change. Spring was at hand, and as always it would bring a rejuvenation of spirit. Such a renascence must have been especially welcome after the trying sessions of the Sixteenth Congress. But there was no time for idleness. With the busy planting season approaching, there were many decisions to make, many details to attend to. He turned to them gladly. During the last several years he had neglected his personal affairs, which now pressed for attention. Poor crops for the past two years and the general agricultural depression that accompanied the Panic of 1819 had forced him into debt.[13] He must redouble his efforts to recover.

As soon as the crops had been planted, Barbour traveled to Richmond to visit members of the Junto, with whom he had not had a chance to talk since the Missouri debates. He found them in an angry mood. They were still seething over the Supreme Court's recent ruling in the *Cohens* vs. *Virginia* case. That ruling, in which the Court emphatically affirmed its appellate jurisdiction over state courts, had set off a new wave of militant states' rights sentiment in Virginia. Spencer Roane, parading as the Mosaic guardian of the constitutional tablets, rushed immediately into public print with a series of essays challenging the Court's right of jurisdiction. Others joined him in the attack. Ritchie denounced the decision as a grave threat to state sovereignty and expressed the opinion that the Court should be replaced with an elective tribunal composed of mature statesmen of Jefferson's and Madison's caliber. At issue in the contest, of course, were the basic and persistent questions of the nature of the Union and the location of the authority to act as final arbiter in disputes between state and federal authority.[14]

The intensity of feeling he witnessed among Junto members could not but have concerned Barbour. It is hard to imagine how, in this hostile environment, he could have escaped the conclusion that the country faced difficult times ahead. It must have given him cause for reflection, not only about Virginia's and the nation's future, but about his own as well. In a sense, his political position seemed fairly secure. With the backing of the Junto, he had recently been reelected to another six-year term in the Senate, having received all but 14 of the 188 votes cast in the General Assembly.[15] But given his nationalist leanings and Virginia's reactionary mood, he must have had serious misgivings about his ability to continue to represent his conservative political constituency.

The Seventeenth Congress assembled on December 3, 1821. Barbour took lodging this session at Brown's Hotel on Pennsylvania Avenue, where his brother Philip Pendleton and a large number of Virginia and New York congressmen were staying.[16] By comparison with earlier congressional sessions, this was to be a relatively quiet and uneventful sitting. An issue that generated a great deal of interest at this time and later was internal improvements. The question had lain dormant since 1817, when Barbour had tried unsuccessfully to secure a constitutional amendment and the House had decided that Congress had an appropriating but not a jurisdictional power over internal improvements. The issue undoubtedly would have arisen again had not the Panic of 1819 and the Missouri Controversy diverted Congress's attention. But internal improvements were too vital a concern to remain suppressed for long. In late April 1822 the House passed and forwarded to the Senate a bill authorizing the federal government to erect turnpikes on the Cumberland Road, with gates and tolls, and to enforce the collection of tolls by sanctioning penalties for evasion. With this action the House, over the objections of the recently elected Speaker Philip Pendleton Barbour and other strict constructionists, conceded the power of jurisdiction it had denied the national government four years earlier.[17]

Despite Virginia's strong opposition, Barbour supported the bill when it came before the Senate. In doing so, he refused to debate the constitutional question. Instead, he took the eminently practical position that it was foolish not to maintain a road that had already been built. Under three presidents Congress had spent almost $2 million on the road's construction but had done nothing to maintain it. Ravaged by the weather and by vandals, it was virtually impassable at places. For Congress to refuse the necessary funds for its repair and maintenance was "absurd and ridiculous." Unlike his brother Philip and other doctrinaire Virginians, he was unwilling in this instance to sacrifice the national good to some "fastidious technicality." Passing over the constitutional question of whether Congress had jurisdiction in the matter, he argued that common sense, if nothing else, dictated that Congress maintain what, at no small expense, it had created. Because the bill involved the appropriation of no federal funds but simply authorized the collection of tolls— "a little pittance . . . [from the users] to keep it in repair"—he did not regard the constitutional objections as important. Sounding like the nationalist of earlier years, he concluded by reminding his listeners of the benefits, both present and future, that this "great artery of communication between East and West" provided. It was a "noble monument" to the vitality, strength, and unity of the nation, the abandonment of which would be a great loss to posterity.[18]

Although the Senate approved the bill, President Monroe considered it unconstitutional. He accompanied his veto with a long paper in which it appeared that he was willing to approve appropriations for internal improvements, provided that the states through which the projects passed assumed the jurisdictional responsibility for building and maintaining them.[19] Encouraged by this faint hope, nationalists renewed their efforts in 1824 with the General Survey Bill.

The evident purpose of the General Survey Bill was to prepare the way for appropriations for internal improvements on a national scale. Although the bill simply provided funds for the specific purpose of conducting surveys, its passage would imply approval of a national system of roads and canals. The bill encountered strong opposition in the House, especially from the Virginia delegation. Philip Pendleton Barbour, whose recent defeat by Clay in the speakership contest had in no way diminished his role as one of the House's most able and vigilant defenders of the states' rights doctrine, led the attack.[20] In a closely reasoned argument that by now was painfully familiar to his colleagues, he defined the respective roles and powers of the state and national governments and warned that unless the Constitution was rigidly followed, the general government, "like Aaron's serpent, would soon swallow up the State governments." He emphatically denied that Congress possessed any jurisdiction over internal improvements or, for that matter, that it was empowered even to appropriate funds for them, as Monroe believed.[21]

Other Old Republican members of the Virginia congressional delegation, including John Randolph, followed Philip Pendleton Barbour, monotonously reiterating all the strict constructionist arguments they could muster. Randolph warned his southern colleagues that if Congress acceded to the power implied in the General Survey Bill, the Constitution would become a mere scrap of paper. Congress might then do anything it pleased, including emancipating every slave in the country.

> Should this bill pass, one more measure only requires to be consummated; and then we, who belong to that unfortunate portion of this Confederacy which is south of Mason and Dixon's line, and east of the Allegheny mountains, have to make up our mind to perish like so many mice in a receiver of mephitic gas, under the experiments of a set of new political chemists; or we must resort to the measures which we first opposed to British aggressions and usurpations—to maintain that independence which the valor of our fathers acquired, but which is every day sliding from under our feet.[22]

It was a frightening specter. But southern conservatives did not need to be reminded of the uses to which the "new political chemists" might put the doctrines of loose construction and implied powers. The conservatives were solidly opposed to the bill. Their opposition was not enough, however, for the measure passed the House in February by a comfortable margin.[23]

In the Senate the bill was stoutly opposed by such southern conservatives as Nathaniel Macon, John Gaillard, and John Taylor, who were joined by John Holmes of Maine and Martin Van Buren. Its sharpest critic was John Taylor. Since his arrival in Washington in 1822, when he replaced Virginia's junior senator James Pleasants, Taylor had become, in John Randolph's words, "quite a lion" among the states' rights congressional delegation. Vying with one another for his company during Washington's long winter evenings, they looked to him as the oracle of political wisdom, the fountainhead of true republican principles.[24] He did not disappoint them in his speech against the General Survey Bill. That measure, he thought, could be likened to the wooden horse prepared by the cunning Greeks, which the foolish Trojans regarded as harmless and admitted into the walls of their city. "Does this bill contain in its womb fewer combustibles, or such as are less likely to inflame geographical interests, and destroy the Union, should we provide for their introduction, by levelling those outworks by which the constitution is defended?" He answered with an emphatic "No!" He then examined and dismissed, one by one, the various constitutional provisions on which nationalists claimed that the power to construct internal improvements was based. He challenged the nationalist argument that Senator Barbour and others had used earlier in defense of roads and canals—the argument that they would serve to bind the nation together into a happy and prosperous whole. "Improvements which may chain the States together," he said, were a poor substitute for "the decaying principles" of the Constitution, which alone were the bond of union. It was a dangerous notion that the states, "when they cease to be united by the Constitution, may be kept together by roads and canals."[25]

Barbour presided over the Senate debate on the General Survey Bill and took no active part in the discussion. In his opinion the constitutional issue was more clearly defined in this measure than it had been in the 1822 bill. The question was not whether Congress should repair and maintain a road it had already built, but whether it should prepare the way for a general system of internal improvements financed by the federal government. However desirable and beneficial such a system might be, he was not willing to have Congress, which had rejected a constitutional amendment that would have obviated the problem, exercise the disputed power. Consequently he voted with the Senate minority against it.[26]

Although Monroe signed the bill, strict constructionists ultimately forced Congress to abandon all plans for a national system of roads and canals. It adopted instead a policy of appropriating funds to the individual states for this purpose. In the years ahead many states, especially those in the West, preferred to undertake their own canal- and road-building programs and turned to the federal government for the necessary financial assistance. Representatives from these states entered into logrolling agreements to secure mutual support for appropriations for state-owned improvements. Even the Cumberland Road itself was soon turned over to the states through which it passed. Thus the controversy about internal improvements resulted in a significant victory for state sovereignty and decentralization. As Barbour and others clearly understood, a national system of internal improvements would have provided a powerful and much needed force for the unification of the nation. But the countervailing forces of strict construction and state sovereignty proved too powerful. In yielding to those pressures, which in Virginia were perhaps irresistible, Barbour lost the opportunity to create what might have constituted an important obstacle to the course of southern sectionalism.

In addition to internal improvements and the tariff, an issue that continued to command the attention of Congress during Monroe's second administration was Anglo-American commercial relations. Great Britain had responded rather contemptuously to the United States' Navigation Acts of 1817, 1818, and 1820. Lord Castlereagh in the Foreign Office had exclaimed that he would rather see Great Britain's West Indian subjects starve than change her mercantilist policy. But for some years forces beyond his control had been at work in England undermining the old commercial order. Those forces achieved a notable victory in 1822 when Liberal Tories on the Board of Trade succeeded in obtaining a bill which embodied the principle of reciprocity vis-à-vis the American–West Indian trade.[27]

The United States' reception of this act, known as the American Trade Act of 1822, was hardly what England had expected. In late August 1822 President Monroe issued a proclamation that appeared to revoke the nation's restrictions on British commerce and to open American ports to British vessels. But he did not remove the tonnage duties or the 10 percent ad valorem levy upon imports customarily charged against vessels not privileged by treaty stipulations. The British ambassador, Stratford Canning, appealed to Secretary of State Adams to correct what he thought must have been an oversight. But Adams put him off. Not long afterward the Senate Foreign Relations Committee, which Barbour still chaired, reported yet another navigation act that was far more stringent and bolder than anything previously attempted.[28]

The Navigation Act of 1823, sometimes called the "Elsewhere Act," did not originate with the Senate Foreign Relations Committee. In December 1822 the committee took under consideration a House bill which lifted most of the restrictions against British commerce. Barbour, Rufus King, and several other committee members thought the bill was premature and unwise. They proceeded to draft a measure of their own that was far less generous.[29] While they were refining the details of their bill, Secretary of State Adams gave Barbour a bill that he had been evolving during a period of months and asked him to consider it in committee. Accordingly, the committee set its bill aside and took up Adams's proposal. Their attention was drawn particularly to the second section of the bill, which insisted upon the right of American ships and goods to enter British colonial ports on the same terms as those from the British Empire. This was indeed a bold demand, described by that Liberal Tory William Huskisson, perhaps the foremost British advocate of free trade, as a "pretension unheard of in the commercial relations of independent states."[30] In effect, the bill sought to compel Great Britain to abandon its centuries-old mercantile policy.

Questioning whether the intent of the administration was what it appeared to be, Barbour conferred on two occasions with Adams to determine the precise views of the government. Assured by him that the bill meant exactly what it said—that the United States did indeed propose to trade in British colonial ports on equal terms with England and her dominions—and that the cabinet was in full accord on the subject, Barbour reported back to the committee.[31] After exhaustive deliberation the committee unanimously approved the bill. Barbour then presented it to the Senate and acted as its chief advocate. In March 1823 it passed. With its passage the commercial nationalism of the United States, which Barbour, King, and others had worked so hard since 1815 to promote, reached a new height.[32]

Barbour's unequivocal advocacy of protection for American commerce did not extend to industry. He did not want the United States to be a helpless agrarian market for British manufactured goods, but he could not bring himself to support the high tariff that protectionists were calling for. In 1824 high tariff advocates, rallied by the Philadelphia publicist Matthew Carey and the Baltimore editor Hezekiah Niles, and led in Congress by Henry Clay, managed to squeeze through the House a new tariff that increased protection.[33] Barbour opposed the bill when it was discussed in the Senate. He was not opposed to the principle of protection, he said, but he did object to the oppresive burden the high rates would impose on the South. He tried without success to reduce the rates. Despite the solid opposition of the South, the bill passed in mid-May by a vote of 25 to 21.[34]

Barbour's opposition to the tariff of 1824 was more moderate than that of Randolph, Taylor, and other Old Republicans who reflected more accurately than he the true sentiments of the Old Dominion. Randolph's friend James M. Garnett saw the tariff issue as "the last chance which we agriculturalists shall have of making head against Northern and Eastern encroachment." Its passage, he predicted, would "consummate our temporal misfortunes as a community. . . . The South must become a tributary to the North, and hold their property according to the principles which . . . [the tariff] will establish, at the will and pleasure of men who have little or no common interest with us."[35] Randolph himself went much further when he warned House colleagues of the possible consequences of a protective system. "If, under a power to regulate trade, you prevent exportation; if, with the most approved spring lancets, you draw the last drop of blood from our veins; if . . . you draw the last shilling from our pockets, what are the checks of the Constitution to us? A fig for the Constitution! When the scorpion's sting is probing to the quick, shall we stop to chop logic? . . . There is no magic in this word *union*."[36]

Although the recurring questions of the tariff, internal improvements, and commerce occupied much of his time in the Senate, Barbour did involve himself with other issues. He was particularly concerned about some of the country's social problems. One of the most serious of these, he believed, was that of imprisonment for debt, a practice he called the "undisputed progeny of a barbarous age."[37] With considerable difficulty he managed in 1822 to steer through the Senate a bill ameliorating the laws concerning insolvent debtors in the Federal District.[38] Two years later he urged his colleagues to adopt a law abolishing the practice throughout the nation. He observed that according to his statistics, no fewer than 1,442 people of 40,000 living in the city of Boston were incarcerated for debts in 1820. For the country as a whole he estimated that the number was not below 13,000. The practice, he said, was a cancerous blight on the character of the nation and should be removed. Drawing on Lockean philosophy, he argued that the great object of the social compact was to guarantee man liberty and the right of its full enjoyment. Poverty was a misfortune, not a crime. The honest debtor deserved sympathy, he said, not punishment. "Let us not ... steel our hearts against the unfortunate—their cup of life is made sufficiently bitter by their misfortune—tis cruelty alone that will administer an additional drug. And yet these victims of misfortune are the subjects of your punishment." It was a moving appeal. The Senate responded by approving a bill which paved the way to the abolition of the practice.[39]

Barbour advocated and supported other measures which attested to his strong social concern. Long opposed to dueling, he unsuccessfully sought congressional action that would have curtailed, if not abolished, the evil.[40] He was active in securing passage of numerous measures aiding the indigent, pensioners, war veterans, and other unfortunates. Typical was his support of a group in New York interested in obtaining land and funds for the construction of an asylum for the deaf and dumb.[41] In addition, he championed or supported many measures designed to advance education.

He vigorously opposed a money-saving cut in postal facilities because he believed it would have hindered the diffusion of knowledge. He was instrumental in securing a charter for present-day George Washington University, and Jefferson turned to him for assistance in obtaining funds which enabled the University of Virginia to open its doors in 1825.[42] In short, Barbour's interest in these and similar matters attested to his deeply benevolent and humanitarian spirit.

During a congressional career spanning barely a decade, Barbour perceived powerful forces working to alter the old political structure of national politics. As a Virginian accustomed to his state's long domination of the presidency and to its correspondingly powerful voice in national affairs, he was disturbed by the shift of political power to other quarters. While the population of the Old Dominion was declining, that of many other states was growing rapidly, bringing a corresponding increase in political power. The dynamic of national expansion was effecting changes that were everywhere apparent, as Barbour was well aware. "The Revolutionary generation," he wrote in 1820, "has passed away. The new presents so many who are equal or think themselves so (which is the same thing) that every section of the union will have its claims—except Virginia. She by common consent is to repose on the recollection of what she has done."[43]

Barbour's lament was not the only one heard in Virginia during the 1820s. Indeed, before the decade was out, he was joined by a veritable chorus of voices from political leaders whose discordant plaints reflected the general malaise and pessimism that had settled on the state. And some of them undoubtedly remembered an earlier voice in the wilderness, that of John Randolph, whose prophetic warnings against abandoning old paths for new had been ignored for so long. How often had his attacks on those in power, his dolorous tirades against constitutional latitudinarianism, fallen on amused but unreceptive ears? But concerned Virginians ignored him no longer. They heralded him as their modern Jeremiah. His public utterances became their sacred tablets. Though not unwilling to accept the new stature accorded him, Randolph thought it was too late for him or anyone else to rescue the republic. "So far has the country moved away from true Republican principles that I fear it is now too late to call upon Minority men for aid." The ruin of his native state, he said, lured by the national inducements proffered by Monroe, Clay, Barbour, and others, "I have long forseen & I await it as my aboriginal ancestors would the torture of their captors." Like King Lear, the once-noble state of Virginia was now nothing more than "an old and feeble monarch" abandoned by her children.[44] Randolph's confidant James M. Garnett had not yet been brought to the same point of despair, but he did concede that if the Old Dominion was "not yet quite dead," it was certainly "in very bad odor at Court."[45]

As Barbour presciently observed, the reelection of Monroe in 1820 marked the end of an era. For four more years the Virginia Dynasty would continue, but the scepter of power, as he noted, had "departed from Judah." Virginia's hegemony in national politics was at an end. The Old Dominion had been supplanted by New York, which in turn would soon be challenged by other states.[46] The leaven of new social and economic forces was hard at work, altering the old order. A nascent modern capitalism, with its factories and urban workers, was beginning to emerge. Throughout the country, pressures were mounting for a broader franchise, equal representation, and greater political and economic democracy. The 1820s displayed a democratic urgency that not everyone saw. John Randolph did. But with a cynicism that carried a distinctly Hamiltonian ring, he could only deplore the stirring of "that monster, the multitude."[47] Jackson sensed it. Intuitively he played to the dissatisfied in America, who rallied to his standard in unprecedented numbers. Barbour saw, not always clearly, perhaps, but better than most. He recognized the benefits that would accrue from the growth of business enterprise, the development of manufacturing, and the physical expansion of the nation, all facilitated by a comprehensive system of roads and canals. But what was the cost? He had been born to the older agrarian world. He believed strongly in its virtues, and he could not easily abandon its ideals. In supporting much of the nationalist legislation after the War of 1812 he had already stretched his agrarian philosophy to the breaking point. He was willing to embrace aspects of the new order, for he believed it would provide greater economic and political opportunities for the American people, but he did not want to sacrifice agrarianism in the process.

Barbour's ambivalent feelings about the new age suggest the strains he and other agrarians felt when their society, resting on what they believed were the natural human relationships of a landed order, was threatened by the seemingly artificial and materialistic values of modern capitalism. The confrontation between the cultural values of the rival systems left them without compass or guide. As long as Jeffersonians controlled the national government, Barbour was confident that agrarian values and republican institutions were secure. That confidence even allowed him to employ Hamiltonian means to expand the benefits of union. But the contest over slavery and the imminent demise of the Virginia Dynasty, coming at the same time that economic changes of a fundamental order were transforming society, left him disoriented and uncertain about the future. At issue once again, it seemed, were the old questions debated by Federalists and Republicans in the 1790s: what form of government and type of society should America have?

Barbour grappled earnestly with these questions as he tried to come to terms with the realities of the new age. And in his struggle we see something of the drama of America's confrontation with her own traditions. Barbour was caught precariously between traditional concerns rooted in an agrarian past and the changing, unpredictable demands of an expansive commercial future. Although neither he nor anyone else really understood the historical and economic forces that were reordering society, he was aware of being caught between two worlds, and he tried to embrace the best of both. The result was that he—like the rival Federalist and Republican parties, which after 1801 seemed so close to switching sides on many political issues—appeared to act from expediency rather than principle. His Old Republican colleagues, by contrast, adhered rigidly to principle. Ill at ease with practical politics, resentful of political or social change of any type, inflexible and uncompromising, they seemed almost to oppose America itself. In the end they were disinherited by their inability to meet the changed requirements of a world in flux. Barbour's instincts were too liberal, his feet too firmly planted in the real political world of his day—he could not be won over to their simplistic, undeviating arguments. He adopted instead an open, inquiring approach, knowing that free government evolved, at least in part, by trial and error. Only in this fashion could the nation stay on the course so hopefully charted by the revolutionary generation.

But the course was not always clearly marked. Occasionally Barbour took a wrong tack, as, for example, in 1824, when he supported the Southerner William H. Crawford as the presidential candidate most likely to pursue the policies and spirit of Jeffersonian Republicanism. In the election contest of that year, which saw the disintegration of the congressional caucus and of one-party rule, he campaigned indefatigably for Crawford and staunchly defended the caucus system against its many critics. There was great irony in his action. By advocating internal improvements and other nationalist measures, he was encouraging increased economic and social mobility for the American people, objectives which he consciously and repeatedly affirmed. But in championing the antiquated and undemocratic caucus system, he acted, whether he intended to do so or not, to restrict political mobility.

President Monroe had no sooner taken the oath of office and made plans for his second term of office than presidential hopefuls began to plan for 1824. Within a short time the number of aspirants was, in Barbour's words, "like Falstaff's reasons—as thick as blackberries."[48] Secretary of State Adams, Speaker of the House Clay, Secretary of War Calhoun, Secretary of the Treasury Crawford, and General Jackson—all began to marshal their forces in preparation for the next election.

By 1822 the campaign was in full swing. State legislatures and mass meetings, scorning the caucus system of nomination, which had been under attack since 1816, began to advance their favorites. The South Carolina legislature, after the death in 1822 of favorite son William Lowndes, backed Calhoun, who was confident of carrying most of the middle states. His hopes were dashed when Pennsylvania, which he had expected to carry, swung to Jackson in 1824. Afterward he concentrated on the vice-presidency.

Neither Clay nor Jackson had a large political following at the beginning of the campaign. Clay's nationalism had attracted support in some sections of the country, and he was hopeful of carrying portions of the North—New York especially—along with the West. But in Virginia his American System was anathema, and he had almost no following there, though he was generally liked personally. Even in the western portion of the state he was a poor third to Adams and Jackson.[49] His chief weakness lay in the fact that he was competing with a powerful foe from his own section. Jackson was initially considered an even weaker contender than Clay. Barbour thought the General possessed none of the qualifications for office and, like most other Virginians, dismissed him as a "mere military man."[50]

But a few Virginians were favorably disposed to the General. Much to the chagrin of his conservative colleagues, John Taylor, a few months before his death in the fall of 1824, began to gravitate to the Jackson camp. When Taylor voted for a five-year military appropriations bill early in the year, a disgruntled John Randolph charged that "the army candidate has got the length of . . . [Taylor's] foot." Taylor's friend and Senate colleague Nathaniel Macon accused him at the time of having "forgotten his own book, and advised him to read it again."[51] The General's campaign was skillfully managed in a manner calculated to appeal to all sections and to the common man in particular. By the end of 1823 it had gained a momentum that seemed irresistible to many observers.

Adams had a large following in the Northeast and had some strength in the Northwest. In Virginia he was preferred after Crawford. Most of his support in Virginia, however, came from the western part of the state, where nationalist sentiment was strong.[52] He was distrusted by the Richmond Junto, whose candidate until his death in 1822 was the archconservative Spencer Roane. Early in the campaign the *Richmond Enquirer* expressed its disapproval of the New Englander. By mid-1822, when the secretary of state had still done nothing to promote his candidacy among the "caucus-mongers" and had "neither Captain nor Sergeant to recruit" for him, Ritchie declared that he was "hors de combat."[53]

The leading candidate during the early phase of the campaign was Crawford, who was still somewhat bitter because he had not received the nomination of his party in 1816. Although Barbour had been one of the principals in preventing his nomination at that time, he had since become a close friend of the handsome and personable Georgian. Barbour hoped to see Crawford succeed Monroe.[54] As early as 1821, Barbour was lamenting the rise of opposition to his favorite. Presidential candidates, he wrote Charles Tait, were "multiplying like the leaves of the forest."[55] During the next few years he worked untiringly to advance the candidacy of the secretary of the treasury.

Although Crawford had a large following in Virginia, the political conservatives, especially the members of the Junto, were surprisingly slow to support him. Barbour used his personal influence with Ritchie and others to promote Crawford.[56] It was not until after Roane's death that he made much headway. Gradually Ritchie was won over. By early 1823 the editor was beginning to devote space in the *Enquirer* to explanations of Crawford's occasional lapses from the Virginia doctrines, especially his support of the tariff and the national bank. The attitude of Virginia conservatives, most of whom ultimately supported the Georgian, was that he was acceptable only because his opinions were less unconstitutional than those of the other candidates.[57] As election time drew nearer, Ritchie increased his efforts on Crawford's behalf. Feeling "so much gorged with mere trash" on the election campaign, he entreated Barbour to "execute your design of addressing the people on the pretensions and merits of W.H.C." If Barbour would provide him with a series of weekly essays possessing the same "eloquence and force" with which he customarily wrote, he would publish them in the *Enquirer*, with confidence that they would have the desired effect on the public mind. In the months ahead Barbour not only provided the desired essays but also joined with Van Buren and other Republican strategists in leading Crawford's election campaign.[58]

But in September 1823 a hard blow was struck Crawford. While visiting Barbour at his recently completed country seat in Orange, the presidential hopeful suffered a paralytic stroke. For more than six weeks he remained immobile at Barboursville, partially paralyzed and almost blind. He was treated by the local physician for bilious fever and bled almost daily, but he did not recover sufficiently to leave until November. His condition then was so bad that it was months before he was able, even on a limited basis, to resume his official duties in the Treasury.[59]

Crawford nevertheless remained in the contest. His partisans, Barbour included, remained optimistic about his chances for a full recovery. When Congress convened in December 1823, Barbour, Van Buren, and other Republican strategists finished their plans for the campaign. Hoping that the prestige of a caucus nomination would serve to rally and unite the badly divided Republican party behind the Georgian, they sought to secure his selection as soon as possible.[60] It was poor strategy, for the caucus, under sharp attack as an undemocratic process, was doomed. Instead of uniting the party, it polarized the various factions. For the remainder of the campaign the caucus's action would hang like an albatross about Crawford's neck.

The congressional caucus of 1824, the last ever to be held for the purpose of nominating a president, met on the evening of February 14 in the chamber of the House of Representatives. A pall hung over the assembly. Only sixty-six congressmen, four fewer than Barbour had predicted, appeared, and almost half of them were from Virginia and New York.[61] Many Crawford supporters, such as Taylor and Randolph of Virginia and Macon and Willie Mangum of North Carolina, refused to attend because they objected to the system. Despite what Barbour called a "troubled scene," the caucus proceeded. Crawford was duly nominated, though not by a unanimous vote. In an effort to give the ticket something of the flavor and credibility of the Republican party of old, they named Albert Gallatin as vice-president. Barbour favored this move, thinking it might serve to unify the party on its old principles.[62] But like the caucus itself, Gallatin's selection was a mistake. Gallatin was not to be well received, especially among the members of the Richmond Junto. And the initial displeasure would increase as time went on. Before the summer had passed, by which time it had become apparent that the Pennsylvanian would not be able to carry his own state against Jackson, supporters would try unsuccessfully to persuade Crawford to dump Gallatin in favor of Clay, whose politics they disliked but who at least would strengthen the ticket in the West.[63] Thus the congressional caucus failed dismally, not only in terms of attendance, but also in its attempt to unite the party under a single standard.

Disappointed though he was by that failure, Barbour did not give up the fight. He corresponded with key political figures in a number of states and did everything he could to advance Crawford's candidacy.[64] The futility of his efforts was illustrated in William Henry Harrison's response to his request for help in the West. Harrison wrote that his state was adamantly opposed to Crawford. He could see not even the remotest possibility that the Georgian would carry Ohio or any of the other western states. If Clay were to withdraw from the race, Harrison would be willing to offer himself as a Crawford elector, but so great was Jackson's popularity in his state that he doubted that Crawford would win. The Jackson advocates, he wrote, "do not appeal to the judgements of the people but to their passions, hence the difficulty of arresting their progress."[65] Other correspondents, for one reason or another, declined to join the Crawford camp.

By early summer Barbour had abandoned all hope of victory. It was apparent to everyone in Washington that although Crawford had resumed some of his official duties, he was a long way from full recovery. Adams was holding his own, and Jackson was weekly gaining ground. Although Barbour considered throwing his support to the secretary of state when Crawford's defeat became certain, he continued publicly to support the secretary of the treasury.[66] Unlike a number of Crawford partisans in Congress, he refused to engage in the attempt of May 1824 to embarrass and discredit Adams by opposing the slave-trade convention he had recently negotiated with Great Britain. The opposition of the Crawford forces to this convention was engineered by Van Buren and John Holmes of Maine and was intended solely as an electioneering maneuver. Adams wrote that Barbour "behaved with great magnanimity and honestly supported the convention." Indeed, in the opinion of John Taylor, who was so ill and weak that he could barely climb the steps to the Senate chamber, he delivered an eloquent and very able speech in its support.[67]

Nor, for that matter, did Barbour engage in any of the countless political electioneering maneuvers Van Buren and other Crawford men in Congress engineered to advance their candidate at the expense of the administration. During the last two years of the election contest they repeatedly attempted to promote Crawford by blocking appointments, opposing administration measures, and in other ways embarrassing Monroe and the presidential aspirants in his cabinet. Throughout the canvass Barbour remained on good terms with the administration and continued to serve Monroe as political adviser and confidant.[68] There is no indication, however, that Monroe, Adams, or anyone else interpreted his refusal to engage in these rather shabby electioneering tactics as an abandonment of Crawford.

In the election of fall 1824, none of the four candidates received the necessary majority. Jackson won a plurality of the popular vote and ninety-nine electoral votes, enjoying substantial support everywhere except in New England. Adams's eighty-four votes came chiefly from New York and New England. Crawford's forty-one came from the Southeast, largely from Virginia and Georgia, and Clay's thirty-seven came chiefly from Kentucky and Ohio. Since none of the candidates received a majority in the electoral college, the final choice would be made by the House of Representatives.

On December 22 Barbour visited Adams and for several hours discussed the impending vote. At this time he stated his personal feelings and those of his state in unequivocal terms. Crawford remained Virginia's first choice. The state's delegates in the House would stand firmly by him so long as there was any hope of success. If it became obvious that he could not be elected, Virginia would then shift its vote to Adams. Before leaving, Barbour questioned the secretary of state on his views regarding the tariff and internal improvements, to which Adams replied that he found the existing tariff satisfactory and that he was more inclined to seek a reduction in its protective level than an increase. As to internal improvements, he informed Barbour that his opinion in favor of them remained unchanged.[69]

At noon on February 9, 1825, Barbour and the other members of the Senate, braving a heavy snowstorm that immobilized the city, filed into the hall of the House of Representatives.[70] The electoral votes were read, and the president of the Senate announced that there was no election, except for Calhoun, who had received 182 of the votes for vice-president. The Senate then retired, and the House proceeded with the balloting for president. When the balloting began, Adams was assured the vote of twelve states. He needed one more for election. New York, wavering until the last minute between Crawford and Adams, cast the decisive ballot for the New Englander. House tellers John Randolph and Daniel Webster read the vote: Adams 13, Jackson 7, and Crawford 4. "It was impossible to win the game, gentlemen," Randolph said, "the cards were stacked."[71] Adams's election by the indirect vote of the House, without a leading majority of either the popular or electoral college votes, did not augur well for his administration.

During the years 1815–1825 Barbour sat in six Congresses. Throughout that period he was one of the most powerful and influential members of the upper house. When he resigned his Senate position in March 1825 to accept a cabinet post in the Adams administration, he could look back over a constructive record. The role he had played in helping to launch the nationalistic ship of state in the years after the Treaty of Ghent had been significant; and when this proud, refurbished vessel was in danger of foundering on the shoals of the Missouri Controversy, he had appeared at the helm along with Clay and others to help pilot it through the danger. Although he had been swept along by the particularistic wave of reaction after 1820, his reaction was tempered by the nationalistic sympathies he had imbibed. In light of the extreme sectional feelings aroused in Virginia after 1819 by the decisions of the Supreme Court, by agricultural depression and general economic displacement, and by the slavery question, his reaction had been moderate. To be sure, his nationalistic tendencies were somewhat dormant after 1820, but they were to come to life again during the Adams administration.

8

To Save
the Red Man

*A*lthough Barbour had good reason to think that a victorious Crawford
would have offered him a cabinet position, he had no reason to
expect Adams to do so.[1] As chairman of the Senate Foreign Relations
Committee he had worked amicably with Secretary of State Adams, who
had a good opinion of him. In mid-February Kentucky's senator Richard M.
Johnson urged Adams to consider bringing Barbour into his government,
saying that he would be a good choice for either the War or Treasury
departments.[2] Soon thereafter Adams offered him the war portfolio. The
president-elect did not confide to his introspective diary the motives
behind his action. In light of the fact that Crawford earlier had declined to
continue in the Treasury, he may have been prompted by a desire to win
over the powerful Crawford interests in Virginia. If so, it was one of the few
politically motivated appointments he made during his presidency.[3]

Barbour did not accept the offer immediately. He was not sure that he
wanted to continue in public life. A year earlier he had said that he would
not accept a position in the new administration if one were offered him. In
April 1824 he had written despairingly of the troubled political atmosphere in Washington and expressed a desire to retire. "My wishes," he
wrote, "are all at home." A month later he wrote in a similar vein: "It has
been six months since I was home. My private affairs suffer greatly. Nothing but a sense of duty keeps me in public life."[4] Apparently the long
summer and fall at Barboursville following congressional adjournment in
May restored his spirits, however, for he did not spurn Adams's overtures.

Having received assurances from the president-elect that he contem-
plated no radical departures from the policies of his predecessors and that
the goal of his administration would be to reconcile divergent sectional
interests by harmonizing, conciliating, and bringing "the whole people
together in sentiment as much as possible," Barbour consulted with a
number of his political associates in Virginia.[5] He received divided coun-

sel. Some of his friends advised him to accept the offer. Others demurred. Ritchie was one who objected. But another respondent advised Barbour to ignore the petulant editor, whose influence in Virginia, he thought, was daily declining: "Ritchie scribbles away sometimes without guide or compass and really, it would seem, without knowing what he is writing about." Another wrote that "many approve and many condemn." But after receiving assurances from Andrew Stevenson and others that they would keep an open mind toward the administration and would judge it on the basis of its merits and accomplishments, Barbour decided to accept.[6]

Adams's inauguration on Friday, March 4, 1825, in the opinion of one veteran observer, was the most impressive ceremony of its kind ever witnessed in Washington. Thousands of festive-spirited citizens thronged the city, lining Pennsylvania Avenue and crowding the halls and chambers of the House of Representatives. The day began on a solemn note for Adams himself. After two successive sleepless nights, he entered upon the day with a supplication to heaven, praying devoutly that he and "those connected with my good name and fortunes" might lead the nation wisely and well.[7] Shortly after noon he entered the House chamber in the Capitol and delivered his inaugural address to a crowded assembly. From his chair in front of the Speaker's rostrum, where he sat with members of the Supreme Court and Congress, Barbour listened attentively as Adams reiterated the credo of nationalism, spoke of preserving the liberty and unparalleled prosperity of the nation by maintaining a proper balance between the powers of the state and federal governments, and reviewed the accomplishments of his predecessor. Loud applause from the crowded chamber and galleries followed. Chief Justice John Marshall administered the oath of office, after which the new president retired from the chamber. Salutes were fired from the Navy Yard and Arsenal as Adams was escorted to his home on F Street. There, for several hours, he received congratulatory calls and hospitably provided his well-wishers, who included Barbour, with punch and wine.[8]

If many hailed what seemed to them the auspicious beginning of the new administration, there were some who felt otherwise. Ritchie reacted immediately to the nationalist tenor of the address. "This broad, this vague, this sweeping exposition of the powers of the General Government," he warned, "is no very agreeable prognostic of the course which we, Virginians, are to anticipate from the present administration." A few days later, after he had had time to read the address more carefully, he sounded the alarm more loudly.

> Mr. Adams is a complete latitudinarian in his construction of the Constitution. . . . He lays down a vague and new fangled rule that "whatsoever directly

involves the rights and interests of the federative fraternity, or of Foreign Powers, is the resort of the General Government". . . . Once go to sea with your speculative ideas of this federative fraternity; once give up your good old chart of certain delegated ends, . . . and there is scarcely . . . one power which may not be directly usurped. . . . What will the Republicans of '98 and '99 say to this sweeping doctrine? What will Thomas Jefferson and James Madison say? . . . Throw Jefferson's Kentucky Resolutions and Madison's Report into the flames. Let us have roads and canals that shall "rival in magnificence and splendor the public works" of ancient Rome. Let us have a National University that shall eclipse the splendor of Oxford and Cambridge. . . . Let us build up a *magnificent and splendid* national government upon the ruins of the Constitution.[9]

This was but the first alarm. Others from all parts of the country would soon follow.

The administration might have endured well enough the southern protests against nationalism, loud and cacophonous though they were. But their coalescence with the charge of "corrupt bargain" created a din which drowned out the president's voice and rendered his government impotent. In appointing Clay secretary of state, Adams doomed his administration from the start. Whether there was an understanding between the two men, by which Adams agreed to appoint the Kentuckian to the State Department in exchange for his support in the House contest, is really beside the point. What matters is the opinion of the people, and they thought that a bargain had been made. In a short time the cries of "corruption and bargain" became quite irrepressible. Overnight Clay became the "Judas of the West" who had unconscionably compromised himself to obtain a better stepping-stone to the presidency. "The combination unheard of till then, of the puritan with the blackleg," as John Randolph put it, did much to assure Jacksonians of victory in 1828.[10]

Adams's presidency was a tragic episode in an otherwise brilliant public career. Few presidents have ever brought to office his breadth of political experience and knowledge of government. Motivated by the highest moral principles and political ideals, he possessed a vision of greatness for the American nation shared by only a few men of his day. With the assistance of a strong national government willing to use its power to administer the country's resources for the improvement of the general welfare, he envisioned a powerful republic stretching for the length and breadth of the continent, sustaining a happy and prosperous people blessed with a measure of liberty never before witnessed among any civilized people.[11] Surrounded by capable secretaries in the principal executive departments, men whose collective vision of America's future was not significantly different from his own, Adams and his colleagues lacked nothing in commitment to the public good. What they did lack was close contact with popular opinion. Without it they were unable to persuade the country to follow their lead. And that was the great tragedy of the Adams administration.

Adams rejected the only hope he had of leading the nation. As a minority president, he could not reasonably expect to unite a badly factionalized populace under his standard of nationality and continental power unless he was willing to engage in the give and take of practical politics. By combining his adversaries and their patronage under his leadership, he might have prevented the majority from uniting against him. But he would not resort to what he considered political legerdemain. Like his illustrious father, he was dogmatic and inflexible, completely lacking in practical political skills. He might have compensated for this deficiency by drawing upon the talents of his cabinet, especially upon the gifts of Clay and Barbour, both of whom were consummate politicians. But he declined to do so. Like Washington and Monroe, he aspired to be the leader not of any party or group of interests but of the whole people. The fact that he did not believe in parties or sections was his undoing, for they had become the essential reality of American politics. He had no party behind him and, scorning the use of patronage, made no effort to create one. He reappointed to office men who worked against him. When vacancies occurred, he appointed Jackson men to demonstrate his public virtue. Had he been less unbending, or had his colleagues in the cabinet been more persuasive, he might have forged in four years a political coalition comparable to that of the Jackson-Calhoun-Crawford party. He refused to play the politicians' game, however. For four years he presided over the destinies of the nation, but that was all he could do. He was the victim of his own ideals and of a surging political democracy that made Jackson its chief beneficiary.[12]

In forming his government Adams tried to be conciliatory, hoping thereby to bring the country together in national sentiment and outlook. Apparently he could not see, or would not believe, that the Era of Good Feelings was dead. He retained as many of his predecessor's appointments as possible. Thus William Wirt continued as attorney general, and two Calhoun men, Secretary of the Navy Samuel L. Southard and Postmaster General John McLean, stayed on at their posts. Although the latter was not a cabinet position, it was an important source of patronage. Adams reappointed McLean knowing that he was openly sympathetic to Jackson. The Treasury office was given to the nationalist-minded Richard Rush. The Crawford interests were represented, at least initially, by Barbour. But Adams was not oblivious to the fact that his secretary of war, despite his traditional Jeffersonian politics, had strong nationalist sympathies. Clay, of course, was his own man. To the important diplomatic post of minister to

England, Adams yielded to the importunities of the Federalists and appointed the aged Rufus King after DeWitt Clinton of New York turned down the position.[13]

The administration thus constructed may not have conformed completely to the president's design for national harmony, but under the circumstances it was as broadly based as any he could design. Even so, it was not broad enough to reconcile and unite the opposing factions that were beginning to coalesce under Jackson and Calhoun. Vice-President Calhoun would soon gloat that Adams's "folly" in trying to win over the powerful Crawford interests in Virginia by bringing Barbour into his government had "wholly failed. They are deadly hostile to him [Adams] and his administration almost to a man."[14]

Soon after the Senate, on March 7, confirmed his appointment, Barbour decided to purchase a house in Washington. Tired of living in the comfortless boardinghouses of the capital, and no longer able to spend the summer and fall months at Barboursville as he had done during the congressional recesses over the past decade, he decided to bring his family to Washington. To accommodate them and to provide a place for the entertaining that went with office, he purchased for $10,000 a house located near the War Department. A few months after taking office he moved his family—Lucy and the two youngest children, Frances Cornelia and Benjamin Johnson, along with several servants—into the residence, leaving James at Barboursville to manage the farm.[15]

On March 8 Barbour moved into his office in the War Department building, a fairly new, two-story, white brick structure conveniently located on Pennsylvania Avenue a short distance west of the White House.[16] In a drab but spacious office warmed in winter by a large, ornate fireplace, the secretary would spend many long hours during the next three years poring over maps, studying Indian treaties, and attending to the many details of his new office.

The War Department was no longer the inefficient office it had been during the War of 1812. During Calhoun's able tenure it had become probably the best organized and most efficiently administered of all the executive departments. Barbour, whose experiences with the department during the War of 1812 had been frustrating in the extreme, welcomed these improvements. During his three-year tenure he made additional refinements in administrative practices which further enhanced effectiveness and helped make his department the model after which other departments would be patterned for years to come.[17]

Though not very large, the War Department was second in size only to the Treasury and was probably the most complex of the executive departments. There were at this time about thirty clerks in all who were engaged in routine correspondence, record keeping, and processing accounts and claims of former officers and enlisted men. Most of them had standing assignments and were proficient in their particular area of responsibility. All worked under the immediate supervision of Chief Clerk Christopher Van Deventer, the former deputy quartermaster general for the southern division of the U.S. Army. Van Deventer, a Calhoun partisan who had served as chief clerk since 1812, had experience and competence that made Barbour's job easier than it might otherwise have been.[18]

The War Office was responsible for two broad administrative operations: the management of army business which, in addition to the routine and purely military concerns, included the supervision of internal improve-ments, and the conduct of Indian affairs. The volume of army business had decreased somewhat since the congressional reduction of the army from 12,000 to a little over 6,000 men in March 1821. In 1825 there were seven infantry and four artillery regiments and a small engineer corps stationed in outposts scattered from northern Maine south to St. Augustine, Florida, and west to Council Bluffs, Missouri (now Iowa). The army was divided at this time into two geographical divisions: the Eastern Department, under the command of Bvt. Maj. Gen. Edmund Pendleton Gaines, and the West-ern Department, under the command of Bvt. Maj. Gen. Winfield Scott. The ranking officer in the army and chief of the General Staff since 1821 was Maj. Gen. Jacob Brown.[19]

To conduct Indian business a separate civilian office, the Bureau of Indian Affairs, existed, the head of which was Thomas L. McKenny, who had been associated in an official capacity with Indian affairs since 1816. The supervision of Indian affairs, the volume of which was at times overwhelming, was a task of no little magnitude. Despite the existence of the bureau, Barbour was called upon almost daily to draft or approve a treaty, to receive a visiting Indian delegation, or to attend to some detail of Indian business. Complaining of the heavy demands which these duties placed upon his office, he urged Congress to delegate to the Bureau of Indian Affairs full responsibility in its area, but Congress declined to act.[20]

Indian affairs occupied a disproportionate amount of both Barbour's and Adams's time and had a dramatic impact on public opinion of the admin-istration. It is ironic that the president, in outlining to Congress in Decem-ber 1825 an ambitious and unprecedented program for national development, should have treated so superficially the question of national Indian policy. For it had become patently obvious by the mid-1820s that the philanthropic policy pursued by every president since Washington, now under sharp attack in the South and West, had approached a point of crisis. The humanitarian expectation that the Indian could be civilized and that the two societies, red and white, could be happily merged, had not been fulfilled. And no system of national planning that did not cope with this fundamental reality was likely to succeed. To turn a deaf ear to the increasingly strident demands of aggressive elements in the dominant white society for changes in the Indian policy—changes which acknowledged their insatiable hunger for new land—was to court political disaster.

But Adams was not one to seek the politically expedient course. The Indian policy which his government pursued, as unpopular as it was altruistic, resulted in a major clash between national and state authority and contributed significantly to his party's political defeat in 1828. The real irony is that Adams, in principle, was no more opposed to Indian removal than was the old Indian fighter Andrew Jackson.[21] Local and sectional interests, determined to take Indian lands by whatever means were necessary, found a ready sympathizer in Jackson. And it was he who benefited politically from the administration's Indian policy.

The Indian problem itself was not of Adams's own making. It was the question, basic, persistent, and inherited from previous administrations, of how to treat the numerous sovereign Indian tribes still residing east of the Mississippi River. Following the War of 1812, when fears of Indian wars receded, white settlers began to encroach boldly on Indian lands. The hapless native had become too dependent on white civilization to resist effectively. He could only appeal to his great white father in Washington to protect him from white cupidity. Those whites who saw the Indian only as an obstacle to the advance of civilization also appealed to the national government, not to protect native rights, but rather to remove the red man, whose ultimate extinction they welcomed, from the path of settlement.

The fundamental problem, arising from the clash between rival civilizations, probably admitted of no real solution. There were few who even understood it and none who could offer a solution. Certainly no one in the Adams government could do so. The majority of Adams's cabinet, including the president himself, believed that removal was the only answer. But that opinion, at least initially, was not shared by Barbour, who subscribed to the humanitarian belief that the red man should and could be assimilated into the dominant white culture. His views, which were essentially those held by other philanthropists, guided the administration's policy.[22]

When he became secretary of war, Barbour had had little direct contact with Indian affairs. His views concerning federal Indian policy were only vaguely developed. But he set to work at once studying and reassessing the policy so as to be able to help direct the administration. He perceived his task to be the difficult one of charting a course that would combine justice and humanity for the red man with the evident destiny of white predominance throughout the width and breadth of the continent. Before he had time to proceed very far in his labors, however, the state of Georgia made a preemptive move which diverted him from his task. For the better part of a year he was preoccupied with the situation in Georgia and was unable to make much progress in developing an administration policy. In the interim his conduct of Indian affairs was based not so much on a coherent national policy as on his and the administration's notions of fair play and national honor.[23]

The controversy with Georgia originated in 1824 when Gov. George M. Troup, greedily eyeing some 5 million acres of Creek Indian land within the state, began to press the federal government to remove the Indians forcibly. This President Monroe refused to do, but he did authorize two Georgians to negotiate a treaty of purchase. The fraudulent Treaty of Indian Springs that they negotiated, which was approved by a minority faction of the tribe and was signed by President Adams shortly after he took office, provoked a loud outcry from the Creek nation.[24] Although the treaty pleased land-hungry Georgians, the majority faction of Creek leaders executed the minor chiefs who had sold tribal land and refused to acknowledge the venal agreement. Barbour convinced Adams and a majority of the cabinet that the treaty should be abrogated because of the bribery involved. When the secretary of war instructed Governor Troup to stay off Creek lands, the ensuing controversy developed into a major contest between the sovereign rights of Georgia (as Georgians perceived them) and the authority of the national government. The significance of that controversy in the states' rights movement of the period has not been fully appreciated. Coming as it did midway between the Missouri Controversy and the nullification crisis of the Jacksonian period, it served to keep alive regional antipathies and gave impetus to the development of southern sectionalism.[25]

Barbour's determination to protect the Creeks from Georgia's cupidity incensed Troup. He broke off all discourse with the federal government's agents in the state and dashed off a series of inflammatory letters to the secretary of war, causing Barbour to conclude that the governor was a "madman."[26] Protesting vehemently the federal government's interference in the internal affairs of Georgia, Troup wrote that his people were caught between "the bayonet on your part, and the tomahawk and scalping knife on the part of the Indians." He went on to warn that Georgia was prepared to defend its rights by taking up arms if all else failed.[27] Barbour cautioned the militant governor against precipitate action and reminded him that "there are duties, not only of justice but of humanity, which the government of the United States is bound to fulfill towards the unhappy aboriginal inhabitants of this country."[28]

For months the war of words between Barbour and Governor Troup continued. In late November 1825 a delegation of Creeks, appointed by the Creek nation in a general council, arrived in Washington to present their case personally to the president and to negotiate a new treaty. Barbour was responsible for conducting the talks. Motivated by a desire to treat the Indian claims justly, he hoped at the same time to acquire the Creek lands and thereby to resolve the crisis. After weeks of discussion, the Creeks finally agreed to cede all but a small portion of their Georgia lands for equal acreage in the West and a sizable money payment. They returned home satisfied that justice had been done.[29]

The Treaty of Washington was discussed in a cabinet meeting in late January. Clay thought it was far less advantageous to the United States than the earlier Indian Springs Treaty, which he apparently favored recognizing despite its irregularities. Barbour, however, objected strongly, as he did to Clay's opinion that the Indians, a race "inferior to the Anglo-Saxon" and not "worth preserving," could never be civilized. Adams supported his secretary of war and finally forwarded the treaty to the Senate for approval, accompanying it with an explanation that it replaced the fraudulent Indian Springs Treaty.[30]

Angered by the new treaty, the Georgia delegation, led by John Forsyth, began looking for some way to discredit it. They soon found it in Barbour's disclosure that Creek leaders intended to hold back for their own use a large part of the purchase money. In informing the House Committee on Indian Affairs of their intent, Barbour expressed regrets that they would thus defraud their people. He went on to say that while he did not condone their scheme, and indeed had refused to make it a part of the document he had framed, he was powerless to interfere with their private actions. Georgia's congressmen were delighted by the revelation. Joined by other southern representatives, including many Jacksonians who had sided with Georgia during the controversy, they used the disclosure as a pretext for denouncing the new treaty as a "stupendous fraud." They charged Barbour with duplicity and denounced the administration for its role in the matter.[31]

But Barbour's defenders outnumbered his critics. The chairman of the House Committee on Indian Affairs, along with representatives from Massachusetts, Kentucky, and other states, defended him.[32] Charles F. Mercer of the Loudoun District became effusive in repelling the attacks on his fellow Virginian: "If, as a great poet has proclaimed, 'an honest man's the noblest work of God,' then James Barbour is entitled to that high eulogy. No man on earth would more proudly scorn to commit, or to conceal a fraud, than the present Secretary of War."[33]

Barbour's own defense was simple. The government, he told the Committee on Indian Affairs, had acted honestly and fairly in its negotiations with the Indians. It had refused to bribe or coerce them in any way. That the recognized tribal leaders should choose to act dishonestly was unfortunate, but that was a matter for the Indians alone. The federal govern-ment, he concluded, had no authority or jurisdiction over the actions of the chiefs, nor had it tried to conceal their deception. After a long debate Congress, at the end of May 1826, passed the appropriation necessary to put the treaty into effect, but it included a provision, designed to thwart the Creek leaders, requiring that the money payment be distributed in a full national council.[34]

To the administration's dismay, the Treaty of Washington failed to quiet Georgians. Troup defiantly wrote that the United States had no authority to annul the first treaty. Georgia had declared the inviolability of that com-pact and the invalidity of any later agreement designed to supersede it. Georgia, he continued, intended to occupy the Creek territory in accor-dance with the terms of the original treaty. In response, Barbour, using more forceful language than Adams would have liked, ordered Troup to stay out of the disputed territory.[35] Once again a crisis loomed.

Troup did not stop here, however. In a message to the state legislature at the end of 1826 he declared that "harmony could not continue" if the Indians remained in Georgia. Upon the governor's prompting, the legisla-ture condemned the course the national government had pursued. In a move strikingly similar to that taken by the South Carolina legislature a few years later, it then declared the Treaty of Washington illegal and uncon-stitutional. With the full backing of the legislature, Troup contemptuously ignored the recent treaty and sent surveyors into the Creek territory. The Indians seized the surveyors and in turn were threatened with attack by a Georgia cavalry unit.[36]

Alarmed by the dangerous impasse, President Adams hastily convened his cabinet. Clay recommended that federal troops be called up to protect the rights of the Creeks. Adams dissented, fearing that such a response could only end in violence. Barbour, like Clay, believed that force might ultimately be necessary to defend the Indians, but he was willing to employ it only as a last resort. He persuaded the cabinet to try a final appeal.[37] Accordingly, he wrote Troup warning him that the administration would use whatever means were necessary, including military force, to uphold and execute the laws of the land.[38] Troup's defiant response was characteristic: "I feel it my duty to resist to the utmost any military attack which the Government of the United States shall think proper to make upon the territory, the people, or the sovereignty of Georgia. . . . From the first decisive act of hostility you will be considered a public enemy . . . because you, to whom we might have constitutionally appealed for our own defense against invasion, are yourselves the invaders, and, what is more, the unblushing allies of the savages whose cause you have adopted."[39] To demonstrate that this was no idle threat, Troup then ordered two divisions of militia to be held in readiness to resist any attempt by federal troops to occupy the state.[40]

As the crisis deepened, Adams resolved to seek the advice and support of Congress. On February 5 he sent to that body a special message which, by his own admission, was "the most momentous" he had ever written. The situation in Georgia, he informed Congress, had reached a critical stage. If Georgia continued upon its present course, he would be compelled to uphold the treaty rights of the Indians with force, which could result in armed conflict. He asked Congress to make recommendations.[41]

Congress supported the president less than the Georgia legislature had its governor. Select committees in both houses studied the problem. The Senate committee, dominated by antiadministration men and headed by Thomas Hart Benton, whom Barbour had angered during the Washington Treaty negotiations by spurning his suggestion that the government bribe the Creek leaders, took a position favorable to Georgia. The House committee somewhat lamely backed the administration by upholding the recent treaty but would go no further. Both committees agreed that the government should make every effort to obtain the small tract of land in Georgia that had been withheld by the Creeks in the last treaty. Barbour accordingly resumed negotiations and at length succeeded in purchasing it.[42] The Creek Indians thereupon prepared to migrate to their new home west of the Mississippi.

The conflict between the Indians and whites of Georgia was but another instance of the unhappy clash between Indian and white cultures that had characterized relations between the two races from the time of their first contact. In trying to resist the encroachment of their white neighbors, the Creeks sought to defy a fundamental law of civilization. The inert Indian society was inevitably overcome by the superior force of the aggressive white civilization.

The Indians were not the only losers, however. The Adams government also lost in a contest which, whatever else it may have been, was clearly a collision between state and national powers. And in no previous contest had a state triumphed so completely as when Georgia invoked states' rights, defied national authority, and called out its troops to back its position. South Carolina would not be so successful a few years later. Despite its desire to preserve and protect the rights of the Creeks, the Adams administration in the end yielded to pressures to remove the Indians as the only way of averting armed conflict. Even so, the administration was widely criticized, and not by Georgians alone, for its actions during the controversy. The *Philadelphia National Chronicle* pretended to see in its assertion of federal authority a disturbing tendency toward tyranny and despotism. Another paper of the same city accused it of a grand design to subvert the rights of the states and to destroy the Constitution.[43] While Virginia, on the whole, was less sympathetic to Georgia than most of the other southern states, it did not pass up the opportunity to join with them in criticizing the federal government's conduct.[44] Despite the unpopularity of the administration's stand, which Jacksonians used to good political advantage, Barbour never doubted its correctness, nor did he make excuses for it. Throughout he maintained a thoroughly nationalist position.

The clash between rival civilizations in Georgia, and the accompanying confrontation between the state and federal governments, dramatically demonstrated to Barbour the urgency of redefining the national Indian policy so as to minimize conflicts of that sort in the future. He turned his attention willingly, though naively, to the task. Like every good Jeffersonian whose sensibilities had not been brutalized by the barbarities of frontier warfare, he rejected the notion held by most denizens of the backcountry that extinction of the native was the best and the only final solution. He held still to the optimistic belief that the two races could exist side by side until the latter could be brought into the pale of the white man's civilization. It was a humanitarian creed to which few men of his day any longer subscribed.[45]

For more than a generation the policy of the national government, endorsed by a substantial portion of civilized opinion, had been to convert the Indian from his aboriginal ways and to transform him into a useful member of the dominant society. From the time of Washington's administration, continuing efforts had been made to persuade Indians to give up their hunter-warrior culture for the more settled pursuits of agriculture and husbandry. Missionaries had been sent among the various tribes, schools established, and instructions offered in the ways of farming. In some cases progress had been made. A number of tribes, particularly the Cherokees, Creeks, and Choctaws, had adopted some of the manners and artifacts of the white civilization. Jefferson, who best embodied the philanthropic approach to the Indian problem, had been greatly encouraged during his presidency by what he interpreted to be a willingness on the part of the native to embrace agriculture. But the humanitarian approach was also highly paternalistic. It exacted a heavy toll from the native culture, subjecting it to stresses that tended to infantilize the Indian and to destroy the integrity of his social order. More often than not the native was left with little or nothing of his own proud culture and with the worst elements of the white culture—thievery, drunkenness, debauchery, and moral dissipation. By the mid-1820s it had become clear to all but a few that the process of acculturation was proceeding much too slowly to accommodate the rapid advance of the frontier and that philanthropy must yield to compulsion.

Both Monroe and his secretary of war, Calhoun, had recognized this reality in 1824 when they concluded that the only solution was removal.[46]

When Barbour first began considering the problem in 1825, he opposed removal. It seemed to him an inhumane approach which ignored the rights of the Indian, guaranteed by countless treaties, to the possession of his land. The first step to resolving the problem, he thought, was to define clearly the status and relationship of the native to the state and national governments and then to pledge the power and authority of the federal government to protect his rights under the law. Barbour's own opinion was that the United States should cease treating the tribes as sovereign nations. With a view to their ultimate assimilation, which he optimistically believed was still possible, they should be incorporated into the states where they resided and should be made subject to the laws of the states and nation. The philanthropic goals should not be abandoned, but the process of amelioration needed to be hurried along.[47]

Several times during the summer and fall of 1825, when the crisis in Georgia was at its height, he discussed his views with the cabinet. Both Clay and Adams thought they were impractical. The secretary of state was particularly vocal in his objections, arguing that the Indian was an "unimprovable breed" whose "disappearance from the human family . . . would be no great loss to the world." Barbour was shocked. But from conversations he had with others in Washington during the following months, he came to realize that Clay's views were more representative of majority opinion than were his own: few people believed any longer that the Indian could or would adopt the white man's culture.[48]

While the controversy with Georgia was going on, Barbour spent many long hours in the dusty archives of the War Department reviewing and studying the problem. From his own reading of the voluminous correspondence between hundreds of Indian agents and the War Office, dating back to 1789, and his study of reports of missionaries, government agents, and others commenting on conditions in the Indian country, he concluded that changes were needed in federal Indian policy. He could not ignore the incontrovertible evidence of the decline and disruption of native culture. However benevolent and altruistic the intentions of the policy may have been historically, he was compelled to concede that it had not fulfilled its promise. There had been no happy coalescence of the two societies but only a wasting attrition of native vitality. Moreover, the aggressive and uncontrollable force of frontier society, as indicated by events in Georgia, would continue to erode Indian society until it collapsed completely, as much from decay within as from pressures without.[49]

By the beginning of 1826 Barbour, with the help if not the full concurrence of Thomas L. McKenney, head of the Bureau of Indian Affairs, had developed the essential elements of a policy which the administration reluctantly endorsed. Although it included some new features and reordered some of the old priorities, it essentially reaffirmed the ideal, though not the reality, of the philanthropic policy. Incorporation of the red man and social homogenization of the two races remained the ultimate objective. The civilizing process was to be given a time extension, however, and a more hospitable environment in which to run its course. Although Adams thought that the plan was "full of benevolence and humanity" and possessed "many excellent observations," he doubted it would work. Most of the cabinet shared his misgivings. But in the absence of a better proposal, which no one could offer, it became the administration's policy recommendation to Congress.[50]

In January 1826 Barbour presented the plan to Congress. The chairman of the House Committee on Indian Affairs, John Cocke, asked him to review and comment on a bill his committee had drafted providing for the preservation and civilization of the Indian.[51] Barbour did not regard the bill as satisfactory. He then submitted his proposal, accompanying it with a long report reviewing and evaluating the history of federal Indian policy.[52] He was critical of that policy, as least as it had operated. Though it had been founded on benevolent and humanitarian principles, in practice it recognized "power as the only standard of right, and fraud and force as perfectly legitimate" instruments for the acquisition of Indian land. "From the first discovery of America to the present time, one master passion, common to all mankind, that of acquiring land, has driven in a ceaseless succession, the white man upon the Indian. The latter reluctantly yielding to a force he could not resist, has retired from the ocean to the mountains, and from the mountains to more inhospitable recesses, wasting away by sufferings and by wars ... till a wretched fragment only survives of the numerous hordes once inhabiting this country."

The distinguishing features of good government, Barbour continued, should be justice, moderation, and humanity. But "sordid selfishness," not liberal principles, had characterized the nation's relations with the Indian. In the history of those relations, there was "but little on which the recollection lingers with satisfaction"; even less was honorable or worthy of a democratic government. Missionaries had been sent among the Indians, and schools for the instruction of their youth had been established.

> They have been persuaded to abandon the chase—to locate themselves, and become cultivators of the soil—implements of husbandry and domestic animals have been presented them, and all these things have been ... accompanied with professions of a disinterested solicitude for their happiness. Yielding to these temptations, some of them have reclaimed the forest,

planted their orchards, and erected houses, not only for their abode, but for the administration of justice, and for religious worship. And when they have so done, *you* send *your* Agent to tell them they must surrender their country to the white man, and recommit themselves to some new desert.

Barbour suggested to Cocke the outlines for a bill that would provide a more stable environment in which acculturation could occur. He proposed that the unorganized territory west of the Mississippi, along with part of the Michigan Territory lying east of the Mississippi but west of Lakes Huron and Michigan, be set aside as the exclusive abode of the Indian. To this territory he would be encouraged, but not compelled, to go. To discourage land speculators and to protect the individual Indian against unscrupulous leaders who, yielding to coercion or bribery, might sell tribal lands, removal should be by individuals or families rather than by tribes. The property rights of those who chose not to emigrate should be protected by the federal government, though it was hoped that the Indians who remained behind on old tribal lands would soon be assimilated into the states in which they resided. Barbour hoped that eventually the tribal structure itself would disappear. Communal ownership of property, which in his opinion had been a major contributing factor to the Indian's failure to make greater progress toward civilization, would in time be abolished. At that time land and other property would be distributed among the Indians according to some equitable formula.

For the new Indian territory a government, which was to be essentially the same as any other territorial government, would be established and maintained by the federal government. In time the territory would be admitted into the Union as a separate and equal state. Indians residing there would enjoy self-government and would exercise the same rights and privileges as citizens of other states. No longer would the various tribes be treated as so many sovereign nations. The end of this practice, Barbour believed, would do much to discourage the dominant white society from taking unfair advantage of the weaker native society.

The merit of Barbour's proposal did not rest on its uniqueness. Incorporation and assimilation had always been the objective of the philanthropic policy. Nor was the concept of a separate Indian territory new, although provisions for its admission into the Union as a sovereign state in which the Indian would enjoy all the rights of self-government were. In the last analysis, the proposal represented a final but unsuccessful attempt to achieve the objectives of philanthropy.

As Adams observed, the plan was commendable for its benevolence. But benevolence was not enough. However good the intentions of Barbour and his colleagues in the administration may have been, they emanated from an unsophisticated understanding of the ways in which different cultures interact. Certainly Barbour misunderstood the nature of Indian society. The plan he offered was based on the assumption that the Indian, once he was adequately exposed to and understood the ways of the white man, would automatically recognize their superiority and would adopt them for himself. The plan required that the Indian abandon his hunter-warrior ways, the communal ownership of land, and the tribal order. Barbour could not see the cultural shock that such a fundamental rear-rangement of native society would have caused. His limitation, in which most humanitarians of his day participated, was one of understanding, not of intent. For the Indian he wanted only the best. But what was best for the white man was not necessarily the best for the native. Therein lay the great tragedy of Indian-white relations.

The House Committee on Indian Affairs substituted a bill incorporating Barbour's recommendations for the one it had initially prepared. But the House, after a short debate, rejected it.[53] Thus the administration's Indian policy, like so many of its other recommendations, was never imple-mented. The defeat of the administration's Indian plan represented, in the final analysis, a rejection of the philanthropic philosophy. There were people other than Barbour who continued to cling to the old view, it is true, but their influence on Indian policy in the future would be minimal. The goal of transforming the Indian and incorporating him into the domi-nant society became, for all practical purposes, unattainable. With no place for the red man in the civilized East, there was very little likelihood, once he was removed beyond the pale of white civilization, that he could ever be induced to accept the white man's ways. The House action in rejecting the administration's proposal signaled the beginning of a new era in Indian relations. Hereafter the frontier attitude, exemplified by Georgia and other states with a large Indian population, triumphed. The policy of forcible removal adopted by Jacksonians would be characterized by un-mitigated harshness.

The Adams government's Indian problems were not limited to the Creeks alone. The Cherokees, Choctaws, Seminoles, and other tribes, pressured by encroaching white settlers, appealed to the administration to uphold their treaty rights. In the summer of 1827 the Cherokees, hoping to arrest Georgia's cupidity and to forestall demands for removal by present-ing evidence of civilization, adopted a written constitution patterned after that of the United States. In it they asserted that they were a sovereign and independent nation with complete jurisdiction over their own territory.[54] But Georgia would not tolerate this action. The legislature condemned the federal government for having failed to extinguish Cherokee land titles and claimed that all Indians within the state, both Cherokees and Creeks, were merely tenants at will. Because all lands in the state belonged absolutely to Georgia, it could abolish that tenancy at any time. Other states with large Indian populations followed Georgia's lead.[55] In the face of this adamant opinion, there was little that Barbour or any executive official of the national government could do but yield.

Nevertheless, for as long as he was in office, Barbour conducted Indian affairs with as much humanity as circumstances permitted. He continued to lobby, without success, for an Indian policy that would have eliminated some of the worst abuses of the coercive and irregular system of removal. When treaty rights were violated and tribal lands seized by whites, he defended the Indians, and in negotiating with them he consistently opposed intimidation and fraud. In aiding the displaced Indians in Florida and Alabama, he demonstrated a benevolence which, if nothing else, did honor to the defunct Jeffersonian philosophy.[56] But neither he nor anyone else could stand against the advancing tide which swept before it the hapless remnants of a once-proud people.

9

For a Prosperous
and Enduring Union

A *lthough* Indian affairs occupied much of his time as secretary of war, Barbour entered actively into the discussion of other matters and had an important hand in shaping government policy. Adams had strong opinions and fixed ideas about the direction his government should take and could be very dogmatic, but he did not ignore the opinions of his cabinet, which he convened regularly. Its meetings were characterized by a free and open exchange. Barbour and Clay were its most vocal members; they were also the ones most likely to disagree with the president. Rush rarely differed with Adams on any issue of substance. Because Wirt was frequently away on government business, and Southard normally contributed little or nothing to cabinet discussions, Barbour, Clay, and Rush were the principal influences.[1] On the whole the cabinet was an able group of hardworking men who, along with the president, set an example of vigorous, imaginative, and faithful public service which has generally been obscured by the political partisanship of their day.

Differences in personalities and political philosophies among the cabinet members sometimes resulted in heated exchanges, but they seem rarely to have personalized their disagreements. Within a year of working together they reached something of a consensus on the broad outlines of government policy. They continued to differ on details, but their agreement on the essential elements of national policy was significant. With each representing different constituencies and different sections of the country, their coalescence signified what was happening to political parties nationally. It also presaged the emergence of the Whig party. Barbour, a somewhat reluctant nationalist ever since the Missouri Controversy, finally embraced the American System in its entirety during his years of close association with Adams, Rush, and Clay. He forged particularly strong political ties with Clay, which linked them closely in their common efforts for the Whig party during the years ahead.[2]

168

Despite their differences in personality and temperament, Barbour and Adams worked well together. Barbour's relationship with the president went beyond the weekly cabinet meetings. Almost daily, and sometimes several times during the day, he consulted with Adams on some administrative problem. Sometimes the burden of tiresome administrative details prevented him during the day from conferring with the president. On such occasions he might call at the White House during the early evening hours, occasionally accompanied by his young son Benjamin, to discuss some pressing issue with Adams over a game of billiards, one of the president's few leisure indulgences.[3] Adams seemed to value his secretary of war's practical political skills and commonsense approach to problems. He appreciated, too, Barbour's personal principles, which like his own, were high-minded, as well as his unfailing sense of humor, which included the ability—which Adams lacked—to laugh at himself.[4]

Throughout 1825 Barbour tried to influence Adams to adopt a politically realistic posture, one that would enable the administration to broaden and strengthen its political base. He recognized that the coalition that had elected Adams president would need help to contain the Jacksonians. Both he and Wirt, and to a lesser extent Clay, were especially sensitive to public opinion in Virginia, which they were anxious not to alienate. Hoping to strengthen the administration there and in the rest of the South, Barbour urged the president to chart a middle course that would be acceptable to the section of the country whose political mood he understood probably better than did any other member of the cabinet.[5] His failure to accomplish this goal reflected the fact that the administration, and the president in particular, were out of touch with popular opinion. The leadership Adams tried to provide was selfless and patriotic, but it was not one to which the people coud respond emotionally. And neither he nor any of his cabinet, Barbour included, understood the intellectual and social ferment that was Jacksonian democracy.

The Adams government enjoyed a brief honeymoon of goodwill that encouraged Barbour and others to hope that they might succeed in their objective of broadening its political base. Even in Virginia, public opinion did not become overtly hostile for almost a year. Although Thomas Ritchie had been quick to condemn both the inaugural address and the "corrupt and vile bargain" between Clay and Adams, he had been somewhat restrained thereafter in his comments about the government. As late as the fall of 1825, indeed, he professed a willingness to judge the administration solely on the basis of its merit and actions: "Principles and not men," he said, would be his standard.[6] A year later Gov. John Tyler wrote Barbour that it was immaterial to him whether "the man at the head of affairs shall come from this or the other side of the Tweed." What was important was that the government be administered on correct principles. "In interpreting the constitution I would neither be liberal [n]or parsimonious, but would take the instrument as I find it written—giving to its terms their ordinary acceptation in their plain and obvious meaning. So far as the government is administered on this principle it shall have my support—and of consequence my opposition when upon any other."[7] In light of these attitudes, it was perhaps not unrealistic for Barbour and others to hope that they might succeed in bringing Virginia solidly into the Adams camp. Whatever basis they may have had for such hopes, however, was destroyed by the president's first Annual Message to Congress in December 1825.

In his message Adams left no doubt, if any ever existed, of his belief that the national government possessed the power to undertake all things. His political theory carried him far beyond the "niggardly doctrines" of limited government espoused by Jefferson, whom he accused of being satisfied with the least when the most was at hand. He advocated an "enlarged nationalism" in which the national government would play a directing role in "promoting the improvement of agriculture, commerce, and manufactures, the cultivation and encouragement of the mechanic and of the elegant arts, the advancement of literature, and the progress of the sciences, ornamental and profound." Freedom was the essence of the best society, he believed, but it should not be allowed to become sterile. "While dwelling with pleasing satisfaction upon the superior excellence of our political institutions," he said, "let us not be unmindful that liberty is power." Power carried with it a moral obligation to administer the resources of the country for the improvement of society and the happiness of each of its members. "While foreign nations less blessed with that freedom which is power than ourselves are advancing with gigantic strides in the career of public improvement, were we to slumber in indolence or fold up our arms and proclaim to the world that we are palsied by the will of our constituents, would it not be to cast away the bounties of Providence and doom ourselves to perpetual inferiority?"[8] The American System as Adams envisioned it was clearly more than a political program: it involved a comprehensive approach to economic, social, and cultural, as well as political, planning, all of which would later become the basic Whig doctrine.

In another age, such a vast extension of governmental authority might have been acclaimed. But in that simpler age in which Adams lived, when many Americans believed that the most sacred of trusts consisted in restricting rather than expanding the powers of the national government, his views were anathema. As Nathaniel Macon astutely observed, "the administration might have got along probably tolerable well, had it been content to have traveled a plain and well known road. But . . . the attempt to make the constitutional way as wide as the world, has and will embarrass it."[9]

It was hardly politic of the president to warn Congress against being palsied by the will of its constituents. That admonition was an affront to those who believed that their will had already been palsied by the Adams-Clay coalition that defeated Jackson and elevated the New Englander to the presidency. Moreover, Adams's intense nationalism gave currency to the old canard that "all Adamses are monarchists" as well as to John Randolph's charge that "the cub is a greater bear than the old one."[10] Jefferson saw in the address a new chapter in Federalist history. With grave concern he wrote that the younger Federalist recruits, "having nothing in them of the feelings and principles of '76, now look to a single and splendid government of an aristocracy, founded on banking institutions, and moneyed incorporations under the guise and cloak of their favored branches of manufacturers, commerce and navigation, riding and ruling over the plundered ploughman and beggared yeomanry."[11]

Adams's colleagues anticipated these denunciations. When the message was discussed in several cabinet meetings in late November, both Barbour and Clay raised objections. For the president to present so nationalistic a program at this time would be, they feared, an act of political suicide. Both attempted to tone down the message by suggesting numerous alterations and deletions. Barbour opposed the ambitious proposal for a comprehensive system of internal improvements, which he feared would ruin the administration in Virginia and the rest of the South. Clay supported Barbour and added his own objections to the portions of the message proposing a national university and a new executive department. Adams considered yielding to his two vocal secretaries, but Rush, who had enthusiastically endorsed the president's views from the beginning, persuaded him not to do so. After several meetings and protracted discussion, Barbour and Clay were won over finally to a grudging acceptance of the general principles of the message, though they "scrupled a great part of the details."[12]

Barbour's acquiescence in the majority cabinet opinion was significant. It signaled an end to the reactionary phase of his public career caused by the Missouri Controversy and by Virginia's subsequent sectional drift. Severing his remaining ties, tenuous though they had become, with the Old Republican leadership of the state, he now embraced the American System, including internal improvements and the protective tariff. His decision to do so indicates a tacit recognition of the futility of finding a middle ground between nationalism and sectionalism. He was compelled to concede that those fruits of union he had desired for the American people from the time he first entered the Senate—freedom, prosperity, and unity—could not be attained except with a broader nationalist political philosophy than his Virginia colleagues were willing to accept. In adopting the American System, many essential elements of which he had long espoused, he acknowledged the inevitability of a political schism within his native state.[13] There was simply no way that Ritchie, Randolph, and other conservative Republicans, or Radicals, as they were now called, could be persuaded to abandon their reactionary stance or could be induced to see the merits of the administration's nationalist policies. Turning his back on the influential Junto, he made the irrevocable decision to align himself with the nationalist element of the state which in the 1830s would combine with other anti-Jackson factions to form the Whig party.[14]

Barbour's acceptance of the American System involved no dramatic or sudden changes in his political philosophy. The principles of the American System had been evolving gradually over the years, and it was by degrees that he embraced them. No visionary, he was a political realist who responded to each new national need as he saw it developing. He had championed a national bank after the War of 1812 because the fiscal chaos that followed the closing of the first bank's doors in 1811 had demonstrated beyond question the need for such an institution. His advocacy of other nationalist measures during the following years—internal improvements, a powerful army and navy, and a strong commercial and foreign policy— had stemmed no less from a desire to respond positively and constructively to the compelling needs of a dynamic and heterogeneous society. Each measure that he supported had been based on a demonstrable need that would serve some real rather than imagined national interest.

It was in this context that Barbour now supported internal improvements and a protective tariff. He had always stressed the value of the former and had been their principal advocate in the years immediately after the War of 1812. Only his reservations about constitutionality, after he had failed to secure a constitutional amendment, had caused him to vote against internal improvements. Even so, he had continued to argue that they were important for a prosperous and enduring nation. In supporting a comprehensive program of roads and canals now, he explained away the constitutional problem by saying that the highest authority in any republic, the people themselves, by their consent over the years to various projects, had sanctioned the exercise of the questionable power. This approval obviated his own reservations. He now supported what he had always advocated.[15]

The constitutionality of the tariff Barbour had never questioned, though he had consistently voted against a high level of protection, which seemed to him to be a government subsidy paid to northern manufacturers from the pockets of southern planters and farmers. In supporting the tariff at this time, he simply modified his notion of an acceptable level of protection. Although he would never have endorsed the special interests incorporated into the Tariff of Abominations, passed about the time he resigned from the cabinet, he did approve the moderate level of protection recommended by Adams. He supported that tariff, which was higher than any he had previously endorsed, because he finally accepted it as a necessary part of the system of national planning the administration had adopted. To encourage the increase of population and the physical expansion of the nation, to which he was irrevocably committed, a higher standard of living and a higher wage scale for urban workers were needed. These the tariff promised to provide. No longer the narrow agrarian particularist he had been at the outset of his political career, he acknowledged, as Jefferson and Madison had done earlier, the need for a balance among agriculture, commerce, and industry. These three primary employments of the American people ought to be allowed to advance together, with equal encouragement and advantages. With careful planning, the government could promote not only the economic and political supremacy of the republic but, indeed, supremacy in all fields of human endeavor.[16]

Having made the commitment to support the American System, Barbour used his office to good advantage to promote its nationalist ends. He pushed ahead as secretary of war with various internal improvement schemes, conscientiously directing the construction of post roads and canals and supervising the improvement of navigable streams and harbors. With equal vigor he moved ahead with the extension of the Cumberland Road. And when Ritchie's attacks on the administration's policies became irksome, he defended them in public print. His defense indicated how complete his conversion to the American System was.[17]

Barbour's prediction that Virginia would react angrily to the president's annual message was quickly fulfilled. Because he defended the message, Barbour was held partially responsible for its nationalist thrust. Ritchie professed to be "completely bewildered" and astonished by its "alarming and unsound doctrines" and peremptorily inquired where Barbour had been when it was penned.[18] Rising to the challenge to defend the Constitution against the "heresies of J.Q.A.," the caustic editor warned that if the president's views were correct, "no powers are left to the State Governments worth having." The message "sweeps down at once the powers of the State Governments, and asserts the right and power of . . . [the national government] to do whatever it may deem expedient to promote the general welfare!"[19] Ritchie urged Jefferson and Madison to use their influence to arrest the tendencies toward consolidation and called upon the legislature to appoint someone to Barbour's old seat in the Senate who would uphold the principles that were dear to Virginia. The assembly responded by electing John Randolph, whose unwavering attachment to those principles and genius at defending them were unrivaled in his day.[20]

Once in the Senate Randolph gave the administration no quarter. As erratic and brilliant as ever, though hovering on the borderline between sanity and insanity, he was still the master dialectician whose pungent phrase and terrible invective could, rapierlike, pierce to the heart. He attacked Adams and his government with a vengeance. "I bore some humble part," he said, "in putting down the dynasty of John the First, and, by the Grace of God, I hope to aid in putting down the dynasty of John the Second." The president, he continued, "has come out with a speech and a message and with a doctrine that goes to take the whole human family under his special protection. Now, sir, who made him his brother's keeper? . . . I say God send him a safe deliverance, and God send the country a safe deliverance from his policy."[21]

The administration might have endured the diatribes of Randolph and other critics and might have secured congressional approval of at least part of its program if it had commanded a broad political base in Congress. Such support it did not have. The narrowness of its base was revealed when the newly elected Nineteenth Congress met in December 1825 and proceeded to elect a Speaker. Adams was committed to John W. Taylor of New York, author of the bill prohibiting slavery north of the line 36°30′, whose influence had helped swing New York's crucial vote in the recent presidential contest. Taylor won the speakership contest by the slender margin of two votes. Although Clay exulted that Taylor's victory was evidence of the administration's strength in Congress, others were less sanguine. Practical-minded men like Barbour knew only too well that Taylor, with his unmistakable antislavery label, could never be an effective administration spokesman with southern congressmen.[22]

Daniel Webster ought to have been a natural spokesman for the administration. But Adams was unwilling to offer any rewards substantial enough to induce that self-interested New Englander to join his cause. With Calhoun controlling committee assignments in the Senate and Taylor too weak to align the House behind the administration, Adams was unable to control either house of Congress. The South's revolt against his nationalist program, the movement of the Radicals into the Jackson camp, and the president's obstinate refusal to use executive patronage or influence to forge a national political party loyal to him, provided the opposition with all it needed to hamstring his administration. "The great effort of my administration," Adams later ruefully acknowledged, "has failed." He could secure only a few small bills for particular improvement projects here and there. Much to his chagrin, the nation "cast away instead of using for the improvement of its own condition, the bounties of Providence."[23]

The nationalist program that Adams proposed to Congress in 1825 was but one club that he and his colleagues gave the opposition forces to use against them. The decision to send delegates to the Congress of American Republics at Panama was another. Convened by the South American patriot and liberator Simon Bolivar for the purpose of forming a South American federation, the Panama congress proved to be almost as divisive an issue as the president's domestic proposals. When Mexico and Colombia first made overtures in the spring of 1825 asking the United States to participate, Adams was wary. He was reluctant to join in a congress whose purpose and outcome were uncertain.[24] Barbour and Clay strongly favored sending delegates. They had no doubts that such a gathering would afford an excellent opportunity for extending the influence of the United States throughout the Western Hemisphere and promoting hemispheric cooperation. From the beginning the two secretaries were in accord on the question and worked together to convert the president to their position.[25]

In December 1825 Adams finally yielded to their persuasion. In announcing his decision to send delegates, he assured Congress that he had no intention of involving the United States in any entangling alliances. Rather he hoped to secure better commercial relations with the Spanish American countries, their agreement to the rights of neutrals, and a pledge that they would resist colonization by any European country.[26]

Adams's announcement aroused strong opposition both within and outside Congress. Isolationists invoked Washington's farewell address, and Southerners denounced the Panama congress as a menace to slavery, specifically because it might recognize the Negro republic of Haiti and might abolish slavery throughout South America.[27] In the Senate the decision encountered unexpected resistance. Randolph held the project up to scorn. The invitation to send delegates, he boldly charged, was a blatant forgery conceived and executed by Adams and Clay, whom he likened to Henry Fielding's Blifil and Black George, the "combination unheard of till then of the puritan with the blackleg."[28] Van Buren seized the occasion to strengthen the emerging political coalition between southern planters and "plain republicans of the North."[29] After a long and acrimonious debate, the Senate finally approved the delegates. But this first and only victory of the administration proved empty. One of the delegates died en route to the congress, and the other did not arrive until after it had adjourned. The administration gained nothing from the contest, while the opposition forces in Congress used it to great advantage to consolidate their strength.[30]

Throughout the contest Barbour never wavered in his belief that the United States should use the congress as a means of promoting cooperation with Latin American neighbors and strengthening the nation's influence in the Western Hemisphere. He ignored Virginia's vehement opposition to the mission and exposed himself further to Radical censure by traveling to Oak Hill, where he tried to persuade Monroe to accept an appointment as one of the American plenipotentiaries. Unwilling to leave his sick wife, Monroe declined.[31] In supporting the Panama congress, Barbour was prompted by the same motives that had caused him, as chairman of the Senate Foreign Relations Committee, to work so hard for the commercial independence of the United States and to advocate the Monroe Doctrine. He saw the congress as a means of promoting the national power of his country in its relations with the other countries of the world, and to that goal, whatever the personal cost, he was firmly committed.

While Barbour, as a member of the president's cabinet, did not limit his activities solely to the business of the War Department, that office did make heavy demands on his time and energy. But routine matters, though time consuming, did not prevent him from addressing broader administrative problems. Although his predecessor Calhoun had done much to make the department a model of administrative efficiency, he saw room for further improvements. When he took office, the quartermaster general's department was badly in need of a general reorganization. It was seriously understaffed, responsibility within the office was delegated in a rather haphazard and irregular fashion, and the system of accounting for public property was subject to abuse. Barbour recommended and obtained from Congress a bill providing for the more effective organization of the department and for a more efficient system of accounting for supplies and equipment issued to the army.[32]

To expedite internal improvement projects, Barbour reorganized and improved the efficiency of the Department of Topographical Engineers. He secured congressional authorization to increase the size of the department, suggested measures designed to reduce the large number of desertions from the army, and was responsible for the formulation and enactment of a uniform system of cavalry and artillery tactics and field maneuvers which was acclaimed by Thomas Metcalfe, chairman of the House Committee on the Militia.[33]

In supervising construction of the Cumberland Road from Wheeling, Virginia, to Zanesville, Ohio, Barbour introduced a number of beneficial changes. After a careful analysis of official documents and engineering reports relating to the portion of the road that had already been completed, he drew several conclusions that caused him to alter operating procedures: first, the cost of construction, which averaged $13,000 per mile for the entire section from the Potomac to the Ohio rivers, had been too high; second, the road had fallen into disrepair too rapidly; and third, the government had been plagued by countless unnecessary complaints and property damage suits from individuals through whose land the road had passed. To remedy the first problem, the secretary of war exercised greater care in the letting of contracts. He allowed less generous terms to road contractors and utilized local materials to a greater extent. To improve the quality and durability of the road, he was more careful with its specifications, requiring the superior macadam-type roadbed and surface. As a result of close supervision and good management, the road from Wheeling to Zanesville was completed at an average cost per mile of only $3,400, a substantial savings over earlier costs even if we allow for the fact that sections completed under Barbour traversed less difficult terrain than had the previously completed sections.[34]

Barbour's attempts to implement changes in the militia system, the deficiencies of which had been repeatedly revealed, were less successful. In November 1826 he submitted to Congress a report, the product of months of work, embodying proposals for a general reorganization of the militia.[35] He recommended that the force be reduced to one-third of its existing size, that an adjutant general be attached to the War Department with authority to standardize procedures among the various state units, that service schools be established for officers, and that a uniform field manual be adopted. He justified his call for reform by saying that the popular notion which identified the militia, closely controlled by state authority, as the only safe means of protecting the republic was a myth. The defects of the system, he argued, were serious. In the interest of national security they should be corrected. The report and its recommendations were favorably received by the House Committee on the Militia, which drew up a bill to implement them. But a reluctant Congress tabled the bill and thereby postponed indefinitely the badly needed reforms.[36] Throughout, Barbour and other advocates of reform and of a stronger military establishment were stymied by a national tradition resistant to change. The jealousy of the states and the absence of administrative means of compelling them to establish a uniform and well-disciplined citizen army thwarted every attempt at significant reform.

The volume and diversity of the tasks that Barbour was called upon to perform in the War Office were great. Treaty negotiations with numerous Indian tribes, military courts, disputes among army officers over rank and seniority, regulations for military contracts, reports to Congress, the supervision of internal improvements and military fortifications—these and other matters required his attention. He worked late into the nights, exhausting his energy and succumbing to several long bouts with illness.[37] Washington, especially in July and August, was unhealthful. Adams observed that the debilitating climate "wears out the spirits, and produces defection and weariness of life, with nervous irritability, and a fermentation of the blood bordering upon insanity."[38] Adding to Barbour's health problems were personal and financial difficulties. In the spring of 1825 his father died at the age of ninety. A year later his mother passed away.[39] Crop failures resulting from periodic droughts followed by torrential rains continued to plague him. In July 1826 excessive rains throughout the Virginia Piedmont caused several thousand dollars of irreparable damage to his tobacco and grain crops at Barboursville.[40] But he learned to live with these and other distractions and, mastering the demands of office, established a creditable administrative record during his tenure in the War Office.

Life in Washington was not all drudgery. Probably no city in the country had a more active social life than the national capital. Almost every evening following dinner, which was universally at five o'clock, someone in the city hosted a party. There was, wrote Lucy Barbour, a constant round of parties where ladies, attired in their finest gowns of velvet and satin, flirted or engaged in small talk with the great men of the nation.[41] "All Washington is nightly compressed into some fashionable drawingroom," she said, "in which the temperature approaches fever heat, and the confusion of tongues to that of Babel. We see the same faces, the same dances, and hear the same music at every place, still the good people seem never tired of attending."[42] On alternate Wednesday evenings when Congress was in session, Mrs. Clay and Mrs. Adams gave balls in their homes, attended by such crowds that one had the choice of trying to dance "in a space no bigger than a cheese plate" or observing and being "crushed up to the wall." Refreshments were normally served on such occasions, the greater part of which "was devoured by the most ordinary of the company, who pounced upon the trays like those not much accustomed to such fare."[43]

Like other cabinet members and congressional leaders, the Barbours had their own salon. Every Saturday evening they opened their home to visitors and friends. The aristocratic Mrs. Basil Hall, wife of a British naval officer, commented on one of those soirees she attended in January 1828. "We went last night to Mrs. Barbour's. . . . Such a crowd and such heat I have seldom been exposed to. Mrs. Barbour told me that in consequence of the badness of the night, which was truly one of the blackest and darkest I ever saw, she had had innumerable apologies, which I am sure she must have been thankful for as I know not possibly how she could have stowed away any more people."[44] Mrs. Hall, whose consistent criticism of American manners and society incurred the wrath of all, likened these gatherings, including the Barbours', to a "three shilling ticket ball at a second rate tavern" and marveled that they were so highly regarded by the Americans. They were certainly not to her taste. At one "particularly squeezy party" at the Southards', her low opinion of American manners was confirmed in a rather dramatic manner. As she was walking up the stairs, her partner began clearing his throat. "This I thought ominous," she said. "However, I said to myself, 'Surely he will turn his head to the other side.' The gentleman, however, had no such thought but deliberately shot across me. I had not the courage to examine whether or not the result landed in the flounce of my dress."[45] The Americans, of course, did not share Mrs. Hall's opinions. Margaret Bayard Smith, arbiter of Washington society, reveled in these gatherings. And she thought the Saturday evening parties at the Barbours', which she attended regularly, especially enjoyable.[46]

If these social gatherings provided pleasant diversions from the oppressive political climate of Washington, they were only momentary. There was no escaping, for any length of time, the grim reality that the Adams government was under siege. Almost every political issue to arise during the New Englander's presidency, whether internal improvements, the tariff, Indian affairs, or the Panama mission, was skillfully manipulated by the Jacksonians, adroitly led by Van Buren, to advance the candidacy of Old Hickory. Adams's administration was, in reality, one long election campaign in which constructive political action of any sort became virtually impossible and national legislation took a back seat to partisan politics and campaign polemics. Into this campaign Barbour, along with fellow-sufferer Clay, was inexorably drawn.

Few critics of the administration were harsher or more persistent than Thomas Ritchie. From late 1825 until Jackson's election three years later, the *Enquirer* kept up a steady barrage against the government, scrutinizing its every action, questioning its motives, and denouncing its nationalism. The recurring theme of his editorials was that the administration had forfeited any claim to republican character by its repeated and flagrant disregard of the Constitution, especially by its frequent resort to the doctrine of implied powers.[47] In November 1826, after the *Enquirer* had been at its task for more than a year, Barbour wrote several lengthy essays defending the administration for publication in the *National Intelligencer*.[48] These essays revealed just how wide the chasm between him and his old Junto associates had become, as well as the extent to which he had embraced the American System.

Lamenting the "violent gusts of prejudice and party spirit" that the *Enquirer*'s unrelenting attacks against the government had caused, Barbour argued that those powers which Ritchie and his friends denied the government were essential to its health and vitality. Without them it would be reduced from the strongest and most effective in the world to "the most imbecile and insignificant." A literal interpretation of the Constitution, he argued, would mean that Congress could do little more than lay and collect taxes, raise and support an army and navy, and pay the salaries of a host of public officials. Of what practical benefit was the power to levy taxes if the government could not apply them to some beneficial purpose? Where was the logic in a governmental charter that authorized Congress to erect lighthouses for navigation but denied it authority to build observatories; or that empowered it to establish a military academy but not a national university? There was none. It was his firm conviction, he said, that the Founding Fathers had never intended the Constitution to be construed in such a fashion.

He went on to argue that the *Enquirer,* in advancing such absurd and "new-fangled interpretations," was simply playing to party spirit in the hopes of effecting a "revolution in the settled policy and regular action of the General Government." Every major proposal advocated by the Adams government, he continued, had its origin in the presidencies of earlier Virginians, whose very administrations Ritchie was now using as proof against the "innovations and usurpations" of John Quincy Adams. It was Jefferson, he noted, who had first proposed that Congress erect an observatory; George Washington who first advocated a national university. Jefferson had begun construction of the Cumberland Road, the continuation of which the *Enquirer* was now vehemently assailing. Madison had been the architect of the nation's first tariff in 1789, and he had endorsed the principle of protection in 1816.

If Ritchie invoked the political philosophy of Jefferson and Madison as proof against the Adams administration's nationalist program, Barbour appealed to the actual political practices of those Republican leaders for sanction. He argued that solid precedents existed in their administrations for every measure now advocated by the Adams government. It was impossible, he said, for the national government to function effectively without employing the general powers sanctioned in the Constitution. In advocating the doctrine of implied powers, he cited sound Republican authority. Madison himself, he said, at the time Congress was debating what became the Tenth Amendment to the Constitution, had successfully argued that it was "impossible to confine this Government to the exercise of express [enumerated] powers, and there must necessarily be exercised powers by implication."

Barbour believed with Madison that the people themselves, by approving and sanctioning the exercise of a questionable power, could decide the question. It was on this ground that he rested his case. In the interpretation of the Constitution, he said, there are certain powers that every honest man

> must admit are granted or withheld—portioned, according to their charac-
> ter, between the General and the State Governments—there are others of so

mixed and doubtful a character, and so difficult to be properly distributed, . . . [that it is impossible] to assert the precise line of separation. That upon these dubious powers great diversity should prevail . . . is what was reasonably to be expected; and, indeed, it is no matter of surprise that the same individual should occasionally differ from himself, at different and distant periods. What rule of construction, then, shall be adopted when one of these difficult questions presents itself for a decision? If it is entirely new, the text and opinions of the Fathers offer the safest standard. But if it be one that has been again and again decided upon by the People, what other standard of construction can we resort to but those decisions? The People made the Constitution—they will interpret it as to them seems right.

Barbour's arguments had a distinctive Madisonian ring.

If those arguments bore little resemblance to the ones Barbour had espoused in 1798, it must be remembered that the times had changed. The issues were different. The critical question now was whether the country could overcome the centrifugal sectionalist forces operating to prevent it from attaining those benefits of union that he, no less than Adams and Clay, coveted: "peace and liberty and union, and in their train, the prosperity and glory of my country."[49] If Barbour had not always seen these as the transcendent goals of the American nation, he did so now.

During the election contest of 1828, in which he participated actively, Barbour exerted every effort to arrest the sectionalist tendencies that had become so pronounced in Virginia and elsewhere in the South. He warned that the *Enquirer,* in posing as the "oracle of new and hitherto-unthought-of constructions of the Constitution," was engaging in a deception that threatened the ruin of the nation. Those static, outmoded principles which Radicals hoped to impose on the national government represented a myopic view of what the nation required. "They mislead others because they themselves are misled," he said. "When the *Enquirer* calls upon the People to assert their rights, *we* call upon them to open their eyes, and no longer be led blindfold to the precipice, where yawns beneath them, to use a recollected phrase of the *Enquirer,* the *gulf of consolidation*: for there is no road so certain to consolidation as through the mazes of disunion, which the *Enquirer* seems disposed to thread [*sic*]."[50]

Barbour's efforts during the campaign to redirect the thinking of his fellow Virginians came to nothing. He was no more successful in persuading Ritchie to abandon his "heedless course." Indeed, the editor's incantations against the government became even more persistent and vitriolic, greatly contributing to the extraordinarily bitter tone of the election contest.[51] Ritchie was joined by other editors who collectively engaged in smear tactics on an unprecedented scale. Duff Green, editor of the scurrilous *United States Telegraph*, surpassed even Ritchie in the zeal and venom with which he attacked Adams. The Jacksonian press held no monopoly on slander tactics. The Adams press at times outdid the Jacksonians. Few restraints were exercised by either side. There is no evidence that Barbour, Clay, or any other members of Adams's cabinet were involved in the character assassination of Jackson, but the General believed they were jointly responsible.[52]

No novice to political fights, Barbour actively entered the lists against Jackson. He attempted to convince others, through private conversations and letters to friends and political acquaintances throughout the country, that the General was unfit for the presidency. He encouraged friends in Kentucky to call anti-Jackson conventions, while in Virginia he advocated the formation of a pro-Adams political organization.[53] When Postmaster General McLean blatantly used his patronage power to assist the Jacksonians, Barbour joined with Clay in urging the president to dismiss him. That the administration should have to contend with enemies outside its camp was to be expected; that it should contend with enemies within was unthinkable. But Adams, refusing to play the politician's game, would not remove the Calhoun partisan. Placing principles above practical consideration, regardless of consequences, he seemed bent on an austere and noble martyrdom. Barbour and Clay were confounded.[54]

Despite the president's intransigence in this matter, both Barbour and Clay remained optimistic about the administration's chances for victory. As late as mid-1827 both men, minimizing disquieting reports from every quarter of the country, remained hopeful.[55] Barbour had been particularly encouraged earlier in the year when Randolph was not returned to the Senate. In January 1827 a coalition of about thirty administration supporters in the Virginia assembly joined with a group of states' rights Republicans unhappy with Randolph's bizarre behavior to elect John Tyler to the Senate. Tyler had been a compromise candidate to whom the assembly turned only after Philip Pendleton Barbour refused to become a candidate for his brother's old seat.[56] And while Tyler's politics were essentially the same as Randolph's, Barbour and other members of the administration must have found him eminently more acceptable than the acerbic and unpredictable Randolph. Moreover, Tyler, who had supported Adams in the previous election, had not yet moved into the Jackson camp.

But Tyler was one of only a few Virginia Radicals who had not yet cast their lot with Jackson. Before the year was out he too would join Randolph, Ritchie, Littleton W. Tazewell, Andrew Stevenson, William C. Rives, and Philip Pendleton Barbour in endorsing the Old Hero.[57] Actually, by mid-1827 there was very little for Barbour to be optimistic about where the administration's future in Virginia was concerned. In the spring of the year

Tazewell, who had replaced John Taylor in the Senate, was won over by Van Buren's blandishments. A few weeks later Ritchie publicly endorsed Jackson, and other prominent Virginians began to fall in line shortly thereafter.[58] William C. Rives expressed the feelings of most Virginia Jacksonians when he recorded his reasons for supporting the Tennessean. "Jackson is the most orthodox & thoroughfaced republican of the Jefferson School. . . . He declares his attachment to the *rights of the states* & to a strict construction of the federal constitution. . . . He is opposed to foreign political connections—to an extension of executive patronage, . . . public debt, . . . [and to] a navy & standing army."[59]

Barbour followed developments closely in Virginia throughout 1827. It must have been a source of personal disappointment to him that his cousin and former law apprentice, John S. Barbour, now a representative in Congress, joined his brother Philip as a "zealous Jacksonian."[60] Barbour's hopes were buoyed momentarily in January 1828, when an anti-Jackson convention, over which his friend Archibald Stuart presided, convened in Richmond and drew up an Adams electoral slate with James Madison at its head. Barbour immediately wrote the retired statesman urging him to accept the nomination. He was confident that an electoral ticket with the venerated name of Madison at its head would carry Virginia and would "save the country from Jackson." When Madison declined to accept, Barbour's hopes, like those of Clay, began to wane appreciably.[61]

There was talk in late 1827 of nominating Barbour as Adams's running mate. Clay had given some thought earlier to offering himself for the position, but he subsequently decided, not altogether selflessly, that Barbour was the preferred choice. Adams favored Barbour, and Clay thought the Virginian would strengthen the ticket. Barbour briefly considered the possibility but decided that he was not interested.[62] Weary of the troubled political climate of Washington, which had exacted its toll, and bothered still by poor health, he began once again to think of retirement. But when Albert Gallatin, in late 1827, resigned his position as minister to England, Barbour decided to seek the post.

Sometime before March 1828, Barbour discussed with Clay his interest in being minister. Rush and Webster were also interested, however, and the secretary of state submitted all three names to the president for consideration. In late March Barbour broached the subject with Adams, whom he assured that, while he was interested in the post, he did not wish to have his pretensions embarrass the administration in any way.[63] Adams delayed making a decision. In early May, when he still had not acted, Clay urged him to appoint Barbour. The secretary of state's political instincts were as strong as ever. It was because he thought Barbour's appointment would arouse less political opposition than the appointment of either of the other two candidates that he pressed Adams.[64] The president saw several objections to the appointment: first, the problem of finding a suitable replacement for him in the War Department; and second—and more important—the effect his resignation would have on the administration. It would, he confided in his diary, "be universally considered by friend and foe as an abandonment of the Administration." He believed that the mission to England was desired by Barbour, Webster, and Rush alike as "a harbour from the storm":

> The secret of Gov. Barbour's anxiety to go to England is to save himself from the wreck. Mr. Rush has the same desire, and it is not inoperative upon Mr. Clay's recent propensities to resign. As the rage of the temptest increases and the chances grow desperate, each one will take care of himself. I know not that I could do better than to gratify Gov. Barbour, who has rendered faithful service to the country, and whose integrity and honor are unsullied. In my political downfall I am bound to involve unnecessarily none of my friends.[65]

Yielding to these sentiments and to the urging of Clay and other cabinet members who thought Barbour the best choice, Adams finally submitted his name to the Senate. A few days later, on May 23, that body voted 27 to 12 to confirm him. Although not every Jacksonian opposed him, both of Virginia's senators, Tazewell and Tyler, voted against him. Their negative vote, however, was a reflection less of their personal estimate of Barbour's merit than of the will of the state's Radical leadership, which considered Barbour's political apostasy unforgivable.[66] If Ritchie and other Radicals were critical of Barbour's appointment, others defended it. The *Richmond Whig* wrote: "It is the fashion in Virginia to depreciate James Barbour for the purpose of dispensing a larger share of praise to his brother, Philip P. Barbour, who has so successfully cultivated the regard of that political club [the Richmond Junto], which has so long ruled things with despotic sway. To deny that Governor Barbour has fine talents, only proves the weakness of those who make the objections."[67] In the new party lines forming in Virginia, it was clear that Barbour would have a new group of political associates.

Adams acted selflessly in appointing Barbour minister to England. He clearly foresaw the adverse effect his appointment would have on the election contest. True to his prediction, Jacksonians quickly claimed that the administration had acknowledged defeat and that Barbour, who probably would be followed by others, had abandoned the cause.[68] If Barbour did not anticipate these charges, he should have. At the very least, he showed a regrettable lack of sensitivity to Adams's quandary and to the political implications of his action.

Certainly Adams's belief that his secretary of war was seeking a harbor from the storm is credible. Barbour denied that he was simply trying to save himself. His reason for wanting the post, he said, was that he was on the verge of retiring and he saw the appointment as a capstone to thirty years of public service. It was, admittedly, a political plum but not a sinecure. Because his confidence in Adams's reelection had significantly abated, he believed his mission would be a short one—one or two years at the most. It would afford him an opportunity to end his public career in a politically untroubled and meritorious capacity.[69]

The president's belief that Barbour was trying to salvage his political career was predicated on the assumption that something remained to be salvaged. In fact, as far as the dominant party in Virginia was concerned, he had no career left to save. From the moment he became a convert to the American System, he was a political outcast in his native state. He had not made his decision blindly.[70] With full awareness of the implications of his actions, he had embraced the administration's nationalist program, had used the powers of his office to promote and implement certain aspects of it, and had unequivocally defended it in public print. By the president's own admission he had loyally and effectively supported the administration's policies. Thus the real test of loyalty, it would seem, came at the outset of the administration, not at its end.

When Barbour turned over the War Department to his successor, Peter B. Porter of New York, he left behind a creditable record as an administrator. He had also contributed in an important way to the formulation of government policy. His effectiveness as a member of the cabinet stemmed, at least in part, from his many years of experience in domestic politics. This advantage he would not have in his new capacity as U.S. minister to England, for he had never traveled abroad nor held a diplomatic assignment. The diplomatic challenges that awaited him, if less momentous than the political issues with which he had dealt, were a great deal more perplexing.

10

An Abortive

Mission

*O*N a humid Friday on the first of August 1828, the packet *Pacific* slipped quietly out of New York harbor and set its course for Liverpool. On board was the new U.S. envoy extraordinary and minister plenipotentiary to Great Britain, accompanied by his wife, Lucy, and three of their children—James, who was to serve as secretary of the mission; sixteen-year-old Frances Cornelia, who must have been saddened to leave behind the young friends with whom, for the past three years, she had shared the excitement of Washington's parties and balls; and seven-year-old Benjamin Johnson, whose excitement about the trip undoubtedly infected the older members of the family.[1]

Barbour and Lucy looked forward to the prospect of a quiet and restful voyage, during which they hoped to recuperate from the hectic activities of the past two months. They had both been very busy since May. In preparation for their departure, Barbour, in addition to making extensive travel arrangements, had had to attend briefings with Secretary of State Clay and to wind up his affairs in the War Department, which included familiarizing his successor with the business of the office. He had also made a trip to Barboursville, where he had made arrangements so that his son-in-law, John Taliaferro, could look after his plantation and business affairs during his absence. The final weeks had been filled with a round of public and private dinners, given by friends in Orange, Fredericksburg, Baltimore, and New York.[2] The hopes he had for a well-deserved rest on the voyage to England were soon disappointed, however, because six days out they encountered a severe storm. Unable to find his sea legs, he and other members of the party became sick and remained so for the duration of the crossing. At long last, on August 19, the *Pacific* reached the southwest coast of Ireland and sailed up the Irish channel. It was much to the relief of all that they disembarked at Liverpool two days later.[3]

After spending several days in the bustling port city, the Barbours took a coach for London. In sharp contrast to their sea voyage, the trip overland was pleasant. They made stops in Manchester, Leeds, York, and Birmingham, where the extremes of poverty caused Barbour to conclude that the industrial system was approaching a "fearful crisis." But the countryside, with its heavy luxuriant growth, was impressive. Although excessive rains had greatly injured the year's grain and potato crops, the farms appeared prosperous—much more so, indeed, than the typical American farm. Agricultural practices, Barbour noted, were much more advanced than in the United States.[4]

Upon arriving in London, then a city of some 1 million people, the Barbours rented a house on Devonshire Place, located between Regent's and Hyde parks.[5] For the next several weeks they were busy settling into their comfortable residence. Lucy attended to most of the domestic details; Barbour found little time initially for anything except business. A stranger to the diplomatic role, he spent most of the month of September acquainting himself with the problems and responsibilities of his mission, a task made unnecessarily difficult by the absence of official diplomatic records. "I regret to find," he wrote Secretary of State Clay shortly after his arrival in London, "that Mr. Gallatin carried his instructions to America without leaving a copy in the office of the Legation."[6] Indeed, Barbour's predecessor had taken with him all the official papers relating to his unhappy mission, and the new envoy found the legation's archives bare. Lacking a record of Gallatin's social and diplomatic activities, he was seriously handicapped from the beginning, because Clay had referred him to the former minister's instructions for explicit views of the American government on the diplomatic issues between the two countries. To make matters worse, William B. Lawrence, the valuable secretary of the legation whose familiarity with British diplomatic personnel and protocol would have been a great aid to the new envoy, resigned soon after Barbour's arrival.[7] Although he was able to avoid some of the inconveniences resulting from Lawrence's departure by filling the vacancy temporarily with his son James, he was unable to enter into any serious discussions with the Foreign Office until he received either a copy of Gallatin's instructions or an entirely new set explaining fully his government's position.[8] On this awkward footing his mission began.

It was not a promising mission. Anglo-American relations had been strained for years, and efforts of the Adams administration to settle long-standing differences between the two countries had met with only limited success. Upon his accession to the presidency, Adams had sent Rufus King to replace Richard Rush as the American minister to England. After nine months of futile talks with Foreign Secretary George Canning, the venerable Federalist resigned, his health too precarious to permit him to engage in protracted and unpromising negotiations.[9] His successor, Gallatin, after more than a year of negotiations with the Foreign Office, had succeeded in reaching agreement in several areas: the Oregon country would be occupied jointly by the United States and Great Britain; the northeastern boundary dispute between the United States and Canada would be referred to some friendly or sovereign state for arbitration; and American claims for slaves carried off by British forces during the War of 1812 would be paid. But on other matters—impressment of American seamen, the West Indies trade, and commercial rights of neutral nations—no agreement could be reached.[10] The British government, in a rather unfriendly mood, had declined to negotiate any treaty or convention concerning these persistent problems. Where the astute and experienced Gallatin had failed, it was unlikely that the inexperienced Barbour would succeed.

But a few signs augured well for his mission. From changes that had recently occurred in the composition of the British government, Barbour saw reason for hope. George Canning, the late prime minister and former foreign secretary who had peremptorily rejected Gallatin's proposal for settling the West India trade question, had died in the late summer of 1827, and the new government, formed in January 1828 by the Duke of Wellington, was more favorably disposed toward the United States than had been the Canning and Lord Liverpool governments.[11] "The Duke of Wellington," Barbour wrote, "is friendly toward the United States and desires the best relations."[12] Indeed, in his desire to cultivate closer friendship, the prime minister called on Barbour in person shortly after the American envoy arrived in London, a departure from protocol that surprised former minister Rush.[13]

Before he left Washington, Barbour had been given a list of subjects, consisting mainly of problems that had long been at issue between the two countries, to discuss with the Foreign Office if the opportunity arose: privateering, impressment, commercial rights of neutral nations, the Maine–New Brunswick boundary, the recovery of fugitive slaves escaping to Canada, trade with the West Indies, and a grievance which had just arisen—a discriminatory British import duty prejudicial to certain American goods, especially cotton.[14] Unfortunately Clay had neglected to instruct Barbour explicitly on these topics, referring him instead to the detailed instructions given earlier to Gallatin. Lacking these documents, Barbour could do very little until additional instructions were sent. For several months, therefore, he could only make the best of an embarrassing situation.

On October 1 Barbour had his first formal audience with Lord Aberdeen, the secretary of state for foreign affairs. Finding Aberdeen, like the Duke of Wellington, a broad-minded statesman favorably disposed to the United States, he told the British official that he hoped they might find solutions to a number of problems that had long exacerbated Anglo-American relations. Two questions in particular were urgent—impressment and West India trade.[15] Conversation then turned to a general discussion of the commercial policies of the two countries with special reference to the West Indies question.

Lord Aberdeen began by reviewing recent developments in this area. In the early years of the decade, the liberal commercial ideas espoused by William Huskisson, a moderate free-trader and important member of Lord Liverpool's unofficial but influential economic cabinet, had come into the ascendent in England, the consequence of which had been a significant modification of British restrictions on American trade with the West Indies. But Congress, and particularly the Senate Foreign Relations Committee chaired by Barbour, had deemed these concessions insufficient and had demanded more. President Adams had recently reaffirmed the position his country had taken in 1823 when it passed the Elsewhere Act. In March 1827 he had attempted to secure for American shipping unrestricted access to the islands by closing American ports to British ships coming from principal British ports in the Western Hemisphere.[16] This move, along with the tariff of 1828, had been highly injurious to British shipping. The United States, Lord Aberdeen charged, had treated Great Britain scurvily.[17]

Barbour answered sharply. Great Britain, he said, should be the last to complain of discriminatory treatment. The American commercial policy had been inspired by that of England, and the chief difference between the two was that the former was less discriminatory than the latter. "I replied that Great Britain...had taxed our principal staples from 200 to 600 percent, that our tobacco paid the latter sum, that our grain was interdicted except in times of imperious necessity, our rice, lumber, turpentine, etc., are labouring under the most onerous impositions, that cotton alone of our principal staples was exempt from these heavy burdens, *to the cause of which exemption it was unnecessary I should refer.*"[18]

Barbour's blunt riposte placed the foreign secretary on the defensive. Lord Aberdeen admitted that he was not very familiar with the question, but he was certain that Huskisson could make a strong case for the British policy.[19] Barbour seized upon the allusion to Huskisson to question the liberality of that statesman's commercial philosophy. Huskisson, he said, had professed very liberal principles and had called himself an apostle of free trade, but his theories and principles had not been consistent with his practice. "I shall be glad to be advised of one act of his, in reference to the United States, in any degree calculated to sustain his pretensions to having liberalized our intercourse."[20] One authentic deed, he declared, was more important to the United States than all Huskisson's liberal professions.

Discussion of the trade question ceased when Barbour, having been asked by the foreign secretary to open formal correspondence on the subject, indicated his willingness to do so only if some assurance could be given that a reasonable prospect of success existed. This Aberdeen could not or would not give, though he did promise to take up the question with Lord Wellington. The conversation then turned to the topic of fugitive slaves in Canada.[21]

Runaway slaves, Barbour observed, escaping from the southern states via the Underground Railroad, found refuge in Canada, where they were beyond the legal reach of their former masters. Slaveowners clamored for an agreement with England which would enable them to retrieve the fugitives. Aberdeen replied that while he personally would be willing to accommodate the request, public opinion in England would not allow it. An even greater obstacle was a parliamentary law granting freedom to every slave taking refuge on British soil. Barbour questioned the existence of the law, saying that according to his information the practice of giving freedom to fugitives stemmed from a judicial decision, not from an act of Parliament. Admitting that there was some ambiguity concerning the law, the foreign secretary insisted that it did exist. Whatever the case, all doubt concerning the question would soon be removed, for the head of the Colonial Department, Sir George Murray, was preparing to bring the whole matter before Parliament. Until that time further discussion of the question would be pointless.[22] Barbour's first audience with Lord Aberdeen then ended.

In subsequent sessions the commercial question was again discussed, and each time Barbour insisted upon the right of American ships to trade with the West Indies on equal terms with the British. The talks were complicated in November by the interposition of another problem—a parliamentary law, passed in July 1828, requiring American vessels transporting American cotton to British ports to pay a higher duty than was required of British ships carrying the same item. Secretary of State Clay, alleging that the preferential duty violated existing trade agreements between the two nations, instructed Barbour to protest.[23] This he did in a formal note to the foreign secretary dated November 27. But the Foreign Office was unmoved. Lord Aberdeen, commenting that the duty had no doubt been prompted by the American tariff of 1828, which he called "an unfriendly measure toward Britain," could see no possibility of an adjust-

ment until the United States modified its policy.[24] When Barbour persisted
in his protests, Aberdeen referred him to the Board of Trade, the president
of which discussed the matter openly, but the result of the meeting was the
usual story—friendly desires but no action.[25] And so Barbour's remonstrances came to nothing.

For the balance of his mission Barbour remained alert to signs of British
willingness to negotiate commercial differences seriously, but the signs
never appeared, or at least they were too faint to offer much hope of
success. Having been instructed to let the Foreign Office make the first
overtures, he could only bide his time patiently. Consequently, such discussion as did take place was indirect, desultory, and inconsequential. The
truth was that Great Britain was not yet ready to negotiate, and there was
little point in pressing the issue. Moreover, Britain considered President
Adams's attitude on the whole question dogmatic and unrealistic: that the
United States should be granted special trading privileges with the West
Indian colonies without making equivalent concessions was, as yet, unthinkable.[26]

On November 24, while government leaders were meeting in a cabinet
session at Windsor Castle, Barbour had his first audience with George IV.
An audience would have been arranged earlier, but the king, suffering
from what Barbour surmised was either dropsy or the gout, had been too
ill to perform the duties of state. Having been told earlier by the Duke of
Wellington that His Majesty's condition was so poor, and his loss of weight
so great that the royal waistcoats had been taken in almost three feet in
girth, Barbour expected to find a weak and emaciated sovereign. To his
surprise the king appeared robust and healthy.[27] Lord Aberdeen, who
accompanied Barbour to the king's closet, presented the American envoy.
After they exchanged greetings, Barbour presented his credentials and
briefly conveyed his personal desire and that of his country for amicable
relations, to which the king responded: "You may assure the President of
the United States that I am anxious to preserve the most friendly relations
with them, and that my conduct will ever be directed by this sentiment. For
the handsome manner in which you have expressed your private feelings, I
assure you of my satisfaction that the appointment has fallen upon you."[28]

About the time of his audience with King George, an incident occurred
off the coast of Ireland that caused Barbour to remonstrate strongly. The
New York packet *John Jay,* under Capt. Nathan Haldrege, was stopped by
the British sloop *Pearl* and was searched by Capt. George C. Blake. Immediately after the incident Captain Haldrege filed a complaint with the
American consul at Liverpool charging the British officer with illegal
search and personal abuse. Barbour registered the complaint with the
British government and demanded an investigation. The Admiralty Board

investigated and reported that Captain Blake had not exceeded his orders. Having been instructed to be on the lookout for an American vessel fitting the description of the *John Jay* and engaged in smuggling off the Irish coast, the British naval officer had stopped the ship and had searched it for illegal cargo. Upon finding everything in order, he had released it and had allowed it to proceed. The Admiralty Board expressed regrets that the incident had occurred and hoped that the explanation given would be satisfactory to the American government. This Barbour doubted, though a pledge that similar incidents would not occur in the future would surely be acceptable.[29]

Barbour used the *John Jay* incident as opportunity to mention the old problem of impressment. Since December 1825 there had been four separate instances of impressment. Two seamen from the Boston brig *Pharos* had been abducted in the port of Freetown, Sierra Leone, in December 1825; two from the Boston brig *Monroe* and two more from the New Bedford sloop *June* had been impressed off the coast of Africa in the spring of 1828; and two from the brig *Telegraph* had been seized at the Bay of Campeche, Mexico, in September of the same year.[30] Barbour protested against the practice in the strongest possible terms, warning Lord Aberdeen that the United States would not submit indefinitely to such flagrant violations of its rights and honor.

The foreign secretary contended that in at least two of the instances, those at Freetown and the Bay of Campeche, the American sailors had volunteered to join the British navy. American evidence indicated otherwise, Barbour retorted, and even if the allegation had been true, the sailors in question were bound by existing contracts with their American captains which, the British must have recognized, took precedence over any subsequent agreements with another party. In any event, this explanation did not apply to the two instances of impressment on the high seas.[31] Aberdeen could provide no defense of British conduct in the latter cases. Despite Barbour's protests, the British government refused immediately to forswear the practice. But his firm remonstrances, joined with those of his predecessors, who for years had been pressing the British on the subject, undoubtedly had some effect in persuading the government soon afterward to abandon the practice.[32]

Barbour spent much time discussing the Maine–New Brunswick boundary dispute with Lord Aberdeen. Gallatin had concluded a convention with the British in 1827 in which it was agreed that the king of the Netherlands would be called in to act as an arbiter of the disputed points. This service the Dutch sovereign had willingly agreed to perform, but the absence of necessary documents and maps—some of which had been carried off by Gallatin when he terminated his mission, others of which

had not yet been furnished by the British government—resulted in interminable delays. The situation was further complicated by ambiguities in
the convention, delayed dispatches from Washington, and countless other
inconveniences which greatly hindered discussion. Consequently, little
progress was made, and the dispute went unsettled until 1842.[33]

Barbour broached other issues with the Foreign Office during his brief
mission. He sought to secure recognition of the right of American vessels
to navigate the St. Lawrence on equal terms with the British. He tried to
obtain a better definition of the rights of neutral nations during time of
war, and he pressed the British to settle American claims for property they
had seized during and after the War of 1812.[34] On some of these issues
Great Britain indicated a willingness to negotiate that had not been evident earlier. In several meetings with the Duke of Wellington in the fall
and winter of 1828 Barbour found the prime minister friendly and anxious
to reach agreement on the disputed points.[35] In one interview, Barbour
wrote, the prime minister declared that "he had no object more at heart
than to cherish and strengthen the amicable relations between us and to
remove every cause calculated to influence them prejudicially."[36] A thaw in
Anglo-American relations was taking place, and Barbour had good reason
to think that agreement might soon be reached on many of the issues that
had gone unresolved for so many years.

But the negotiations called for time that Barbour did not have. After
Andrew Jackson's overwhelming victory in November 1828, the envoy
knew that he would soon be recalled. He certainly had no reason to expect
the president-elect to allow him to remain in London. He had been a
severe critic of the military chieftain, skeptical of his abilities and fearful of
the political consequences of his leadership. In a letter to John H. Pleasants, a Jackson opponent and later a prominent figure in the Whig party in
Virginia, Barbour summed up his feelings concerning the Tennessean and
described the European reaction to his election: "His first pretensions
excited my ridicule, his success my apprehension—but the support given
him by the People produced almost despair. . . . All Europe heard of his
election with astonishment, and every liberal man with regret. . . . My only
consolation was that it might be a temporary paroxysm, and when the
fascination subsided they would resume again their sober senses."[37]
Barbour's views were not unknown to Jackson, who lost no time in
replacing him with a loyal supporter.

Before Jackson's inauguration, John Taliaferro wrote his father-in-law
that in the matter of official changes a violent revolution was in the making
and that his removal was almost certain.[38] In April 1829, John Quincy
Adams wrote that according to rumors, Littleton W. Tazewell, Virginia's Old
Republican senator who had actively supported Jackson, had been offered

the mission to England. Barbour thought he should resign. But Adams, Clay, Taliaferro, and others advised him to remain at his post until he was recalled.[39] He did not have long to wait. In May he received a letter from Secretary of State Van Buren informing him that Louis McLane of Delaware had been appointed his successor.[40]

Had he been given more time, Barbour might have successfully concluded negotiations on at least some of the outstanding issues between the two countries. The friendly attitude of both the Duke of Wellington and Lord Aberdeen gave substance to his belief that success was imminent. But when his mission ended in May 1829, he had nothing concrete to show for his labors of nine months.

It would be a mistake to say that Barbour's mission was a complete failure. If he failed to settle long-standing diplomatic problems, he did contribute to the growth of better feelings between the two countries. He made a concerted effort to ameliorate British prejudices against the United States by "mingling freely with the people" and "engaging them in intelligent conversation."[41] Such socializing plainly did not influence the attitude or stance of the government. Still, his social conduct, his guileless and direct personal manner, and the firmness with which he asserted the American position, won the respect of the foreign secretary and perhaps contributed in some small way to clear the troubled atmosphere that had so long enshrouded Anglo-American relations.[42]

Lord John Russell, who in 1852 was to succeed Lord Palmerstone as secretary for foreign affairs, suggested as much when, at the annual meeting of the British and Foreign School Society in July 1829, he said:

> In former days, the mission on which he [Barbour] comes was little else than to watch and observe, with every kind of envy, the prosperity of the nation where he was sent to reside, and to take all possible precaution and means for marring that prosperity. But, it is our good fortune to see a Minister of America, among us who thinks differently; who as a member and representative of the United States, thinks nothing more fitting than to foster and favor the progress of this country in all the arts of social life.[43]

Whether Russell's estimate of the function of earlier American ministers was accurate may be questioned, but his belief that Barbour helped to dispel some of the old prejudices and suspicions was not without foundation. And if the favorable impression he made in London contributed to the development of a friendlier attitude toward the United States, as apparently it did, this in itself was an important achievement. The Jackson administration would take full advantage of the new posture of Anglo-American relations to settle old problems.

Although most of Barbour's time in England was spent on his official duties, he did manage to sandwich in other activities. He attended meetings of the Medico-Botanical Society of London and found time to call on the famous agriculturalist Sir John Coke of Norfolk, with whom he had a visit of "rare enjoyment" discussing agricultural problems in which they shared a common interest.[44] In May, suffering from eye problems, he pushed aside his tedious paperwork and took a trip with his family through portions of England and Wales, collecting rock specimens with his friend Joshua Bates of the famous banking house of Baring Brothers and Company.[45]

Before he left England in July 1829, the University of Oxford honored Barbour by awarding him the degree of doctor of civil laws.[46] Shortly afterward he journeyed to France, where for several weeks he toured the countryside with his family, taking in the sights which attracted tourists. In Paris he purchased some items for Madison and bought several pieces of furniture for Barboursville.[47]

From Paris the Barbours traveled to La Grange, where they spent several days visiting with Lafayette, whom Barbour had known since October 1824, when he, along with a large group of other prominent Virginians, had dined at the Eagle Hotel in Richmond with the Frenchman during his triumphal tour of the United States. From Richmond Lafayette had traveled to Washington, stopping en route at Montpelier and Barboursville, where he had been entertained by Madison and Barbour.[48] It was to repay this hospitality that the Marquis had written him in April 1829, inviting him and his family to come to France.[49] To the aged friend of America, who was now in his seventies, Barbour presented as a token of his personal esteem a fine copying machine, similar to the ones used by Jefferson, upholstered in leather and trimmed with brass.[50] After leaving La Grange, the Barbours spent another week touring the French countryside. As always, Barbour showed a strong interest in agriculture, especially in the French vineyards. By the middle of August the party was back in England, and on October 1, just thirteen months after leaving New York, the Barbours sailed for America.[51]

On the long return voyage, which was much more pleasant than the first crossing, Barbour must have reflected at length on the events of the past four years. He did not understand the political ferment of those years. The surging political democracy that had borne Andrew Jackson to the presidency and the new generation of politicians now coming to power seemed completely alien to him. He could not ignore the fact that a new political era had dawned. The sun had unmistakably set on the fortunes and political ascendency of the Jeffersonian Republicans. He had come into political prominence with the Jeffersonian revolution of 1800; with the Jacksonian revolution of 1828 he was forced into retirement.

Barbour had made a momentous decision in 1825 when he accepted a position in the Adams government. His identification with the enlarged nationalism of that administration had been complete, and his alienation from the old political leadership of Virginia, which, clinging to the Old Republican creeds, had moved into the Jackson camp, was final. His advocacy of the American System, and his opposition to Jackson, made reconciliation unthinkable. To his group of former political associates— Ritchie, Tazewell, Giles, Stevenson, and others who for so long had domi-nated Virginia politics—he was a political outcast.

But the hold of the Richmond Junto on Virginia politics was weakening. New elements of opposition, both to Jackson and to the Old Republicans, were emerging in Virginia. Soon many diverse factions, united only in their common opposition to the Jackson administration, would coalesce to form the Whig party. In the organization of that party, both in Virginia and in the country as a whole, Barbour would play a leading role. But all political activity in which he engaged after 1829 was secondary to the main pursuit of his final years—agriculture. In May 1829 he had written Sen. Charles Tait that he was anxious to return to Barboursville where he would devote himself completely to agriculture.[52] After three decades of activity in state and national politics, he turned now to the pursuits of the gentle-man farmer.

11

The Elusive
Goal

*U*pon their return to the United States, the Barbours stopped in Richmond to visit a few days with friends. There Barbour was honored with a public dinner, attended by a large number of old acquaintances and political associates. Some of the more distrustful members of the Junto saw sinister political overtones in the gathering. Thomas Ritchie charged that it was an electioneering maneuver intended by Barbour's friends to bring him before the public and legislature and to promote his election as governor.[1] Although political issues were undoubtedly discussed during the evening, the gathering was not, as Ritchie suspected, political. Thoroughly disillusioned by the triumph of Jackson and by the apparent repudiation of nationalism, Barbour looked forward to retirement from public life.[2]

The Barbours reached home at the height of the fall season. The brilliant reds and golds of the Piedmont hills blended with the muted, mist-veiled hues of the distant mountains, giving the flame-streaked October sunsets an unsurpassed beauty. It must have been a happy homecoming. The family was greeted by daughter Lucy Maria and her husband, John Taliaferro, as well as by grandchildren and a large slave family.[3] The Barbours settled quickly into the old routine. The weary politician was especially happy to be back home among the familiar hills his grandfather had first cultivated a century earlier. Throughout his long political career his attachment to the land that sustained him, his fondness of things agrarian, had not diminished. Having always accepted as a basic article of faith the proposition that the farmer was the noblest of God's creatures, he again became one without regrets and pursued the elusive goal of reforming Virginia agriculture.

Barbour was a highly successful planter at a time when success did not come easily. His plantation was a model of good management and progressive farming. One of the wealthiest planters of his region, he owned in

1830, at the time of his retirement, more than 20,000 acres of land, some of which was in scattered parcels in areas as distant as Florida and Mississippi. His main plantation, Barboursville, contained some 5,000 acres in the vicinity of the Southwest Mountains in Orange and Albermarle counties. A smaller plantation located to the north on the Rapidan River consisted of 2,000 acres of rich bottomland. To work the plantations he maintained a large labor force which in 1830 numbered eighty-one adult slaves. Including land, slaves, livestock, buildings, and other improvements, he possessed at this time property worth at least $300,000, the greatest part of which he had acquired through his own labors and that of his bondsmen rather than through inheritance. These figures in themselves are convincing evidence of his success as a planter.[4]

Few public figures ever retired to more comfortable circumstances than Barbour. His plantation, with its commanding view of the Blue Ridge Mountains, its well-kept fields, and its handsome buildings, was one of the most impressive in Virginia. Dominating the estate was an imposing neo-classical home, one of Jefferson's most beautiful and successful creations. The house was a splendid structure of dark red brick and contrasting white Doric columns. On both fronts, facing north and south, were large pediment porticoes adorned with massive columns. Like Monticello, Barboursville was built where a slight declivity in the land made it possible to give a two-story structure a single-story effect when approached from the principal north entrance. From the central portion of the house extended east and west wings in which four large bedrooms were located.[5]

The interior of the house was equally imposing. From the large north portico the main entrance was into a beautiful hexagonal salon with an elegant domed ceiling. Two corridors containing narrow stairways extended transversely from either side of the salon and formed an unbroken passage through the house. Adjoining the salon and projecting onto the south portico was an even more ornate two-story octagonal drawing room. A large state dining room made up the remainder of the house's central portion.[6]

Accessible from the south portico was a three-acre formal garden, laid out geometrically and surrounded by serpentine brick walls like those at the University of Virginia. Walks lined with grass and flanked by double rows of boxwood crisscrossed the garden, and a small flower-bordered stream spanned by three rustic bridges meandered lazily through. A short distance from the main house stood a number of smaller structures—an ice house, a carriage house, a long row of stables, and the slave quarters.[7] As a whole, the plantation had the appearance of a small, neat, well-ordered community.

Although he entertained frequently, Barbour rarely allowed overnight guests to interrupt his routine. At daybreak each morning, except Sundays,

The north, or main, entrance to
the Barboursville ruins, c. 1937.
Courtesy of the University of Virginia Library.

Barboursville with its later additions, c. 1880,
several years before its destruction by fire.
Courtesy of the University of Virginia Library.

he mounted his horse and made his rounds of the plantation. Several hours later he met with guests and family for a leisurely breakfast, after which he continued his rounds until about noon. In mid-afternoon he usually retired to his study, where he read or wrote letters. Dinner in the elaborate dining room was more formal. Afterward guests and family retired to the drawing room, where lively conversation followed. An engaging conversationalist and a generous host, Barbour dispensed hospitality with a graciousness characteristic of gentleman farmers in the age of Jefferson.[8]

Barbour's success as a planter was due in no small part to the early interest he took in published works on scientific agriculture. When at the turn of the century an increasingly profitable legal practice provided him with the financial resources to acquire land and to establish a plantation, he began to add agricultural treatises to his library—Arthur Binn's *A Treatise on Practical Agriculture,* several works by the noted English farmer Arthur Young, and copies of transactions from various agricultural societies.[9] Always anxious to acquire studies that would increase his scientific knowledge, he read widely and profited from the information gleaned, showing none of the traditional reluctance of farmers to adopt new techniques or to benefit from the experiences of others. Learning from Humphrey Davy's *Agricultural Chemistry* that soil acidity was responsible for the small benefit derived from vegetable manures, he sought a remedy in liberal applications of lime. John Taylor's *Arator* confirmed his belief in the efficacy of deep plowing and crop rotation. He showed a keen interest in the experiments with marl made by his friend Edmund Ruffin and obtained an early edition of *An Essay on Calcareous Manures.* He subscribed to a number of pioneer farm journals and frequently contributed articles to Ruffin's *Farmers' Register* and to John S. Skinner's *American Farmer.*[10] In short, he believed that solutions to some of the agricultural problems of his day could be found on the printed page.

Virginia agricultural practices in 1800, when Barbour began to establish himself as a planter, had improved little since colonial days. Generally the old system of the seventeenth and eighteenth centuries persisted, and the same exhaustive methods of planting were widely practiced. With a tenacity that defied explanation, Virginians of all ranks, planters and yeomen alike, clung to the past, seeking only to produce the largest possible crop at the greatest profit, without regard to the impact such exploitative practices had on the soil. The Tidewater area, where grain crops now dominated, had yielded its position as the tobacco-growing center to the more recently settled Piedmont, but an increase in the price of tobacco resulted almost invariably in a rapid return throughout the Tidewater to the old staple. The persistence of tobacco culture saw also the continuation of all its attendant evils. New land was cleared and planted for three or four years in tobacco, followed by five or six years of corn, and was then abandoned to sorrel, sage, and pine.[11]

Statements made by travelers in Virginia during the late eighteenth and early nineteenth centuries gave ample evidence of the continuation of exhaustive cultivation, of wasted lands and abandoned fields, of the air of poverty and despair that had settled on much of the state. To some, it was as if an "angel of desolation had cursed the land." Landowners generally were "in low circumstances, the inferior rank of them wretched in the extreme," while agriculture had reached its "lowest grade of degradation."[12] The Duc de La Rochefoucauld-Liancourt observed that in sixty miles of travel around the city of Richmond, he found not a single well-cultivated field. Depleted by long tobacco cultivation, the land was poor and barren; soil untreated by manures created a condition "inferior to [that of] almost all the other states of America."[13] Large areas of the state, both in the Tidewater and Piedmont, were described as scenes of ruin and desolation that "baffle description—farm after farm . . . worn out, washed and gullied, so that scarcely an acre could be found in a place fit for cultivation."[14] Although there were many "gullied fields interspersed with broom straw and stunted pines," there were "no meadows, no luxuriant fields of clover, no rich crops of grain, no large and fat cattle, and indeed nothing that indicates good husbandry."[15]

By 1800 the day had clearly passed when the Virginia farmer could readily buy new land more cheaply than he could improve the old. Indeed, the old system had been so exploitative that good land was virtually nonexistent. A planter had the choice of either improving the old lands or moving to the newer regions of the West and lower South where virgin soil was abundant. Although Orange County, more recently populated than the Tidewater, suffered less extensively from abusive agricultural practices than the older areas, it too had been subjected to many of the same ruinous practices. Much of the land that Barbour acquired in Orange and Albemarle consisted of farms that had been exhausted by their owners before they migrated to new regions. Because he equated the well-being of republicanism and, consequently, the future of America's unique experiment in self-government with the health and vigor of the agrarian sector, Barbour devoted himself to the elusive goal of reforming agriculture. His interest in scientific farming and his commitment to agricultural improvement did much during his lifetime to restore soil fertility and prosperity in depressed areas of the state.

One of the major factors contributing to soil exhaustion was the mode of plowing. Plows generally used in Virginia at the turn of the century were inadequate instruments which, by turning a superficial furrow, loosened the topsoil but left an unbroken hard stratum beneath, thus creating a shallow surface which heavy summer rains quickly washed away. Although deep plowing was known, it was seldom practiced. Beginning about 1800 Barbour experimented extensively with new types of plows and new methods of plowing. He acquired and used new, improved iron models capable of penetrating the subsoil and by 1804 was using large plows requiring three- to five-horse teams that cut the earth to a depth of eight to ten inches. He experimented also with winged plows, iron moldboards, "duckbill" colters, and improved hillside plows. Those which proved most effective he put into general use.[16]

In addition to his experimentation with deep plowing, Barbour devised new ways to fight soil erosion. He abandoned the ruinous system of cross-plowing, which was employed widely on corn lands, and planted instead by drill. Although he used plows of special design, such as Randolph's hillside plow, and followed the horizontal method of cultivation on the rolling hills, these measures in themselves were not sufficient to prevent washing of the steeper slopes. The unusually heavy summer rains to which the Piedmont was subject continued to cause great damage, and in August 1813 the "disastrous effect" of ten inches of rain falling in a twelve-hour period prompted him to seek additional preventive measures. After considerable study and observation, he devised an effective system of hillside ditching which involved the digging of trenches at suitable intervals on the steeper hillsides to carry off the storm water and to drain the horizontal furrows. This system stopped erosion even on the steepest slopes. "The land within or below these ditches," he informed members of the Albemarle Agricultural Society, "becomes almost as valuable as the valleys, and when cured of their galls is worth $100 the acre."[17]

A major task which confronted Barbour and his neighbors was that of restoring and maintaining soil fertility. To accomplish this Barbour experimented widely with various systems of fertilization and crop rotation. Manure production and liberal applications of various forms of fertilizer were basic components of his agricultural system. In the first decade of the century he began experimenting with animal manure, plaster, and cover crops. Animal manure, though highly beneficial, was always in short supply. When practicable, he penned his livestock and mulched the offal with straw and cornstalks, but the quantity produced, though carefully conserved, was never sufficient for general use.[18] In the second decade of the century he conducted small-scale experiments with marl, but he found an equally effective and less expensive substitute in the form of lime, which he employed successfully for a while. He finally settled on gypsum or plaster, a mineral which, when applied liberally to his wheat fields and used in conjunction with clover cover crops, increased yields by as much as 100 percent. He employed this same system successfully with other grain crops such as corn, rye, and oats.[19]

Deep plowing and fertilization produced the best results when used in conjunction with a judicious system of crop rotation, and Barbour incorporated all three practices into his agricultural system. Sufficiently familiar with the works of Arthur Young to know that crops differ in their demands on soil nutrients, he sought to develop a system of rotation which would give maximum yields without exhausting the soil and at the same time would provide continuity of employment for the labor force and work stock. Although he never devised a system which could be applied uniformly to all his land, he did employ a number of systems which produced good results. These ranged from the simple but effective three-field system to a more elaborate seven-field system. The former, which he employed on certain of his upland wheat fields, consisted simply of two years of wheat followed by a year of ungrazed clover. The difficulty with this system was that it entailed heavy use of plaster and could be applied only to the better lands. On less fertile upland ground he followed a more involved six-field system of corn, wheat, clover, clover, wheat, and clover. Occasionally tobacco was included in a more complex seven-field system, but generally it was grown on the rich bottomlands of his river plantation where the richer soil permitted a less elaborate system of rotation (tobacco was followed by wheat and two years of clover).[20] In an age when the expansive, speculative nature of Virginia agriculture caused the typical planter to rely heavily on productive new lands, Barbour served as a much-needed model of the success that could come with the careful maintenance and improvement of the old.

Barbour did not abandon tobacco, as did some of his neighbors, but neither did he make it the cornerstone of his plantation economy; rather he integrated it into an intelligent system of general farming which included wheat and other grains.[21] Indeed, by 1800 wheat had become for him a more important money crop than tobacco. In wheat as in tobacco production, he was careful to employ scientific techniques. In contrast to those farmers who simply scattered seed on unprepared ground, he tilled the soil carefully, planted with drills, and fertilized heavily. Through wise use of cover crops and plaster, he consistently harvested yields much greater than the Piedmont average of seven bushels per acre.[22]

Along with many other progressive farmers, Barbour constantly sought ways to combat more effectively the diseases and insects, such as the smut and Hessian fly, which menaced wheat crops. From his friend John S. Skinner, editor of the *American Farmer,* and from neighboring farmers he obtained many varieties of wheat seed with which he conducted carefully controlled experiments in the period 1813–1819, hoping to discover a seed resistant to both the fly and the smut.[23] Early experiments were disappointing. It appeared that every variety of seed was subject to the ruinous fly, which seemed a "calamity without remedy." When Barbour sought a solution by delaying planting from August to October, he found that winter frosts killed much of the crop, but in 1815 he began to meet with encouraging results. In the fall of that year he planted on an experimental basis twenty pounds of Columbian, or Lawler, wheat, which produced a crop totally free of the insect. Subsequent tests showed that Lawler wheat resisted the fly when other varieties were almost totally destroyed. Encouraged by these findings, he planted most of his wheat acreage with the Lawler seed in 1817. The results were gratifying; the crop was large and unblighted.[24]

In 1819 Barbour reported to the Albemarle Agricultural Society the results of his experiments with Lawler wheat and warmly extolled its fly-resistant qualities. It was far more resistant than the more popular purple straw and bearded wheats, and the quality and size of its yields were comparable and perhaps superior to those of the other varieties. The danger lay in late planting. If planting were delayed beyond the proper season by as much as a single week, the crop became subject to heavy damage from smut and rust.[25]

Next to the Hessian fly, the greatest enemy of Virginia wheat was smut. Although Barbour had not been previously troubled by that blight, he noticed it for the first time in his early wheat in the spring of 1816, and by the following year it had become a major problem. To combat the disease he soaked the seed wheat in a saline solution immediately before planting. Imperfect or diseased seeds floated to the surface and were removed. He then mixed with each bushel of seeds a gallon of slaked or hydrated lime and a bushel of plaster, and the whole was thoroughly mixed and immediately planted. Of the many elaborate tests that he conducted to find a smut-resistant seed, this procedure, he informed neighboring farmers at a meeting of the Albemarle Agricultural Society, had proved the most successful. Seeds prepared in this manner produced crops almost totally free of smut, while similar control seeds, omitted from the process, produced heavily blighted crops.[26]

Although wheat and tobacco were his chief money crops, Barbour produced other items which, taken as a whole, constituted an important source of income. Corn was grown in large quantities, not only for feeding his slaves and livestock but also for sale on the commercial market. He maintained a large herd of merino sheep, whose wool brought good prices. He distilled whiskey and brandy and produced a popular chewing tobacco for sale locally.[27] The sale of thoroughbred horses also provided an important source of farm income. About 1800, when he acquired a stallion of local fame named Hyflyer, Barbour began to raise racing stock and fine riding horses. In time his stables became famous throughout the South. His horses won top honors at many state fairs, and some of them developed into outstanding racers. One of them, an Arabian thoroughbred named Camel, was reputedly among the fastest in the country. He sold stock to men throughout the lower South, including Henry Clay, who paid him $1,500 for a fine brood mare. Some of his stallions commanded handsome stud fees. Truffles, a large, dark bay stallion imported from England, serviced mares from across the South and earned as much as $5,000 annually.[28] Such diversification allowed Barbour to hedge against losses in wheat and tobacco and at the same time to use his labor force efficiently.

Although scientific argricultural techniques were a sine qua non for nineteenth-century Virginia farmers, nothing was more essential to successful large-scale farming than a reliable, stable labor force. During most of his adult life, Barbour owned between 100 and 150 slaves and succeeded, through careful management and efficient utilization of labor, in making the "peculiar institution" profitable.[29] His plantation records do not support the assertion that slavery was unprofitable, nor is there anything in his experience to suggest that the institution, by its very nature, precluded soil reclamation, crop diversification, or agricultural innovation. Moreover, the agricultural adjustments that he made were not contingent upon capital derived from the sale of surplus slaves to the lower South. Through profits obtained from routine farming operations he was able to invest in fertilizers and improved equipment, to experiment with new methods, and to diversify his crops without reducing his labor force.[30]

Speculation about whether or not slave labor was as profitable as free labor can only be termed an exercise in futility, since adequate materials for comparison do not exist. The many variables of climatic conditions, nature of crops, and cost accounting systems preclude significant comparisons between the free labor farms of the North and West and the slave plantations of the South.[31] Certainly the thesis that slaveowners made money in spite of slavery rather than because of it does not apply in Barbour's case, nor, we may suspect, does it apply to many of his neighboring planters. Except in unusual years, such as those following the Panic of 1819, Barbour rather consistently earned profits that, by any method of cost accounting, represented a good rate of return on his capital investment.[32] And this statement does not take into account such concealed sources of profit as personal services rendered by domestics, natural increase of slaves, and appreciation of land values resulting from improvements wrought by slave labor.

Barbour encountered no insuperable obstacles in training his labor force to perform the different tasks required by scientific and diversified farming. Admittedly, it might have been easier to train and supervise hands in the routine chores of staple production alone, and the temptation, especially when tobacco prices were good, to resort to the one-crop system must have been great; but experience and business acumen suggested that diversification held the greatest promise. Barbour's success indicates that slave labor proved far more adaptable than many scholars have believed.[33] Good management was essential for success in any complex agricultural operation such as Barbour's, and its absence, rather than any inherent limitation of slave labor, seems to have been the decisive factor in the failure of other southern plantations.

The efficiency of slave labor depended to a large extent upon the health and morale of slaves, a fact of which Barbour was well aware. Within obvious limits, he did all he could to keep his chattels happy. A firm master who tempered judgment with benevolence, he believed that humanity, no less than the simple dictates of self-interest, demanded good treatment. He held a deep affection for his "people" and showed a genuine concern for their well-being. His close attention to their physical needs and his sympathetic treatment were designed to win their affection, for he felt that a close personal attachment between slave and master was mutually beneficial.[34]

Proper treatment of bondsmen, Barbour informed members of the Albemarle Agricultural Society, involved, among other things, careful attention to their basic physical needs. They should be well fed, properly clothed, carefully attended in sickness, and adequately housed. Revealing what may have been a better understanding of nutritional requirements than was possessed by those planters who fed their slaves only cornmeal and salt pork, he urged fellow planters to include milk, garden vegetables, and daily allotments of lean meat in the slaves' diet. Each hand, he continued, should be allowed at least three suits of clothing per year—a durable, warm suit for winter and two linen suits for summer. In sickness or in the infirmities of old age, the slaves had an incontestable claim to the immediate and humane attention of the master. When medical attention was needed, the master should "give of his stores" and affection with "no sparing hand." The raising of children should be entrusted to elderly nurses who, uniting kindness with firmness, would assume primary responsibility for their care. The careful attention Barbour gave to proper diet, sanitary living quarters, and treatment of the sick paid handsome dividends; for more than twenty-five years he lost not a single adult through illness, a remarkable record. Not only was his slave family healthy, it also doubled in size in fewer than twenty-five years. With his policy of humane treatment, Barbour combined a program of special rewards. He, like other imaginative planters, compensated for the natural lack of incentive among slaves by providing incentives of his own—extra food, drink, holidays, and other bonuses which he awarded to the most industrious of his hands. The cost of such a policy was trifling, he said, and the effect was "manifestly beneficial." It "inspired gratitude toward the master" and was a "stimulus to good conduct."[35]

Like so many of his contemporaries, Barbour in principle condemned the institution of slavery, but he could see no practical means of dismantling it. It was, he believed, a necessary evil. Echoing Aristotle and anticipating the arguments of such proslavery spokesmen as John C. Calhoun and George Fitzhugh, he said that a laboring class, "whether bond or free, white or black," must exist in every community, for it constituted "the indispensable foundation of the social fabric." Any attempt to alter the social fabric, he argued, would be disastrous. "Our own daily experience teaches us that the condition of the slaves, when well treated, is infinitely preferable to that of free people of color . . . , who, ignorant, insolent, and demoralized . . . , are reduced to prostitution, theft . . . , and begging."[36] Thus he helped to lay the groundwork for one of the most persistent themes formulated to defend slavery: that bondage was good for the slaves.[37] In this way, too, he rationalized what he knew was immoral and contradictory, an affront to the conscience and principles of a free people. He was simply unwilling to sacrifice an aristocratic life-style that depended on slave labor. Beyond treating his Negroes as humanely as possible, he did nothing to ameliorate the baneful effect of the despised institution in the life of his state and nation.

One of the most persistent and troublesome problems of running a large plantation in Barbour's day was that of finding capable managers. The overseer system so widely employed was almost universally condemned. In an address to the Virginia Agricultural Convention in 1836, Barbour expressed the sentiment of most intelligent farmers when he noted the evils of the system.

Were I to select the most disastrous of all causes which have contributed to our misfortunes, I would say at once, it was the lack of capacity of proprietors to manage their estates. Instead of personally superintending them . . . , they have deputed their management to hireling superintendents, not infrequently as ignorant as themselves—and to complete their ruin, have paid these hirelings with a share of the crop. These, as was natural, looked only to the present year—the future being left to take care of itself. The lands capable of producing, were annually cultivated till exhausted; improvements of every kind neglected, and in effect, the whole country by this simple process was as though it had been under an annual rack-rent—with no restrictions on the tenants, and with no supervision by the proprietors.[38]

Barbour did not share the conviction held by a majority of planters that overseers as a class were vicious and unreliable. Undue prejudice, he believed, was expressed against them, and this in turn contributed to the evils of the system by robbing the overseer of self-respect and creating unnecessary suspicion between proprietor and manager. These attitudes combined with penurious salaries to create in the overseer a continual restlessness and a disposition to annual change.[39]

To combat the evils of the managerial system, Barbour believed that the overseer should be treated with greater respect and understanding and that the proprietor should make every effort to inculcate in him a sense of responsibility and self-respect. Nor should the proprietor expect too much of the overseer too soon. "Indeed it is impossible that he can succeed so well the first year—he has to learn the wishes of his employer, and the disposition of the hands under him—the capacity of the latter for labor—the different kinds of soil he has to cultivate, and a long list of details which cannot be acquired in a year."[40] For the evils of the system, he believed that the proprietor was as culpable as the overseer.

Barbour himself sought to achieve managerial stability by giving his overseers a stake in their work in the form of liberal wages, substantial bonuses, and indulgences of various sorts. "Instead of grudging them their wages," he said, "I rejoice that while they are securing my independence, they are acquiring one for themselves." As a result of this approach, he encountered far less difficulty than most of his neighbors in obtaining and keeping able managers. His principal manager stayed with him for more than twenty years, performing his tasks with "honesty, industry and zeal."[41]

The steadily declining condition of agriculture in Virginia in the early 1800s, dramatized by a rising tide of emigration to the lower South that threatened to depopulate the older areas, gave a sense of urgency to the activities of agricultural reformers like Barbour who, seeking to preserve the agrarian order, joined together in cooperative self-help societies designed to explain and improve the economy of their section. One of the most popular ventures was the agricultural society. Although many such groups were organized in Virginia during this period, none was more successful than the one centering in Albemarle and embracing the neighboring counties of Orange, Amherst, and Fluvanna. Organized in 1817, the Albemarle Agricultural Society— "perhaps as brilliant for the number assembled as had ever gathered in the name of agriculture"—did much in the 1820s and 1830s to improve farming practices. Its goal was to sustain the life of rural virtues and to promote the agricultural prosperity vital to the country's republican character. Barbour, along with Jefferson, Madison, John H. Cocke, Joseph C. Cabell, and Thomas Mann Randolph, was a leader of the group.[42]

At the society's organizational meeting a committee of five was appointed to draw up rules and objectives. Serving on the committee were John Patterson, Jefferson, Cocke, Cabell, and Barbour. During the summer the five men worked at their assignment, and in October they presented to the organization a list of ten "Objects for the Attention and Enquiry of the Society." First, and principally, was the cultivation of the primary staples of wheat, tobacco, and hemp for market. Next came the subsidiary articles for the support of the farm: corn, barley, oats, and other grains; peas and beans; turnips, potatoes, and "other useful roots"; and grapes and other fruit. Third were the care and utilization of animals for saddle or draught and the destruction of noxious insects, reptiles, fowls, and quadrupeds. The report encouraged the discovery and promotion of improved agricultural techniques through experimentation with crop rotation, the adoption of new implements of husbandry, and the use of manures, plaster, green dressings, and fallow. Members were urged to keep close records of their experiments and were invited to report the results to the society.

After approving these objectives, the society organized with Madison as president, Thomas Mann Randolph and John H. Cocke as vice-presidents, Peter Minor as secretary, and Isaac Cole as treasurer. The steering committee included Randolph, Cabell, Cocke, and Barbour. A sort of agricultural catechism to be used by the members in reporting their farming practices, including questions about crop rotation, yield per acre, methods of fertilization, and labor-saving machines, was then adopted. Plans were made for the establishment of a nursery from which members might secure plants and trees; a committee was appointed to examine the possibility of importing blooded horses to improve Virginia racing stock; and other measures were proposed to improve agriculture.[43]

For the next several decades the society was an active agent in promoting reform. It held agricultural fairs that awarded premiums to outstanding exhibitions, conducted plowing contests to determine the most effective types of plows, gave bonuses to its members for significant agricultural innovations, established a manufactory for farm implements, and supported internal improvements designed to improve markets of the section. Barbour was a leading spirit in the organization. He served on most of the important committees during the early years of its existence and attended the meetings with as much regularity as his duties in Washington permitted. He presented several important papers on various agricultural experiments that he had conducted, delivered speeches on other topics of interest, and exchanged ideas with members of the society. In recognition of his contributions to scientific farming, the society in 1825 elected him to succeed Madison as president.[44]

Throughout the 1820s and 1830s Barbour maintained a lively interest in agricultural reform. With prominent farmers from other sections and countries, including the famous English agriculturalist Sir John Coke of Norfolk, he discussed agrarian problems and urged neighboring farmers to adopt new, improved methods.[45] But farmers as a group were slow to abandon traditional practices. Old evils persisted, and for Barbour and other progressive farmers this was a matter of growing concern. From such concern grew the Virginia Agricultural Convention of 1836.

The convention, called for the specific purpose of discussing agricultural problems and proposing solutions, met in Richmond in January 1836. Progressive farmers from all parts of the state attended. Barbour, who had been instrumental in the convening of the assembly, was chosen president.[46] In the major address to the delegates he pointed to the magnitude of the agricultural problems confronting Virginia and proposed several remedies.

> I call your attention to a spectacle without an example in any other part of the globe. Vast regions, once the abode of a numerous population, of plenty, and of social happiness, have been recommitted to the forest—and their original inhabitants, the wild beasts, re-established in their primitive dominion. That a result of this kind has occurred where a barbarous conqueror, Attila-like, has swept the face of the country with the besom of desolation, or where dread misrule has caused the population to recede before the rod of the oppressor is true—but in no instance where the hoof of the conqueror has not defiled the land, and where peace and freedom have held undisturbed sway as in our case, has such a thing occurred. Other large portions of the commonwealth . . . still present the most discouraging prospects—wasted fields, houses threatening their inhabitants with their fall—and depopulated districts—while our people by the tens of thousands, are leaving us. . . . When and how these great mischiefs are to be stayed in their career, are questions that address themselves with an irresistible pathos to every lover of his mother land.

Many factors had contributed to the plight of Virginia's "tillers of the soil." The greatest of these, Barbour believed, was the failure of proprietors to manage their own estates. They turned management over to "hireling superintendents" who, with no restrictions or supervision, butchered the land and laid waste once-fertile fields. The overseer system, as practiced by most Virginians, was a primary cause for agricultural decline. Another contributing factor was emigration. Virginia, Barbour noted, had been for more than half a century "the great hive from which have gone numerous swarms of emigrants to the south and west." Two groups remained behind: "the well-to-do who are too comfortable to move, and the indigent who are too poor to move. . . . The head and tail of society are thus left; the vital part attends the emigrants."

The reluctance of farmers to adopt improved agricultural techniques worsened the situation. Despite the development of improved practices and methods, old customs persisted. Exhausting crops were planted until the soil was capable of producing nothing but sorrel, persimmon, and weeds. Little or no effort was made to ameliorate the land by fertilization or rotation.

In enumerating the causes of agricultural paralysis and decline, Barbour contended that the state of Virginia society could not be overlooked. For many years it had been passing through a "violent revolution." Ancient and wealthy families, once a numerous class, had disappeared. Young men raised in the "luxurious indulgence" of the wealthy families all too often lacked enterprise and motivation. Sticking "like suckers to the parent stock, . . . they have exhausted it, and all have gone down together."

Barbour was confident that Virginians possessed the means to correct these evils. Although there existed no quick remedy to the waste of centuries, a judicious program of reform perseveringly pursued would, in time, bring a return of prosperity to the agricultural community. He then proposed to the convention two measures that he believed would help bring about improvement. A state agricultural board, composed of outstanding agriculturalists and representing the agrarian interest of the state, should be created to promote and coordinate reform and to act as a pressure group to secure from the legislature laws aiding agriculture. Second, an agricultural professorship and an experimental farm should be established at the University of Virginia. The professor should be a man of broad experience and training, capable of applying scientific knowledge from many fields to the exclusive domain of agriculture. The experimental farm would serve as the proving ground for new farming methods and techniques. Experiments with different soil types, fertilizers, and improved varieties of seeds and plants might be conducted to great advantage on such a farm and the results made known throughout the state. By fostering reform and seeking to determine the best farming practices, the agricultural professor and the experimental farm would perform a great service to farmers of the state.[47]

The Agricultural Convention adopted Barbour's recommendations, incorporating them into a petition addressed to the General Assembly. But the legislature, as in the past, took no action, and the efforts of Barbour and other reformers came to nothing. The House of Delegates did debate a bill in 1839 which would have established a board of agriculture, but the measure failed.[48]

Although Barbour was not the first Virginian to propose an agricultural professorship, he was apparently the first to stress emphatically the value of an experimental farm. Of both ideas he was the foremost and ablest champion. As early as 1825, when he became president of the Albemarle Agricultural Society, he had strongly urged that both be created; and despite the failure of numerous petitions to move the legislature to action, he had continued to advocate the move, adding proposals for the establishment of an agrarian press for the state.[49] In 1830–1831, when he had been briefly a member of the legislature, he had submitted a bill embodying his schemes, only to see it rejected.

> It was in vain I urged that in a society boasting of its exclusive agricultural character, the legislature had never dispensed the slightest aid to its encouragement; that while the tillers of the earth had paid ninety-nine hundredths of the cost of the University, their particular interests had been entirely overlooked.... To my mortification ... the proposals ... which have long been favorite objects with me ... fell still-born. They appeared as scandal to the Jews, and folly to the Greeks. There was a headlong member ... who condescended merely to denounce them as smelling too strong of the tariff.[50]

Although the legislature declined to act upon Barbour's proposal for an agricultural professorship and experimental farm, it did finally respond favorably to the pressure that he and others exerted for a state board of agriculture. Created by the General Assembly in 1841, the Virginia Board of Agriculture was composed of eight prominent agriculturalists representing the Tidewater, Piedmont, Valley, and Trans-Allegheny regions of the state, who were to meet annually to suggest measures of agricultural improvements.[51]

In December 1841, when the board held its first and only meeting, Barbour was elected president and Edmund Ruffin corresponding secretary.[52] In a report to the General Assembly, Barbour gave a brief summary of the board's goals, the foremost of which was "to remove the blighting evil of injudicious agriculture." To promote improvement, it would attempt to draw together and assimilate the vast store of agricultural knowledge and, after careful study, would incorporate it into an agricultural code to serve as a guide and encyclopedia for farmers. By embodying the best knowledge that science and experience could offer, the code would serve, he hoped, as a "tool of inestimable value" to both the experienced and the inexperienced farmer. To promote further reform, advisory committees composed of outstanding husbandmen would be created in each county. Farmers of the county might address inquiries to this committee, and each individual member would serve as a sort of county agent, encouraging reform and advising farmers of his respective district. Finally, the board hoped to give new direction to the course of Virginia agriculture and society.

> Agriculture should be the first object of civilized man; its condition is a fair test of the state of society; when it is defective all conditions suffer—when it prospers all partake of its prosperity. Every patriot should esteem it among his first duties to do all in his power for its advancement: the apathy too prevalent everywhere should cease—a new impulse should be imparted by the zealous friends of agriculture—and the public mind, diverted from an engrossing devotion to party politics, should be made to perceive that this great interest has claims on its attention. For while the bickering, the rise and fall of heated partisans, and their baneful influence on society shall be forgotten, or be remembered only to be deplored, the achievements of agriculture, by the aid of science and experience, will endure forever, and in their progress will dispense blessings in all coming time to human kind. The board indulges the hope that its labors will not be altogether unavailing in producing this new direction of sympathies and feelings, so propitious to the success of agriculture.[53]

Apparently the legislature was unimpressed by this statement; it abolished the board in 1843. Although Barbour did not live to see this action taken, the board's demise would have been for him a great personal disappointment. Believing as he did that the noblest of God's creatures was the tiller of the earth, and fearful that Virginia's agricultural decline presaged ruin of the agrarian society, he was particularly anxious to see the legislature extend every encouragement to farmers of the state.

Legislative enactment of those measures which he and fellow reformers urged undoubtedly would have abetted agricultural progress, yet the real obstacle to reform was not the legislature but rather the farming masses, who seemed utterly resistant to change. Farmers as a group were notoriously slow to abandon practices, however ruinous, that carried the weight of custom. Few would admit, or seemingly could recognize, that the exploitative methods of their fathers and grandfathers could not be continued without disastrous results. Rather than change their habits, they chose instead to emigrate to the virgin lands of the Southwest where they could profitably continue the soil-mining form of agriculture traditionally practiced. A large percentage of those who remained behind were subsistence farmers unable to raise the capital necessary to move. It was they, also, who were generally the most resistant to change. In the final analysis, the availability of cheap land elsewhere may well have been the greatest single obstacle to agricultural reform in Virginia.

If we view Barbour's own experience as an example of what might have been accomplished within the limits of a slave society, we must conclude that the potential for developing a sound agricultural economy based on slave labor was great. It is a mistake to assume that such labor was adaptable only to staple crop production, that the wasteful methods of exploitative farming are attributable exclusively to it, or that the institution of slavery, impervious to reform, was on the road to extinction by the 1830s. It is true that agricultural reform in Virginia was largely unsuccessful until the supply of fresh land in the South and West was exhausted and until economic depression, resulting from declining staple prices and rising production costs on worn-out soil, forced planters to choose between reform or ruin. But when the time came, it was slaveholders like Barbour, Edmund Ruffin, and John H. Cocke who generally took the lead. They sounded the call for reform, promoted agricultural societies and fairs, experimented with crop rotation and fertilizers, devised new farming methods, employed and sometimes designed improved implements, and in general demonstrated that slaves could be used successfully in a system of scientific, diversified farming. In demonstrating the superiority of this type of agriculture over the old system of monoculture, Barbour and a few other progressive farmers prepared the way for a new era of productive agriculture in Virginia.

Unlike many of his day who sensed but did nothing to arrest the decline of their society, Barbour tried to analyze its causes and advocated positive steps for recovery. A healthy agricultural sector was essential to republicanism, but so too was an educated citizenry, without which the country's free character could not be preserved. He was as much concerned about the dearth of educational opportunities as he was about agricultural decline. An educated and informed populace, he said, was the bedrock of republican government, "the indispensable guarantor of liberty."[54] He was deeply disturbed by Virginia's failure to provide better educational opportunities for its youth. Throughout his public life he sought to remedy this deficiency. While a member of the General Assembly he sponsored the Literary Fund and the Orange Humane Society, both devoted to improving elementary education. During his governorship he tried unsuccessfully to persuade the legislature to establish a state university.[55]

In the following years when he was in Washington, Barbour did not lose interest in establishing an institution of higher learning in Virginia. With Jefferson and others he pressed the legislature to act. Finally in 1819 it passed a bill creating the University of Virginia, but to Barbour's dismay no less than to Jefferson's, it declined to appropriate necessary construction funds. A protracted struggle for funding followed, in which Barbour played a major role. Against the formidable array of local interests and legislative obstinance, friends of the university were unable to make much headway. To Jefferson, who began to despair of ever establishing the institution on the grand scale he envisioned, progress seemed excruciatingly slow. When it appeared that opponents of the university would triumph, Barbour entered the contest. In the spring of 1823 he wrote, under the pseudonym Henry, a series of five open letters addressed to the people of Virginia that were published in the *Richmond Enquirer*.[56]

In the letters Barbour appealed to Virginians to support what he believed would be a "noble monument" to the people's liberality and vision. The legislature's "niggardly parsimony" in refusing to fund the university was highly detrimental to Virginia's future. He believed that for individuals no less than for nations, knowledge was power. Without it men were shackled slaves of ignorance. It was as essential to free governments as liberty was to personal happiness. Legislative myopia forced scores of Virginia's brightest and most talented young men to leave the state each year to pursue their education elsewhere, many of them never to return. In the race for distinction, he continued, Virginia was being badly outstripped by her sister states. Though once "the most conspicuous star in the constellation," she now emitted "but a feeble and secondary light."

Has your once proud spirit . . . become so abased? Is it indeed so low, as to behold without a blush, the degrading comparison which awaits us, when placed in the national councils by the side of our more fortunate brethren; whose intellectual acquirements, the offspring of a more liberal policy in their native states, shall throw us completely into the shade? Or, my fellow citizens, have you duly weighed the disastrous consequences of that ill-timed economy which threatens to deprive Virginia in the day of trial . . . of her Solomons in council and her Sampsons in the field? Are you content to weigh and accept as an equivalent, dollars and cents, against some future Henry, whose mind reared to power and grandeur by your fostering care, might, by his sublime eloquence, redeem a sinking state? Let me conjure you, then, to rise to the exigency of the occasion, and perform the part expected of you by your best and most enlightened citizens. . . . Endow [the university] so liberally as to invite the best talents of the old and the new world to preside over the education of your rising youth; throw open its doors to the rich and poor alike; fulfill the design of the fathers of the Literacy Fund, by attaching to the university ample funds for the maintenance of genius in poverty.[57]

Although Ritchie thought the force and eloquence of Barbour's letters, which he said had a strong effect on the public mind, would move the legislature to action, it still refused to provide the necessary funding.[58] In March 1824, however, it did empower the university's governing board to receive for the university's benefit $50,000 that the federal government owed the state for military expenditures during the War of 1812—provided that they could persuade Congress to recognize the claim. Jefferson quickly enlisted Barbour's support. Barbour subsequently introduced a reimbursement bill in the Senate, but the committee to which it was referred, chaired by Andrew Jackson, reported against it. Disappointed by this setback, Barbour renewed his effort at the next congressional session. This time he succeeded. On March 2, 1825, he exultantly wrote Jefferson that the bill had been approved. With these and additional monies from the Literary Fund the university was finally able to open its doors.[59]

Barbour continued to support the university actively. Although he declined an invitation to join its faculty as a professor of law, he did everything within his power over the years to promote its success.[60] It was, he believed, his generation's most valuable and enduring bequest to posterity, a living monument to learning. His efforts to encourage education and promote the diffusion of knowledge were not limited to Virginia, however. Colleges in other states benefited from his support, both privately and publicly. A number of them, including Princeton, acknowledged his contributions by making him an honorary member of their literary societies. The trustees of Columbian College, later George Washington University, formally thanked him for the "many acts of beneficence" and the "uniform influence" he exerted on behalf of higher education. In promoting knowledge, which he called "that living and everflowing fountain of happiness," Barbour revealed a progressive and enlightened spirit that did honor to his Jeffersonian heritage.[61]

In a society that in many ways had become static, Barbour was an advocate of change and progress. While he believed strongly in the basic virtues of his society, he was not blind to its faults. Unlike those of his contemporaries who loudly lamented Virginia's decline but did nothing to arrest it, he urged constructive action. He accepted as a basic article of faith the proposition that society, like the individual, was capable of improvement. Because human nature was malleable, both it and society could be shaped and bettered. It was the government's responsibility to use its power and resources to promote the social and economic changes on which progress depended. By supporting public education, encouraging agricultural improvement, and fostering economic development for all citizens, urban as well as rural, government could free individuals to achieve their full potential and thereby redeem society.

12

The Enduring Challenge

In retirement Barbour remained active politically. He kept abreast of public affairs, maintained close contact with many of the nation's political leaders, and was closely associated with the development of the country's second major party system. Many of his friends, regretting his retirement, unsuccessfully urged him to return to public life. John H. Pleasants, editor of the *Richmond Whig*, exhorted him to seek elective office again and "prepare to take post under President Clay in 1833."[1] Samuel L. Southard believed that if he remained before the public he would be the logical running mate for Clay in 1832. There was talk in 1829–1830 of running him for governor or perhaps for his old Senate seat.[2] Some Virginia Jacksonians, who may simply have been voicing the pride that most Virginians felt in eminent fellow Virginians, regardless of their politics, expressed the opinion that his experience and talents would be missed in government councils.[3] One of them, who thought that Barbour was still "the best debater I think I ever heard," wished there were some way to redirect his thinking and utilize his political talents in the Jackson government.[4]

But Barbour had little interest in seeking political office again and none whatever in joining the Jacksonian movement. Indeed, he abhorred the bitter partisanship and unseemly scramble for political place which, in his mind, epitomized Jackson's administraion. He was one of the government's most outspoken and inveterate critics. It was a terrible judgment on the times, he said, that an "impetuous military man, worn out by the toils, infirmities, and the natural progress of age, had been elevated to the country's highest elective office"—a position for which, "by education and character, he was totally unfit." As if this were not enough, the president had surrounded himself with a clique of "inept and designing politicans" motivated wholly by "blind cupidity and vindictive party spirit." Repulsed by Jackson's policies and conduct in office, Barbour feared that they would result in a "disastrous, perhaps a fatal, revolution."[5] With a rhetoric that became increasingly overwrought and strident as time wore on, he denounced Jackson as an imperious demagogue whose arbitrary actions and political excesses imperiled the republic. To help save the country from "fearful despotism" and restore the "reign of reason" of earlier years, he pledged his unremitting efforts.[6] In the course of his fight against Jacksonian democracy, Barbour emerged as a principal organizer and leader of the Whig party.

While he was yet in England, Barbour was warned by several Virginia correspondents that a "violent revolution" in American politics would follow Jackson's "Waterloo rout" of Adams. "The newspapers," wrote John H. Pleasants, "do not give any idea of the horror and detestation caused by the President's proscriptive system and despotic exercise of his power."[7] Having been forewarned, Barbour lost no time following his return to the United States in joining the lists against Jackson. In the late fall of 1829 he traveled to Richmond, where the constitutional convention was in progress, to consult with politicians from across the state on an appropriate political strategy for the next presidential election. The administration, he discovered, was very solicitous of its standing in the Old Dominion. Van Buren was conspicuously present, earnestly courting Ritchie and others. Barbour learned that although the "mania for Jackson" had not subsided, there was enough antiadministration sentiment to give substance to his hope that the Democratic party could be defeated in 1832, at least in Virginia. Both Clay and Calhoun had a significant following in the state, and there were intimations, weak but nonetheless hopeful, that major defections might soon occur from the Jackson ranks.[8]

In the months ahead that prospect brightened. Many Radicals who had supported the General in 1828 began to abandon him when it became apparent that he was more sympathetic to northern and western entrepreneurs than he was to conservative southern agrarians. John Floyd, who had worked hard for Jackson in 1828, led the way. Disappointed at not having been rewarded for his efforts with a government post, he turned against the administration with a vengeance that suggests how much Virginia politics had been infected by the new spoils contagion. Jackson, he ruefully observed, had thrown him overboard, spurning not only his own claim to office but also ignoring his recommendations for the appointment of others.[9] To John S. Barbour, a fellow worker for Jackson in 1828, he wrote: "I do not know how it is with you, [but] for myself, I must say, it has been like the apples of the Dead Sea—fair to the eye, but all bitterness and ashes within."[10] He went on to say that the president had not lived up to his advanced billing as "the most orthodox and thoroughbred republican of the Jefferson School," an advocate of states' rights and strict construction. "To my chagrin and mortification, every principle and every power claimed by Adams and Clay, as belonging to the Federal Government, has been acted on and claimed by President Jackson."[11]

There were other influential Virginians—William C. Rives, John S. Barbour, James Pleasants, Littleton W. Tazewell, and John Tyler—who, like Floyd, had supported Jackson in 1828 because they believed he would adhere more closely to the "Principles of '98" than would Adams. Although they acknowledged Jackson's limitations, they thought his administration, guided by such likely cabinet members as Philip Pendleton Barbour, Tazewell, and Van Buren, would chart a course acceptable to the Old Dominion.[12] When they were disappointed in this expectation, most of them joined Floyd and others in opposition. Senator Tazewell, disgusted by what he considered the incompetence of both the president and his cabinet, did so in 1831. Before the election of the next year, he was joined by former governor Pleasants, Senator Tyler, and Cong. John S. Barbour.[13]

To James Barbour, an astute student of Virginia politics, these defections may have come as no surprise, but they must certainly have pleased him. While the Democrats struggled with their divisive internal problems, both in Virginia and elsewhere, Barbour joined with other National Republicans in the search for a viable presidential candidate. Clay was his first choice. But he feared that public prejudice was too deeply entrenched against the Kentuckian to render his candidacy acceptable. Someone under whose standard National Republicans and anti-Jackson elements might unite was needed. If his nationalist posture could be modified and made acceptable to the South, Daniel Webster, he thought, might be such a man. With this in mind, he had several interviews with Webster in late 1829. From these and other talks with politicians in Virginia and elsewhere he concluded that the New Englander was less acceptable than Clay. "I learned that everywhere you alone promise anything like successful opposition," he wrote his old friend.[14] He went to work immediately thereafter to promote the Kentuckian's candidacy.

The Clay campaign was actively launched in Virginia in March 1830, when the *Lynchburg Virginian* declared that "for ourselves, we shall stand by Henry Clay for next President."[15] Later in the year the *Richmond Whig* added its endorsement, lauding Clay as "the most highly endowed public man, not of this country only, but of the age."[16] In the Shenandoah Valley and the western counties, where sentiment for the American System was strong, citizens held mass meetings and public rallies where they enthusiastically endorsed him.[17] Jacksonians were quick to challenge the Clay campaign. Ritchie took the lead. "Does Henry Clay hold one great constitutional principle in common with Virginia? . . . Will they prefer the Father of the American System to one who declares himself in favor of a temperate tariff? Will they prefer an active friend of the Bank of the United States and the Latitudinarian Advocate of Internal Improvements; they who have boasted so much of their attachment to States Rights?"[18] Other Jacksonians were equally zealous in defending the administration against its critics and working for the president's reelection.

Both National Republicans and Democrats found themselves confronting a growing Calhoun faction as the election approached. Many influential Virginians, finding neither Clay nor Jackson acceptable, turned to Calhoun, whose appeal as the new champion of states' rights they found irresistible. Thomas W. Gilmer tried unsuccessfully to establish a Calhoun paper in the state, and in March 1831 Gov. John Floyd honored the South Carolinian with a public dinner attended by many legislators. Indeed, Calhoun had greater support in the General Assembly than either of the other candidates.[19]

In Barbour's home district Calhoun had no significant following. The Orange electorate was about equally divided between Jackson and Clay partisans. Early in 1830, just as the campaign was beginning, a number of Clay supporters approached Barbour about running for the assembly, where his experience and influence, they argued, could be used to good advantage to advance Clay's candidacy. Though reluctant to stand, Barbour was finally persuaded to do so. He was opposed by a zealous Jacksonian, Thomas Davis, the son of Barbour's old friend and fellow legislator Isaac Davis, who was now also a Jacksonian. Davis campaigned actively throughout the county, charging his opponent with the political crime of being a part of the Adams administration and advocating the American System. Though he did not actively campaign, Barbour won by a narrow margin. In December 1830 he took his seat, but Davis contested the election. When the House Committee on Privileges and Elections, controlled by Jacksonians, indicated it would award the election to Davis, Barbour resigned. Although the committee's decision was based largely on partisan political considerations—one member justified its action on the ground that public sentiment in Virginia was against Barbour because of his nationalist views—Barbour accepted the verdict gracefully and without apparent malice.[20]

Though deprived of a political platform, Barbour campaigned actively for Clay, speaking at political gatherings throughout the state, corresponding with key political figures in Virginia and elsewhere, and using his personal influence to promote the National Republican ticket in every way possible.[21] Aware of Barbour's influence in Virginia, Jackson made indirect overtures to him, hoping to draw him away from Clay's camp into his own. On several occasions in Washington, the president expressed to Cong. John S. Barbour his desire to win James Barbour's good will. Congressman

Barbour tried to act as mediator. He urged his old law mentor to "banish all hostile feeling" toward the president who, he said, had taken the first step toward establishing friendly relations. "Whatever you may think of the old man," he wrote, "he is honest and frank. His expressions toward you indicate magnanimity." He went on to say that Jackson had defended Barbour against the criticism of a Virginia office seeker by "speaking very handsomely of you, [and] relating an anecdote of your fellow service in the Senate that was strongly complimentary."[22] But Barbour was unimpressed. He continued to view Jackson as "a dangerous man" whose policies he felt it his "solemn duty" to oppose.[23]

In the early months of the campaign Barbour and other National Republicans were optimistic about their chances. In May 1830, Daniel Webster wrote Barbour from Washington that as Congress adjourned their prospects for victory in 1832 were much improved. Public opinion, he believed, was turning against the administration. The anticipated veto of the Maysville Road bill would hurt Jackson in Maryland and the West.[24] Barbour was encouraged by this and other promising developments. Richard Rush, in response to Barbour's suggestion, promised to try to secure Clay's nomination at the Antimasonic convention that was to meet soon in Philadelphia. Governor Floyd's announcement not long afterward that he was "a sort of Clay man," along with the defection of such important Jacksonians as John S. Barbour, Tazewell, and Tyler, bolstered his hopes. Francis Brooke, who along with Barbour was one of Clay's principal campaign managers in Virginia, exultantly wrote Barbour in the summer of 1831 that public opinion in the Old Dominion was "settling in favor of Clay."[25]

But Clay was more realistic than either Barbour or Brooke. He realized that he had only scattered support in Virginia. The only hope he had of carrying his native state during this period of political realignment, he believed, lay in a fusion ticket that would unite all antiadministration elements.[26] Others shared his view, including John S. Barbour, who by the summer of 1831 had joined the opposition to Jackson. In July of this year Congressman Barbour urged James Barbour to throw his support to Calhoun. The South Carolinian, he wrote, was the "strategical candidate" for Virginia. If he could carry the Old Dominion and several other key southern states, the election might be thrown into the House of Representatives, where Jackson would be defeated. A choice between Calhoun and Clay might then be made. John Floyd also attempted unsuccessfully to lure Barbour into Calhoun's camp.[27]

Although Barbour was unreceptive to the scheme, Clay's friend Francis Brooke was intrigued by the idea. Clay himself considered it. If his southern supporters, he wrote Brooke, supported Calhoun and forced the election into the House, Jackson might indeed be defeated. He had no assurance, however, that the Calhoun party could be trusted at that point to withdraw their candidate and support him. Fearing that the plan had "sprung out of the desperate condition of Mr. Calhoun's prospects," he doubted it would produce the promised results.[28]

Barbour shared Clay's misgivings. Convinced that Virginia's opposition to Calhoun was too great to allow the fusion scheme to succeed, he feared that to run no Clay ticket, as the Calhoun party suggested, would be to give the state to Jackson. With a great many other Virginians, he deplored Calhoun's extreme states' rights views and believed that if Clay's name were withdrawn, his supporters, rather than vote for the champion of nullification, would support Jackson. Like Brooke, he could see "no prospect of compromise between nullification and the American System." The basic differences in political philosophy separating Clay and Calhoun made it virtually impossible for their followers in Virginia to unite. Nor was Duff Green's last-minute effort to persuade the two groups to unite on the Antimasonic candidate William Wirt more successful. The Clay following in Virginia, though small, was loyal. Barbour, along with other Clay men, turned a deaf ear to such siren songs.[29]

As always, personalities played an important role in the presidential election in Virginia, but political issues, more sharply delineated in 1832 than in most previous contests, played an even larger role. Jackson's veto of the Maysville Road and the bank recharter bills provided National Republicans with clear issues for conducting the campaign. Barbour did not hesitate to wage the campaign on the principles of the American System. His efforts did much to clarify the issues in Virginia and to keep the campaign in sharp focus.[30]

In an attempt to make Clay's nationalist principles more palatable to Virginians, the *Richmond Whig*, in November 1831, suggested that the Kentuckian stood for a revenue tariff with only incidental protection. It went on to proclaim his sensitivity to the rights of the states and to argue that there was nothing in his political principles contrary to those upheld by Virginia.[31] The article was misleading, however, for Clay had no intention of abandoning the tariff as a protective device nor, for that matter, of modifying his nationalist stand. The tariff position that he had laid down in Congress for his followers in December 1831 was essentially unchanged. To prevent the administration from extinguishing the public debt and distributing the Treasury surplus among the states, he proposed a reduction of the national revenue. But this was to be accomplished by removing duties on noncompetitive goods, not by a general reduction of duties, which would have destroyed protection.[32]

Barbour applauded Clay's tariff position and publicly defended it in the election campaign. He did not think his party should cloud the issues by trying, as the *Richmond Whig* had done, to portray Clay as a sympathizer of states' rights or as the advocate of a revenue tariff only.[33] Clay was a nationalist. He was the father of the American System, and he stood by its principles in this election. Barbour thought the public should know this and should choose among the candidates accordingly. The National Republicans, he said, advocated a tariff that would provide protection for manufacturing, internal improvements that would facilitate commerce and bind the sections together, and a national bank that would provide monetary stability. These were policies that would benefit all people and all sections. He endorsed them as heartily as Clay, and the National Republican party, win or lose, stood by them now.[34]

In December 1831 National Republicans, following the Antimasonic lead, held a national nominating convention in Baltimore. It was not an open convention like that of the Antimasonic party, which had nominated Barbour's old friend William Wirt. It was intended not to select a presidential candidate but rather to generate popular enthusiasm and support for Clay, who had already been decided upon. Barbour served as an elected delegate from the congressional district that included Orange. Bad weather delayed the meeting several days but did nothing to dampen the enthusiasm of the delegates once they arrived. Barbour, whose activities on behalf of the party and its nominee Clay were well known, was unanimously elected permanent chairman of the convention.[35]

Upon assuming the chair, Barbour thanked the delegates for their vote of confidence and then briefly addressed them on the challenge that awaited. President Jackson, he said, by his extraordinary and unprecedented use of executive power, had embarked upon a perilous course that threatened to destroy republican principles and constitutional government. The delegates' task was to defeat the party in power and to restore sound principles and leadership to the national government. He concluded with a predictable appeal for unity of action: "As yet, we may confide in the peaceful and sure remedy of republican concurrence to the people, a majority of whom I sincerely believe would hail with joy the redemption of the pledge . . . [Jackson made] to retire to private life at the expiration of his present term of service. The union and cooperation of this majority is all that is necessary to enforce . . . the fulfillment of his promise. Let us . . . set an example of the harmony so essential to success, and indulge a hope that its influence will reach the extremities of the republic."[36]

The convention itself was marked by all the harmony Barbour could have hoped for. When the time came to nominate a ticket, he read the delegates a letter he had recently received from Clay urging the convention not to endorse him perfunctorily but to choose the strongest candidate possible. The delegates were of one mind. By acclamation they nominated the Kentuckian. For a running mate they chose John Sergeant of Pennsylvania. This accomplished, Barbour delivered a long address that embodied the party's official platform. He excoriated Jackson for the highly partisan way in which he had employed patronage and executive powers, his harsh policy of Indian removal, his "wanton attack" on the federal judiciary, his wholesale removals from office, and his inconsistent and vacillating stand on such national questions as the tariff and internal improvements. He emphatically affirmed the principles of the American System and praised its principal author, Henry Clay, who, if elected president, would "promote the security and permanence of our political institutions" and would restore to the United States its former "greatness and glory." Following the conclusion of Barbour's "most able and eloquent" speech, which was repeatedly interrupted by cheers and applause, the convention adjourned in high spirits, and the delegates returned home to promote the ticket among their constituents.[37]

Over the next year Barbour and other National Republicans worked hard to secure victory. In February 1832, when the matter of nominating an electoral slate for the party in Virginia arose, Barbour consulted with Clay on an appropriate strategy. They decided after some weeks not to nominate a slate through the legislature but to wait until summer, when the party's central committee would either frame a ticket or call a state convention for that purpose.[38] The reason for this move was to withdraw pressure from the Democratic party and to "accelerate its tumbling to pieces.... The less active the Clay forces are, the less cohesion there will be among the Jackson men ..., for the Clay party acts as a hoop to preserve the cohesion of Jackson's followers."[39]

Barbour and other Clayites were undoubtedly delighted at the division that appeared in the Democratic party when it met in national convention in Baltimore in May 1832. That convention had assembled not for the purpose of choosing a presidential candidate, since Jackson had already been named by scores of state caucuses and conventions throughout the nation, but rather for the purpose of deciding on a vice-presidential candidate. Jackson's choice, of course, was Van Buren. But the "Little Magician" was unpopular in the South, and the strict constructionist southern wing of the party tried to block his nomination by advancing the name of Philip Pendleton Barbour. When the New Yorker won the nomination despite their opposition, the dissident faction launched an independent Barbour-Jackson ticket at a meeting in Charlottesville, Virginia, in June.[40]

Encouraged by this rupture in the Democratic party, National Republicans in Virginia decided to hold a state convention to promote their ticket and to choose a slate of electors. Ninety delegates representing seventeen of the state's twenty-one congressional districts met in the Valley town of Staunton in July 1832. As Barbour had done at the national convention six months earlier, the keynote speaker condemned Jackson for his proscriptive system, his abuse of patronage, his inconsistency on internal improvements, his evasiveness on the tariff, and his veto of the bank bill. Clay was lauded as the panacea for all the nation's ills. A strong electoral ticket on which Barbour was included was then chosen, after which the convention adjourned on the optimistic and hopeful note that victory was attainable.[41]

In August Barbour and his family accompanied Clay to White Sulphur Springs, where they spent several weeks vacationing.[42] The leisurely life at the popular resort spa afforded plenty of opportunities for political discussion, in which they undoubtedly engaged at length. The momentum the independent Barbour-Jackson ticket seemed to be gaining, much to the regret of Ritchie and other regular Democrats, must have been especially pleasing to them. Following his return from the springs, Barbour apparently tried quietly to encourage the movement by helping Duff Green distribute among influential Virginians a special issue of the *Telegraph* calculated to sow discord in the Democracy's ranks. He hoped that the division in the opposition party would combine with a recent franchise extension approved by the constitutional convention to give the state to National Republicans.[43] But his hopes were dealt a severe blow in October when Van Buren announced his opposition to a national bank, internal improvements, and a protective tariff.

Van Buren's announcement prompted Philip Pendleton Barbour to withdraw from the contest, allegedly in the interest of party unity. He may have acted from other considerations, however. Always more interested in law than in politics, he desired an appointment to the federal bench. Shortly after the independent ticket movement began, John S. Barbour, by now thoroughly disaffected with Jackson, predicted that "the fleshpots of Egypt will be put before him [Philip Pendleton Barbour] by the dirty currs that prowl the Executive Kennel."[44] The administration, he told James Barbour, would tempt Philip with a spurious offer of an appointment to the Supreme Court. If such an offer was made, it was not an empty one, for Jackson did name him associate justice in 1836. The collapse of the independent ticket demoralized James Barbour and other Clay partisans in Virginia, who now despaired of carrying the state—for good cause, as events soon proved. The recently enfranchised voters did not, as expected, go for Clay, and in the November election Jackson won easily, carrying the eastern and most of the western part of the state.[45]

Disappointed by this defeat, Barbour turned his energies once again to farming. During the next several years he maintained a fairly active political correspondence and continued to speak out against Jacksonian democracy, awaiting all the while the next presidential election, when he would again join with other antiadministration elements to try to defeat the incumbent party. He also decried the extreme states' rights views being championed now by Calhoun. When the South Carolina convention met in November 1832 and declared the tariff acts of 1828 and 1832 null and void, he denounced its action and vehemently denied that nullification was the progeny of the Virginia Resolutions and the *Report of 1800*. The support some Virginians gave South Carolina at this time tempted him to seek a better public platform from which to oppose the dangerous doctrines. Friends in the legislature approached him again about standing for governor, and a group in his congressional district attempted to persuade him to run for Congress on an antinullification ticket. In the end he declined to do either, but he continued to speak out against both Calhoun and Jackson.[46]

Although Barbour was unrelenting in his criticism of Jackson, he must have approved of the president's firm response to the nullification movement. His proclamation to the people of South Carolina declaring that nullification was unconstitutional, followed by the Force Act, which specifically authorized him to employ the army and navy to uphold federal law, left little doubt in anyone's mind that the president would take whatever steps were necessary to uphold the Constitution. Barbour had favored a similarly vigorous executive response when Georgia, a few short years before, had ignored Creek territorial rights and had openly defied federal authority. The nullification struggle too strongly resembled the earlier contest for him to withhold support from Jackson. At the same time, however, he criticized the president for upholding the Constitution in South Carolina but at the same time encouraging Georgians to disregard it in their contest with the Cherokees.[47]

The president's proclamation to the people of South Carolina was discussed in the Virginia legislature in the middle of December. It hit many administration supporters like a thunderbolt. Its argument, unequivocally nationalistic, lucid, and forceful, struck straight at the heart of the cherished states' rights doctrine. The Richmond correspondent for the *National Intelligencer* wrote that "perhaps the same space of time has never exhibited so marked a revolution of political sentiment as that which we have witnessed among Virginia State-Rights politicians since the receipt of the Proclamation."[48] The proclamation and the Force Act, by driving many Virginia Democrats from the party, gave impetus to the formation of the Whig party. That impetus would undoubtedly have been stronger had not the Compromise Tariff of 1833 made it unnecessary for the president to employ force against South Carolina.

Jackson's decision to remove government deposits from the national bank also had a pronounced political effect on Virginia. Barbour's view that this controversial action represented a dangerous and unprecedented exercise of executive power was shared by many fellow Virginians. Protest meetings were held in Richmond, Norfolk, Fredericksburg, and other places. A number of prominent Virginians, including Junto member William F. Gordon, until now a loyal Jacksonian, abandoned the administration and joined the swelling opposition ranks.[49] His was but one in a succession of defections from the Junto that grieved and alarmed Ritchie. "The Richmond Junto," exulted John S. Barbour, "are broken down and thrown into the most contemptible and spiritless minority. Even Ritchie and Peter V. Daniel are fawning and begging for quarter."[50] The states' rights faction, led by Floyd, Tyler, and Tazewell, stood solidly with Barbour and other nationalists in opposing the president's war on the bank. In the General Assembly the states' rights followers of Calhoun and the nationalist followers of Clay united to pass a resolution condemning his action. They then instructed their senators to work for a restoration of the deposits and to rectify the damage caused by their removal. William C. Rives, a loyal Jacksonian, resigned his seat rather than obey the instructions. Having forced his resignation, they appointed probank Benjamin W. Leigh to the vacancy and elected Tazewell to the governorship.[51]

In their common desire to save the country from Jackson's "executive usurpations and political vagaries," eastern states' rights and western nationalist groups in Virginia found the basis for an uneasy political alliance. The two groups, one supporting Clay and the other Calhoun, formed a coalition from which the Virginia Whig party sprang. Barbour considered the alliance unnatural and doubted that its incongruous elements could work together very long, but lacking a better alternative, he supported it in the hope that it could wrest political control from the Jacksonians.[52] This hope alone gave Virginia Whigs cohesion, for they were an amorphous group who differed sharply among themselves on questions of national policy. They were united only in their conviction that the president's use of patronage, his vetoes, his removal of bank deposits, his claim that he was coequal with Congress in representing the people's will and with the federal judiciary in upholding the Constitution as he interpreted it, were evidence of a tyranny which they must oppose.

That such Radicals as John Floyd, James Pleasants, Littleton W. Tazewell, and John Tyler joined the Whig party was an anomaly. Their nostalgia for agrarian simplicity and for the "Principles of '98" was far more compatible with the political philosophy of Democrats than with that of Whigs. The Democratic party was the heir of Jeffersonian agrarianism and the neo-

Physiocratic ideas of John Taylor. Its stance on the national bank, paper money, the public debt, and internal improvements, together with its drift toward free trade and laissez-faire, should have been much more appealing to them than the nationalistic Whig program. Their actions strongly suggest that some of them, like John Floyd, for example, were unprincipled opportunists whose desire for office outweighed every other consideration. Others simply looked upon the Whig party as a convenient vehicle for opposing a president and a party whose policies, in one way or another, had alienated them.[53]

Unlike his conservative Virginia colleagues, who never progressed beyond the political principles enunciated in 1798, Barbour moved predictably into the Whig party, which was a part of the political continuum that began but did not end for him in 1798. His espousal of strict construction and state sovereignty at that time had been consistent with his belief in limited government resting upon the freely given consent of the people and with his conviction that natural rights must be protected against would-be usurpers. With those principles and rights secured, his progression to a moderate nationalism after the War of 1812, to the American System in the 1820s, and, finally, to Whiggery, was a logical and natural one. He shared completely the Whig optimism regarding the future of the country. That optimism, closely linked to material development, was predicated on the assumption that endless progress was possible under an active, purposeful national government that provided centralized direction to social policy. The Whig program had a coherence and consistency of purpose based on a vision of the United States as an economically diverse, commercially powerful, and politically integrated nation. During his years in Washington, Barbour had helped delineate that vision. Economic growth, the principal instrument of progress, required the fostering hand of a central government in the form of subsidies for internal improvements, protective tariffs for industry, and a national bank for a stable currency. An economically diversified country, in which industry and commerce could take their place alongside agriculture, held out the greatest hope for the betterment of mankind. In short, he and other Whig leaders advocated a "positive liberal state" which, appealing to men's hopes rather than to their fears, promoted the general welfare in such a way as to provide economic, political, and educational opportunities that allowed citizens to realize their full potential. These, Barbour maintained, were "American Principles" which constituted "the creed of every high minded and patriotic" citizen.[54]

If the Whig program was essentially economic in form, it was because Whigs like Barbour believed that economic progress served as the basis for every other kind of progress. They had less faith in political and social than in material changes as the instruments of progress. Their opposition to Jacksonian policies stemmed, at least in part, from their belief that those policies stifled economic growth. A balanced, diversified economy offered the best hope of national prosperity. Despite his agrarian roots, Barbour believed in the complementarity of diverse interests, in the natural harmony of interests between all groups making up American society. Labor and capital were complements of one another. The farmer and urban worker, agriculture and commerce and industry, were parts of the whole. The good of one contributed to the good of all. Contemplating America's great natural resources, the energy and ingenuity of her people, and the rapid progress of technology, Barbour and other Whigs pressed toward their goals of endless progress and prosperity under economic capitalism. And Barbour did not think these goals were a denial of his agrarian roots. Adam Smith in his *Wealth of Nations*, which Barbour had studied, had posited that there was a natural order of economic development in which a nation, as it accumulated capital, would move beyond agriculture to a complex commercialism. Smith approved of the structural consequences of society's commercialization, for in economic change he saw a peaceful way of achieving social improvement. Barbour endorsed these views. Moreover, his own experience with a plantation economy offered convincing proofs of the value of diversification. He was firmly convinced that a strong economy providing a variety of employment for the nation's citizens would promote not only the Whig objectives of progress and prosperity but also, and equally important, the goal of raising the moral and intellectual level of society.[55]

The latter was of special importance to Whigs. They believed that society, like the individual, was capable of improvement through conscious effort. Although economic development promoted by the national government should be the primary vehicle for raising the moral and intellectual level of society, there were other ways of achieving the objective. Barbour's efforts to reform agriculture reflected his concern for social improvement and moral regeneration. Farmers, whose declining condition he viewed with deep anxiety, constituted the dominant element of society. There could be no progress, prosperity, or social redemption unless they, the backbone of the nation and custodians of its moral values, were themselves redeemed. The goal was to better people. His efforts to abolish dueling; his admonitions to his own children to eschew gambling, drinking, and other vices; his advocacy of public education, benevolent societies, prison reform, changes in debtor laws, and asylums for the insane, were all intended to improve the quality of life in America. A society that did not take advantage of opportunities for self-improvement, he said, was victimized by its own apathy.[56]

Although Whigs and Democrats were in basic agreement on the general democratic direction the country had taken, they differed significantly as to how the common goal of political democracy could best be reached. Jacksonians sought to enlarge opportunities for the individual by removing restrictions and special privileges originating in acts of government. By divorcing government from business and freeing people from the burden of taxation, they hoped to regain the "pristine purity" of the early republic. Their narrow view of the function of the national government prevented them from using the government for constructive ends. Whigs, on the other hand, believed that the function of government was to promote the general welfare actively, to administer the affairs of the nation according to its best judgment for the good of the whole and all parts of the whole. Thus taxes, instead of being reduced or eliminated, should be retained and spent on worthwhile improvements. Roads and canals, a protective tariff, and sound banking were worthwhile because they contributed to economic development beneficial to all classes in society. Whigs were not distrustful of wealth and commerce. They sought to promote them not by relying on the invisible forces of the marketplace but by centralized government planning. Economic development, public education, and self-improvement efforts would unleash individual potential and would help establish the equality of condition essential to preserving a sound and vigorous democracy.[57]

Virginia Whigs made their first bid for power in 1834 when they challenged Democrats for control of the General Assembly. Because the next legislature would select a successor to Senator Leigh, whose term expired in 1835, both parties considered the contest vitally important. Barbour campaigned actively for his party's candidates in Orange and neighboring counties. The Whigs won an impressive victory, the consequences of which were predictable. The Whig legislature reelected Leigh to the Senate and deposed Jackson's chief spokesman in Virginia, Thomas Ritchie, from his position as public printer, a lucrative appointment he had held for almost twenty years. "The times," the editor ruefully complained, "are out of joint in politics."[58]

As Barbour knew all too well, the common hatred of Jackson that gave rise to the Whig coalition was a narrow and shaky foundation on which to build a political party. There was little chance, once it came to acting upon any substantive issue such as the national bank or internal improvements, that the incompatible elements making up the party would be able to agree. They were unable to do so, and after a year in power, they were ousted by a determined Democratic majority led by Ritchie and William C. Rives. The Democrats retained control of the legislature for three years. Despite his pessimism about being able to weld the disparate Whig elements into a working party, Barbour was bitterly disappointed by this reversal, temporary though it was. "Since our retrograde movement," he wrote Clay, "I have desponded almost to despair." The unscrupulous methods Ritchie and the dominant party used in winning the election, together with their success in "obscuring the real political issues" and concealing the "designing character" of Jackson's hand-picked successor Van Buren, "seem to me to render our scheme of self-government highly doubtful."[59]

Having regained control of the assembly, Democrats moved to force the state's Whig senators, Leigh and Tyler, to resign. This they attempted to accomplish by instructing them to vote for Thomas Hart Benton's Expunging Resolution. Ever since the Senate, led by Clay and Calhoun, censured the president in 1834 for removing bank deposits, the administration had been awaiting a chance to vindicate itself. Benton's successful resolution expunging the Senate's action from the official record accomplished that end. Before he received the legislature's instructions, which Governor Tazewell, himself a Whig, refused for a while to transmit because he thought they were unconstitutional, Tyler sought Barbour's counsel. Should he resign from the Senate if he could not in conscience obey the instructions? Barbour thought he should not. The instructions, he said, were a partisan attempt to force him from office. "However sacred instructions may be held when honestly and properly given," he wrote, they should not be honored when they were intended for "factious and fatal purposes to break down the Senate." Because the motive of the Virginia assembly had been to make the Senate "a servile body to the executive, and thus give him absolute power, I would not yield . . . , but standing on the Constitution, I would boldly appeal to the people, and disclose the means and ends of the [Democratic] party."[60]

From other Whig leaders Tyler and Leigh received divided counsel. William F. Gordon and Francis Brooke agreed with Barbour that they should not resign, but John H. Pleasants thought they should. If they disobeyed the instructions and refused to step down, said the influential editor of the *Richmond Whig*, the opposition party would immediately and loudly castigate them for disregarding the will of the people. The results for the Whig party would be disastrous. Their hopes of regaining control of the state would "be annihilated at once." All were agreed, however, that they should act in concert whatever they did. Barbour wrote Tyler that "should you and Mr. Leigh divide in your course, it will be the most fatal shock that the Whig party will have received."[61]

Events proved Barbour right. Senator Tyler, after deciding that he could not obey the instructions, resigned and was immediately replaced by the loyal Jacksonian William C. Rives. Leigh, on the other hand, though he disregarded the instructions and voted against the Expunging Resolution, refused to step down. Whigs were thus in the awkward position of having to defend Tyler for resigning and Leigh for not doing so. Quite a few Whigs, including Pleasants, who had advised both to resign, criticized them for not standing together.[62] But the embattled Whigs tried to make the most of a bad situation. Soon after Tyler returned to Virginia they held a dinner honoring him and Leigh, at which toasts were drunk to both men. The irony of the situation did not escape the ever-vigilant Ritchie, who surmised that the toasts offered went as follows:

> John Tyler: His obedience to the requisitions of Legislature, by *resigning*, does honor to his principles.
> Benjamin Watkins Leigh: His firmness in *resisting* the instructions of the Legislature does honor to his principles.
> Mr. Tyler: Honor to him! because he could not with honor retain his seat.
> Mr. Leigh: Honor to him! because he could not with honor relinquish his seat.[63]

The contradictory positions of Leigh and Tyler were simply symptomatic of the conflicting elements within the party itself. The difficulty of reconciling what Barbour feared was irreconcilable explains the anomalous strategy Whigs adopted in the presidential election of 1836.

Divided by fundamental political differences that made it impossible for them to agree upon either a national platform or a single presidential candidate, the Whig party did not hold a national convention in 1836. The strongest faction in the coalition, the National Republicans, in the main favored William Henry Harrison, though in Massachusetts they favored Daniel Webster. Hugh Lawson White of Tennessee, a strict constructionist and antibank man, was the choice of most southern Whigs. By running Webster in the Northeast, Harrison in the West, and White in the South, Whigs hoped to force the election into the House, where presumably they would unite on a single candidate and would defeat Van Buren.[64]

Although White enjoyed the backing of most southern Whigs, in Virginia he was supported only by the states' rights faction. That group, most of whom had been Calhoun partisans in 1832, met in caucus in Richmond in February 1836 and nominated the Tennessean, who until very recently had been a Jacksonian, and named Tyler as his running mate.[65] Ritchie called the caucus "a piebald Coalition" of every hue and description— "a complete Noah's ark of beasts, birds, fishes, and animals of every species . . . , all piggling together on the same truckle bed" for the purpose of defeating the administration.[66] Whigs in the western part of the state later held a convention of their own and nominated Harrison and Tyler. This division among the Virginia Whigs contributed heavily to their failure to carry the state.

Barbour was not happy with either of the men. He did not like White's politics, and he thought Harrison lacked presidential stature. His choice was Clay. But he recognized that the Kentuckian could never carry Virginia, where his stand on the bank alone, to say nothing of internal improvements or the tariff, made him anathema. "I am quite satisfied," he wrote Clay in the summer of 1835, shortly before the ever-hopeful presidential aspirant withdrew his name from consideration, "that no candidate can succeed against him [Van Buren] here, not withstanding his unpopularity, unless it is one maintaining the favorite doctrine of the State, especially one who has been opposed, and is now opposed to, the Bank. . . . Opposition to this institution is now a fixed maxim in the political creed of this State, as much so as the undivided Godhead with a Mohammedan."[67] The orthodoxy of White's political principles, Barbour continued, made him the strongest candidate they could offer. If he carried the state and thereby enabled the Whigs to regain control of the legislature, there would be some consolation in that. The subsequent nomination of Harrison by the western faction of the party, however, destroyed whatever hopes Whigs had of achieving this objective.

Barbour questioned the wisdom of the strategy of running three different candidates on the national ticket, fearing it would provide Democrats with ammunition to use against them. Democratic leaders, he predicted to Clay, would tell "their creatures that the Whigs are playing false; they wish to divide Jacksonians, so as to bring the election into the House (of which they express a holy horror), with a view to elect Webster, yourself, or some other Whig. It is this which constitutes the most formidable obstacle to our success in this state."[68] His prediction proved to be accurate. Ritchie lost no time in sounding the alarm. The "piebald faction," he warned, was plotting to thwart the people's will by running three favorite sons and forcing the election into the House, where the nation's popular favorite, Van Buren, would be defeated.[69] He touched a responsive chord that evoked memories of the corrupt bargain of 1824. The effectiveness of the Democratic campaign, together with the fatal Whig divisions, resulted in a fairly decisive victory for Van Buren. Virginia Democrats, in addition to carrying the state for the Little Magician, retained firm control of the legislature. Having predicted the outcome of the election, Barbour could hardly have been surprised by Van Buren's victory. Nevertheless, he was disappointed, especially by his party's defeat in the state elections.

Barbour was disappointed and saddened by several other events that occurred during the presidential campaign. One concerned the failure of a Florida plantation he had acquired several years earlier and had given to his oldest son, James, in the hopes of establishing him as a successful planter. The venture had begun with great hopes. The 640 fertile acres on the Ancilla River near Tallahassee were well suited to sugar culture, and the fifty slaves and generous financing he advanced his son for building and running the plantation were more than adequate. But a combination of bad weather and poor management forced Barbour to abandon the operation after three years. Once again his hopes for his son, who had failed in so many things, were dashed.[70]

The other event that saddened Barbour, though in a different way, was the death in late June 1836 of his neighbor and mentor James Madison. Their relationship spanning forty years had been a close and particularly enriching one for Barbour. Although they never engaged in an extensive correspondence, in part because their proximity as neighbors made it unnecessary, Barbour frequently visited and talked with Madison when they both were in Orange. He venerated the older statesman, whose counsel and advice he valued and whose life and political principles were a worthy model for his own. On June 29 he served as a pallbearer when Madison's body was laid to rest in the family burial plot near Montpelier. Soon thereafter he delivered a moving tribute to his deceased friend at a well-attended memorial service at Orange Courthouse, and in the months following he helped Dolley settle the estate.[71]

After the unsuccessful Whig bid for power in 1836 Barbour spent less time with politics and more at farming. During the next several years he devoted a great deal of effort to lobbying legislators and other state officials in the hopes of persuading them to enact the reform measures that the Virginia Agricultural Convention, over which he had presided, had recommended in 1836. While he was occupied with other matters, Barbour's Whig associates continued the fight. Their efforts were rewarded in 1838 when they won the state elections. Benefiting from a growing antiadministration sentiment resulting from the Panic of 1837 and from Van Buren's monetary policy, they defeated the demoralized Democrats and regained control of the General Assembly. Encouraged by this victory, which he saw as the harbinger of better days, Barbour resumed his political activities, speaking at numerous Whig political rallies throughout the state and preparing for the presidential election of 1840.[72]

In September 1839 Barbour met with other Virginia Whigs in a state convention at Staunton. A large and enthusiastic delegation heartily approved resolutions condemning the policies of the Van Buren administration and overwhelmingly endorsed Clay and Nathaniel P. Tallmadge of New York for president and vice-president. Delegates from each of the twenty-one congressional districts were chosen to represent Virginia at the national convention, and Barbour and Benjamin W. Leigh were elected delegates at large.[73]

Barbour was undoubtedly pleased with the results of the convention, particularly with the nomination of Clay, who had made himself more acceptable to Virginians in recent years by temporizing his stand on the bank, internal improvements, and the tariff.[74] After the convention concluded its business Barbour returned home and began to prepare for the national convention which was to meet in early December 1839 at Harrisburg, Pennsylvania.

When Barbour arrived in Harrisburg, a large and enthusiastic delegation had already assembled. He was warmly greeted by old friends such as Clay and Tyler, but most of the delegates were younger men who, relatively speaking, were newcomers to the political scene. Most of them knew Barbour, at least by reputation, and looked upon him as something of a senior statesman in the party. They acknowledged his leadership in the party and rewarded him for his long struggle against Jacksonians by electing him permanent chairman, or president, of the convention. Barbour took his chair on the dais at the front of the convention hall. When the applause subsided, he delivered a brief address not unlike the one he had given at the National Republican convention at Baltimore eight years earlier. In what one observer called a "beautiful and lively manner" marked throughout by "eloquence and patriotism," he enumerated the failures of the Van Buren administration and warned that the unresolved problems facing the nation, attributable to the dangerous and capricious policies of the Democrats during the past twelve years, threatened to destroy the country. During the course of his philippic against the administration, he was frequently interrupted by "repeated, loud, and spontaneous bursts of applause."[75]

Following the address the convention turned to the nomination of a presidential candidate. Whig leaders were aware that the outcome of the approaching election depended largely upon their choice of its standard-bearers. If they chose wisely, they stood an excellent chance of defeating Van Buren. Foremost among the candidates being considered were Clay, Harrison, and Gen. Winfield Scott. Barbour favored Clay, as he had in 1832 and again in 1836. Indeed, the Kentuckian was the choice of most of the southern delegates. But many northern Whigs, among them the astute New York politician Thurlow Weed, feared that Clay lacked availability. He could not carry Pennsylvania and New York, and without the votes of those two states he could not win the election. In the end both he and Scott were passed over for Harrison.[76]

Harrison's nomination was accepted with the outward semblance of unanimity. Among Clay's supporters, however, especially those from the South, there was a feeling of bitter disappointment, some of which stemmed from their fear of Harrison's position on slavery. They considered conducting a floor fight to reject him and to nominate Scott, a slaveholder, instead. They believed that New York and several other states that had initially supported Scott would go along with their plan. When several leaders of the movement called on Barbour one morning before breakfast, he advised them strongly against the scheme. He told them that he too was disappointed that Clay had not been nominated, but he could not support a move that he believed would be disastrous. "No," he admonished, "it will not do to reject General Harrison now; the people will not understand how he failed to be nominated after he had been chosen upon full deliberation by the states in the convention; just as they did not understand how Jackson failed to be elected by the House of Representatives after having obtained the highest vote in the electoral college." The convention, he said, should give its unanimous vote to Harrison. The party's only hope of success was to stay with the candidate already named.[77]

Before the assembly later in the day Barbour assumed the role of pacificator. With the hope of uniting the party fully behind its candidate, he addressed the delegates, saying that while many would be disappointed that their favorite had not been selected, the party's good required that they be united. Although he himself had preferred Clay, he yielded gracefully to majority opinion. Expressing complete confidence in the wisdom, talents, and patriotism of Harrison, he promised to do everything in his power to promote his success and urged the other delegates to do likewise.[78]

With Harrison's nomination accomplished, the convention proceeded to choose his running mate. There was general agreement among party leaders that the second place on the ticket, in order to give it balance, should go to someone from a slaveholding state. John Tyler, who was well known to Whig voters because he had been on the Whig ticket with Hugh Lawson White in 1836, and whose warm advocacy of Clay at the present convention would perhaps mollify some of the Kentuckian's diappointed backers, was an obvious possibility. Tyler had strong backing from all the state delegations except Virginia's. The Virginia convention earlier in the year had nominated not Tyler but Tallmadge for vice-president, and the Virginia delegation was not enthusiastic about having the doctrinaire states' righter on the national ticket. Leigh, a member of the convention's nominating committee, favored Barbour over any other Virginian. But Barbour was not interested in the nomination. Tyler was finally chosen, having been endorsed by all of the state delegations except Virginia's, which withheld its vote. With the addition of Tyler's name to the ticket, the work of the convention was complete. After an "appropriate and eloquent" address by Barbour it adjourned, though not with the "utmost harmony and good feeling" reported.[79]

That a semblance of unity and harmony was maintained during the troubled convention was owing in no small part to Barbour's efforts. His presence and personal influence had a moderating effect, and he was instrumental in steering southern delegates away from what may well have proven a disastrous course. Of his role at the meeting, Henry W. Hilliard, a Clay-Tyler delegate from Alabama, wrote: "The choice of Governor Barbour as president was felicitous in every way, personally, geographically, and politically. As a presiding officer he was transcendently fine. In the whole course of a long public service I have never seen a man who could rival him as a presiding officer of a public assembly. His person was commanding, his presence distinguished, his bearing dignified and stately, and his sonorous voice controlled the large body . . . with resistless effect."[80] Age had been kind to Barbour. There had been no diminution of his mental faculties, and his physical presence, in the opinion of many, was simply enhanced by the years, which had mellowed but not impaired his appearance.[81]

In the election of 1840 Whigs borrowed the Democratic appeal to the masses. Fired by the prospect of victory, they conducted a vigorous and enthusiastic campaign which, though colorful, was replete with blatant demagoguery. Throughout the country, Harrison, "the Cincinnatus of the West," was portrayed as the friend of the common man, and the log cabin, the coonskin, and hard cider became the symbols of a spurious Whig democracy. In contrast to the simple farmer from North Bend, Van Buren was portrayed by his opponents as an aristocratic Easterner who wore corsets, slept in French beds, put cologne on his beard, and ate with gold spoons from silver plates—the symbol of executive usurpation, tyranny, and haughty aristocracy.[82]

Virginia had its share of Tippecanoe clubs and log cabins. Throughout the state political rallies were held where log cabins bedecked with coonskins and slogans were conspicuously displayed. Whigs joined heartily in singing campaign songs praising their log cabin candidate and ridiculing "Sweet Sandy Whiskers."[83] Barbour entered actively into the contest in Virginia, attending numerous rallies and conventions, often as a principal speaker. In July he and William Cabell Rives, a recent defector from the Democratic ranks, addressed a Whig rally at Fredericksburg.[84] A short time later, at a rally in Staunton, he spoke at great length defending Whig principles and denouncing the "executive usurpations" of Jackson and Van Buren. Barbour's speech on this occasion, said his Democratic opponent, William Smith, later governor of Virginia, was the best he ever heard from any man.[85] In other towns such as Winchester, Charlottesville, Richmond, and Martinsburg, he took part in political meetings, being credited in the latter town with "the most magnificent burst of eloquence to which the times have given birth."[86] The Whig campaign in Virginia reached its climax in early October when the party convened at Richmond to choose a slate of electors. Along with Leigh, Rives, John Minor Botts, and other Whig leaders, Barbour attended this convention, which had as its distinguished speaker the "godlike" Webster.[87]

Barbour received many invitations to speak at Whig rallies and conventions in neighboring and distant states, including Pennsylvania, Maryland, North Carolina, and Massachusetts. Bostonian Robert C. Winthrop wrote that "your presence would be particularly welcome to the people of New England, to say nothing of the delight with which they would listen to a voice so well known in the annals of popular eloquence."[88] Similarly, a group of North Carolina Whigs wrote: "It would afford us particular gratification to welcome to our State . . . one who, as it were, stands as a connecting link between the present and the past, who has lived through some of the most eventful periods of his country's history and who has ever been found battling for the rights of man."[89] Because declining health would not permit him to travel long distances, he declined all out-of-state invitations, restricting his activities instead to Virginia.

Despite the vigorous campaign Barbour and other Whigs conducted, Van Buren carried Virginia. Harrison and Tyler carried many of the Tidewater counties, most of the central and southern Valley counties, and about half of the western counties. Van Buren carried most of the Piedmont section, including Barbour's home county, the upper Valley counties, and most of southwest Virginia.[90] Despite their defeat in Virginia, Whigs won a decisive national victory, though events would soon prove it to be a Pyrrhic one. The party was too diverse, too lacking in cohesion, to withstand the strains of office.

Shortly after the election Barbour traveled to Baltimore and Philadelphia to seek medical advice. Throughout his long active life, except for an extended illness of several months in the fall of 1825 and another in 1828, he had enjoyed good health. But in 1839 it began to fail, and his exertions during the presidential campaign of that year weakened him. Physicians in Philadelphia told him that his illness was incurable.[91] Rather stoically, he wrote Lucy: "As I suspected, my case is without cure, owing to an increase in the prostate gland of some 1 or 200 percent. Not much can be done—leeches to be applied—medication will ease discomfort."[92] He had but a short time to live.

Until his death sixteen months later, Barbour remained active. His final days were saddened by the illness of his oldest daughter, Lucy Maria, who would die barely a year after him, and by the sudden death in February 1841 of his brother, Philip.[93] Despite their political differences, which were substantial, the two brothers had not allowed the bitter party battles of the last decade and a half to separate them. Barbour grieved at the loss as old friends and neighbors, many of whom he knew would gather at his own funeral, assembled at Frascati, a short distance from Barboursville, to pay their last respects to the distinguished jurist.

After assisting in settling his deceased brother's estate, Barbour traveled to Washington to attend Harrison's inauguration. In an address to a Whig assembly just before the ceremony, he gave no indication of his illness. His speech, according to an observer, was characterized by all "the vigorous thought and fervid eloquence" of earlier years.[94] In the following months his health seemed to improve. In December he embarked on a trip to Baltimore by way of Richmond, where he was to preside over the Agricultural Convention. Exhausted by the convention, he was compelled to return to Barboursville. Throughout the winter he was confined to bed, but by late spring he was feeling strong enough to visit the Virginia springs. His condition worsened in late May, however, and continued to decline until the morning of June 7 when, after an uneasy night of fitful consciousness during which he was barely aware of the family and friends at his bedside, he quietly passed away. Several days later his body, borne by family and servants to the family burial plot nearby, was laid to rest in a simple ceremony attended by a large group of neighbors and acquaintances.[95]

Barbour's death was noted by both state and national newspapers. Some simply printed short obituaries; others carried long eulogies.[96] Of the many public pronouncements, days of mourning, and eulogies, both public and private, in his honor, perhaps none was more to the point than the one attributed to John Quincy Adams. Virginia congressman Alexander H. H. Stuart was alone with Adams in Washington when the former president read a notice of Barbour's death in a local newspaper. Deeply moved, Adams, following a long silence, turned to Stuart and said: "I have been connected with this government in one way or another, almost from its foundation to the present hour. I have known personally nearly all the great men who have been connected with its administration, and I can safely say that I have rarely known a wiser man, and never a better man than James Barbour."[97] It was a fitting tribute to one who had served his country wisely and well.

13

James Barbour:
An Appraisal

*B*arbour's death marked neither the end of an era nor the passing of a generation. The revolutionary generation that he esteemed so much— Washington, Jefferson, Madison, and others—had already passed. The second generation of independent Americans, his own, was fast giving way to younger men, though such illustrious figures as Adams, Clay, Webster, and Calhoun, with whom he had joined to turn the dark night of 1812 into a bright and promising morning, would continue on the political stage a few years longer. His death simply signaled the quiet passing of one who, born to the age of Jefferson, imbibed deeply of its faith, believed firmly in its ideals, and labored untiringly to translate its promise into reality.

Barbour does not stand in the first rank of great men his age produced. But among the second rank, composed of individuals whose activities gave them national stature if not preeminence, he is entitled to a place of prominence. His contributions were notable. In many of the memorable debates on national policy, debates that vitally affected the political, social, and economic future of the country, he played a major role. Throughout an era of momentous change, an uncertain period of transition from sail to steam, from carriage to canal and railroad, he exerted a steady and constructive influence in national councils. His was an optimistic and progressive voice at a time when such voices, at least from the South, were rare. His unshakable faith in the future, and his abiding concern about the quality of life for all Americans, not just those from his native South, qualify him for a place of honor among those men and women whose contributions to their country's good transcend time and place.

Both his and future generations, whether living in the North, South, or West, benefited ultimately from the agricultural reform movement to which he contributed so much. His proposals for an agricultural professorship and experimental farm at the University of Virginia, and for a state board of agriculture to promote scientific farming, foreshadowed our whole national system of agricultural education. In his belief that the ideal society was composed of farmers, and that small farms tilled by independent yeomen were the foundation of the republic, he reflected the values of his agrarian age. To him, farming was more than a means of livelihood. It was the primary source of those traits and virtues most compatible with liberty and self-government. It was essential to the preservation of republican society and institutions, therefore, that farmers be freed from the shackles of ignorance and tradition that bound them to unremitting toil but denied them the fruits of their labor. In pledging himself to the task of bridging the gap between ideal and reality, he was simply reaffirming those values of the agrarian society of which he was so inseparably a part. In promoting agricultural reforms that would benefit not only fellow Virginians but countrymen everywhere, he was, in a sense, espousing the cause of the common man, for the United States in 1830, almost as much as in 1800, was a nation of small farmers.

In other interests and commitments that occupied him in public life, Barbour reflected the liberal spirit of his age: in his humanitarian efforts to promote public education, both at the elementary and university levels, and to make it accessible to bright but impoverished youth; in his attempts to abolish dueling; and in his successful endeavor to abolish imprisonment for debt. His glaring omission, where social issues are concerned, related to slavery. In the abstract he opposed the peculiar institution. He saw it as a serious blight on the American character, a notable failure to achieve fully the ideals of the Revolution. But at the same time he viewed it as an economic necesssity for the South. In this respect he was never able to reconcile ideal to reality. Like others of his generation, he was active in the colonization movement, but he never emancipated his own slaves. He unsuccessfully urged Madison to free his, saying that such an act would endear him to posterity, which would remember him, along with Jefferson, as the foremost advocate of individual freedom and the rights of man.[1] Barbour's failure to make the leap of faith reflected both personal and societal shortcomings. To his credit, Frances Cornelia, one of his two children who lived to see the Civil War, possessed the courage to act on the liberal faith her father transmitted and freed her slaves during the turbulent 1850s.[2]

Politically Barbour embodied the best of both the spirit and the practice of Jeffersonian democracy. He was committed to the basic principles of the freedom and happiness of man—above all, to personal liberty. The role of government, he believed, was to preserve liberty and protect property, which alone could guarantee to man the social stability and individual opportunities that were due his limitless potential. Since men are created equal and live in society, to promote the social welfare was also to promote individual welfare. Unlike many of his day, he recognized that the means of securing the ends of government did not remain constant. What was appropriate in 1798 was inappropriate in 1816 or 1826. That he was able in the course of a lifetime to respond in a politically realistic way to changing national conditions and expectations, without losing sight of republican objectives or abandoning his basic Jeffersonian faith, did honor to his party, to his country, and to his age.

Throughout his life Barbour acted from political principles that were dynamic rather than static. He was pragmatic, not dogmatic, a realistic politician who fully understood that in a free society politics is the art of the possible. Politically he avoided both radical and reactionary extremes, recognizing that American democracy combined a basic faith in man's capacity for self-government with an experimental process. While the goals were fixed, the process itself, because it was experimental, must remain flexible. In this conviction he showed the marked influence of Madison. Many of his Old Republican colleagues, including his brother, Philip Pendleton, acted from other influences. These men looked principally to John Taylor, a man who never overcame his Antifederalist beginnings, for political inspiration and constitutional arguments to use in defending a fast-evaporating society to whose values they were irrevocably committed. They could only rail at the engines of change and look back wistfully to a nostalgic golden age which in fact existed only in their imaginations. Barbour was like them in some ways. His roots, his language, and some of his sentiments, like theirs, were those of the romantic. But his political actions were those of the practical-minded politician, not of the romantic ideologue. The romantic mode of mind offered no solutions to the real problems of his day, problems which he earnestly sought to solve. The essential difference between Barbour and his conservative contemporaries was that for him the philosophy with which they all began was an organic, evolving frame of reference, not sacred dogma. His political philosophy grew and changed to meet altered realities; theirs did not.

Beginning his political career at a time when repressive Federalist laws imperiled basic freedoms of speech and press, Barbour feared consolidated government as much as did his doctrinaire Virginia colleagues. He did not think that the United States was immune to those dangers that had destroyed democratic republics of the past. Until the Hamiltonian political engine had been harnessed and the free republican character of the government firmly fixed, he stood by the principles enunciated in the Virginia Resolutions and the *Report of 1800*. His commitment to them was less ideological than practical: he believed they were the surest guarantors of the liberty the republic had been created to preserve. Fifteen years of experience in Virginia government, coterminous with the benign republican rule of Jefferson and Madison and the disappearance of the Federalist threat to personal freedom, convinced him that the old creeds were inadequate for the nation that emerged from the War of 1812. He clearly recognized that the new nation was no longer the simple agrarian republic he and others had idealized in 1800. A nascent industrial order, buttressed by a political nationalism inherited from Hamilton, had made its appearance and would soon begin to challenge the weakened but not defunct agrarian order. Of agrarian primacy he was by birth and practice an advocate, and to the end of his days agriculture remained the occupation nearest to his heart. But in the newly emerging order he saw much that was indispensable to the national welfare. He did not think the new banking and industrial interests could or should be ignored. Strong as his loyalties to the agrarian life were, he believed that his role as a public servant in national government was to advance the interests of all the people. Accepting the pragmatic premise that changed conditions require new responses, and believing that the inflexible creeds of the Old Re-publicans were inadequate for governing a country that had changed dramatically since 1800—in size, in constituency, and in expectations—he embraced nationalism.

The goal had not changed. It remained the preservation of the liberty that would enable men throughout the country to realize their full potential by capitalizing on expanded economic, social, and political opportunities. Only the means of achieving it had changed. If a decentralized government of limited powers seemed to provide the surest means in 1798, a strong Union whose cooperative power would release new energies and opportunities for individual fulfillment provided a better means in 1816. Political independence, without which there could be no individual liberty, could be secured only by economic independence. On this ground he advocated a national bank, internal improvements, a strong navy and navigation policy to encourage commerce, and a moderate protective tariff. Although the Missouri Controversy caused him to retreat from his nationalist position, it was a temporary retreat only. As a member of the Adams government a few years later he favored an enlarged nationalism in which the central government would employ its powers and resources to promote the economic life and the internal development of the nation. For almost two decades, until his death, he held to this position.

In responding to the new and sometimes baffling challenges of his age, Barbour, far more than most of his southern contemporaries, acted from national rather than sectional commitments. To the perpetuation of the Union he was no less pledged than to the preservation of personal liberty, for he believed the two were synonymous. Whenever the Union was imperiled, as it was by the Missouri Controversy, he was among the first to urge the necessity of compromise. In politics he, like Clay, was a pacifica-tor. He believed that mutual accommodation and political compromise were the basic working tools of democracy. His efforts during the crisis of 1820 to reconcile clashing interests and to temper the reaction of angry constituents to the compromise once it was obtained, served his country well.

Borne forward by the vision of a strong, undivided country that shel-tered under its standard a free, happy, and prosperous people, Barbour pointed the way to an affluent and enduring nation. He believed that North and South, agriculture and commerce and industry, could coexist. Old creeds and philosophies would have to be modified, and mutual conces-sions among the various interests and sections would be required, but the great experiment in self-government need not founder on the rocks of sectionalism. Unfortunately, the generation that followed him ignored his moderate voice and wise counsel. Had his conciliatory spirit survived into the 1850s, the Civil War could have been avoided. For when compromise failed, the Union failed. Nevertheless, Barbour deserves to be remem-bered as a man whose defense of personal freedom, and of the Union that promised the fullest measure of human happiness, contributed to the progress of mankind.

Abbreviations and
Short Forms

Annals	U.S. Congress, *Annals of Congress*
ASPIA	U.S. Department of State, *American State Papers,* Class 2, *Indian Affairs*
ASPMA	U.S. Department of State, *American State Papers,* Class 5, *Military Affairs*
BP NYPL	James Barbour, Papers, New York Public Library
BP UVA	Barbour Family, Papers, University of Virginia
CVSP	Commonwealth of Virginia, *Calendar of Virginia State Papers*
DMGB	U.S. Department of State, Despatches from the United States Ministers to Great Britain
Duke	William R. Perkins Library, Duke University, Durham, N.C.
EC	Commonwealth of Virginia, Executive Communications
ELB	Commonwealth of Virginia, Executive Letter Book
EP	Commonwealth of Virginia, Executive Papers
IOLB	U.S. Department of War, Indian Office, Letter Books
JB	James Barbour
JHD	Commonwealth of Virginia, *Journals of the House of Delegates of the Commonwealth of Virginia*
LC	Library of Congress, Washington, D.C.
NYPL	New York Public Library, New York City
OCD	Orange County, Deed Books
OCL	Orange County, Land Books
OCM	Orange County, Minute Books
OCO	Orange County, Order Books
OCP	Orange County, Personal Property Books
UVA	University of Virginia Library, Charlottesville, Va.
VHS	Virginia Historical Society, Richmond, Va.
VMHB	*Virginia Magazine of History and Biography*
VSL	Virginia State Library, Richmond, Va.
WMQ	*William and Mary Quarterly*

Source Notes

Chapter 1. The Virginia Heritage

1. Barbour Family Bible and Barbour Family Genealogy, BP UVA; Louise P. du Bellet, *Some Prominent Virginia Families,* 4 vols. (Lynchburg, Va.: J. P. Bell, 1907), 2:394–95.

2. Barbour Family Bible, BP UVA; Raleigh Travers Green, *Genealogical and Historical Notes on Culpeper County, Virginia, Embracing a Revised and Enlarged Edition of Dr. Phillip Slaughter's History of St. Mark's Parish* (Culpeper, Va.: n.p., 1900), pt. 2, p. 135; Virginia Patent Book, No. 14, p. 196, VSL. Some writers have suggested, though without conclusive evidence, that the family was descended from John Barbour, the fourteenth-century Scottish poet who wrote "The Brus." See Green, *Culpeper County,* pt. 2, p. 135, and William S. Long, "James Barbour," *John P. Branch Historical Papers of Randolph-Macon College,* 4 (June 1914):3.

3. Philip Slaughter, *A History of St. Mark's Parish, Culpeper County, Virginia* (Baltimore: Innes, 1877), p. 118; Margaret Vowell Smith, *Virginia 1492–1892 . . . with a History of the Executives of the Colony and the Commonwealth of Virginia* (Washington, D.C.: W. H. Lowdermilk, 1893), p. 321; W. W. Scott, *A History of Orange County, Virginia* (Richmond: E. Waddey, 1907), pp. 26–27.

4. Barbour Family Bible and Barbour Family Genealogy, BP UVA. The old Barbour home was near the hamlet of Liberty Mills in present-day Madison County.

5. OCD, 1762–95, and OCL, 1762–95, Orange County Clerk's Office; OCP, 1782–93, VSL. Other personal property during the years 1782–95 included some fifteen to twenty horses, twenty-five to thirty head of cattle, and a pleasure carriage, one of approximately twelve in the county.

6. OCO, 7:365, Orange County Clerk's Office, Orange, Virginia; Bishop William Meade, *Old Churches, Ministers, and Families of Virginia,* 2 vols. (Philadelphia: J. B. Lippincott, 1872), 2:89–90; *VMHB,* 4 (1896):383.

7. *Journals of the House of Burgesses of Virginia, 1766–1769,* ed. John Pendleton Kennedy, pp. xxxix–xlii.

8. Ibid., *1766–69,* pp. xxxix–xlii, and *1770–72,* pp. xxvii–xxxi; *Virginia Gazette,* May 25, 1769.

9. Richard Henry Lee to James Gordon, Feb. 26, 1788, in Richard Henry Lee, *The Letters of Richard Henry Lee,* ed. James Curtiss Ballagh, 2 vols. (New York: Macmillan, 1911–14), 2:460–63; Green, *Culpeper County,* pt. 2, p. 136.

10. Charles Washington Coleman, "The County Committees of 1774–1775 in Virginia," *WMQ,* 1st ser., 5 (April 1897):247; James Madison to William Bradford, July 28, 1775, in James Madison, *The Papers of James Madison,* ed. William T. Hutchinson, William M. E. Rachal, Charles F. Hobson, and Robert A. Rutland, 13 vols. to date

(Chicago and Charlottesville: University of Chicago and University of Virginia presses, 1962–), 1:147n, 148n, 159–61, 162n; *Virginia Gazette,* Jan. 28, March 11, 15, 1775.

11. Green, *Culpeper County,* pt. 1, p. 47; James Madison to William Bradford, June 19, 1775, in Madison, *Papers,* ed. Hutchinson, 1:147n, 148n, 151–53; *Virginia Gazette,* May 19, 1775, supp., p. 3; Bessie Grinnan, "A Sketch of Colonial Orange, 1734–1776," *Tyler's Quarterly Historical and Genealogical Magazine,* 4 (1923):109–14; Robert Douthat Meade, *Patrick Henry,* 2 vols. (Philadelphia: J. B. Lippincott, 1957–69), 1:139ff.; Ralph Ketcham, *James Madison, A Biography* (New York: Macmillan, 1971), pp. 63–65; Orange County Committee of Safety to Patrick Henry, May 9, 1775, and Madison to William Bradford, May 9, 1775, in Madison, *Papers,* ed. Hutchinson, 1:144–47.

12. *Heads of Families at the First Census of the United States Taken in the Year 1790: Records of the State Enumerations: 1782 to 1785* (Baltimore: Genealogical Publishing, 1966), p. 9. (The figures for Orange County were compiled in 1782.) There were 551 Orange landowners in 1787, excluding women and estates, according to the manuscript tax lists of the county. (See OCL, 1787, VSL.) The land records for 1782 are somewhat mutilated, but the total number of landowners appears to be about the same. The census records for 1782 do not give a specific number for adult white males. There were 1,317 white males sixteen and older and 1,426 younger than sixteen, for a total of 2,743. Approximately 40 percent of that number, or 1,097, may be assumed to have been twenty-one or older. See Charles S. Sydnor, *American Revolutionaries in the Making: Political Practices in Washington's Virginia* (New York: Collier Books, 1962), app. 2 and p. 141, 17n; also see *Heads of Families at the First Census,* p. 9. Because tenantry was not very common in the county before 1800, it is likely that the majority of unlanded adult males were sons of landowners who had not yet established themselves on their own property and were still working the family farms.

13. OCL and OCP, 1786, 1787, VSL. In addition to Baylor and the Madisons, only William Stannard owned more than 3,000 acres of land in 1787, which appears to be a typical year for the decade.

14. These conclusions are based on an examination of the OCL and OCP for the years 1782–1800, particularly the years 1782, 1787, 1795, and 1800. OCM, 1784–1800, at the Orange County Clerk's Office, Orange, Virginia, contain lists of county officers and minutes from the proceedings of the county court. See also the manuscript Register of Justices and Other County Officers, Orange County, 1777–1833, VSL.

15. Madison, *Papers,* ed. Hutchinson, 1:148, n. 2; *Heads of Families at the First Census,* p. 96. For a description of a typical Virginia plantation and home in the 1780s, see Johann David Schoepf, *Travels in the Confederation, 1783–1784,* trans. and ed. Alfred J. Morrison, 2 vols. (Philadelphia: W. J. Campbell, 1911), 2:32–33.

16. OCP, 1785. Some of the most common slave names, repeated with great monotony in the slave lists of the Orange County planters, were Tawney, Pompey, Cuffey, Silvey, Sukey, Sambo, Daphne, Reuben, and Cato.

17. Barbour Family Genealogy, BP UVA; du Bellet, *Virginia Families,* 2:396; Ketcham, *Madison,* pp. 62–63.

18. Barbour Family Genealogy, BP UVA.

19. Francis Taylor Diary, 1786, 1788, VSL.

20. Ibid., 1785–95, passim; James Madison, Sr., to Thomas Barbour, Feb. 15, 1800, Madison Papers, NYPL.

21. Francis Taylor Diary, 1785–99, passim.

22. Ibid.; Meade, *Churches, Ministers, and Families of Virginia,* 2:90–95.

23. Francis Taylor Diary, 1785–99, passim; Ketcham, *Madison,* p. 13.

24. A number of recent monographs provide excellent treatment of the English origins of Virginia political philosophy and of the influence of country ideology in Jeffersonian Virginia. See especially Robert Dawidoff, *The Education of John Randolph* (New York: W. W. Norton, 1979); Robert E. Shalhope, *John Taylor of Caroline, Pastoral Republican* (Columbia: University of South Carolina Press, 1980); Lance Banning, *The Jeffersonian Persuasion: Evolution of a Party Ideology* (Ithaca: Cornell University Press, 1978); Drew R. McCoy, *The Elusive Republic: Political Economy in Jeffersonian America* (Chapel Hill: University of North Carolina Press, 1980); and Richard Buel, Jr., *Securing the Revolution: Ideology in American Politics, 1789–1815* (Ithaca: Cornell University Press, 1972).

25. Scott, *Orange County,* p. 127.

26. *Virginia Gazette,* Jan. 28, March 11, April 15, 1775; Coleman, "The County Committees of 1774–1775," p. 247; OCO, 8:353–56, and OCM, 2:158–60, Orange County Clerk's Office; Thomas Barbour to Colonel Davis, Nov. 1781, *CVSP,* 2:607.

27. OCM, 1783–89, passim, especially the entry of Aug. 14, 1789.

28. Scott, *Orange County,* p. 127.

29. *Dictionary of American Biography,* 1st ed., s.v. "James Wadell"; William Wirt, *The Letters of the British Spy* (New York, 1832), pp. 195–202.

30. [George Watterson], *Letters from Washington, on the Constitution and Laws; with Sketches of Some Prominent Public Characters of the United States. Writings during the Winter of 1817–1818 by a Foreigner* (Washington, D.C.: J. Gideon, 1818), pp. 128ff.

31. Henry Lee to James Madison, Dec. 20, 1787, in Madison, *Papers,* ed. Hutchinson, 10:339–40.

32. Andrew Shepherd to James Madison, Dec. 22, 1787, James Madison, Sr., to James Madison, Jan. 30, 1788, James Gordon, Jr., to James Madison, Feb. 17, 1788, and Joseph Spencer to James Madison, Feb. 28, 1788, in ibid., 10:344–45, 446–47, 515–16, 540–41.

33. Francis Taylor Diary, 1789; Irving Brant, *James Madison,* 6 vols. (Indianapolis: Bobbs-Merrill, 1941–61), 3:188; James Gordon, Jr., to James Madison, Feb. 17, 1788, and Joseph Spencer to James Madison, Feb. 28, 1788, in Madison, *Papers,* ed. Hutchinson, 10:515–16, 540–41. Joseph Spencer wrote that Barbour "misrepresents things in such horred carrecters that the weker clas of the people are much predegessed agains it [the Constitution] by which meens he has many [people] which as yet, appears grately in favour of him, amoungs his friends appears, in a general way the Baptus's."

34. Francis Taylor Diary, 1789; Brant, *Madison,* 3:188.

35. Joseph Jones to James Madison, July 23, 1787, in Madison, *Papers,* ed. Hutchinson, 10:111–12; Brant, *Madison,* 3:188; Avery O. Craven, *Soil Exhaustion as*

a Factor in the Agricultural History of Virginia and Maryland, 1606–1860, University of Illinois Studies in the Social Sciences, 13:1 (Urbana: University of Illinois Press, 1926), 72–73; W. A. Low, "The Farmer in Post-Revolutionary Virginia, 1783–1789," *Agricultural History,* 25 (July 1951):123ff.

36. OCD, 19:135, 325, 384, 425, 511, 20:28, 145, Orange County Clerk's Office; Samuel Shepherd to JB, May 12, 1808, and Thomas Barbour to Benjamin Johnson, Oct. 6, 1792, BP NYPL; Business and Financial Papers, 1783–1810, passim, BP UVA.

37. Inventory of Books, 1805, BP UVA; Richard Beale Davis, *Intellectual Life in Jefferson's Virginia, 1790–1830* (Chapel Hill: University of North Carolina Press, 1964), p. 366.

38. Watterson, *Letters from Washington,* p. 128; Inventory of Books, 1805, BP UVA.

39. JB to Thomas W. White, April 22, 1829, BP UVA; Armistead C. Gordon, *William Fitzhugh Gordon, A Virginian of the Old School: His Life, Times, and Contemporaries, 1787–1858* (New York: Neale, 1909), pp. 52–53. The name of the lawyer and the length of time Barbour studied under him are not known.

40. Charles Warren, *A History of the American Bar* (Boston: Little, Brown, 1911), pp. 175–78.

41. *CVSP,* 5:449; Seth Spencer to JB, June 25, 1792, BP UVA.

42. OCM, 1793, Orange County Clerk's Office.

43. See the manuscript Orange County Court Dockets for the years 1793–95, Orange County Clerk's Office.

44. This description of Barbour is taken from later accounts of his personal appearance. See Stephen Collins, *Miscellanies* (Philadelphia: Carey and Hart, 1845), p. 226; Robert C. Winthrop to William Wirt Henry, Jan. 24, 1876, William Wirt Henry Papers, VHS.

45. Albemarle County Order Book, 1793–95, p. 194, Albemarle County Clerk's Office; Louisa County Order Book, 1792–97, p. 237, Louisa County Clerk's Office; Fluvanna County Order Book, 1792–96, p. 562, Fluvanna County Clerk's Office.

46. William Wirt to Francis Walker Gilmer, Aug. 29, 1815, Gilmer Letter Book, UVA.

47. John Pendleton Kennedy, *Memoirs of the Life of William Wirt, Attorney General of the United States,* 2 vols. (Philadelphia: Lee and Blanchard, 1850), 1:66–68.

48. Ibid., 1:69–72.

49. Francis Taylor Diary, 1789–95, passim; OCM, 1785–1800, and Orange County Register of Marriages, 1:38, Orange County Clerk's Office; Barbour Family Genealogy, BP UVA.

50. OCL, 1788, 1797–1800, VSL; OCM, 1797, and OCD, 1:306, Orange County Clerk's Office; Deed of Sale between Andrew Stainton and JB, Sept. 18, 1799, BP UVA. In May 1798, Francis Taylor recorded in his diary that James Barbour purchased "two square tables, a tea table, and looking glass" from him.

51. OCM, 1796, Orange County Clerk's Office; OCP, 1798, VSL.

52. Francis Taylor Diary, 1798; Brant, *Madison,* 1:306; JB to James Barbour, Jr., May 7, 1825, BP UVA.

53. In four elections conducted in Orange between 1786 and 1790, an average of 273 men voted. The electorate at this time numbered 551 men, or 50 percent of the 1,100 free white males twenty-one and older residing in the county. By 1800 the electorate had grown to 640, representing 53 percent of the adult white male

population. In the election of 1800, when voter interest was high, 344 persons, or 54 percent of those meeting the fifty-acre freehold qualification, voted. The fifty-acre freehold required for the franchise was not large for a landed society in which only a few landowners, fewer than one-half of 1 percent in Orange, possessed fewer than fifty acres, but about half of the adult white males owned no land at all and were thus disfranchised. The votes for the elections during the period 1786–90 can be found in the Francis Taylor diary and in Sydnor, *American Revolutionaries,* pp. 121–23. I determined the size of the electorate from the OCL, 1787 and 1800, and from the published *Second Census of the United States,* 1800. For the election returns of 1800, see *Virginia Argus,* Dec. 2, 1800.

54. Francis Taylor Diary, 1798. For a good description of local elections in Virginia during this period, see Anthony F. Upton, "The Road to Power in Virginia in the Early Nineteenth Century," *VMHB,* 62 (July 1954):259–79.

Chapter 2. In Defense of Republicanism

1. James Morton Smith, *Freedom's Fetters: The Alien and Sedition Laws and American Civil Liberties* (Ithaca: Cornell University Press, 1956), pp. 5–6; Richard Beeman, *The Old Dominion and the New Nation, 1788–1801* (Lexington: University Press of Kentucky, 1972), pp. 173–77.

2. Ketcham, *Madison,* pp. 393–97; Dumas Malone, *Jefferson and His Time,* 6 vols. (Boston: Little, Brown, 1948–81), 3:395–401.

3. Malone, *Jefferson,* 3:399–401.

4. Harry Ammon, "The Republican Party in Virginia, 1789–1824" (Ph.D. diss., University of Virginia, 1948), pp. 176–77; *Richmond Observatory,* Aug. 27, Oct. 1, 1798; *Virginia Gazette and General Advertiser,* Aug. 14, Sept. 25, Oct. 2, 1798; *Virginia Argus,* Oct. 12, 26, 1798; *Philadelphia Aurora,* Nov. 20, Dec. 1, 7, 1798.

5. *Virginia Argus,* Oct. 12, 1798; *Philadelphia Aurora,* Dec. 1, 1798; Collins, *Miscellanies,* p. 216.

6. Francis Taylor Diary, 1798.

7. Ibid.; Ketcham, *Madison,* pp. 394–95; *Virginia Argus,* Oct. 12, 1798; *Philadelphia Aurora,* Dec. 1, 1798; *Richmond Whig and Public Advertiser,* July 4, 1842; James Barbour, *Eulogium Upon the Life and Character of James Madison* (Washington, D.C.: Gales and Seaton, 1836), passim.

8. Francis Taylor Diary, 1798; *Virginia Argus,* Oct. 12, 1798; *Philadelphia Aurora,* Dec. 1, 1798; *Richmond Whig and Public Advertiser,* July 4, 1842.

9. *Virginia Gazette and General Advertiser,* Aug. 14, 1798.

10. Ibid., Sept. 25, 1798.

11. Beeman, *Old Dominion,* pp. 196–98; *Virginia Gazette and General Advertiser,* July 10, Aug. 14, 28, Sept. 25, 1798; Charles Henry Ambler, *Sectionalism in Virginia from 1776 to 1861* (Chicago: University of Chicago Press, 1910), pp. 65–68; Frank Maloy Anderson, "Contemporary Opinion of the Virginia and Kentucky Resolutions," *American Historical Review,* 5 (Oct. 1899):46; *VMHB,* 29 (April 1921):174–75; Dice R. Anderson, *William Branch Giles: A Study in the Politics of*

Virginia and the Nation from 1790 to 1830 (Menasha, Wisc.: George Banta, 1914), p. 62.

12. *Virginia Argus,* Dec. 4, 1798; Samuel Mordecai, *Virginia, Especially Richmond, in By-Gone Days; With a Glance at the Present; Being Reminiscences and Last Words of an Old Citizen* (Richmond: West and Johnson, 1860), pp. 55–70; Duc de La Rochefoucauld-Liancourt, *Travels Through the United States of North America, the Country of the Iroquois and Upper Canada, in the Years 1795, 1796, and 1797,* 2 vols. (London: R. Phillips, 1799), 2:30–32; Schoepf, *Travels in the Confederation,* 2:64; Charles Henry Ambler, *Thomas Ritchie: A Study in Virginia Politics* (Richmond: Bell Book and Stationery, 1913), p. 17; Barbour, *Eulogium Upon Madison,* pp. 19–20.

13. *Richmond Whig and Public Advertiser,* July 4, 1842; Brant, *Madison,* 3:461; Jeremiah Morton, *Eulogy Upon the Late Governor Barbour* (Richmond: n.p., 1842), p. 7.

14. Anderson, *Giles,* p. 63; Ambler, *Sectionalism in Virginia,* p. 68; *Virginia Argus,* Dec. 27, 1799.

15. Beeman, *Old Dominion,* p. 189; *Philadelphia Aurora,* Aug. 6, 1798.

16. Beeman, *Old Dominion,* pp. 189–90; *JHD,* 1798–99, p. 3.

17. *The Virginia Report of 1799–1800 Touching the Alien and Sedition Laws, Together With the Virginia Resolutions of December 21, 1798* (Richmond: J. W. Randolph, 1850), pp. 22–23, 148–50; Adrienne Koch, *Jefferson and Madison: The Great Collaboration* (New York: A. A. Knopf, 1950), pp. 191–92; Ketcham, *Madison,* pp. 396–97; Adrienne Koch and Harry Ammon, "The Virginia and Kentucky Resolutions: An Episode in Jefferson's and Madison's Defense of Civil Liberties," *WMQ,* 3d ser., 5 (April 1948):160–61.

18. Koch and Ammon, "The Virginia and Kentucky Resolutions," pp. 159–60; Malone, *Jefferson,* 3:407–408; Brant, *Madison,* 3:459–63; *Virginia Report,* pp. 228–32.

19. *Virginia Report,* pp. 24–28, 29–39, 51; Shalhope, *John Taylor,* p. 101.

20. Henry H. Simms, *Life of John Taylor* (Richmond: William Byrd Press, 1932), p. 81; *Richmond Whig and Public Advertiser,* July 4, 1842; Koch and Ammon, "The Virginia and Kentucky Resolutions," p. 162; Koch, *Jefferson and Madison,* p. 193; Morton, *Eulogy on Barbour,* p. 7. The following analysis and quotations from Barbour's speech are from the *Virginia Report,* pp. 54–70.

21. Koch, *Jefferson and Madison,* pp. 188–94; Koch and Ammon, "The Virginia and Kentucky Resolutions," pp. 159–62. John Taylor asserted the right which Jefferson implied. See Buel, *Securing the Revolution,* pp. 217–23, and Shalhope, *John Taylor,* p. 80.

22. Koch, *Jefferson and Madison,* pp. 191–93; Ketcham, *Madison,* p. 396.

23. *Virginia Report,* pp. 71–180, passim.

24. Ibid., p. 75.

25. Ibid., pp. 56–57, 118–21, 134–39.

26. Ibid., pp. 104, 157–58.

27. Ibid., pp. 157–58; Beeman, *Old Dominion,* p. 194.

28. *Virginia Report,* pp. 71–76.

29. Ibid., pp. 54–57, 62–65.

30. Ibid., p. 69; Buel, *Securing the Revolution,* pp. 219–21; Banning, *Jeffersonian Persuasion,* pp. 269–88; Shalhope, *John Taylor,* p. 80.

31. *JHD,* 1789–99, p. 52; Francis Taylor Diary, 1798; Beeman, *Old Dominion,* p. 195.

32. Beeman, *Old Dominion,* pp. 196–98.

33. *JHD,* 1798–99, pp. 6–7, 17.

34. See below, chapter 3.

35. *Richmond Whig and Public Advertiser,* July 4, 1842; *Virginia Argus,* Oct. 12, 1798.

36. Simms, *John Taylor,* p. 81; *Virginia Report,* p. 71; JB to Jefferson, Jan. 20, 1800, Jefferson Papers, LC.

37. Anderson, "Contemporary Opinion of the Virginia and Kentucky Resolutions," pp. 45–63, 225–36; Francis Taylor Diary, 1799; Ames to Christopher Gore, Jan. 11, 1799, in Fisher Ames, *Works of Fisher Ames,* ed. Seth Ames, 2 vols. (Boston: Little, Brown, 1854), 2:249–51.

38. Meade, *Patrick Henry,* 2:446–48; *Columbian Mirror,* April 23, 1799; *Virginia Report,* pp. xiv–xvi.

39. Francis Taylor Diary, 1799; John Page to Henry Tazewell, n.d., Tazewell Family Papers, VSL; Beeman, *Old Dominion,* p. 204; Joseph C. Cabell to David Watson, June 7, 1799, in *VMHB,* 29 (1921):263–64.

40. Beeman, *Old Dominion,* pp. 204–209.

41. Koch, *Jefferson and Madison,* p. 195; John Taylor to Creed Taylor, April 10, 1799, Creed Taylor Papers, UVA; Barbour, *Eulogium Upon Madison,* pp. 19–20; Brant, *Madison,* 3:465.

42. Francis Taylor Diary, 1799.

43. Jefferson to Archibald Stuart, May 14, 1799, in Jefferson, *The Works of Thomas Jefferson,* ed. Paul Leicester Ford, 12 vols., Federal ed. (New York: G. P. Putnam's Sons, 1904–1905), 9:66–68.

44. Barbour, *Eulogium Upon Madison,* pp. 19–20; Madison to Jefferson, Dec. 29, 1799, in James Madison, *The Writings of James Madison,* ed. Gaillard Hunt, 9 vols. (New York: G. P. Putnam's Sons, 1900–10), 6:342–44.

45. *Virginia Gazette and General Advertiser,* Dec. 6, 10, 1799; *JHD,* 1799–1800, pp. 2–4; Harry Ammon, *James Monroe: The Quest for National Identity* (New York: McGraw-Hill, 1971), p. 173.

46. Malone, *Jefferson,* 3:410–18; Ammon, *James Monroe,* p. 171; Barbour, *Eulogium Upon Madison,* pp. 19–21; Francis Taylor Diary, 1799.

47. *Virginia Report,* pp. 189–232; Ketcham, *Madison,* pp. 399–403.

48. JB to Jefferson, Jan. 20, 1800, Jefferson Papers, LC; *JHD,* 1799–1800, pp. 49, 72, 79; *Virginia Report,* pp. 236–37.

49. Noble E. Cunningham, Jr., *The Jeffersonian Republicans: The Formation of Party Organization, 1789–1801* (Chapel Hill: University of North Carolina Press, 1957), pp. 129–44; Koch, *Jefferson and Madison,* pp. 210–11; Beeman, *Old Dominion,* pp. 217–20; *Virginia Argus,* Jan. 21, 1800; *JHD,* 1799–1800, pp. 83, 91.

50. Although Republicans in the House outnumbered Federalists two to one, the electoral law passed by the margin of only five votes (JB to Jefferson, Jan. 20, 1800, Jefferson Papers, LC; *Virginia Federalist,* March 19, 1800).

51. *Virginia Argus,* March 11, 25, 1800; Cunningham, *The Jeffersonian Republicans,* pp. 145–46.

52. The other committee members were Littleton W. Tazewell of James City, Samuel Tyler of Charles City, John Mercer of Spotsylvania, and either William Daniel, Jr., of Cumberland or Robert B. Daniel of Middlesex (*CVSP,* 9:75; Cunningham, *Jeffersonian Republicans,* pp. 150–51).

53. *CVSP,* 9:75; Philip Norborne Nicholas to Jefferson, Feb. 2, 1800, Jefferson Papers, LC.

54. Beeman, *Old Dominion,* p. 224.

55. *CVSP,* 9:85.

56. *Virginia Argus,* Dec. 2, 1800.

57. Albert J. Beveridge, *The Life of John Marshall,* 4 vols. (Boston: Houghton Mifflin, 1919), 4:576–77; *JHD,* 1799–1800, pp. 4, 14, 34, 41.

58. *Virginia Report,* p. 69; JB to the Freeholders of Orange County, Jan. 1803, BP UVA.

Chapter 3. An Expanding World

1. Barbour Family Bible, BP UVA.

2. James Waddell to JB, Nov. 21, 1806, and JB to James Barbour, Jr., 1810–20, passim, BP UVA; John C. Underwood to Cornelia Barbour, July 9, 1860, John C. Underwood Papers, LC.

3. See below, chapter 11.

4. OCD, 1800–10, Orange County Clerk's Office; OCL and Albemarle County Land Books, 1800–10, VSL; Will of Benjamin Johnson, Sept. 1801, Philip Pendleton Barbour Papers, VHS.

5. OCP, 1795–1810, VSL.

6. James Barbour, *Address of James Barbour, Esquire, President of the Agricultural Society of Albemarle at Their Meeting of the 8th of November, 1825* (Charlottesville: C. P. M'Kennie, 1825), pp. 9–10; see below, chapter 11.

7. Barbour, *Address to the Agricultural Society of Albemarle,* pp. 9–11; Edward Coles to H. B. Grigsby, Dec. 23, 1854, Edward Coles Papers, Historical Society of Pennsylvania.

8. Charles D. Lowery, "James Barbour, A Progressive Farmer of Antebellum Virginia," in *America: The Middle Period; Essays in Honor of Bernard Mayo,* ed. John B. Boles (Charlottesville: University Press of Virginia, 1973), pp. 168–87.

9. Davis, *Intellectual Life in Jefferson's Virginia,* p. 353.

10. Memoirs of Philip Pendleton Barbour, manuscript written May 23, 1834, Ambler Family Papers, UVA; Notes on PPB's Legal Practice, Philip Pendleton Barbour Papers, VHS; William Wirt to Dabney Carr, March 28, June 26, 1803, William Wirt–Dabney Carr Correspondence, VSL.

11. Barbour Ledger, 1800–12, BP UVA; Thomas Jefferson Account Book, 1796–1806, pp. 671, 716, UVA; Thomas Jefferson to James Madison, Aug. 29, Sept. 17, 1800, Madison Papers, LC; Robert E. Winthrop to William Wirt Henry, Jan. 24, 1876,

William Wirt Henry Papers, VHS; JB to Smith Thompson, n.d., Smith-Thompson Family Papers, LC; JB to Isaac Davis, Jan. 20, 1818, Isaac Davis Papers, UVA.

12. Barbour Account Book, 1805, BP UVA; *Richmond Enquirer,* Jan. 3, 1805; A Traveller [Anne Royall], *Sketches of History, Life, and Manners in the United States* (New Haven: Printed for the Author, 1826), pp. 115–17; Robley Dunglison Diary, pp. 473–74, UVA; Francis G. Ruffin Diary, p. 105, VHS.

13. Barbour Account Book, 1805, BP UVA.

14. James Barbour, "Address to the Agricultural Convention of Virginia," *Farmer's Register,* 3 (March 1836):685–89; Francis Taylor Diary, 1798–99; JB to James Barbour, Jr., May 9, 1825, April 28, 1826, BP UVA; Linn Banks to Thomas Davis, Dec. 31, 1830, and Charles Yancey to Thomas Davis, Dec. 31, 1830, Isaac Davis Papers, Duke University; Political Circulars, 1800–10, BP UVA.

15. I determined Barbour's wealth relative to that of other legislative leaders on the basis of land and slaves owned in the years 1800, 1805, and 1810, consulting the Land and Personal Property Books for these years in the VSL.

16. OCM, 1822, Orange County Clerk's Office; Register of Justices and Other County Officers, 1777–1833, OC, VSL. The role of local government as a training ground for higher political office is discussed in Sydnor, *American Revolutionaries,* pp. 100ff.

17. Beeman, *Old Dominion,* pp. 28–32; Jackson Turner Main, "The One Hundred," *WMQ,* 3d ser., 11 (July 1954):365–67; J. R. Pole, "Representation and Authority in Virginia from the Revolution to Reform," *Journal of Southern History,* 24 (Feb. 1958):16ff. Daniel P. Jordan, in his dissertation "Virginia Congressmen, 1801–1825" (University of Virginia, 1970), argues that there was little change in the social standing and wealth of Virginia's political leaders during the Jeffersonian, or Dynasty, era. His study focuses on the state's congressional membership, however, not on that of the General Assembly, which I examine below. He and I hold somewhat divergent views, reflecting the study of groups which, though different, overlap in many important ways.

18. The leaders referred to here have been identified by Beeman and are listed in *Old Dominion,* app. 1, pp. 250–52. Actually there are thirty-three men in the group, but the six whose principal residence was in a town, and whose wealth was therefore more likely to be in property other than land and slaves, have been excluded.

19. Main, "The One Hundred," pp. 354ff.

20. These figures include land and slaves owned by legislative leaders in the county of their principal residence only. The task of compiling accurate and complete figures for all property owned outside the home county is so immense as to be prohibitive and would probably be impossible. The figures used here are drawn from the Land and Personal Property Books, 1795, VSL (or the nearest date possible when records for a particular individual and county are not extant). Main's figures in "The One Hundred" include property owned in all counties, but only ten of the legislative leaders of the period 1788–1800 are included in his group. Beeman's figures are mixed, including in some instances total property owned by leaders in all counties and in other instances that owned only in their home county. Hence his figures could not be used in this computation.

21. I used the Land and Personal Property Books for 1810, or for the nearest available date, VSL, in determining the wealth of this group of legislative leaders. The smaller number of men in the later group of leaders should not be construed to mean that leadership in the 1800–15 period was more exclusive. It simply reflects a greater diversity of leadership with fewer individuals holding positions of power for any length of time.

22. Land and Personal Property Books, 1810, VSL.

23. Main, "The One Hundred," p. 364.

24. Included among the group were two ministers, four judges, two customs collectors, one law professor, and two merchants, some of whom pursued other careers in addition to their principal one.

25. Sydnor, *American Revolutionaries,* p. 88; Beeman, *Old Dominion,* pp. 44–48.

26. By 1800 the six standing committees of the late colonial period had been reduced to four, and it was not until 1806, when the Committee on Finance was elevated to standing committee status, that there were five. The three men with four-year tenures were Edmund Harrison of Amelia, Robert Stanard of Richmond, and William Noland of Loudon (*JHD,* 1800–15, passim).

27. Sydnor, *American Revolutionaries,* p. 88; *JHD,* 1786–99, passim.

28. *JHD,* 1800–15, passim. Other speakers during this period included Andrew Stevenson of Richmond, Larkin Smith of King and Queen, Hugh Holmes of Frederick, and Peter Johnston of Prince Edward.

29. *JHD,* 1800–15, passim.

30. Ibid.

31. Main, "The One Hundred," pp. 366–67.

32. Ibid.

33. In 1820 Barbour exceeded the average wealth of the One Hundred in real and personal property in the home county. He fell below the average in the size and number of working plantations in neighboring counties, though not in the number of acres held for speculative purposes (OCL and OCP, 1805, 1820, VSL; Inventory of Real and Personal Property, 1820, BP UVA).

34. During the formative period of the new nation, Virginia's senators were more likely than her congressmen to be from the old ruling elite. Some of the former, however, such as William B. Giles, possessed only moderate taxable wealth. In 1795 he owned only 400 acres of land in his home county and twenty-three slaves (Amelia County Land and Personal Property Books, 1795, VSL).

35. The occupations of political leaders for the period before 1800 are listed in Main, "The One Hundred," pp. 368–83, and Beeman, *Old Dominion,* pp. 250–52; those after 1800 have been drawn from tax lists, court records, newspapers, wills, and scattered other sources.

36. Upton, "The Road to Power in Virginia," p. 271.

37. Hugh A. Garland, *The Life of John Randolph of Roanoke,* 2 vols. (New York: D. Appleton, 1850), 2:225. For a similar opinion, see Archibald Stuart to Creed Taylor, Jan. 19, 1812, Creed Taylor Papers, UVA.

38. Beeman, *Old Dominion,* pp. xii–xiii, 48–55.

39. *JHD,* 1797–1812, passim; Petitions of Frederick County (Nov. 18, 1796), Greenbrier County (May 12, 1797), and Ohio County (Dec. 26, 1798), Legislative

Petitions, VSL; *Virginia Argus,* Dec. 29, 1801, Jan. 19, Feb. 19, 1802; *Examiner,* Feb. 5, 1802; John Campbell to David Campbell, Jan. 30, 1811, Campbell Family Papers, Duke University; *JHD,* 1810–11, p. 85; JB to John H. Pleasants, July 7, 1829, BP UVA. J. R. Pole discusses the reform question in detail in "Representation and Authority," pp. 31–39.

40. James Barbour, "On the Improvement of Agriculture and the Importance of Legislative Aid to That Object. Description of the South West Mountain Lands," *Farmers' Register,* 2 (April 1835):705; Barbour, *Address to the Agricultural Society of Albemarle,* pp. 9–12; *JHD,* 1809–12, passim; *Niles' Register,* 39:464; *Washington National Intelligencer,* Nov. 28, 1826.

41. *JHD,* 1800–1801, pp. 4, 13; 1801–1802, pp. 1, 6, 12, 13, 16; 1802–1803, pp. 1, 6, 9; 1804–1805, pp. 1, 16, 61; 1807–1808, pp. 1, 4, 58; 1808–1809, p. 105.

42. Brant, *Madison,* 4:248; *JHD,* 1804–1805, pp. 8, 45; 1807–1808, p. 58; *Richmond Enquirer,* Jan. 7, 1808; JB to Madison, Dec. 11, 1807, Madison Papers, LC; Harry Ammon, "The Richmond Junto, 1800–1824," *VMHB,* 61 (Oct. 1953):399–408.

43. Speech of James Barbour, Dec. 31, 1804, BP UVA; *Richmond Enquirer,* Jan. 3, 1805.

44. William Wirt to Littleton W. Tazewell, Dec. 30, 1804, Tazewell Family Papers, VSL. For other contemporary opinions of Barbour's speeches in the assembly, see John Campbell to Elizabeth Campbell, Dec. 4, 1810, Campbell Family Papers, Duke University, and Thomas Davison to JB, Feb. 24, 1812, BP UVA.

45. *JHD,* 1802–1803, 1805–1807, passim; JB to Freeholders of Orange County, Jan. 1803; Barbour Family Bible, BP UVA.

46. Mordecai Barbour to JB, Sept. 2, 1806, BP UVA.

47. Bills, Receipts, and Miscellaneous Papers, 1807, BP UVA; JB to Jefferson, March 29, 1817, Jefferson Papers, LC; Fiske Kimball, *Thomas Jefferson, Architect* (Boston: Riverside Press, 1916), pp. 73–74; Ketcham, *Madison,* p. 455.

48. David Robertson, *Reports of the Trial of Colonel Aaron Burr for Treason and for a Misdemeanor,* 2 vols. (Philadelphia: n.p., 1808), 1:1–5; *Richmond Enquirer,* April 10, 15, 1807; *Virginia Argus,* April 7, 1807; *Norfolk Gazette and Public Ledger,* June 24, 1807.

49. *Richmond Enquirer,* June 29, July 1, 3, 1807.

50. Ibid., June 27, July 1, 27, 1807.

51. Ibid., July 24, 1807.

52. Ibid., June 3, Dec. 27, 1807, Jan. 7, 1808; *JHD,* 1807–1808, p. 58.

53. *JHD,* 1807–1808, p. 58; *Richmond Enquirer,* Jan. 7, 1808.

54. *Richmond Enquirer,* Oct. 30, Nov. 3, 10, 17, 1807, Jan. 12, 14, 1808; Speech of JB, Jan. 6, 1808, BP UVA.

55. *Richmond Enquirer,* Jan. 3, 1805.

56. Ammon, "Richmond Junto," pp. 403–405; Brant, *Madison,* 5:421; *Richmond Enquirer,* Jan. 19, 1808; Norman K. Risjord, *The Old Republicans: Southern Conservatism in the Age of Jefferson* (New York: Columbia University Press, 1965), p. 88; Creed Taylor to [n.n.], Dec. 21, 1807, Creed Taylor Papers, UVA; Shalhope, *John Taylor,* p. 124.

57. Ammon, *James Monroe,* pp. 270–73; *Richmond Enquirer,* Jan. 19, 1808.

58. *Richmond Enquirer,* Jan. 19, 23, 26, 1808; Harry Ammon, "James Monroe and the Election of 1808 in Virginia," *WMQ,* 3d ser., 20 (Jan. 1963):44–47; Risjord, *The Old Republicans,* pp. 88–90.

59. *Richmond Enquirer,* Jan. 13, 16, 19, 23, 26, Feb. 11, March 1, 1808; Ammon, "The Election of 1808," pp. 47–48; Ammon, *James Monroe,* pp. 275–77; *Virginia Argus,* Nov. 11, 17, 25, 1808.

60. Spencer Roane to Wilson Cary Nicholas, Jan. 5, 1809, Wilson Cary Nicholas Papers, LC; Ammon, "The Election of 1808," pp. 54–55; *Richmond Enquirer,* Dec. 31, 1808, Feb. 7, 1809; Ammon, "Richmond Junto," pp. 411–12.

61. *JHD,* 1808–1809, pp. 4, 18, 87, 97.

62. Archibald Stuart to Creed Taylor, Nov. 27, 1802, Creed Taylor Papers, UVA; Larkin Smith to Littleton W. Tazewell, Aug. 17, 1804, Tazewell Family Papers, VSL.

63. *JHD,* 1798–1812, passim. The two western delegates Barbour appointed to standing committee chairmanships were James McFarlane of Russell County and Thomas Preston of Rockbridge (ibid., 1809–1810, pp. 9–10).

64. Ibid., 1809–10, pp. 3, 5–9, 74, 94, 108; JB to William Cabell Rives, Feb. 21, 1818, William Cabell Rives Papers, LC; JB to Gen. Francis Preston, July 3, 1825, Campbell-Preston Family Papers, LC; Wiley E. Hodges, "Pro-Governmentalism in Virginia, 1789–1836: A Pragmatic Liberal Pattern in the Political Heritage," *Journal of Politics,* 25 (May 1963):333–42; Philip Alexander Bruce, *History of the University of Virginia, 1819–1919: The Lengthened Shadow of One Man,* 5 vols. (New York: Macmillan, 1920), 1:86; C. J. Heatwole, "Origin and Sacredness of the Literary Fund," *Virginia Journal of Education,* 23 (April 1930):329–31. Barbour's interest in education is shown also by his successful efforts in 1811 to secure from the legislature a charter for the Orange County Humane Society, which was given control over a special fund to be used exclusively for the education of the indigent. From the beginning a trustee and for many years the president of the society, he played a large role in educating hundreds of poor children in the county (JB to John S. Pendleton, Feb. 1839 [n.d.], cited in Scott, *History of Orange County,* p. 182).

65. *Richmond Enquirer,* Jan. 6, 20, 1810; *JHD,* 1809–10, pp. 50, 71; John H. Cocke to Joseph C. Cabell, April 18, 1803, Joseph C. Cabell Papers, UVA.

66. *Richmond Enquirer,* Jan. 17, 1811; Ammon, *James Monroe,* pp. 285–86; *JHD,* 1811–12, p. 13; John Campbell to David Campbell, Dec. 3, 1811, Campbell Family Papers, Duke University.

67. Richard M. Johnson to JB, Dec. 9, 1811, BP NYPL.

68. *Richmond Enquirer,* Dec. 28, 1811–Jan. 6, 1812; *JHD,* 1811–12, p. 62.

Chapter 4. "War's Wild Alarm"

1. St. George Tucker, *Blackstone's Commentaries: With Notes of Reference, to the Constitution and Laws, of the Federal Government of the United States; and of the Commonwealth of Virginia,* 5 vols. (Philadelphia: William Young Birch and Abra-

ham Small, 1803), app. C, 1:122–24. The *Richmond Enquirer,* Jan. 28, 1806, contains a good statement on the powers of the executive branch.

2. JB to Jefferson, Jan. 14, 1812, Jefferson Papers, LC; Jefferson to JB, Jan. 12, 22, 1812, BP NYPL.

3. Jefferson to JB, March 22, 1812, Jefferson Papers, LC.

4. Virginius Dabney, *Richmond: The Story of a City* (New York: Doubleday, 1976), pp. 74–89.

5. Mary Newton Stanard, *Richmond: Its People and Its Story* (Philadelphia: J. B. Lippincott, 1923), pp. 104–13; Dabney, *Richmond,* pp. 78–81, 84–89.

6. Dabney, *Richmond,* pp. 78–80; *The Executive Mansion* (Richmond, n.p., 1961, pp. 5–7.

7. *Richmond Enquirer,* Jan. 21, 1812; *The Executive Mansion,* pp. 5–7; Lyon Gardiner Tyler, *Letters and Times of the Tylers,* 3 vols. (Richmond: Whittet and Shepperson, 1884–96), 1:219.

8. *The Executive Mansion,* pp. 8–9.

9. Dabney, *Richmond,* pp. 79–92; Stanard, *Richmond,* pp. 109–11; Clayton Torrence, "War's Wild Alarm," *VMHB,* 49 (July 1941):217–27. Frances Cornelia was the second daughter given this name. The first, born in June 1801, had died in August 1802 (Barbour Family Bible, BP UVA). The quotation is from Dabney, *Richmond,* p. 92.

10. *JHD,* 1812–13, p. 1; *Richmond Enquirer,* June 27, 1807, Jan. 7, 1808; JB to Madison, Jan. 29, 1812, Madison Papers, LC; JB to Isaac Davis, Aug. 27, 1812, A. L. Hench Collection, UVA.

11. ELB, March 31, 1812.

12. Barbour to the Speaker of the House of Delegates and [the President of the] Senate, Jan. 27, 1812, ELB; *JHD,* 1811–12, pp. 104–105; *Acts Passed at the General Assembly of the Commonwealth of Virginia, 1811–1812* (Richmond, 1812), p. 6.

13. Robert Quarles to JB, Feb. 11, 1813, *CVSP,* 10:191; ELB, Jan.-March 1812, passim; Council of State Journals, 1811–12, VSL; EC, Jan.-April 1812; *Richmond Enquirer,* April 17, 24, 1812.

14. John Campbell to David Campbell, Oct. 17, 1812, Campbell Family Papers, Duke University.

15. Journals of the Council of State, 1812–14, passim, VSL; J. W. Randolph, comp., *History of William and Mary College* (Richmond: J. W. Randolph, 1874), pp. 98–103; Lawrence Burnette, Jr., "Peter V. Daniel: Agrarian Justice," *VMHB,* 62 (Oct. 1954):289–90; John Dawson to James Monroe, Jan. 19, 1800, Monroe Papers, NYPL; *JHD,* 1800–12, passim.

16. JB to Peyton Randolph, April 24, 1812, EP; *CVSP,* 10:131–42; JB to the Council of State, May 12, 1812, EP.

17. JB to the Council of State, May 12, 1812, JB to Secretary of War William Eustis, May 14, 19, 1812, and Secretary of War Eustis to JB, April 30 and May 20, 1812, EP; *JHD,* 1812–13, p. 20.

18. ELB, May 12–30, 1812; *Richmond Enquirer,* June 2, 1812.

19. Marshall Smelser, *The Democrat Republic, 1801–1815* (New York: Harper and Row, 1968), pp. 227–29; Russell F. Weigley, *History of the United States Army* (New York: Macmillan, 1967), pp. 118–19; Raymond Walters, Jr., *Albert Gallatin: Jefferso-*

nian Financier and Diplomat (New York: Macmillan, 1957), pp. 246–50, 254–56; Alexander Balinky, *Albert Gallatin: Fiscal Theories and Policies* (New Brunswick: Rutgers University Press, 1958), pp. 164ff.; Shaw Livermore, Jr., *The Twilight of Federalism: The Disintegration of the Federalist Party, 1815–1830* (Princeton: Princeton University Press, 1962), pp. 10–11.

20. JB to the Speaker of the House of Delegates and [the President of the] Senate, Nov. 30, 1812, and JB to Secretary of War William Eustis, April 17, May 19, Aug. 21, 1812, ELB.

21. JB to Monroe, Sept. 11, 1812, Monroe Papers, LC; ELB, Sept.-Dec. 1812; JB to Isaac Davis, Aug. 27, 1812, A. L. Hench Collection, UVA; *CVSP,* 10:157; General Orders, Sept. 3, 1812, ELB.

22. The Quids were the Tertium Quids, or a "third something" between the Federalists and Republicans. In 1806 John Randolph declared in Congress that he was no longer a Republican but a member of a third party called "Quids" (Risjord, *Old Republicans,* p. 166).

23. Francis Fry Wayland, *Andrew Stevenson, Democrat and Diplomat, 1785–1857* (Philadelphia: University of Pennsylvania Press, 1949), pp. 23–24; Ambler, *Thomas Ritchie,* pp. 57–59; EC, 1812, passim; *Richmond Enquirer,* June-Dec. 1812, passim. Initially there had been considerable opposition in the state to war. For example, of twenty-two Virginia representatives elected in 1811 to the Twelfth Congress, five were Federalists from the Valley, transmontane, and Loudoun-Fairfax districts. Led by Daniel Sheffey of the Valley and Joseph Lewis of the Loudoun-Fairfax district, they voted consistently against war and war measures. At the same time, Virginia Quids, led by John Randolph, elected three antiwar congressmen from the Tidewater. Only three Virginia Republicans elected in 1811 unequivocally favored war (Ambler, *Sectionalism in Virginia,* pp. 90–92; Risjord, *Old Republicans,* pp. 123–24, 146).

24. Edward Jones, Lieutenant Colonel, and all other officers of the 100th Regiment to the Adjutant General, Nov. 29, 1813, *CVSP,* 10:291–93; *Richmond Whig and Public Advertiser,* July 4, 1842; John Campbell to David Campbell, June 12, Oct. 5, 17, 1812, Campbell Family Papers, Duke University; EP, 1812–14, passim. Among the most laudatory of these resolutions were those adopted by the citizens of Patrick County on July 4, 1812.

25. *JHD,* 1812–13, p. 41; *Richmond Enquirer,* Dec. 8, 1812.

26. *JHD,* 1812–13, pp. 1–3; JB to the Speaker of the House of Delegates and [the President of the] Senate, Nov. 30, 1812, ELB.

27. William Sharp to JB, Feb. 4, 1813, *CVSP,* 10:184–85; *JHD,* 1812–13, p. 153; *Norfolk Gazette and Public Ledger,* June 1, 1816; James Semple to JB, March 22, 1813, EP; *CVSP,* 10:204ff.; EC, Feb.-April 1813.

28. *Acts Passed at a General Assembly of The Commonwealth of Virginia, 1812–1813* (Richmond, 1813), pp. 13, 18; *JHD,* 1812–13, p. 138.

29. *Norfolk Gazette and Public Ledger,* Feb. 12, April 17, 1813; *CVSP,* 10:190, 376, 381; *JHD,* 1812–13, pp. 5–6; William Wirt to Dabney Carr, March 31, 1813, Wirt-Carr Correspondence, VSL.

30. Robert B. Taylor to JB, March 24, 1813, and James Semple to JB, March 22, 1813, EP; *Norfolk Gazette and Public Ledger,* March 17, 20, April 14, 1813; St. George

Tucker to JB, March 19, 1813, *CVSP,* 10:206, 214; General Orders, March 9, April 1, 1813, ELB; *Norfolk Argus,* June 22, 1855; ELB, March-April 1813.

31. *JHD,* May 1813, pp. 2–4; *Acts of the General Assembly Begun on May 17, 1813* (Richmond, 1813), p. 4.

32. *CVSP,* 10:225ff.; *Norfolk Gazette and Public Ledger,* June 23, 1813; *Norfolk Argus,* June 22, 1855; Littleton W. Tazewell to JB, June 22, 1813, and Robert G. Scott to JB, June 25, 1813, EP; *JHD,* 1813–14, p. 3; JB to Sir John Borlase Warren, June 30, 1813, ELB.

33. *CVSP,* 10:240–47; EP, June-July 1813; Torrence, "War's Wild Alarm," pp. 217–18; S. Bailey Turlington, "Richmond during the War of 1812; The Vigilance Committee," *VMHB,* 7 (Jan. 1900):226–27, 408–409; Journals of the Council of State, July 1813, VSL; *Richmond Enquirer,* July 1813, passim.

34. "Richmond during the War of 1812," pp. 229ff., 409.

35. James McDowell to JB, July 25, 1813, EP; *CVSP,* 10:266–68.

36. *JHD,* 1813–14, pp. 7–8.

37. EP, 1812–14, passim; Harry L. Coles, *The War of 1812* (Chicago: University of Chicago Press, 1965), pp. 266–67; Smelser, *The Democratic Republic,* pp. 227–30; Leonard D. White, *The Jeffersonians: A Study in Administrative History, 1801–1829* (New York: Macmillan, 1951), pp. 211–20.

38. JB to Eustis, April 17, May 19, Aug. 21, 1812, ELB; *CVSP,* 10:184ff.; JB to Madison, Oct. 4, 1813, and Madison to JB, Feb. 26, 1814, Madison Papers, LC.

39. Charles Everette to James Monroe, Sept. 29, 1814, *CVSP,* 10:392; *JHD,* 1814–15, pp. 22ff.; Gordon, *William Fitzhugh Gordon,* p. 78; EC, June-Nov. 1814, passim; *Richmond Whig and Public Advertiser,* July 4, 1842.

40. *JHD,* 1813–14, p. 4. By large majorities in both houses the legislature voted on Jan. 7, 1814, to assume Virginia's portion, fixed at $369,018.44. To raise this money the legislature voted to increase the overall tax rate by one-third. Although this measure passed the House of Delegates by a safe margin, it passed the Senate only with the deciding vote of the president (ibid., pp. 111–12, 117; *Richmond Enquirer,* Feb. 10, 12, 1814).

41. *Richmond Whig and Public Advertiser,* July 4, 1842; *Baltimore Weekly Register,* Dec. 18, 1813; John Campbell to David Campbell, June 18, 1813, Campbell Family Papers, Duke University; Francis Preston to John Preston, Dec. 16, 1813, Preston Family Papers, LC.

42. John Campbell to David Campbell, July 16, 1813, Campbell Family Papers, Duke University.

43. Francis Preston to John Preston, Dec. 16, 1813, Preston Family Papers, LC.

44. *Baltimore Weekly Register,* Dec. 18, 1813; *JHD,* 1813–14, p. 50.

45. *JHD,* 1814–15, pp. 5–6; *CVSP,* 10:358ff.

46. JB to Gen. James Singleton, May 26, 1812, *CVSP,* 10:376, 381, 391; *JHD,* 1814–15, p. 6; *Richmond Enquirer,* Aug. 27, 1814.

47. Robert Porterfield to JB, Sept. 2, 1814, *CVSP,* 10:382–84; *JHD,* 1814–15, pp. 5–7, 607.

48. *Acts of the General Assembly, 1814–1815* (Richmond, 1815), pp. 40–52; *Richmond Enquirer,* Jan. 18, 1815.

49. JB to the Commandants of the Virginia Militia Regiments (Circular), March 31, 1812, ELB; JB to the Speaker of the House of Delegates and [President of the] Senate, Dec. 6, 1813, ELB.

50. JB to the Speaker of the House of Delegates and [President of the] Senate, Oct. 10, 1814, ELB.

51. William F. Gordon to Mrs. Gordon, July 31, 1814, quoted in Gordon, *William Fitzhugh Gordon,* p. 78; William Eustis to JB, April 30, May 20, 1812, EP; James Monroe to JB, Oct. 23, 1813, *JHD,* 1813–14, p. 6; Robert Quarles to JB, Feb. 11, 1813, *CVSP,* 10:191; Spencer Roane to JB, Feb. 19, 1820, John Tyler Papers, LC.

52. John Campbell to David Campbell, June 12, 1812, Campbell Family Papers, Duke University.

53. *Virginia Argus,* Dec. 7, 1812; *Baltimore American,* quoted in Brant, *James Madison,* 4:269–70.

54. Resolutions, July 4, 1812, EP.

55. *Richmond Enquirer,* Dec. 5, 1812; Hodges, "Pro-Governmentalism in Virginia," pp. 342–50.

56. JB to the Speaker of the House of Delegates and [President of the] Senate, Nov. 30, 1812, JB to Charles F. Mercer, Oct. 14, 1812, and JB to the President of the James River Canal Company, Potomac Company and Dismal Swamp Canal Company, Oct. 4, 1812, ELB; William Cammack to JB, Jan. 13, 1813, EC; *Norfolk Gazette and Public Ledger,* June 11, 1814; *Acts of the General Assembly, 1813–1816,* passim.

57. *JHD,* 1812–13, p. 2; *Richmond Enquirer,* Dec. 5, 1812. Barbour's efforts on behalf of the University of Virginia are discussed in chapter 11.

58. Ammon, "The Richmond Junto," pp. 399–400.

59. Ammon attributes greater power to the Junto in the period before the war than I do. See Ammon, "The Richmond Junto," pp. 395–405, and Ammon, *James Monroe,* pp. 277, 283–84.

60. Ammon, "The Richmond Junto," pp. 400, 412–13. Barbour's relationship to the Junto is best revealed in a group of letters written to him by members of the group at the time of the Missouri Controversy, published in the *WMQ,* 1st ser., 10 (July 1901):5–24.

61. William Wirt to Dabney Carr, Dec. 10, 1814, Wirt-Carr Correspondence, VSL; Philip Pendleton Barbour to JB, Nov. 17, 1814, BP UVA; Ammon, *James Monroe,* p. 285; *Richmond Enquirer,* Jan. 14, 1811, Jan. 4, 1812.

62. William Wirt to Dabney Carr, Dec. 10, 1814, Wirt-Carr Correspondence, VSL. Neither the house journals nor the newspapers record details of the contest. In the absence of other letters providing information about the election, there has been heavy reliance on Wirt's five-page letter, though it is admittedly biased. My account of the contest is drawn from this source.

63. Ibid. Neither the house journals nor the newspapers give a division of the vote. Dabney Carr thought it was 127 to 80; Wirt recorded 107 to 80.

64. Ibid.; Philip Pendleton Barbour to JB, Nov. 17, 1814, BP UVA.

65. *JHD,* 1814–15, p. 140.

Chapter 5. The Lure of Nationalism

1. Quoted in Henry S. Randall, *The Life of Thomas Jefferson,* 3 vols. (New York: Derby and Jackson, 1858), 3:5.

2. The details of this experience and the quotations are from [Royall], *Sketches,* pp. 116–17.

3. Margaret Bayard Smith, *The First Forty Years of Washington Society, Portrayed by the Family Letters of Mrs. Samuel Harrison Smith (Margaret Bayard) from the Collection of her Grandson, J. Henley Smith,* ed. Gaillard Hunt (New York: C. Scribner's Sons, 1906), pp. 109–10; William Wirt to Mrs. William Wirt, Oct. 14, 1814, William Wirt Papers, Maryland Historical Society, Baltimore. For descriptions of Washington during this general period, see Joseph West Moore, *Picturesque Washington, Pen and Pencil Sketches . . .* (Providence: J. A. and R. A. Reid, 1884), pp. 26ff.; John C. Proctor, ed., *Washington, Past and Present,* 4 vols. (New York: Lewis Historical Publishing, 1930), 1:95–97; Constance McLaughlin Green, *Washington: Village and Capital, 1800–1878* (Princeton: Princeton University Press, 1962), 1:56–80; James Sterling Young, *The Washington Community, 1800–1828* (New York: Columbia University Press, 1966), passim. Barbour's feelings upon first viewing the ruins of the capital were expressed in his speech advocating a stronger military establishment, delivered in the Senate on Feb. 25, 1817, in *Annals,* 14th Cong., 2nd sess., pp. 152–58.

4. *Annals,* 13th Cong., 3rd sess., p. 165.

5. Hugh Blair Grigsby, "Sketches of the Members of the Constitutional Convention of 1829–1830," *VMHB,* 61 (July 1953):331; Collins, *Miscellanies,* pp. 217, 226; Watterson, *Letters from Washington,* pp. 127–29; Robert E. Winthrop to William Wirt Henry, Jan. 24, 1876, William Wirt Henry Papers, VHS; Smith, *Washington Society,* p. 137; John W. Bell, comp., *Memoirs of Governor William Smith, of Virginia* (New York: Moss Engraving, 1891), p. 14; John Campbell to Elizabeth Campbell, Dec. 4, 1810, Campbell Family Papers, Duke University.

6. Watterson, *Letters from Washington,* p. 131.

7. Smith, *Washington Society,* pp. 137–38, 208–209; William Cabell Rives to Mrs. Rives, Dec. 24, 1823, William Cabell Rives Papers, LC; James Monroe to JB, Jan. 3, 1820, "Missouri Compromise: Letters to James Barbour, Senator of Virginia in the Congress of the United States," *WMQ,* 1st ser., 10 (July 1901):17; [Royall], *Sketches,* pp. 115–17; Collins, *Miscellanies,* pp. 226–27; Robley Dunglison Diary, pp. 473–74, UVA; Francis G. Ruffin Diary, p. 105, VHS; John Campbell to David Campbell, June 20, 1821, and David Campbell to Elizabeth Campbell, Dec. 4, 1810, Campbell Family Papers, Duke University.

8. [Royall], *Sketches,* p. 115; Smith, *Washington Society,* pp. 137, 208.

9. Ralph C. H. Catterall, *The Second Bank of the United States* (Chicago: University of Chicago Press, 1903), pp. 1–11; Bray Hammond, *Banks and Politics in America from the Revolution to the Civil War* (Princeton: Princeton University Press, 1957), pp. 228ff.; J. Van Fenstermaker, "The Statistics of American Commercial Banking, 1782–1818," *Journal of Economic History,* 25 (Sept. 1965):400–13.

10. The most influential Virginia Republican, other than Barbour, to support the Bank actively was James Pleasants, but several members of the Junto, including

Thomas Ritchie, yielded to the nationalist spirit and raised only feeble protests against the move to create a national bank (*Annals,* 13th Cong., 3rd sess., pp. 1043–45; Ambler, *Thomas Ritchie,* p. 72; Risjord, *Old Republicans,* p. 177).

11. Roane to JB, Jan. 4, 1816, BP NYPL. See also Hugh Nelson to Charles Everett, Jan. 3, 1815, Hugh Nelson Papers, LC.

12. Watterson, *Letters from Washington,* p. 129; Hammond, *Banks and Politics,* pp. 230–37; Catterall, *Second Bank,* pp. 7–17; *Annals,* 13th Cong., 3rd sess., pp. 119–26, 164–74, 1024–83, 1120. In the House, Philip Pendleton Barbour was one of the foremost opponents of the bank, which he had consistently opposed for years (Philip Pendleton Barbour to JB, Nov. 17, 1814, BP UVA).

13. *Richmond Whig and Public Advertiser,* July 4, 1842; Charles M. Wiltse, *John C. Calhoun, Nationalist, 1782–1828* (Indianapolis: Bobbs-Merrill, 1944), p. 100; Risjord, *Old Republicans,* p. 156; *Annals,* 13th Cong., 3rd sess., pp. 226, 232, 1168.

14. Shaw Livermore, Jr., *The Twilight of Federalism: The Disintegration of the Federalist Party, 1815–1830* (Princeton: Princeton University Press, 1962), pp. 11ff.; Risjord, *Old Republicans,* pp. 161–64; Ketcham, *Madison,* pp. 602–605; Banning, *Jeffersonian Persuasion,* pp. 296–302.

15. George Dangerfield, *The Awakening of American Nationalism, 1815–1828* (New York: Harper and Row, 1965), pp. 3–17; Ketcham, *Madison,* pp. 602–606; James D. Richardson, ed. and comp., *A Compilation of the Messages and Papers of the Presidents, 1789–1897,* 10 vols. (Washington, D.C., 1896–99), 1:565–68.

16. JB to James Barbour, Jr., Dec. 5, 1815, BP NYPL.

17. Risjord, *Old Republicans,* pp. 160–74; Ketcham, *Madison,* pp. 603–604.

18. *Annals,* 14th Cong., 1st sess., pp. 494–505; Wiltse, *Calhoun, Nationalist,* pp. 108–109.

19. *Annals,* 14th Cong., 1st sess., pp. 1207–19.

20. Ibid., pp. 236–38.

21. Ibid., pp. 241–44.

22. Ibid., pp. 244–81.

23. *Richmond Enquirer,* March 9, July 31, 1816; Ambler, *Thomas Ritchie,* p. 67.

24. *Annals,* 14th Cong., 1st sess., pp. 241–44; *Richmond Enquirer,* March 9, 1816.

25. Richardson, *Messages and Papers of the Presidents,* 1:555; *Annals,* 14th Cong., 1st sess., p. 241.

26. Frank W. Taussig, *The Tariff History of the United States* (New York: Putnam, 1892), pp. 68ff.; Dangerfield, *Awakening of American Nationalism,* pp. 12–13; *Annals,* 14th Cong., 1st sess., pp. 960, 1257ff., 1362. The Virginia delegation opposed the tariff 13 to 6. It appears that many of the southern nationalists, including Calhoun and William Lowndes of South Carolina, supported the tariff from a desire not to see manufacturing develop in the South but to raise additional revenue for the national government and to protect the limited industry that had been established. The latter consideration was especially important to Calhoun, who feared a new war with Britain (Norris W. Preyer, "Southern Support of the Tariff of 1816—A Reappraisal," *Journal of Southern History,* 25 [Aug. 1959]:306–22).

27. *Annals,* 14th Cong., 1st sess., pp. 326–31; JB to John J. Crittenden, May 31, 1820, John J. Crittenden Papers, Duke University. Barbour's views on the subject of protection are more fully developed in his lengthy speech concerning a navigation

bill delivered in the Senate in April 1818. See *Annals,* 15th Cong., 1st sess., pp. 313–24.

28. JB to Crittenden, May 31, 1820, John J. Crittenden Papers, Duke University; *Annals,* 14th Cong., 1st sess., pp. 326–31.

29. *Annals,* 14th Cong., 1st sess., pp. 326–27.

30. Ibid., pp. 326–31, 334.

31. Ammon, *James Monroe,* p. 353; Ambler, *Thomas Ritchie,* pp. 63–64; J. E. D. Shipp, *Giant Days; or, The Life and Times of William H. Crawford* (Americus, Ga.: Southern Printers, 1909), pp. 142–45; Robert V. Remini, "New York and the Presidential Election of 1816," *New York History,* 31 (Sept. 1950):308–23.

32. Ammon, *James Monroe,* p. 354; Remini, "New York and the Presidential Election," p. 319; James Barbour, James Pleasants, Armistead T. Mason, Hugh Nelson, Thomas Newton, and William Roane to [the Virginia Legislature], Feb. 9, 1816, BP NYPL; *Richmond Enquirer,* March 20, 1816.

33. JB et al. to [the Virginia Legislature], Feb. 9, 1816, BP NYPL.

34. *Richmond Enquirer,* Feb. 20, March 20, 1816; Ambler, *Thomas Ritchie,* p. 64; Ammon, *James Monroe,* pp. 353–54.

35. Ambler, *Thomas Ritchie,* pp. 63–64; *Richmond Enquirer,* March 20, 1816; Ammon, "The Richmond Junto," p. 406; Roane to JB, Feb. 12, 1816, BP NYPL; *National Intelligencer,* March 14, 1816; Remini, "New York and the Presidential Election of 1816," pp. 320–21; Ammon, *James Monroe,* p. 356.

36. *Richmond Enquirer,* March 20, 1816; Ammon, *James Monroe,* p. 354.

37. *Annals,* 14th Cong., 1st sess., pp. 159, 165–66, 178, 253, 275–79, 300, 305, 318, 336, 341, 363, 368.

38. *Congressional Directory,* 14th Cong., 2nd sess. (Washington, D.C., 1816), p. 77; William C. Rives to Mrs. Rives, Jan. 3, 1817, Rives Papers, LC.

39. Barbour Family Genealogy and Barbour Family Bible, BP UVA.

40. JB to James Barbour, Jr., July 7, Nov. 8, Dec. 22, 1815, March 21, Nov. 18, 1816, BP UVA.

41. Barbour Ledgers, Account Books, and Business Papers, passim, BP UVA.

42. OCP and OCL, 1816–17, VSL; Barbour Account Books, 1816–19, BP UVA; Barbour, "Address to the Agricultural Society of Albemarle," p. 12; Thomas Jefferson to JB, March 5, 1816, Jefferson Papers, Massachusetts Historical Society.

43. JB to James Barbour, Jr., May 7, 1817, BP UVA; Thomas Jefferson to Albert Gallatin, Sept. 8, 1816, in Jefferson, *Works,* ed. Ford, 12:34–39.

44. Henry Bradshaw Fearon, *Sketches of America. A Narrative of Journey of Five Thousand Miles Through the Eastern and Western States of America* ... (London: Longman, Hurst, Rees, Orme, and Brown, 1818), p. 311; John M. Duncan, *Travels Through Part of the United States and Canada in 1818 and 1819,* 2 vols. (London: Hurst, Robison, 1823), 1:268.

45. *Annals,* 14th Cong., 2nd sess., pp. 21–22.

46. Ibid., pp. 296–97, 361, 851–923, 933–34; Wiltse, *Calhoun, Nationalist,* pp. 132–36. The Virginia delegation voted 14 to 6 against the bill, with only two Republicans, neither of whom was orthodox, favoring it.

47. *Annals,* 14th Cong., 2nd sess., pp. 166–80, 186–91; Caspar N. Nevin to JB, June 29, 1827, BP UVA.

48. *Annals,* 14th Cong., 2nd sess., pp. 165–70, 177–80.

49. Richardson, *Messages and Papers of the Presidents,* 1:584–85; Risjord, *Old Republicans,* pp. 172–74.

50. *Richmond Enquirer,* March 11, Dec. 27, 1817.

51. *Richmond Enquirer,* March 11, 1817. See also the issues of March 9 and July 31, 1816.

52. *Richmond Enquirer,* Jan. 9, March 11, Dec. 27, 1817; Ambler, *Thomas Ritchie,* pp. 72–73; Ammon, "The Richmond Junto," pp. 406–407.

53. *Annals,* 15th Cong., 1st sess., pp. 17–22.

54. Ibid., pp. 451–60.

55. *Richmond Enquirer,* Dec. 27, 1817.

56. *Annals,* 15th Cong., 1st sess., pp. 1114–40, 1385–86; Risjord, *Old Republicans,* pp. 200–201.

57. *Annals,* 15th Cong., 1st sess., pp. 10, 22, 292; 15th Cong., 2nd sess., p. 171; 16th Cong., 1st sess., p. 655. For a good study of the internal improvements issue, see Joseph H. Harrison, Jr., "The Internal Improvements Issue in the Politics of the Union, 1783–1825" (Ph.D. diss., University of Virginia, 1954).

58. *Annals,* 14th Cong., 2nd sess., pp. 124–30, 152–58, 164.

59. Ibid., 16th Cong., 2nd sess., pp. 365–75, 449, 758–99, 802–41, 936–37; Wiltse, *Calhoun, Nationalist,* p. 225; Risjord, *Old Republicans,* pp. 191–96.

60. *Annals,* 14th Cong., 2nd sess., pp. 19–20, 30–32; JB to Daniel Webster, Feb. 17, 1832, in George Ticknor Curtis, *Life of Daniel Webster,* 2 vols. (New York: D. Appleton, 1870), 1:425n.

61. John Quincy Adams, *Memoirs of John Quincy Adams, Comprising Portions of His Diary from 1795 to 1848,* ed. Charles Francis Adams, 12 vols. (Philadelphia: J. B. Lippincott, 1874–77), 3:391–94; F. Lee Benns, *The American Struggle for the British West India Carrying-Trade, 1815–1830,* Indiana University Studies, 10:56 (March 1923), pp. 40–51; *Annals,* 14th Cong., 2nd sess., pp. 356–57, 15th Cong., 1st sess., pp. 307–15, 866–70; Rufus King to JB, Aug. 18, 1818, BP NYPL; Robert Ernst, *Rufus King, American Federalist* (Chapel Hill: University of North Carolina Press, 1968), pp. 354–57.

62. Benns, *The American Struggle for the British West India Carrying-Trade,* pp. 7–36; *Niles' Register,* Feb. 1, 1817.

63. Barbour's speech, from which the quotations and analysis that follow are drawn, is in *Annals,* 15th Cong., 1st sess., pp. 313–24.

64. Quoted in the *Charleston Courier* (South Carolina), July 30, 1818. See also James Madison to JB, April 16, 1818, BP UVA.

65. *Annals,* 15th Cong., 1st sess., pp. 234–41, 1720. Negative votes in the Senate were cast by John W. Eppes of Virginia and James L. Wilson of New Jersey.

66. Monroe to JB, March 3, 1817, Feb. 3, 1820, June 14, 1823, March 14, 16, 1824, BP NYPL.

67. *Annals,* 15th Cong., 2nd sess., p. 232.

68. *Annals,* 14th Cong., 1st sess., p. 47; Watterson, *Letters from Washington,* pp. 130–31; Smith, *Washington Society,* pp. 137–38, 208–209, 227–28; Fearon, *Narrative of a Journey,* p. 312; Robley Dunglison Diary, pp. 473–74, UVA.

69. Grigsby, "Sketches of the Members of the Constitutional Convention of 1829–30," p. 331; James Pleasants to William Cabell Rives, Jan. 1, 1817, Rives Papers, LC.

70. Quoted in William Cabell Bruce, *John Randolph of Roanoke, 1773–1833,* 2 vols. (New York: G. P. Putnam's Sons, 1922), 2:202.

71. Perceval Reniers, *The Springs of Virginia: Life, Love, and Death at the Waters, 1775–1900* (Chapel Hill: University of North Carolina Press, 1941), p. 131; Watterson, *Letters from Washington,* p. 130; Adams, *Memoirs,* 4:226–27; John H. Eaton to Harrison Gray Otis, March 23, 1824, Harrison Gray Otis Papers, Massachusetts Historical Society, Boston; Robley Dunglison Diary, p. 473, UVA.

72. John P. Little, *Richmond, The Capital of Virginia: Its History* (Richmond: Macfarland and Fergusson, 1851), pp. 96–97, 129.

73. E. B. Williston, *Eloquence of the United States,* 5 vols. (Middletown, Conn.: E. and H. Clark, 1827); Wirt to Littleton W. Tazewell, Dec. 30, 1804, Tazewell Family Papers, VSL.

74. Francis G. Ruffin Diary, p. 105, VHS; Bell, ed., *Memoirs of Governor William Smith,* p. 14.

75. Watterson, *Letters from Washington,* p. 130; Adams, *Memoirs,* 4:226, 506.

76. Fearon, *Narrative of Journey,* p. 312.

77. Watterson, *Letters from Washington,* p. 129; William Faux, *Memorable Days in America, Being a Journal of a Tour to the United States* (London: N. Simpkin and R. Marshall, 1823), p. 369.

78. Adams, *Memoirs,* 4:506.

79. Banning, *Jeffersonian Persuasion,* pp. 269, 285; Shalhope, *John Taylor,* pp. 44, 104; Dawidoff, *Education of John Randolph,* pp. 159, 237–38.

80. James Madison to William Eustis, May 22, 1823, Madison, *Writings,* ed. Hunt, 9:135–37.

81. *Annals,* 14th Cong., 1st sess., p. 47.

82. Ibid., 14 Cong., 2nd sess., p. 158.

Chapter 6. A Dream Shattered

1. *Richmond Enquirer,* Dec. 19, 1818.

2. *Annals,* 15th Cong., 1st sess., pp. 71–80, 94–108, 1675, 1740–44.

3. *Richmond Enquirer,* May 19, Aug. 18, 1818; Ambler, *Thomas Ritchie,* pp. 73–74; Spencer Roane to JB, Jan. 30, Feb. 16, 1819, BP NYPL.

4. *Richmond Enquirer,* April 13, 1819.

5. Thomas Ritchie to JB, Jan. 4, 1819, BP NYPL.

6. JB to John J. Crittenden, Feb. 6, 1820, quoted in Mrs. Chapman Coleman, *The Life of John J. Crittenden, with Selections from His Correspondence and Speeches,* 2 vols. (Philadelphia: J. B. Lippincott, 1871), 1:41; *Annals,* 16th Cong., 1st sess., p. 107.

7. *Annals,* 15th Cong., 2nd sess., pp. 238, 251, 1166–70, 1433–38.

8. Ibid., 16th Cong., 1st sess., pp. 107, 335.

9. Ibid., p. 107; *Richmond Enquirer,* Nov. 23, Dec. 3, 21, 1819.

10. *Annals,* 16th Cong., 1st sess., pp. 103–107; Ammon, *James Monroe,* pp. 450–53.

11. Ammon, *James Monroe,* pp. 452–53; Glover Moore, *The Missouri Controversy, 1819–1821* (Lexington: University of Kentucky Press, 1953), pp. 94–95.

12. *Annals,* 16th Cong., 1st sess., p. 54; Cecil B. Egerton, "Rufus King and the Missouri Question: A Study in Political Mythology" (Ph.D. diss., Claremont Graduate School, 1967), pp. 145–48.

13. *Annals,* 16th Cong., 1st sess., pp. 103–105; Monroe to JB, Feb. 3, 1820, in "Missouri Compromise: Letters to James Barbour," p. 9.

14. *Annals,* 16th Cong., 1st sess., p. 841.

15. Ibid., pp. 35–36, 47, 54–55, 85.

16. John Holmes to William King, Jan. 1, 1820, William King Papers, Maine Historical Society; Monroe to JB, Feb. 3, 1820, in "Missouri Compromise: Letters to James Barbour," p. 9; Ammon, *James Monroe,* p. 452; *Richmond Whig and Public Advertiser,* July 4, 1842.

17. Christopher Gore to Rufus King, Jan. 29, 1820, quoted in *The Life and Correspondence of Rufus King,* ed. Charles R. King, 6 vols. (New York: G. P. Putnam's Sons, 1894–1900), 6:261; Anonymous to JB [n.d.], BP UVA.

18. *Annals,* 16th Cong., 1st sess., pp. 85–118; W. P. Preble to John Holmes, Jan. 16, 1820, John Holmes Papers, Maine Historical Society.

19. *Annals,* 16th Cong., 1st sess., pp. 86–99, 732–36, 802–804, 937; John Holmes to William King, Jan. 5, 1820, and Mark Langdon Hill to William King, Jan. 6, 1820, William King Papers, Maine Historical Society.

20. *Annals,* 16th Cong., 1st sess., pp. 101–108.

21. Ibid., pp. 86–88, 93–99, 118.

22. *Washington National Intelligencer,* Jan. 22, 1820; Adams, *Memoirs,* 5:40; Smith, *Washington Society,* pp. 148–49.

23. *Annals,* 16th Cong., 1st sess., pp. 86–118; William Plumer, Jr., to William Plumer, March 4, 1820, in *The Missouri Compromises and Presidential Politics, 1820–1825, from the Letters of William Plumer, Jr.,* ed. Everett Somerville Brown (St. Louis: Missouri Historical Society, 1926), pp. 13–14.

24. James Monroe to [George Hay], Feb. 10, 1820, Monroe Papers, NYPL.

25. *Annals,* 16th Cong., 1st sess., pp. 119, 313–35. The quotations that follow are from this source.

26. Ernst, *Rufus King,* p. 370.

27. *Annals,* 16th Cong., 1st sess., p. 330.

28. Ibid., pp. 232, 236, 238, 321, 389–417; Moore, *Missouri Controversy,* pp. 97–98; Thomas Hart Benton, *Thirty Years' View; or, A History of the Working of the American Government for Thirty Years, from 1820 to 1850,* 2 vols. (New York: D. Appleton, 1854–56), 1:20; Rufus King to Christopher Gore, Jan. 30, 1820, in *Rufus King,* ed. King, 6:263.

29. *Annals,* 16th Cong., 1st sess., pp. 259–75, 343, 418–24.

30. Ibid., p. 239; John Tyler to Henry Curtis, Feb. 5, 1820, John Tyler Papers, LC; Calvin Colton, ed., *The Private Correspondence of Henry Clay* (New York: A. S. Barnes, 1855), p. 61.

31. Adams, *Memoirs,* 5:13.

32. Ibid., 4:502–503, 525–26, 531, 5:12; Brown, *Missouri Compromises,* pp. 11–14; Moore, *Missouri Controversy,* p. 93; Monroe to [George Hay], Feb. 8, 1820, Monroe Papers, NYPL; *Annals,* 16th Cong., 1st sess., p. 209.

33. *Annals,* 16th Cong., 1st sess., pp. 335, 338–39.

34. George Hay to Monroe, Dec. 24, 1819, Monroe Papers, LC; James Madison to JB, Feb. 14, 1820, BP NYPL; JB to John J. Crittenden, Feb. 6, 1820, in Coleman, *Crittenden,* 1:41; "Missouri Compromise: Letters to James Barbour," pp. 5–24, passim; Ammon, "The Richmond Junto," p. 412; *Richmond Whig and Public Advertiser,* July 4, 1842.

35. Monroe to JB, Feb. 3, 1820, in "Missouri Compromise: Letters to James Barbour," p. 9; JB to Crittenden, Feb. 6, 1820, in Coleman, *Crittenden,* 1:41; *Richmond Enquirer,* Feb. 17, 1820; Ammon, *James Monroe,* p. 452.

36. *Annals,* 16th Cong., 1st sess., pp. 424, 427; Monroe to JB, Feb. 3, 1820, in "Missouri Compromise: Letters to James Barbour," p. 9; Ammon, *James Monroe,* pp. 452–53.

37. *Richmond Enquirer,* Feb. 10, 17, 1820; Charles Yancey to JB, Feb. 10, 1820, in "Missouri Compromise: Letters to James Barbour," p. 10; JB to Crittenden, Feb. 6, 1820, in Coleman, *Crittenden,* 1:41.

38. JB to Crittenden, Feb. 6, 1820, in Coleman, *Crittenden,* 1:41; *Annals,* 16th Cong., 1st sess., pp. 161, 329; "A Gentleman in Washington to His Friends in Richmond," Feb. 12, 1820, in *Richmond Enquirer,* Feb. 17, 1820. Jefferson, Madison, and Monroe shared Barbour's distrust of Federalist motives (Don E. Fehrenbacher, "The Missouri Controversy and the Sources of Southern Separatism," *Southern Review,* 14 [Oct. 1978]:661).

39. *Annals,* 16th Cong., 1st sess., pp. 966–90, 1243.

40. *Richmond Enquirer,* Jan. 20, Feb. 17, 1820; JB to Crittenden, Feb. 6, 1820, in Coleman, *Crittenden,* 1:41; *Annals,* 16th Cong., 1st sess., pp. 161, 329; JB to James Madison, Feb. 10, 1820, Madison Papers, LC.

41. Moore, *Missouri Controversy,* pp. 179–83; Ernst, *Rufus King,* pp. 373–74; Livermore, *Twilight of Federalism,* pp. 88–112.

42. JB to Crittenden, Feb. 6, 1820, in Coleman, *Crittenden,* 1:41; JB to Madison, Feb. 10, 1820, Madison Papers, LC; Monroe to Madison, Feb. 5, 1820, Rives Papers, LC; Clay to Leslie Combs, Feb. 5, 1820, in Henry Clay, *The Papers of Henry Clay,* ed. James F. Hopkins, 6 vols. to date (Lexington: University of Kentucky Press, 1959–), 2:774; *Richmond Enquirer,* Jan. 20, 1820; Monroe to [George Hay], Jan. 5, Feb. 8, 1820, Monroe Papers, NYPL; Shalhope, *John Taylor,* pp. 198–99.

43. "A Gentleman in Washington to His Friends in Richmond," Feb. 12, 1820, *Richmond Enquirer,* Feb. 17, 1820.

44. JB to Crittenden, Feb. 6, 1820, in Coleman, *Crittenden,* 1:41; JB to Madison, Feb. 10, 1820, Madison Papers, LC; "Missouri Compromise: Letters to James Barbour," pp. 5–24, passim; *Richmond Enquirer,* Feb. 10, 1820; Madison to JB, Feb. 14, 1820, BP NYPL.

45. *Annals,* 16th Cong., 1st sess., p. 105.

46. Thomas M. Bayly to Monroe, Feb. 15, 1820, Monroe Papers, NYPL; *Richmond Enquirer,* Feb. 10, 1820; Ammon, "The Richmond Junto," pp. 412–13.

47. Yancey to JB, Feb. 11, 1820, Roane to JB, Feb. 19, 1820, and William F. Gordon to JB, Feb. 18, 1820, in "Missouri Compromise: Letters to James Barbour," pp. 10, 17–18; Joseph C. Cabell to Henry St. George Tucker, Feb. 10, 1820, Tucker-Coleman Papers, College of William and Mary; Chapman Johnson to Peachy R. Gilmer, Feb. 17, 1820, Gilmer Papers, VSL; Ammon, "The Richmond Junto," pp. 212–13; *Richmond Enquirer,* Feb. 10, 12, 1820; *Boston Columbian Centinel,* Feb. 19, 1820.

48. *Richmond Enquirer,* Feb. 8, 10, 1820.

49. Yancey to JB, Feb. 9, 1820, John Tyler Papers, LC; Tucker to JB, Feb. 11, 1820, in "Missouri Compromise: Letters to James Barbour," pp. 10–11 and passim; *Richmond Enquirer,* Feb. 10, 1820; Ammon, *James Monroe,* p. 455.

50. Tucker to Barbour, Feb. 11, 1820, in "Missouri Compromise: Letters to James Barbour," pp. 10–11.

51. Roane to JB, Feb. 16, 1820, BP NYPL; Roane to Monroe, Feb. 16, 1820, quoted in Ammon, *James Monroe,* p. 455.

52. "Missouri Compromise: Letters to James Barbour," pp. 5–24, passim; Ammon, "The Richmond Junto," pp. 412–13.

53. Yancey to JB, Feb. 16, 17, 1820, in "Missouri Compromise: Letters to James Barbour," pp. 13–16.

54. Gordon to JB, Feb. 18, 1820, and Banks to JB, Feb. 20, 1820, in "Missouri Compromise: Letters to James Barbour," pp. 18–22.

55. Ammon, *James Monroe,* p. 456, attributes the letters to both men.

56. *Richmond Enquirer,* Feb. 17, 1820.

57. Chapman Johnson to Peachy R. Gilmer, Feb. 17, 1820, Gilmer Papers, VSL; *Richmond Enquirer,* Feb. 19, 1820; William Fitzhugh Gordon to JB, Feb. 18, 1820, and Charles Yancey to JB, Feb. 17, 1820, in "Missouri Compromise: Letters to James Barbour," pp. 16–19; Ammon, "The Richmond Junto," pp. 413–14.

58. *Richmond Enquirer,* March 7, 1820.

59. Chapman Johnson to Peachy R. Gilmer, Feb. 17, 1820, Gilmer Papers, VSL; Henry St. George Tucker to St. George Tucker, March 8, 1820, Tucker-Coleman Papers, College of William and Mary; Roane to JB, Feb. 19, 1820, in "Missouri Compromise: Letters to James Barbour," pp. 17–18.

60. William Fitzhugh Gordon to JB, Feb. 18, 1820, Linn Banks to JB, Feb. 20, 1820, and Spencer Roane to JB, Feb. 19, 1820, in "Missouri Compromise: Letters to James Barbour," pp. 17–22.

61. JB to John J. Crittenden, Feb. 6, 1820, in Coleman, *Crittenden,* 1:41; JB to Madison, Feb. 10, 1820, Madison Papers, LC; *Annals,* 16th Cong., 1st sess., p. 428.

62. *Annals,* 16th Cong., 1st sess., p. 428; JB to Crittenden, Feb. 6, 1820, in Coleman, *Crittenden,* 1:41; JB to Crittenden, May 31, 1820, Crittenden Papers, Duke University.

63. *Preamble and Resolutions on the Subject of the Missouri Question, Agreed to by the House of Delegates, and the Amendment of the Senate, Proposed Thereto* (Richmond, 1820); *Niles' Register,* 17:343–44, 416–17; *Richmond Enquirer,* Jan. 27, Feb. 3, 10, 17, 1820; Roane to JB, Feb. 16, 1820, BP NYPL; "Missouri Compromise; Letters to James Barbour," p. 6.

64. Moore, *Missouri Controversy,* pp. 245–49; *Annals,* 16th Cong., 1st sess., pp. 428, 1587–88; Tait to John Walker, May 20, 1820, John W. Walker Papers, Alabama Department of Archives and History.

65. Craven, *Soil Exhaustion,* pp. 17–19; Ammon, "The Richmond Junto," pp. 407–11; Risjord, *Old Republicans,* pp. 177–78; Samuel Reznack, "The Depression of 1819–1822: A Social History," *American Historical Review,* 39 (Oct. 1933):32–33.

66. Ammon, "The Richmond Junto," pp. 407–409; Rex Beach, "Judge Spencer Roane: A Champion of States Rights" (M.A. thesis, University of Virginia, 1941), pp. 73ff.; Ambler, *Thomas Ritchie,* pp. 80–83; Anderson, *William Branch Giles,* pp. 208–209.

67. Ritchie to JB, Jan. 4, 1819, BP NYPL; Simms, *John Taylor,* pp. 173–95; Ambler, *Thomas Ritchie,* pp. 80–81; Shalhope, *John Taylor,* pp. 196–202.

68. *Annals,* 16th Cong., 1st sess., pp. 428–30, 444, 457–59, 1457, 1558.

69. Ibid., pp. 467–69, 1572–77.

70. Ibid., pp. 471–72; Glyndon G. Van Deusen, *The Life of Henry Clay* (Boston: Little, Brown, 1937), pp. 139–40; Moore, *Missouri Controversy,* pp. 102–103.

71. *Annals,* 16th Cong., 1st sess., pp. 314–35, 411; JB to Charles Tait, Jan. 7, 1821, Tait Family Papers, Alabama Department of Archives and History; "A Gentleman in Washington to His Friends in Richmond," *Richmond Enquirer,* Feb. 17, 1820.

72. Fehrenbacher, "Missouri Controversy," p. 667; Merrill D. Peterson, *Thomas Jefferson and the New Nation: A Biography* (New York: Oxford University Press, 1970), p. 998.

73. *Annals,* 16th Cong., 1st sess., pp. 581–82, 655–72.

74. Barbour Family Bible, BP UVA; JB to James Barbour, Jr., Sept. 15, 1817, BP NYPL.

75. *Congressional Directory,* 16th Cong., 2nd sess. (Washington, D.C., 1820), p. 115.

76. *Annals,* 16th Cong., 2nd sess., p. 33.

77. Moore, *Missouri Controversy,* pp. 142–46; Brown, *Missouri Compromises,* pp. 29–33.

78. *Annals,* 16th Cong., 2nd sess., pp. 31, 41.

79. Ibid., pp. 41, 44–50, 102.

80. Ibid., pp. 116, 119.

81. Ibid., pp. 982, 1027, 1078–80, 1116–17; Van Deusen, *Henry Clay,* pp. 141–43.

82. *Annals,* 16th Cong., 2nd sess., pp. 267, 288, 341–47, 1058–59, 1147–66; Moore, *Missouri Controversy,* p. 152; Brown, *Missouri Compromises,* pp. 35–38; Adams, *Memoirs,* 5:276.

83. *Annals,* 16th Cong., 2nd sess., pp. 353–54, 363–64.

84. Ibid., pp. 381–82.

85. Ibid., p. 1228; Moore, *Missouri Controversy,* pp. 155–59; William Plumer, Jr., to William Plumer, Feb. 26, 1821, in Brown, *Missouri Compromises,* p. 42.

86. Hugh Nelson to Charles Everette, Feb. 26, 1821, Hugh Nelson Papers, LC; *Annals,* 16th Cong., 2nd sess., pp. 1238–40.

87. Adams, *Memoirs,* 5:308; William Plumer, Jr., to William Plumer, Feb. 26, 1821, in Brown, *Missouri Compromises,* p. 42.

88. *Annals,* 16th Cong., 2nd sess., pp. 388–90.

89. JB to John J. Crittenden, Feb. 6, 1820, in Coleman, *Crittenden,* 1:41.

90. JB to Charles Tait, Jan. 7, 1821, Tait Family Papers, Alabama Department of Archives and History.

Chapter 7. Between Two Worlds

1. Risjord, *Old Republicans,* pp. 178–80, 223–27; Ammon, "The Richmond Junto," pp. 407–12; Ambler, *Sectionalism in Virginia,* pp. 102ff.; Simms, *John Taylor,* pp. 173ff.; *Richmond Enquirer,* Feb. 25, 1819, Feb. 8, 10, 1820; Shalhope, *John Taylor,* pp. 193–202; Dawidoff, *Education of John Randolph,* pp. 240–44.

2. Roane to Archibald Thweat[t], Dec. 11, 1821, in "Roane Correspondence, 1799–1821," ed. William E. Dodd, *John P. Branch Historical Papers of Randolph-Macon College,* 2 (June 1905):140–41.

3. James M. Garnett to John Randolph, Dec. [n.d.] 1819, Randolph-Garnett Papers, LC, quoted in Risjord, *Old Republicans,* p. 226; Thomas Ritchie to JB, Jan. 4, 1819, BP NYPL; *Richmond Enquirer,* Nov. 17, 1820; *Annals,* 17th Cong., 2nd sess., p. 56.

4. James M. Garnett to John Randolph, Dec. 1819, Dec. 12, 1825, Randolph-Garnett Papers, LC.

5. Jefferson to Archibald Thweat[t], Jan. 19, 1821, and Jefferson to Edward Livingston, April 4, 1824, in Jefferson, *Works,* ed. Ford, 12:196–97, 348–51.

6. See BP NYPL, 1819–24, passim.

7. Roane to JB, Jan. 4, 1816 [misdated 1815], Jan. 30, Feb. 16, 1819, Feb. 22, 1821, Ritchie to JB, Jan. 4, 1819, May 21, 1823, and William Brockenbrough to JB, Jan. 25, 1819, BP NYPL; Roane to James Monroe, March 24, 1821, and John Taylor to JB, Jan. 18, 1824, Monroe Papers, NYPL; John Campbell to David Campbell, June 20, 1821, Campbell Family Papers, Duke University.

8. *Annals,* 16th Cong., 1st sess., pp. 625, 655–72, 2155–56. Barbour was also influenced by the depression. He thought the deficit in the national treasury necessitated retrenchment (JB to Isaac Davis, Dec. 24, 1819, Isaac Davis Papers, Duke University; JB to John J. Crittenden, May 31, 1820, Crittenden Papers, Duke University).

9. Benns, *West India Carrying-Trade,* pp. 64–70; *Annals,* 15th Cong., 1st sess., p. 578.

10. *Annals,* 16th Cong., 1st sess., pp. 579–84.

11. Ibid., pp. 597, 1822, 1836, 2240.

12. Adams, *Memoirs,* 5:317–18; Barbour Family Bible and JB to James Barbour, Jr., 1817–21, passim, BP UVA; Smith, *Washington Society,* p. 137.

13. Financial Papers, 1818–21, and JB to James Barbour, Jr., 1815–19, passim, BP UVA; JB to Isaac Davis, Jan. 22, 1819, A. L. Hench Collection, UVA.

14. John Campbell to David Campbell, June 20, 1821, Campbell Family Papers, Duke University; *Richmond Enquirer,* May 25, 29, June 1, 5, 8, 1821, Jan. 22, 1822; Roane to Archibald Thweat[t], Dec. 11, 24, 1821, "Roane Correspondence," pp. 140–41; Adams, *Memoirs,* 5:264–65; Roane to JB, Jan. 4, 1816 [misdated 1815], Jan. 30, Feb. 16, 1819, BP NYPL; Roane to Monroe, Dec. 13, 1819, Monroe Papers, NYPL.

15. JB to Charles Tait, Jan. 7, 1821, Tait Family Papers, Alabama Department of Archives and History; *Richmond Enquirer,* Jan. 16, 1821. Barbour's reelection, Roane thought, was a "fresh and honorable testimonial of the confidence of Virginia" (Roane to Monroe, March 24, 1821, Monroe Papers, NYPL).

16. *Congressional Directory,* 17th Cong., 1st sess. (Washington, D.C., 1821), passim.

17. *Annals,* 17th Cong., 1st sess., pp. 1690–93, 1734. Philip Pendleton Barbour was elected Speaker of the House in December 1821, unseating the previous Speaker, John W. Taylor of New York. An Adams man and antislavery spokesman in the House, Taylor was opposed by the Van Buren Bucktails in the New York delegation, who were instrumental in arranging Barbour's election (Risjord, *Old Republicans,* p. 231).

18. *Annals,* 17th Cong., 1st sess., pp. 443–44.

19. Monroe's veto message and the paper entitled "Views of the President of the United States on the Subject of Internal Improvements" were published in Richardson, *Messages and Papers of the Presidents,* 2:142–83.

20. After serving two terms as Speaker of the House, Barbour, whose political opinions were too conservative for the majority of the House, was overwhelmingly defeated by Clay, 139 to 42 (JB to Madison, Dec. 3, 1823, Madison Papers, LC).

21. *Annals,* 18th Cong., 1st sess., pp. 1005, 1014. Philip Pendleton Barbour and Roane were of one mind on this matter. See Roane to Monroe, July 1, 1822, "Roane Correspondence," p. 180.

22. *Annals,* 18th Cong., 1st sess., p. 1310.

23. Ibid., pp. 1468–69.

24. John Randolph to James M. Garnett, Dec. 30, 1822, Jan. 9, Feb. 10, Sept. 10, 1823, Randolph-Garnett Papers, LC.

25. *Annals,* 18th Cong., 1st sess., pp. 559–65.

26. Ibid., pp. 570–71.

27. George Dangerfield, *The Era of Good Feelings* (New York: Harcourt, Brace, 1952), pp. 254–63.

28. Benns, *West India Carrying-Trade,* pp. 87–94.

29. JB to Daniel Webster, Feb. 17, 1832, in Curtis, *Life of Daniel Webster,* 1:425n; Rufus King to Charles King, Dec. 28, 1822, Jan 7, 1823, in *Rufus King,* ed. King, 6:492–93.

30. Dangerfield, *Era of Good Feelings,* p. 483, n. 10.

31. JB to Webster, Feb. 17, 1832, in Curtis, *Life of Daniel Webster,* 1:425n.

32. *Annals,* 17th Cong., 2nd sess., pp. 314–18; Dangerfield, *Era of Good Feelings,* p. 262; Rufus King to JB, Aug. 18, 1818, BP NYPL.

33. Dangerfield, *Awakening of American Nationalism,* pp. 202–205; Taussig, *Tariff History,* pp. 68ff.; *Annals,* 18th Cong., 1st sess., pp. 1480, 1625–27, 1658, 2429.

34. *Annals,* 18th Cong., 1st sess., pp. 658–59, 743–44; JB to Isaac Davis, May 23, 1824, Isaac Davis Papers, UVA.

35. James M. Garnett to John Randolph, Dec. 22, 26, 1823, Randolph-Garnett Papers, LC.

36. *Annals,* 18th Cong., 1st sess., p. 2361.

37. Ibid., p. 283.

38. Ibid., p. 276.

39. Ibid., pp. 227–28, 503–505; Speech of James Barbour on Abolishment of Imprisonment for Indebtedness, Feb. 17, 1824, BP UVA. The Society for the Relief of the Distressed thanked Barbour for his reform efforts and for his "most excellent and most eloquent and feeling speech" (John Mackey et al. to JB, March 23, 1824, BP UVA).

40. *Annals,* 15th Cong., 2nd sess., p. 219.

41. Ibid., 16th Cong., 1st sess., p. 886.

42. Ibid., 18th Cong., 1st sess., pp. 118–19; William Staughton to JB, March 3, 1821, BP NYPL; Jefferson to JB, May 2, Dec. 26, 1824, and Jan. 3, 1825, and JB to Jefferson, May 15, Dec. 31, 1824, and March 2, April 19, 1825, Jefferson Papers, LC.

43. JB to John J. Crittenden, May 31, 1820, Crittenden Papers, Duke University.

44. Randolph to James M. Garnett, Jan. 1, 1824, and Garnett to Randolph, Dec. 12, 1825, Randolph-Garnett Papers, LC; *Proceedings and Debates in the Virginia State Convention of 1829–1830* (Richmond, 1830), p. 231. For a study of attitudes in Virginia concerning the state's decline, see Robert P. Sutton, "Nostalgia, Pessimism, and Malaise: The Doomed Aristocrat in Late-Jeffersonian Virginia," *VMHB,* 76 (Jan. 1968):41–55.

45. Garnett to Randolph, April 10, 1824, Randolph-Garnett Papers, LC. John Taylor joined the chorus in 1824, when, sounding very much like an old warrior going to his last battle, he wrote Barbour: "I assure you that I am not dead. . . . The ague and fever have left me, but have carried off meat of my flesh, so that it will be necessary for me to eat for some time, before I shall be able to perform the achievement of mounting the precipice leading to the Senate chamber. As soon as I can do this, and speak for five minutes, I will be with you. . . . But alas! What can I say towards saving our happy form of government from foes assailing it on all sides?" (Taylor to JB, Jan. 18, 1824, Monroe Papers, NYPL).

46. *Annals,* 18th Cong., 1st sess., p. 389.

47. Randolph to James M. Garnett, Jan. 1, 1824, Randolph-Garnett Papers, LC.

48. JB to John J. Crittenden, May 31, 1820, Crittenden Papers, Duke University.

49. Randolph to Richard Kidder Randolph, Jan. 14, 1824, John Randolph Papers, LC; *Richmond Enquirer,* Jan. 28, Aug. 26, 1823, Nov. 26, 1824.

50. JB to Isaac Davis, Jan. 22, 1819, A. L. Hench Collection, UVA; *Richmond Enquirer,* Jan. 23, 28, Feb. 13, 1823; Ambler, *Thomas Ritchie,* pp. 85–90; Adams, *Memoirs,* 6:466.

51. Randolph to James M. Garnett, April 26, 1824, Randolph-Garnett Papers, LC.

52. Adams, *Memoirs,* 6:356–57, 450–52.

53. John Quincy Adams to Robert Walsh, Jr., June 21, 1822, Adams Family Papers, LC; *Richmond Enquirer,* Jan. 26, 1822; Ambler, *Thomas Ritchie,* pp. 85–87; Risjord, *Old Republicans,* pp. 249–51; Ammon, "The Richmond Junto," pp. 414–15.

54. Crawford to JB, Sept. 18, 1819, July 25, 1821, Monroe to JB, March 3, 1817, Ritchie to JB, May 21, 1823, and Martin Van Buren to JB, Oct. 9, 1823, BP NYPL; JB to James Barbour, Jr., March 13, 1824, BP UVA.

55. JB to Tait, Jan. 7, 1821, Tait Family Papers, Alabama Department of Archives and History.

56. Ritchie to JB, May 21, 1823, BP NYPL; Risjord, *Old Republicans,* p. 250; Ambler, *Thomas Ritchie,* p. 89; *Richmond Enquirer,* Aug. 5, 1823.

57. *Richmond Enquirer,* Jan.-Feb. 1823, passim, and May 20, 25, 1823; Ambler, *Thomas Ritchie,* pp. 86–91.

58. Ritchie to JB, May 21, 1823, and Van Buren to JB, Oct. 9, 1823, BP NYPL; *Richmond Enquirer,* Oct. 7, 1823, Jan 1, 6, 1824; Adams, *Memoirs,* 6:235.

59. Wiltse, *Calhoun, Nationalist,* pp. 277–78; *Richmond Enquirer,* Sept. 26, 1823; Ammon, *James Monroe,* p. 530; JB to Madison, Dec. 3, 1823, Madison Papers, LC; Smith, *Washington Society,* pp. 199–200.

60. JB to Madison, Dec. 3, 1823, Madison Papers, LC; Asbury Dickens to Van Buren, Oct. 28, 1824, Van Buren Papers, LC; Van Buren to JB, Oct. 9, 1823, BP NYPL; *Richmond Enquirer,* Oct. 7, 1823, Jan 6, 1824; Dangerfield, *Awakening of American Nationalism,* pp. 212–15; Adams, *Memoirs,* 6:235.

61. *National Intelligencer,* Feb. 17, 1824; JB to Madison, Feb. 14, 1824, Madison Papers, LC.

62. JB to Madison, Feb. 14, 1824, Madison Papers, LC; Nathaniel Macon to Van Buren, May 9, 1823, and John Taylor to Van Buren, May 12, 1823, Van Buren Papers, LC.

63. Risjord, *Old Republicans,* p. 254; Ambler, *Thomas Ritchie,* pp. 90–95.

64. JB to Isaac Davis, Feb. 24, 1824, Isaac Davis Papers, UVA; William Henry Harrison to JB, April 18, 1824, BP NYPL; Adams, *Memoirs,* 6:235, 242, 450, 456.

65. Harrison to JB, April 18, 1824, BP NYPL.

66. Adams, *Memoirs,* 6:242; JB to Clay, Aug. 14, 1827, Clay Papers, LC.

67. Adams, *Memoirs,* 6:345, 348; John Taylor to JB, Jan. 18, 1824, Monroe Papers, NYPL; Randolph to James M. Garnett, Jan. 10, 1824, Randoph-Garnett Papers, LC.

68. Ammon, *James Monroe,* pp. 493–514; Monroe to JB, June 14, 1823, March 14, 16, 1824, BP NYPL.

69. Adams, *Memoirs,* 6:450–52, 466–67; JB to Philip Pendleton Barbour, Aug. 3, 1830, Philip Pendleton Barbour Papers, VHS.

70. Smith, *Washington Society,* p. 186.

71. Ibid., pp. 186–87; Samuel Flagg Bemis, *John Quincy Adams and the Union* (New York: A. A. Knopf, 1956), pp. 32ff.; Van Deusen, *Henry Clay,* pp. 190–91.

Chapter 8. To Save the Red Man

1. Barbour mentioned his expectation of being offered a cabinet post if Crawford won the election in a letter to Isaac Davis, Feb. 24, 1824, Isaac Davis Papers, UVA.

2. Adams, *Memoirs,* 6:509.

3. Ibid., 6:514–15, 520; William Plumer, Jr., to William Plumer, Feb. 25, 1825, in Brown, *Missouri Compromises,* p. 143; Bemis, *Adams and the Union,* p. 589; Dangerfield, *Awakening American Nationalism,* p. 233.

4. JB to Isaac Davis, Feb. 24, April 26, May 23, 1824, Isaac Davis Papers, Duke University. Barbour also spoke of his desire for retirement in a letter to John H. Cocke, Sept. 18, 1826, John H. Cocke Papers (Shields Deposit), UVA.

5. Adams, *Memoirs,* 6:474; JB to Philip Pendleton Barbour, Aug. 3, 1830, Philip Pendleton Barbour Papers, VHS; William Plumer, Jr., to William Plumer, Feb. 23, 1825, in Brown, *Missouri Compromises,* p. 143.

6. Adams, *Memoirs,* 6:515, 520; JB to Philip Pendleton Barbour, Aug. 3, 1830, Philip Pendleton Barbour Papers, VHS; Andrew Stevenson to JB, March 28, 1825, John Campbell to JB, March 8, 1825, and Francis Brooke to JB, May 13, 1825, BP UVA. Stevenson wrote, "Principles and not men, has heretofore and will continue to be my motto." Nathaniel Macon expressed a similar neutrality. See Macon to Charles Tait, Feb. 23, 1825, Nathaniel Macon Papers, Duke University.

7. Ben Perley Poore, *Perley's Reminiscences of Sixty Years in the National Metropolis,* 2 vols. (Philadelphia: Hubbard Brothers, 1886), 1:26; *Richmond Enquirer,* March 8, 1825; Adams, *Memoirs,* 6:518–19.

8. *Richmond Enquirer,* March 8, 1825; Bemis, *Adams and the Union,* pp. 52–53; Richardson, *Messages and Papers of the Presidents,* 2:292–99; Poore, *Perley's Reminiscences,* 1:26; Adams, *Memoirs,* 6:518–19.

9. *Richmond Enquirer,* March 8, 11, 1825.

10. Bruce, *Randolph,* 1:513; Wiltse, *Calhoun, Nationalist,* pp. 308–12. The bargain created a furor among some members of the Junto in Richmond. Andrew Stevenson's sister wrote, "The good people are run mad here about the presidential election." Many of the Junto, she said, universally denounced Clay and Adams and were prepared to "take Jackson and anybody now in preference to Adams" (Betsy Coles to Andrew Stevenson, Feb. 13, 1825, Andrew Stevenson Papers, LC).

11. Bemis, *Adams and the Union,* p. 61; Dangerfield, *Era of Good Feelings,* pp. 348–53.

12. Adams, *Memoirs,* 7:59–63; Adams to Charles Upham, Feb. 2, 1827, in Henry Adams, *The Degradation of the Democratic Dogma* (New York: Macmillan, 1919), p. 11; Bemis, *Adams and the Union,* pp. 55–70; Dangerfield, *Era of Good Feelings,* pp. 349–52.

13. Bemis, *Adams and the Union,* pp. 56–59; Adams, *Memoirs,* 6:510–20.

14. Calhoun to J. G. Swift, Sept. 2, 1825, quoted in Bemis, *Adams and the Union,* p. 60, n. 21.

15. Adams, *Memoirs,* 6:520, 525–26; L. D. Ingersoll, *A History of the War Department of the United States, with Biographical Sketches of the Secretaries* (Washington, D.C.: F. B. Mohun, 1879), pp. 108–10; James Barbour–James Barbour, Jr., correspondence, 1825, passim, BP UVA; JB to John Floyd et al., Dec. 11, 1830, John Tyler Papers, LC.

16. Ingersoll, *War Department,* pp. 108–10; Adams, *Memoirs,* 6:526.

17. White, *The Jeffersonians,* pp. 246–50; Carlton B. Smith, "John C. Calhoun, Secretary of War, 1817–25: The Cast-Iron Man as Administrator," in *Essays in Honor of Bernard Mayo,* ed. Boles, pp. 132–36.

18. White, *The Jeffersonians,* pp. 234ff.; Young, *The Washington Community,* p. 31.

19. Weigley, *United States Army,* pp. 141–43, 170; *ASPMA,* 2:108–15.

20. White, *The Jeffersonians,* pp. 506–11.

21. Adams, *Memoirs,* 7:113; Bemis, *Adams and the Union,* p. 62; Jennings C. Wise, *The Red Man in the New World Drama: A Politico-Legal Study with a Pageantry of American Indian History,* ed. and rev. Vine Deloria, Jr. (New York: Macmillan, 1971),

pp. 210–11; Lynn Hudson Parsons, "'A Perpetual Harrow upon My Feelings': John Quincy Adams and the American Indian," *New England Quarterly,* 46 (Sept. 1973):344–55.

22. Adams, *Memoirs,* 7:56–57, 89–90, 113. The best study of the philanthropic view of the Indian is Bernard W. Sheehan, *Seeds of Extinction: Jeffersonian Philanthropy and the American Indian* (Chapel Hill: University of North Carolina Press, 1973).

23. Adams, *Memoirs,* 7:3–21, 61–62, 66–69; Edward J. Harden, *The Life of George M. Troup* (Savannah: E. J. Purse, 1859), pp. 481–85; JB to George M. Troup, Aug. 30, 1825, *ASPIA,* 2:814–15.

24. *Niles' Register,* 27:222–23; Annie H. Abel, "The History of Events Resulting in Indian Consolidation West of the Mississippi River," American Historical Association, *Annual Report for the Year 1906,* 2 vols. (Washington, D.C., 1908), 1:335–45; Ulrich B. Phillips, "Georgia and State Rights," American Historical Association, *Annual Report for the Year 1901,* 2 vols. (Washington, D.C., 1902), 2:15–60, passim; *American State Papers, Public Lands,* 1:125–26.

25. Adams, *Memoirs,* 7:3–12; Charles S. Sydnor, *The Development of Southern Sectionalism, 1819–1848* (Baton Rouge: Louisiana State University Press, 1948), pp. 182–85.

26. Adams, *Memoirs,* 7:3–12, 33–35, 66–69, 89–90; JB to Maj. Timothy Andrews, May 19, 1825, IOLB, ser. 2, no. 2, pp. 13–15; Troup to Andrews, June 14, 28, 1825, and Andrews to John Crowell, June 21, 1825, *ASPIA,* 2:803, 807, 852; James W. Silver, *Edmund Pendleton Gaines, Frontier General* (Baton Rouge: Louisiana State University Press, 1949), pp. 116–21.

27. Troup to JB, Aug. 15, 1825, *ASPIA,* 2:810–11; Harden, *Life of Troup,* pp. 485–87; JB to Isaac Davis, Feb. 5, 1826, Isaac Davis Papers, Duke University.

28. JB to Troup, Aug. 30, 1825, *ASPIA,* 2:814–15.

29. *ASPIA,* 2:728–842, passim; Adams, *Memoirs,* 7:61–79, 90; Abel, "Indian Consolidation," p. 350; IOLB, ser. 2, no. 2, p. 388.

30. Adams, *Memoirs,* 7:90, 110.

31. Abel, "Indian Consolidation," pp. 352–53; *Annals,* 19th Cong., 1st sess., pp. 2669–71.

32. *Annals,* 16th Cong., 1st sess., pp. 2673–74.

33. Ibid., p. 2674.

34. Ibid., p. 2673–74; Abel, "Indian Consolidation," p. 353.

35. Troup to Adams, Feb. 11, 1826, Troup to JB, Aug. 16, 1826, and JB to Troup, Sept. 16, 1826, *ASPIA,* 2:737–44.

36. *ASPIA,* 2:731–34; Adams, *Memoirs,* 7:219–20.

37. Adams, *Memoirs,* 7:219–20.

38. *ASPIA,* 2:864–65.

39. Troup to Adams, Feb. 17, 1827, quoted in Harden, *Life of Troup,* pp. 485–87.

40. Ibid.

41. Adams, *Memoirs,* 7:221; Bemis, *Adams and the Union,* pp. 85–86.

42. Benton, *Thirty Years' View,* 1:60; *Annals,* 20th Cong., 1st sess., p. 1534; *ASPIA,* 2:869–72; Abel, "Indian Consolidation," p. 356.

43. *Philadelphia National Chronicle,* cited in *Niles' Register,* 29:5; *Philadelphia National Gazette and Literary Register,* Sept. 1, 1825.

44. *Richmond Enquirer,* Dec. 8, 10, 24, 1825.

45. Adams, *Memoirs,* 7:56–57, 89–90. For contemporary philanthropic opinion, see Sheehan, *Seeds of Extinction,* pp. 213–23, 243–54, and Francis Paul Prucha, *American Indian Policy in the Formative Years: The Indian Trade and Intercourse Acts, 1780–1834* (Cambridge, Mass.: Harvard University Press, 1962), pp. 227–30.

46. Sheehan, *Seeds of Extinction,* pp. 10–12, 121–22, 168–70, 218–20; Prucha, *American Indian Policy,* pp. 227–30.

47. Adams, *Memoirs,* 7:56–67, 89–90.

48. Ibid., 7:90; Prucha, *American Indian Policy,* pp. 227–40.

49. JB to John Cocke, Feb. 21, 1826, *House Executive Documents,* 19th Cong., 1st sess., Doc. 102, pp. 3–12; Sheehan, *Seeds of Extinction,* pp. 212–42, passim.

50. Adams, *Memoirs,* 7:113.

51. Cocke to JB, Jan. 11, 1826, in Office of Indian Affairs, Letters Received (miscellaneous), National Archives, Washington, D.C.

52. JB to John Cocke, Feb. 3, 1826, in *ASPIA,* 2:646–49; JB to John Cocke, Feb. 21, 1826, in *House Executive Documents,* 19th Cong., 1st sess., Doc. 102, pp. 3–12. The quotations and analysis of Barbour's policy are from *ASPIA,* 2:646–49.

53. Report of John Cocke to the House of Representatives, May 20, 1826, *ASPIA,* 2:667–68.

54. Phillips, "Georgia and State Rights," pp. 66–72; Prucha, *American Indian Policy,* pp. 231–32.

55. Prucha, *American Indian Policy,* pp. 232–33, 250ff.

56. Abel, "Indian Consolidation," pp. 363–69; *ASPIA,* 2:614–55; *House Executive Documents,* 19th Cong., 1st sess., Docs. 112, 124, and 161; 19th Cong., 2nd sess., Docs. 17, 28, 39, and 43; 20th Cong., 1st sess., Docs. 44, 74, 104, and 283.

Chapter 9. For a Prosperous and Enduring Union

1. Adams, *Memoirs,* 7: passim.

2. Ibid., 7:59–66; *Washington National Intelligencer,* Nov. 28, 1826; see below, chapter 12.

3. Adams, *Memoirs,* 7:32, 52–386, passim.

4. Ibid., 7:525–26; Bemis, *Adams and the Union,* p. 82; Willie Person Mangum, *The Papers of Willie Person Mangum,* ed. Henry Thomas Shanks, 5 vols. (Raleigh, 1950–56), 1:234–35.

5. Adams, *Memoirs,* 7:59–65; JB to Isaac Davis, Mar. 12, 1826, Isaac Davis Papers, UVA; JB to Isaac Davis [n.d., ca. 1827], Isaac Davis Papers, Duke University.

6. Ambler, *Thomas Ritchie,* p. 99; *Richmond Enquirer,* May 24, Dec. 15, 1825.

7. Tyler to JB, Nov. 20, 1826, BP UVA.

8. Richardson, *Messages and Papers of the Presidents,* 2:299–317.

9. Macon to Bartlett Yancey, Nov. 3, 1827, quoted in Risjord, *Old Republicans,* p. 261.

10. Quoted in Bruce, *John Randolph,* 1:508.

11. Jefferson to William B. Giles, Dec. 26, 1825, quoted in Dangerfield, *Awakening American Nationalism,* p. 238, n. 15.

12. Adams, *Memoirs,* 7:59–65; JB to Isaac Davis, March 12, 1826, Isaac Davis Papers, UVA.

13. See Barbour's essay defending the administration's nationalism in the *Washington National Intelligencer,* Nov. 28, 1826; JB to Isaac Davis, March 12, 1826, Isaac Davis Papers, UVA; James M. Garnett to John Randolph, Dec. 12, 1825, Randolph-Garnett Papers, LC.

14. See below, chapter 12; Henry H. Simms, *The Rise of the Whigs in Virginia, 1824–1840* (Richmond: William Byrd Press, 1929), pp. 66ff.

15. *Washington National Intelligencer,* Nov. 28, 1826; JB to John H. Cocke, Sept. 18, 1826, John H. Cocke Papers (Shields Deposit), UVA.

16. *Washington National Intelligencer,* Nov. 28, 1826.

17. Ibid.; *ASPMA,* 3:161–66, 184–87, 287–302.

18. Ambler, *Thomas Ritchie,* p. 101; James M. Garnett to John Randolph, Dec. 12, 1825, Randolph-Garnett Papers, LC; Benjamin Estill to David Campbell, Dec. 18, 1826, Campbell Family Papers, Duke University.

19. *Richmond Enquirer,* Dec. 10, 15, 1825; Ambler, *Thomas Ritchie,* p. 102.

20. *Richmond Enquirer,* Dec. 10, 15, 1825; Ambler, *Thomas Ritchie,* p. 102; Bruce, *John Randolph,* 1:505; James M. Garnett to John Randolph, Dec. 12, 1825, Randolph-Garnett Papers, LC.

21. Bruce, *John Randolph,* 1:507.

22. Adams, *Memoirs,* 7:70–71; Bemis, *Adams and the Union,* pp. 72–73.

23. Adams to Charles Upham, Feb. 2, 1837, quoted in Adams, *The Degradation of the Democratic Dogma,* p. 11.

24. Adams, *Memoirs,* 7:16, 55, 75, 82; Bemis, *Adams and the Union,* pp. 76–77; Van Deusen, *Henry Clay,* pp. 202–206.

25. Adams, *Memoirs,* 6:542, 7:55, 156–58; JB to James Monroe, Oct. 6, 1826, Monroe Papers, LC.

26. Dangerfield, *Era of Good Feelings,* pp. 356–57; Bemis, *Adams and the Union,* pp. 76–77; Richardson, *Messages and Papers of the Presidents,* 2:318–20.

27. William C. Rives to Francis W. Gilmer, March 27, April 22, 1826, Rives Papers, LC; Van Deusen, *Henry Clay,* pp. 207–208; Dangerfield, *Era of Good Feelings,* pp. 362–64.

28. Quoted in Bruce, *John Randolph,* 1:511–12.

29. Adams, *Memoirs,* 7:112–13, 116–17.

30. Dangerfield, *Era of Good Feelings,* pp. 360–67; Risjord, *Old Republicans,* pp. 260–61; JB to James Barbour, Jr., April 9, 1826, BP UVA.

31. JB to Monroe, Oct. 6, 1826, Monroe Papers, LC; Adams, *Memoirs,* 7:156, 158. Had he accepted the mission, Monroe would have served as a replacement for Richard C. Anderson, who died en route to the congress.

32. *ASPMA,* 3:161–66.

33. Ibid., 3:184–87, 193, 227–40, 278–302.

34. Archer B. Hulbert, *The Cumberland Road* (Cleveland: A. H. Clark, 1904), pp. 54–57, 67–76; *House Executive Documents,* 19th Cong., 1st sess., Doc. 51, pp. 6–10. Barbour was the first secretary of war to specify the macadam road for new construction, though the process had been used earlier (1824) for repairing stretches of the road that had fallen into disrepair (Hulbert, *Cumberland Road,* p. 67).

35. *ASPMA,* 3:388–401, 478–88.

36. *Annals of Congress,* 19th Cong., 1st sess., p. 707; White, *The Jeffersonians,* pp. 534–36.

37. Adams, *Memoirs,* 7:161, 169, 186; Samuel Southard to James Monroe, Nov. 5, 1826, Monroe Papers, LC.

38. Adams, *Memoirs,* 7:39.

39. Ibid., 7:11, 33–37; Adams to JB, Aug. 30, 1826, and Barbour–James Barbour, Jr., correspondence, 1825, passim, BP UVA.

40. Adams, *Memoirs,* 7:118.

41. Lucy Barbour to [James Barbour, Jr.], Feb. 7, 1827, BP UVA. See also William C. Rives to Mrs. William C. Rives, Dec. 24, 1823, Rives Papers, LC; Mrs. Henry Dearborn to Mrs. H. A. S. Dearborn, Feb. 23, 1825, Miscellaneous Bound Collection, Massachusetts Historical Society, Boston.

42. Lucy Barbour to [James Barbour, Jr.], Feb. 7, 1827, BP UVA.

43. Bemis, *Adams and the Union,* pp. 96–99; Adams, *Memoirs,* 7:89–101, 394, 8:89; William C. Rives to Mrs. Rives, Jan. 1, 1825, Rives Papers, LC; Margaret Hunter Hall, *The Aristocratic Journey,* ed. Una Pope-Hennessy (New York: G. P. Putnam's Sons, 1931), p. 169.

44. Hall, *Aristocratic Journey,* pp. 173–74.

45. Ibid., pp. 174, 189.

46. Smith, *Washington Society,* pp. 208–209.

47. *Richmond Enquirer,* Dec. 8, 10, 24, 1825, and Oct.-Nov. 1826, passim; *Washington National Intelligencer,* Nov. 25, 28, 1826.

48. *Washington National Intelligencer,* Nov. 25, 28, Dec. 2, 1826; Adams, *Memoirs,* 7:186. The quotations and arguments that follow are from the *National Intelligencer,* principally from the November 28 issue and from Barbour's long letter to John H. Cocke defending the administration's nationalist policies, Sept. 18, 1826, John H. Cocke Papers (Shields Deposit), UVA. On his views regarding internal improvements, see also John Tyler to JB, Nov. 20, 1826, BP UVA. Adams commented that Barbour's "intentions are kind and friendly, and a great part of the essay was very good. Some passages I thought might be improved, but I thought it best not to object to them" (Adams, *Memoirs,* 7:186).

49. *Niles' Register,* 39:464.

50. *Washington National Intelligencer,* Nov. 28, 1826.

51. Ambler, *Thomas Ritchie,* pp. 101–17.

52. Adams, *Memoirs,* 7:431; Bemis, *Adams and the Union,* pp. 142–46; JB to James Barbour, Jr., April 9, 1826, and Ritchie to JB, Dec. 2, 1825, BP UVA; *Richmond Whig,* May 24, 1828; *Washington Daily National Journal,* March 26, April 12, 1827.

53. JB to Isaac Davis, April 28, 1828, Isaac Davis Papers, Duke University; JB to John H. Pleasants, July 7, 1829, and to James Barbour, Jr., Feb. 11, 1827, BP UVA; Francis Johnson to JB, Aug. 31, 1827, BP NYPL; Adams, *Memoirs,* 7:352–53.

54. Adams, *Memoirs,* 7:535.

55. JB to Isaac Davis, March 12, 1826, Isaac Davis Papers, Duke University; JB to James Madison, Jan. 14, 1828, Madison Papers, LC; JB to Henry Clay, Jan. 28, 1828, Clay Papers, LC; Alfred H. Powell to JB, Sept. 21, 1827, BP NYPL; Van Deusen, *Henry Clay,* pp. 228–29.

56. *Richmond Enquirer,* Jan. 16, Aug. 21, 1827; JB to James Barbour, Jr., Feb. 11, 1827, BP UVA.

57. William C. Rives to Francis W. Gilmer, July 20, 1827, Rives Papers, LC; John Tyler to Henry Curtis, Dec. 16, 1827, John Tyler Papers, LC.

58. Ambler, *Thomas Ritchie,* pp. 108–109; *Richmond Enquirer,* March 6, April 27, 1827.

59. William C. Rives to Francis W. Gilmer, July 22, 1827, Rives Papers, LC.

60. Ibid.

61. JB to Madison, Jan. 14, 1828, Madison Papers, LC; JB to Lucy Barbour, Nov. 3, 1827, and to James Barbour, Jr., April 21, 1828, and Archibald Stuart to JB, Oct. 28, 1827, BP UVA.

62. Adams, *Memoirs,* 7:217, 352, 374.

63. Ibid., 7:410, 468, 485.

64. Ibid., 7:525.

65. Ibid., 7:525–26, 538–39.

66. Ibid., 7:544, 546–47, 8:6–9; *Richmond Whig,* May 26, 1828.

67. *Richmond Whig,* May 24, 1828.

68. *Richmond Enquirer,* May 26, 27, 1828; *New York Evening Post,* May 24, 1828.

69. Adams, *Memoirs,* 7:468, 485.

70. JB to John H. Cocke, Sept. 18, 1826, John H. Cocke Papers (Shields Deposit), UVA.

Chapter 10. An Abortive Mission

1. *Niles' Register,* 34:378. The only member of the immediate family not to accompany the party was Lucy Maria, the Barbour's oldest daughter (JB to John S. Skinner, July 12, 1828, BP UVA).

2. Adams, *Memoirs,* 8:17, 31, 54; JB to James Madison, June 11, 1828, Hook Collection, UVA; Clay to JB, June 3, 12, 13, 1828, Henry Clay Papers, Despatches and Instructions, vol. 7, LC; Citizens of Fredericksburg to JB, July 23, 1828, BP UVA; *Niles' Register,* 34:330; Charles King et al. to JB, July 22, 1828, BP NYPL.

3. JB to Madison, Sept. 29, 1828, Madison Papers, LC; James Barbour, Jr., to James B. Newman, Aug. 24, 1828, BP UVA.

4. JB to Madison, Sept. 29, Nov. 13, 1828, Madison Papers, LC; JB to James Monroe, March 12, 1829, James Monroe Papers, LC; JB to Henry Clay, Aug. 22, 1828, DMGB, vol. 36.

5. JB to Clay, Sept. 5, Oct. 2, 1828, DMGB, vol. 36; J. Dean to JB, Mar. 6, 1829, BP UVA.

6. JB to Clay, Sept. 5, 1828, DMGB, vol. 36.

7. Ibid.; Beckles Willson, *America's Ambassadors to England (1785–1929): A Narrative of Anglo-American Diplomatic Relations* (New York: Frederick A. Stokes, 1929), pp. 181–82. Clay, shocked to learn that Gallatin had removed the official papers, took steps to assure that future ministers would not do the same.

8. JB to Clay, Sept. 5, 1828, DMGB, vol. 36.

9. Ernst, *Rufus King,* pp. 398–401.

10. Walters, *Albert Gallatin,* pp. 332–41.

11. Harry C. Allen, *Great Britain and the United States: A History of Anglo-American Relations, 1783–1952* (New York: St. Martin's Press, 1955), pp. 386–88; Philip Guedalla, *Wellington* (New York: Harper and Brothers, 1931), pp. 365ff.

12. JB to Madison, Nov. 13, 1828, Madison Papers, LC.

13. Rush to JB, Nov. 15, 1828, BP NYPL.

14. Clay to JB, June 3, 12, 13, 1828, Clay Papers, Despatches and Instructions, vol. 7, LC. Clay had left Washington for Kentucky on June 22, 1828, before he had an opportunity to discuss in detail with Barbour the objectives of his mission. He left abbreviated instructions for President Adams to convey to the new minister (Adams to JB, June 26, 1828, BP NYPL).

15. JB to Clay, Oct. 2, 1828, DMGB, vol. 36.

16. Allen, *Great Britain and the United States,* pp. 386–88; Theodore E. Burton, "Henry Clay," *The American Secretaries of State and Their Diplomacy,* ed. Samuel Flagg Bemis, 10 vols. (New York: A. A. Knopf, 1927–29), 4:122–30; Benns, *British West India Carrying-Trade,* pp. 133–38.

17. JB to Clay, Oct. 2, 1828, DMGB, vol. 36.

18. Ibid.

19. Ibid.

20. Ibid.

21. Ibid.

22. Ibid.

23. Clay to JB, Oct. 15, 1828, Clay Papers, Despatches and Instructions, vol. 7, LC.

24. JB to Lord Aberdeen, Nov. 27, 1828, and JB to Clay, Nov. 28, 1828, DMGB, vol. 36.

25. JB to Clay, Jan. 22, 1829, DMGB, vol. 36.

26. Allen, *Great Britain and the United States,* p. 388; Dangerfield, *Era of Good Feelings,* pp. 370ff.

27. *Niles' Register,* 36:65; JB to Clay, Nov. 28, 1828, DMGB, vol. 36.

28. JB to Clay, Nov. 28, 1828, DMGB, vol. 36.

29. James Maury to JB, Nov. 22, 1828, JB to Lord Aberdeen, Dec. 2, 1828, Jan. 18, 1829, George C. Blake to Sir George Paget, Jan. 13, 1829, and JB to Clay, Feb. 6, 1829, DMGB, vol. 36.

30. Clay to JB, Jan 26, 1829, Clay Papers, Despatches and Instructions, vol. 7, LC.

31. JB to Lord Aberdeen, March 12, 1829, DMGB, vol. 36.

32. James Fulton Zimmerman, *Impressment of American Seamen,* Columbia University Studies in History, Economics, and Public Law, 262 (New York: Columbia University Press, 1925):239–44.

33. Clay to JB, Oct. 15, 1828, Clay Papers, Despatches and Instructions, vol. 7, LC; Lord Aberdeen to JB, Oct. 31, 1828, Jan. 1, 29, 1829, JB to Lord Aberdeen, Jan. 3, 1829, and JB to Clay, Nov. 7, 1828, Feb. 21, 1829, DMGB, vol. 36.

34. Clay-Barbour correspondence, Aug. 1828–March 1829, passim, Clay Papers, Despatches and Instructions, vol. 7, LC; Barbour-Clay correspondence, Aug. 1828–March 1829, DMGB, vol. 36; William R. Manning, ed. and comp., *Diplomatic Correspondence of the United States: Canadian Relations, 1784–1860,* 4 vols. (Washington, D.C., 1940–45), 2:763–810, passim.

35. JB to Madison, Nov. 13, 1828, Madison Papers, LC; JB to Daniel Webster, May 17, 1829, BP UVA; JB to Monroe, March 12, 1829, Monroe Papers, LC.

36. Quoted in Willson, *America's Ambassadors to England,* p. 184.

37. JB to Pleasants, July 7, 1829, BP UVA.

38. Taliaferro to JB, Jan. 27, 1829, BP NYPL.

39. Adams to JB, April 1829, Mercer to JB, March 17, 1829, and Clay to JB, Dec. 29, 1828, BP UVA.

40. Van Buren to JB, May 12, 1829, BP NYPL.

41. JB to [Gales and Seaton], July 10, 1829, BP NYPL.

42. Willson, *America's Ambassadors to England,* p. 183; *Niles' Register,* 36:65.

43. *Niles' Register,* 36:340.

44. John P. Yosy to JB, April 20, 1830, BP UVA; Robert A. Brock, *Virginia and Virginians,* 2 vols. (Richmond: H. H. Hardesty, 1888), 1:119.

45. JB to Daniel Webster, May 17, 1829, and Receipts and Miscellaneous, 1829, BP UVA.

46. JB to [Gales and Seaton], July 10, 1829, BP NYPL; *Niles' Register,* 37:69.

47. JB to Lucy Barbour, Aug. 1, 1829, BP NYPL.

48. *Richmond Enquirer,* Oct. 5, 8, 22, 1824.

49. Lafayette to JB, April 12, 1829, BP NYPL.

50. A. M. Perkins to JB, April 30, June 6, 1829, BP UVA.

51. *Niles' Register,* 37:123.

52. JB to Tait, May 10, 1829, Tait Family Papers, Alabama Department of Archives and History.

Chapter 11. The Elusive Goal

1. Hugh Mercer to JB, Jan. 12, 1830, BP UVA; John S. Barbour to JB, Nov. 28, 1829, Jan. 18, 1830, BP NYPL.

2. JB to Charles Tait, May 10, 1829, Tait Family Papers, Alabama Department of Archives and History; JB to John H. Pleasants, July 7, 1829, BP UVA; JB to Henry Clay, Dec. 20, 1829, Clay Papers, LC.

3. John Taliaferro to JB, Feb. 2, 1829, BP NYPL.

4. OCL AND OCP, 1830, VSL; Barbour Account Book, BP UVA.

5. Salma Hale to Arthur Livermore, May 16, 1818, in *Massachusetts Historical Society Proceedings,* 46 (June 1913):404; Robert A. Lancaster, Jr., *Historic Virginia Homes and Churches* (Philadelphia: J. B. Lippincott, 1915), pp. 391–92; Kimball, *Thomas Jefferson, Architect,* pp. 73–74. Barbour's workmen were trained at Monticello (JB to Jefferson, March 29, 1817, Jefferson Papers, Massachusetts Historical Society).

6. Lancaster, *Virginia Homes,* pp. 391–92; I. J. Frary, *Thomas Jefferson, Architect and Builder* (Richmond, 1950), pp. 97–98; Kimball, *Thomas Jefferson, Architect,* pp. 73–74.

7. Frances A. Christian and Susanna W. Massie, eds., *Homes and Gardens in Old Virginia* (Richmond: Garrett and Massie, 1950), p. 325; Frary, *Thomas Jefferson, Architect and Builder,* p. 97; Barbour Account Book, 1817, BP UVA.

8. Francis G. Ruffin Diary, pp. 104–105, VHS; Robert E. Winthrop to William Wirt Henry, Jan. 24, 1876, William Wirt Henry Papers, VHS; Collins, *Miscellanies,* p. 228.

9. List of Books, 1805, BP UVA.

10. Barbour Ledger and Account Book, BP UVA; James Barbour, "On the Improvement of Agriculture and the Importance of Legislative Aid to That Object; Description of the South West Mountain Lands," *Farmers' Register,* 2 (April 1835):705; *Farmers' Register,* 2–9 (1834–41):passim; *American Farmer,* 1–12 (1819–31): passim.

11. W. A. Low, "The Farmer in Post-Revolutionary Virginia, 1783–1789," *Agricultural History,* 25 (July 1951):123–24.

12. William Strickland, *Observations on the Agriculture of the United States of America* (London: W. Bulmer, 1801), p. 49.

13. Cited in Craven, *Soil Exhaustion,* p. 3.

14. *Farmers' Register,* 1 (Aug. 1833):150.

15. Craven, *Soil Exhaustion,* p. 85.

16. Barbour Ledger, Account Book, and Bills, Receipts, and Business Papers, 1800–30, passim, BP UVA; Barbour, "Improvement of Agriculture," pp. 705–706.

17. Barbour, "Improvement of Agriculture," pp. 705–706.

18. Barbour Ledger, Account Book, and Bills, Receipts, and Business Papers, 1800–10, BP UVA.

19. Barbour Ledger, BP UVA; Barbour, "Improvement of Agriculture," pp. 704–705; JB to John S. Skinner, May 5, 1820, *American Farmer,* 2 (May 1820):55.

20. Barbour, "Improvement of Agriculture," pp. 704–705; Barbour Ledger and Sims Brockman to JB, Dec. 22, 1828, BP UVA.

21. Bills, Receipts, and Business Papers, BP UVA; Lewis C. Gray and Esther Katherine Thompson, *History of Agriculture in the Southern United States to 1860,* 2 vols. (New York: P. Smith, 1941), 2:752–69.

22. JB to William M. Barton, Dec. 15, 1824, *American Farmer,* 7 (May 1825):60; Barbour, "The Cultivation of Wheat," *American Farmer,* 1 (Dec. 1819):301–302.

23. JB to Skinner, May 5, 1820, *American Farmer,* 7 (May 1825):60; Barbour, "Cultivation of Wheat," pp. 301–302.

24. Barbour, "Cultivation of Wheat," pp. 301–302.

25. Ibid., p. 302.

26. Ibid.

27. JB to Jefferson, April 13, 1821, Jefferson Papers, LC; Barbour Ledger and Account Book, Bills, Receipts, and Business Papers, 1800–42, passim, BP UVA; JB to John H. Cocke, May 15, 1819, John H. Cocke Papers, UVA.

28. William Bagley to JB, July 21, 1830, Alexander Givens to JB, March 14, 1831, Gabriel Moore to JB, July 17, 1832, William Terrill to JB, Dec. 26, 1833, J. S. Moore to James Barbour, Jr., Nov. 15, 1842, BP UVA; Barbour Ledger and Account Book, BP UVA; *American Farmer,* 12 (Nov. 1830):275; JB to Henry Clay, Aug. 2, 1835, Clay Papers, LC; Clement Eaton, *Henry Clay and the Art of American Politics* (Boston: Little, Brown, 1957), p. 73.

29. OCP, 1800–42, VSL; Barbour Ledger, BP UVA.

30. Barbour Ledger, Account Book, and Bills, Receipts, and Business Papers, 1800–42, passim, BP UVA.

31. See Thomas P. Govan, "Was Plantation Slavery Profitable?" *Journal of Southern History,* 8 (Nov. 1942):513–14.

32. Barbour Ledger, Account Book, and Bills, Receipts, and Business Papers, 1800–42, passim, BP UVA.

33. See especially Eugene D. Genovese, *The Political Economy of Slavery: Studies in the Economy and Society of the Slave South* (New York: Vantage Books, 1967), pp. 124–44.

34. Barbour, *Address to the Agricultural Society of Albemarle,* p. 9.

35. Ibid., p. 10.

36. Ibid., p. 11.

37. James Oakes, *The Ruling Race: A History of American Slaveholders* (New York: A. A. Knopf, 1982), p. 9.

38. "Address to the Agricultural Convention of Virginia," *Farmers' Register,* 3 (March 1836):685.

39. Barbour, *Address to the Agricultural Society of Albemarle,* pp. 11–12.

40. Ibid.

41. Ibid.

42. Rodney H. True, "Early Days of the Albemarle Agricultural Society," American Historical Association, *Annual Report for the Year 1918,* 2 vols. (Washington, D.C., 1921), 1:243–45; Charles W. Turner, "Virginia Agricultural Reform, 1815–1860," *Agricultural History,* 26 (July 1952):81–83.

43. True, "Early Days of the Albemarle Agricultural Society," pp. 244–51.

44. Rodney H. True, ed., "Minute Book of the Albemarle (Virginia) Agricultural Society," American Historical Association, *Annual Report for the Year 1918,* 1:263–349.

45. Brock, *Virginia and Virginians,* 1:119.

46. JB to Edmund Ruffin, July 23, 1835, *Farmers' Register,* 3 (Sept. 1835):274–75; Barbour, "Address to Agricultural Convention of Virginia," p. 685.

47. Barbour, "Address to Agricultural Convention of Virginia," pp. 685–89.

48. Turner, "Virginia Agricultural Reform," p. 85.

49. The Albemarle Agricultural Society in 1822 appropriated $1,000 for the purpose of establishing an agricultural professorship at the University of Virginia. It is not known whether John H. Cocke, who suggested the appropriation, or some

other person initiated the move, but Barbour was an early supporter of the idea (True, "Early Days of the Albemarle Agricultural Society," pp. 253–54).

50. Barbour, "On the Improvement of Agriculture," p. 704; H. G. Good, "Early Attempts to Teach Agriculture in Old Virginia," *VMHB,* 48 (Oct. 1940):345–46.

51. Rodney H. True, "The Virginia Board of Agriculture, 1841–1843," *Agricultural History,* 14 (July 1940):97–98.

52. Ibid., p. 94.

53. Barbour, "Introduction to the Report of the Board of Agriculture to the General Assembly of Virginia," *Farmers' Register,* 9 (Dec. 1841):688–89.

54. Henry [James Barbour], *To the People of Virginia: What Shall be Done for the University?* (Charlottesville, 1823), p. 3.

55. *JHD,* 1809–10, pp. 74, 94, 108; Bruce, *History of the University of Virginia,* 1:85–86; JB to William Cabell Rives, Feb. 21, 1818, Rives Papers, LC; JB to the Virginia House of Delegates and Senate, Nov. 30, 1812, ELB, 1812, VSL; JB to Francis Preston, July 3, 1825, Campbell-Preston Papers, LC.

56. Bruce, *History of the University of Virginia,* 1:232–33, 287ff.; Barbour, *What Shall Be Done for the University?* foreword.

57. Barbour, *What Shall Be Done for the University?* pp. 3–6.

58. Ritchie to JB, May 21, 1823, BP NYPL.

59. Jefferson to JB, May 2, 1824, April 16, 1825, and JB to Jefferson, May 15, Dec. 31, 1824, Jan. 3, March 2, 1825, Jefferson Papers, LC; JB to Madison, Jan. 4, 1825, Madison Papers, LC.

60. Jefferson to Francis Walker Gilmer, June 6, 1825, Jefferson Papers, UVA; JB to Jefferson, March 24, 1825, Jefferson Papers, LC; Madison to JB, Sept. 22, 1828, Feb. 7, 1829, Madison Papers, LC.

61. Barbour, *What Shall Be Done for the University?* p. 3; Samuel L. Southard to JB, June 7, 1825, Washington College Literary Society to JB, March 17, 1840, and Columbian College to JB, July 12, 1824, BP UVA; William Staughton to JB, March 3, 1821, BP NYPL.

Chapter 12. The Enduring Challenge

1. Pleasants to JB, May 30, 1829, BP NYPL.

2. Southard to JB, Dec. 17, 1829, James P. Preston to JB, May 10, 1830, A. Stephenson to JB, Sept. 22, 1832, and John S. Barbour to JB, Nov. 28, 1829, and July 30, 1831, BP NYPL; Hugh Mercer to JB, Jan. 12, 1830, and Fred Harris to JB, Jan. 30, 1830, BP UVA; JB to Isaac Davis [n.d.], Isaac Davis Papers, Duke University.

3. Thomas L. Boyd to Thomas W. Gilmer, Nov. 4, 1830, in *Tyler's Quarterly Historical and Genealogical Magazine,* 1 (1919):49–50.

4. John Campbell to [n.n.], April 23, 1830, Campbell Family Papers, Duke University.

5. *Niles' Register,* 41:308.

6. JB to Henry Clay, Dec. 30, 1829, Clay Papers, LC; JB to John H. Pleasants, July 7, 1829, BP UVA.

7. Pleasants to JB, May 30, 1829, Francis Brooke to JB, Jan. 27, 1829, and John Taliaferro to JB, Feb. 2, 1829, BP NYPL.

8. JB to Clay, Dec. 20, 1829, Clay Papers, LC; Charles Yancey to Thomas Davis, Dec. 31, 1830, Isaac Davis Papers, Duke University; Philip Pendleton Barbour to JB, Dec. 5, 1829, BP NYPL.

9. John Floyd to John Williams, Dec. 27, 1830, John Floyd Papers, LC.

10. John Floyd to John S. Barbour, June 24, 1831, John Floyd Papers, LC.

11. Ibid.; Floyd to Littleton W. Tazewell, May 31, 1832, John Floyd Papers, LC; William C. Rives to Francis W. Gilmer, July 22, 1827, William C. Rives Papers, LC.

12. William C. Rives to Francis W. Gilmer, July 20, 22, 1827, William C. Rives Papers, LC; John Floyd to Littleton W. Tazewell, May 31, 1832, and to John Williams, Jan. 2, 1832, John Floyd Papers, LC; John Tyler to Henry Curtis, Dec. 16, 1827, John Tyler Papers, LC.

13. John Floyd to John Williams, Dec. 27, 1830, John Floyd Papers, LC; John S. Barbour to JB, July 30, Nov. 22, 1831, BP NYPL; Risjord, *Old Republicans,* pp. 274–75.

14. JB to Clay, Dec. 20, 1829, Clay Papers, LC; Francis Brooke to JB, July 2, 1831, Jan. 1, 1832, and Daniel Webster to JB, May 24, 1830, BP NYPL.

15. *Lynchburg Virginian,* March 29, 1830.

16. *Richmond Whig,* Dec. 22, 1830.

17. Simms, *Rise of the Whigs,* p. 40.

18. *Richmond Enquirer,* June 15, 1830.

19. John Floyd to Calhoun, April 16, 1831, John Floyd Papers, LC; John S. Barbour to JB, July 30, Nov. 22, 1831, BP NYPL; Simms, *Rise of the Whigs,* p. 45; Ambler, *Thomas Ritchie,* pp. 135–39. The Richmond correspondent of the *Winchester Republican* wrote that the complexion of the General Assembly was: "Calhoun men 68, whole hog Jackson men 60, and Clay men 48" (*Washington National Intelligencer,* April 21, 1831).

20. JB to Isaac Davis, Feb. 5, 1826, Linn Banks to Thomas Davis, Dec. 31, 1830, and Charles Yancey to Thomas Davis, Dec. 31, 1830, Isaac Davis Papers, Duke University; James P. Preston to JB, May 10, 1830, BP NYPL; *JHD,* 1830–31, p. 4; *Richmond Whig,* Dec. 21, 1830; William Robinson to Philip Pendleton Barbour, May 9, 1830, Ambler Family Papers, UVA.

21. John S. Barbour to JB, March 1, April 2, 1830, Webster to JB, May 24, 1830, Richard Rush to JB, Aug. 7, 1830, Francis Brooke to JB, July 2, 1831, Jan. 1, 1832, BP NYPL; JB to Clay, March 7, 1832, Clay Papers, LC; James King to JB, Jan. 5, 1832, J. C. Gibson to JB, April 11, 1832, BP UVA.

22. John S. Barbour to JB, Jan. 11, 1831, BP NYPL.

23. *Niles' Register,* 41:308–309; JB to Clay, Dec. 20, 1829, Clay Papers, LC.

24. Webster to JB, May 24, 1830, BP NYPL.

25. Brooke to JB, July 30, 1831, and Richard Rush to JB, Aug. 7, 1830, BP NYPL; Charles H. Ambler, ed., *The Life and Diary of John Floyd, Governor of Virginia, an Apostle of Secession, and the Father of the Oregon Country* (Richmond: Richmond Press, 1918), pp. 117–18.

26. Clay to Francis Brooke, April 24, 1830, Henry Clay, *The Works of Henry Clay,* ed. Calvin Colton, 6 vols. (New York: A. S. Barnes and Burr, 1857), 4:362–64; Simms, *Rise of the Whigs,* pp. 48–52.

27. John S. Barbour to JB, July 30, Nov. 22, 1831, BP NYPL.

28. Clay to Francis Brooke, April 1, 1832, Clay, *Works,* ed. Colton, 4:331–34; John Floyd to Calhoun, Dec. 27, 1830, John Floyd Papers, LC; Francis Brooke to JB, July 2, 1831, BP NYPL.

29. John S. Barbour to JB, July 30, 1831, Brooke to JB, July 2, 1831, and Duff Green to JB, Sept. 24, 1832, BP NYPL; Robert B. Semple to JB, March 17, 1833, BP UVA; Simms, *Rise of the Whigs,* pp. 48–51; Morton, *Eulogy Upon Barbour,* p. 16.

30. *Richmond Whig,* Jan. 24, 1832; *Lynchburg Virginian,* Feb. 20, 1832; Simms, *Rise of the Whigs,* p. 58.

31. *Richmond Whig,* Nov. 29, 1831.

32. Van Deusen, *Henry Clay,* pp. 249–50.

33. JB to Clay, March 7, 1832, Clay, *Works,* ed. Colton, 4:328.

34. *Niles' Register,* 41:308–309.

35. Samuel Rhea Gammon, Jr., "The Presidential Campaign of 1832," *Johns Hopkins University Studies in Historical and Political Science,* 40 (1922):60–65; *Niles' Register,* 40:28–29, 41:301–302; Resolutions of an Anti-Jackson Meeting, Oct. 29, 1831, and JB to James Barbour, Jr., Dec. 17, 1832, BP UVA.

36. *Niles' Register,* 41:302.

37. Ibid., 41:306–12.

38. JB to Clay, March 7, 1832, Clay Papers, LC; John H. Pleasants to JB, March 23, 1832, BP NYPL.

39. Pleasants to JB, March 23, 1832, BP NYPL.

40. Arthur Charles Cole, *The Whig Party in the South* (Washington, D.C.: American Historical Association, 1914), p. 14; Risjord, *Old Republicans,* p. 276; *Richmond Whig,* Oct. 26, 1832; John S. Barbour to JB, March 25, 1832, BP NYPL.

41. *Richmond Whig,* July 24, 31, 1832; John H. Pleasants to JB, Oct. 7, 1832, BP NYPL.

42. A. Stephenson to JB, Sept. 22, 1832, BP NYPL.

43. Duff Green to JB, Sept. 24, 1832, and John H. Pleasants to JB, March 23, Oct. 7, 1832, BP NYPL.

44. John S. Barbour to JB, June 27, 1832, BP NYPL.

45. Ibid.; John H. Pleasants to JB, Oct. 7, 1832, BP NYPL; Cole, *Whig Party,* p. 14; Simms, *Rise of the Whigs,* pp. 53–61.

46. John S. Barbour to JB, Nov. 29, Dec. 13, 1832, Jan. 22, 1834, BP NYPL; Robert B. Semple to JB, March 3, 1833, and JB to Robert B. Semple, March 17, 1833, BP UVA; Morton, *Eulogy Upon Barbour,* p. 16.

47. *Niles' Register,* 41:306–308.

48. *Washington National Intelligencer,* Dec. 18, 1832; Simms, *Rise of the Whigs,* pp. 65–67; Risjord, *Old Republicans,* pp. 279–80; Ambler, *Thomas Ritchie,* pp. 150–52.

49. Cole, *Whig Party,* pp. 27–29; Simms, *Rise of the Whigs,* pp. 79–82.

50. John S. Barbour to JB, Jan. 22, 1834, BP NYPL.

51. *Richmond Enquirer,* Jan. 18, 23, Feb. 27, 1834; Oliver P. Chitwood, *John Tyler, Champion of the Old South* (New York: D. Appleton-Century, 1939), pp. 120–23.

52. Simms, *Rise of the Whigs,* pp. 84–86; Cole, *Whig Party,* p. 30; JB to Clay, Aug. 2, 1835, Clay Papers, LC.

53. John Floyd to John Williams, Dec. 27, 1830, and John Floyd to John S. Barbour, June 24, 1831, John Floyd Papers, LC; Glyndon G. Van Deusen, "Some Aspects of Whig Thought and Theory in the Jacksonian Period," *American Historical Review,* 63 (Jan. 1958):318; Richard Hofstadter, *The American Political Tradition and the Men Who Made It* (New York: A. A. Knopf, 1948), pp. 52–56.

54. *Niles' Register,* 41:308; Marvin Meyers, *The Jacksonian Persuasion: Politics and Beliefs,* rev. ed. (New York: Vintage Books, 1960), pp. 3–15; Daniel W. Howe, *The Political Culture of the American Whigs* (Chicago: University of Chicago Press, 1979), pp. 11–20.

55. *Niles' Register,* 41:308–12, 58:251–52; *Washington National Intelligencer,* Nov. 25, 28, 1826; JB to John H. Cocke, Sept. 18, 1826, John H. Cocke Papers (Shields Deposit), UVA; JB to Henry Clay, March 17, 1832, Clay, *Works,* ed. Colton, 4:328; JB to Clay, Aug. 2, 1835, Clay Papers, LC; Speech of JB, *Annals,* 16th Cong., 1st sess., pp. 579–84, and 17th Cong., 1st sess., pp. 443–44; Howe, *American Whigs,* pp. 96–122; Shalhope, *John Taylor,* p. 177; McCoy, *Elusive Republic,* p. 35.

56. Howe, *American Whigs,* pp. 150–80, passim; James Barbour, "Address to the Agricultural Convention of Virginia," pp. 685–89; Barbour Family Correspondence, 1815–28, passim, BP UVA; James Barbour, "Report of the Board of Agriculture to the General Assembly of Virginia," pp. 688–89; Barbour, *What Shall Be Done for the University?* pp. 4–5.

57. Van Deusen, "Whig Thought and Theory in the Jacksonian Period," pp. 315–18; Howe, *American Whigs,* p. 36; Meyers, *Jacksonian Persuasion,* p. 7.

58. Ambler, *Thomas Ritchie,* p. 158; *Richmond Enquirer,* Dec. 9, 1834, Jan. 29, 1835; John S. Barbour to JB, Jan. 22, 1834, BP NYPL; Simms, *Rise of the Whigs,* pp. 86–94.

59. JB to Clay, Aug. 2, 1835, Clay Papers, LC; Ambler, *Thomas Ritchie,* pp. 168–71.

60. JB to Tyler, Jan. 14, 1836, in Tyler, *Letters and Times of the Tylers,* 1:527; Chitwood, *Tyler,* pp. 134–36.

61. JB to Tyler, Jan. 14, 1836, and William F. Gordon to Tyler, Jan. 15, 1836, in Tyler, *Letters and Times of the Tylers,* 1:527–29; *Richmond Enquirer,* March 5, 1836; Chitwood, *Tyler,* pp. 135–39.

62. Chitwood, *Tyler,* pp. 137–39.

63. Quoted in Tyler, *Letters and Times of the Tylers,* 1:542.

64. *Richmond Whig,* Feb. 27, 1835; JB to Clay, Aug. 2, 1835, Clay Papers, LC; *Richmond Enquirer,* Feb. 13, 1836.

65. *Richmond Enquirer,* Feb. 13, 1836; Chitwood, *Tyler,* pp. 148–49.

66. *Richmond Enquirer,* Feb. 13, 1836.

67. JB to Clay, Aug. 2, 1835, Clay Papers, LC.

68. Ibid.

69. *Richmond Enquirer,* Feb. 13, 1836; Ambler, *Thomas Ritchie,* pp. 179–80.

70. JB–James Barbour, Jr., correspondence, 1831–35, and Business and Miscellaneous Papers, 1831–35, BP UVA.

71. Barbour, *Eulogium on Madison,* passim; Ketcham, *Madison,* pp. 669–70; Brant, *Madison,* 6:521–22; JB to Dolley Madison, Dec. 22, 1836, Madison Papers, NYPL.

72. *Washington National Intelligencer,* May 2, 1837; *Richmond Enquirer,* May 1, 11, 1838; Letters of Invitation, 1837–40, BP UVA.

73. *Richmond Enquirer,* Oct. 1, 4, 1839; *Niles' Register,* 57:125–27.

74. Van Deusen, *Henry Clay,* p. 320.

75. *Niles' Register,* 57:248–49. For opinions concerning Barbour's stature in the party, see Letters of Invitation, 1840, especially Tippecanoe Club of Caswell (Milton, N.C.) to JB, Sept. 10, 1840, and James King to JB, Jan. 5, 1832, BP UVA.

76. *Niles' Register,* 57:249–52; Van Deusen, *Henry Clay,* pp. 324–34.

77. Henry W. Hilliard, *Politics and Pen Pictures at Home and Abroad* (New York: G. P. Putnam's Sons, 1892), pp. 9–10.

78. *Niles' Register,* 57:251.

79. Ibid., 57:252; Chitwood, *Tyler,* pp. 167–73; Benjamin W. Leigh to the Editors of the *Richmond Whig* [n.d.], *Tyler's Quarterly,* 9 (1928):94.

80. Hilliard, *Politics and Pen Pictures,* p. 5.

81. Bell, *Memoirs of Governor William Smith,* p. 14; Collins, *Miscellanies,* p. 226; Robert C. Winthrop to William Wirt Henry, Jan. 24, 1876, William Wirt Henry Papers, VHS.

82. Dorothy Burne Goebel, *William Henry Harrison: A Political Biography* (Indianapolis: Historical Bureau of the Indiana Library and Historical Department, 1926), pp. 347–54; Chitwood, *Tyler,* pp. 177–83.

83. Simms, *Rise of the Whigs,* pp. 148–49.

84. Letters of Invitation, 1840, BP UVA; Citizens of Fredericksburg to William C. Rives, June 25, 1840, William C. Rives Papers, LC; JB to Lucy Barbour, Sept. 6, 1840, and JB to James Barbour, Jr., April 26, 1839, BP UVA.

85. Bell, *Memoirs of Governor William Smith,* p. 14.

86. Letters of Invitation, 1840, BP UVA; *Richmond Enquirer,* Aug. 14, 1840; *Richmond Whig,* Sept. 21, 1840.

87. *Richmond Whig,* Oct. 7, 1840.

88. Robert C. Winthrop to JB, Aug. 10, 1840, BP NYPL.

89. Tippecanoe Club of Caswell (Milton, N. C.) to JB, Sept. 10, 1840, BP UVA.

90. Simms, *Rise of the Whigs,* pp. 157–58.

91. Collins, *Miscellanies,* pp. 209–10.

92. JB to Lucy Barbour, March 10, 1841, BP UVA.

93. Barbour Family Bible, BP UVA.

94. Collins, *Miscellanies,* p. 225.

95. Ibid., pp. 210–11; *Richmond Whig and Public Advertiser,* July 4, 1842; Lucy B. Taliaferro to James Barbour, Jr., June 9, 1842, BP UVA.

96. Obituary Notices, 1842, BP UVA.

97. Alexander H. H. Stuart to Robert A. Brock, Jan. 4, 1884, Robert Alonzo Brock Papers, Henry E. Huntington Library, San Marino, Calif.

Chapter 13. James Barbour: An Appraisal

1. Edward Coles to Hugh Blair Grigsby, Dec. 23, 1854, Edward Coles Papers, Historical Society of Pennsylvania; Robert Taylor to JB, July 7, Aug. 13, 1836, and John C. Hansborough to JB, Oct. 17, 1836, BP UVA.

2. John C. Underwood to Cornelia Barbour, July 9, 1862, John C. Underwood Papers, LC.

Bibliography

1. Manuscript Sources

a. Private

Adams Family. Papers. LC; Massachusetts Historical Society, Boston, Mass.

Ambler Family. Papers. UVA.

Ast, William F. Papers. Henry E. Huntington Library and Art Gallery, San Marino, Calif.

Barbour, James. Account Book. UVA.

———. Ledger. UVA.

———. Papers. UVA.

———. Papers. Duke.

———. Papers. Rare Book and Manuscripts Division. The New York Public Library. Astor, Lenox, and Tilden Foundations.

Barbour, Philip Pendleton. Papers. VHS.

Bolling, William. Papers. Duke.

Brock, Robert Alonzo. Collection. Henry E. Huntington Library and Art Gallery, San Marino, Calif.

Bryan, Tennant. Papers. VHS.

Cabell, Joseph C. Papers. UVA.

Cabell, William H. Papers. LC.

Campbell Family. Papers. Duke.

Campbell-Preston Family. Papers. LC.

Clay, Henry. Papers. LC.

Cocke, John Hartwell. Papers. UVA.

Coles, Edward. Papers. Historical Society of Pennsylvania, Philadelphia, Pa.

Crittenden, John J. Papers. Duke.

Davis, Isaac. Papers. Duke.

———. Papers. UVA.

Dunglison, Robley. Diary. Microfilm. UVA.

Floyd, John. Papers. LC.

Garnett, James Mercer. Papers. UVA; VSL.

Gilmer, Francis Walker. Letter Book. UVA.

———. Papers. VSL.

Gilmer, Peachy. Papers. UVA; VSL.

Grinnan Family. Papers. UVA.

Harrison, William Henry. Papers. LC.

Hench, A. L. Collection. UVA.

Henry, William Wirt. Papers. VHS.

Holmes, John. Papers. Maine Historical Society, Portland, Maine.

Jefferson, Thomas. Account Books. UVA.

————. Papers. LC; Massachusetts Historical Society, Boston, Mass.

King, Rufus. Papers. New-York Historical Society, New York City.

————. Papers. NYPL.

King, William. Papers. Maine Historical Society, Portland, Maine.

Leftwich, Joel. Papers. UVA; Southern Historical Collection, University of North Carolina, Chapel Hill, N. C.

Leigh, Benjamin Watkins. Papers. VHS.

Macon, Nathaniel. Papers. Duke.

Madison, James. Papers. LC; NYPL.

Madison-Todd Family. Papers. UVA.

Miscellaneous Bound Collection. Massachusetts Historical Society, Boston, Mass.

Monroe, James. Papers. LC.

————. Papers. Rare Books and Manuscript Division. The New York Public Library. Astor, Lenox, and Tilden Foundations.

Nelson, Hugh. Papers. LC.

Nicholas, Wilson Cary. Papers. LC; UVA.

Otis, Harrison Gray. Papers. Massachusetts Historical Society, Boston, Mass.

Personal Papers, Miscellaneous. LC.

Preston Family. Papers. VHS; LC.

Randolph, John. Papers. LC.

Randolph, John – Garnett, James M. Papers. LC.

Randolph, John – Gilmer, Francis Walker. Papers. VSL.

Ritchie, Thomas. Papers. LC.

Rives, William Cabell. Papers. LC.

Ruffin, Francis G. Diary. VHS.

Smith-Thompson Family. Papers. LC.

Stevenson, Andrew. Papers. LC.

Stuart, Archibald. Papers. VHS.

Tait Family. Papers. Alabama Department of Archives and History, Montgomery, Ala.

Taylor, Creed. Papers. UVA.

Taylor, Francis. Diary. VSL.

Taylor, John. Papers. Duke.

Taylor, John W. Papers. New-York Historical Society, New York City.

Tazewell Family. Papers. Personal Papers Collection, Archives Branch, VSL.

Tucker-Coleman Family. Papers. Earl G. Swem Memorial Library, College of William and Mary, Williamsburg, Va.

Tyler, John. Papers. LC.

Underwood, John C. Papers. LC.

Van Buren, Martin. Papers. LC.

Walker, John W. Papers. Alabama Department of Archives and History, Montgomery, Ala.

Webster, Daniel. Papers. LC.

Wirt, William. Papers. LC; Maryland Historical Society, Baltimore, Md.
Wirt, William – Carr, Dabney. Correspondence. Personal Papers Collection, Archives Branch, VSL.

b. Public

Albemarle County, Va. Deed Books, 1793 – 1842. Albemarle County Clerk's Office.
———. Land Books, 1760 – 1812. VSL.
———. Minute Books, 1793 – 1812. VSL.
Commonwealth of Virginia. Council of State Journals, 1812 – 14. VSL.
———. Executive Communications, 1812 – 14. VSL.
———. Executive Letter Book, 1812 – 14. VSL.
———. Executive Papers, 1812 – 14. VSL.
Culpeper County, Va. Land Books, 1760 – 1842. VSL.
———. Minute Books, 1760 – 1812. Culpeper County Courthouse.
Fluvanna County, Va. Minute Books, 1792 – 1812. Fluvanna County Courthouse.
———. Order Books, 1792 – 1812. Fluvanna County Courthouse.
Louisa County, Va. Minute Books, 1792 – 1812. Louisa County Courthouse.
———. Order Books, 1792 – 1812. Louisa County Courthouse.
Madison County, Va. Deed Books, 1793 – 1812. Madison County Clerk's Office.
———. Minute Books, 1793 – 1812. Madison County Clerk's Office.
Orange County, Va. Court Dockets, 1792 – 1828. Orange County Clerk's Office.
———. Deed Books, 1738 – 1842. Orange County Clerk's Office.
———. Land Books, 1735 – 1842. Orange County Clerk's Office and VSL.
———. Minute Books, 1738 – 1842. Orange County Clerk's Office.
———. Order Books, 1742 – 1842. Orange County Clerk's Office.
———. Personal Property Books, 1782 – 1842. VSL.
———. Register of Justices and Other County Officers, 1777 – 1833. VSL.
———. Register of Marriages, No. 1. Orange County Clerk's Office.
U.S. Department of State. Despatches and Instructions, Great Britain. Vol. 7. National Archives, Washington, D.C.
———. Despatches from the United States Ministers to Great Britain. National Archives, Washington, D.C.
U.S. Department of War. Military Book. Vols. 12 and 13. National Archives, Washington, D.C.
———. Indian Office. Letter Books, Series 2, vol. 104. National Archives, Washington, D.C.

2. Printed Sources

a. Writings of Contemporaries

Adams, John Quincy. *Memoirs of John Quincy Adams, Comprising Portions of His Diary from 1795 to 1848.* Edited by Charles Francis Adams. 12 vols. Philadelphia: J. B. Lippincott, 1874 – 77.

Ames, Fisher. *Works of Fisher Ames.* Edited by Seth Ames. 2 vols. Boston: Little, Brown, 1854.

Bell, John W., comp. *Memoirs of Governor William Smith, of Virginia.* New York: Moss Engraving, 1891.

Benton, Thomas Hart. *Thirty Years' View; or, A History of the Working of the American Government for Thirty Years, from 1820 to 1850.* 2 vols. New York: D. Appleton, 1854–56.

Collins, Stephen. *Miscellanies.* Philadelphia; Carey and Hart, 1845.

Cunningham, Noble E., Jr., ed. *Circular Letters of Congressmen to Their Constituents, 1789–1829.* 3 vols. Chapel Hill: University of North Carolina Press, 1978.

Dix, Morgan, comp. *Memoirs of John Adams Dix.* 2 vols. New York: Harper and Brothers, 1883.

Duncan, John M. *Travels Through Part of the United States and Canada in 1818 and 1819.* 2 vols. London: Hurst, Robison, 1823.

Faux, William. *Memorable Days in America, Being a Journal of a Tour to the United States.* London: W. Simpkin and R. Marshall, 1823.

Fearon, Henry Bradshaw. *Sketches of America. A Narrative of a Journey of Five Thousand Miles Through the Eastern and Western States of America* . . . London: Longman, Hurst, Rees, Orme, and Brown, 1818.

Grigsby, Hugh Blair. "Sketches of Members of the Constitutional Convention of 1829–30." *VMHB,* 61 (July 1953):319–32.

Hall, Basil. *Travels in North America in the Years 1828 and 1829.* 3 vols. London: Simpkin and Marshall, 1829.

Hall, Margaret Hunter. *The Aristocratic Journey.* Edited by Una Pope-Hennessy. New York: G. P. Putnam's Sons, 1931.

Hilliard, Henry W. *Politics and Pen Pictures at Home and Abroad.* New York: G. P. Putnam's Sons, 1892.

Jefferson, Thomas. *Notes on the State of Virginia.* Edited by William Peden. Chapel Hill: University of North Carolina Press, 1955.

———. *Thomas Jefferson's Garden Book, 1766–1824.* Edited by Edwin Morris Betts. Philadelphia: American Philosophical Society, 1944.

La Rochefoucauld-Liancourt, Duc de. *Travels Through the United States of North America, the Country of the Iroquois and Upper Canada, in the Years 1795, 1796, and 1797.* 2 vols. London: R. Phillips, 1799.

"Letters from William and Mary College, 1798–1801." *VMHB,* 29 (April 1921): 129–71.

Martineau, Harriet. *Retrospect of Western Travel.* 3 vols. London: Saunders and Otley, 1838.

Mason, Jeremiah. *Memoirs and Correspondence of Jeremiah Mason.* Edited by G. S. Hillard. Cambridge, Mass.: Riverside Press, 1873.

Morton, Jeremiah. *Eulogy Upon the Late Governor Barbour.* Richmond, 1842.

Perry, Benjamin F. *Reminiscences of Public Men.* Philadelphia: J. D. Avil, 1883.

Poore, Ben Perley. *Perley's Reminiscences of Sixty Years in the National Metropolis.* 2 vols. Philadelphia: Hubbard Brothers, 1886.

Roberts, Jonathan. "Memoirs of a Senator from Pennsylvania," pts. 7–9. *Pennsylvania Magazine of History and Biography,* 62 (July 1938):361–409.

Ruffin, Edmund. "Writers of Anonymous Articles in the Farmers' Register." Edited by J. G. de Roulhac Hamilton. *Journal of Southern History,* 23 (Feb. 1957):90–102.

Sargent, Nathan. *Public Men and Events from the Commencement of Mr. Monroe's Administration in 1817, to the Close of Mr. Fillmore's Administration in 1853.* 2 vols. Philadelphia: J. B. Lippincott, 1875.

Schoepf, Johann David. *Travels in the Confederation, 1783–1784.* Translated and edited by Alfred J. Morrison. 2 vols. Philadelphia: W. J. Campbell, 1911.

Smith, Margaret Bayard. *The First Forty Years of Washington Society, Portrayed by the Family Letters of Mrs. Samuel Harrison Smith (Margaret Bayard) from the Collection of her Grandson, J. Henley Smith.* Edited by Gaillard Hunt. New York: C. Scribner's Sons, 1906.

Sparks, William Henry. *The Memoirs of Fifty Years.* Philadelphia: Claxton, Remsen and Haffelfinger, 1870.

Traveller, A. [Royall, Anne]. *Sketches of History, Life, and Manners in the United States.* New Haven: Printed for the Author, 1826.

Tucker, St. George. *Blackstone's Commentaries: With Notes of Reference, to the Constitution and Laws, of the Federal Government of the United States; and of the Commonwealth of Virginia.* 5 vols. Philadelphia: William Young Birch and Abraham Small, 1803.

Virginian, A. *Letters on the Richmond Party.* Washington, D.C., 1823.

[Watterson, George]. *Letters from Washington, on the Constitution and Laws; with Sketches of Some Prominent Public Characters of the United States. Writings during the Winter of 1817–1818 by a Foreigner.* Washington: J. Gideon, Jr., 1818.

Wirt, William. *The Letters of the British Spy.* New York: J. and J. Harper, 1832.

b. Letters of Contemporaries

Calhoun, John C. *Correspondence of John C. Calhoun.* Edited by J. Franklin Jameson. In American Historical Association, *Annual Report for the Year 1899,* vol. 2. Washington, D.C., 1900.

———. *The Papers of John C. Calhoun.* Edited by Robert L. Meriwether. 14 vols. to date. Columbia: University of South Carolina Press, 1959– .

Clay, Henry. *The Papers of Henry Clay.* Edited by James F. Hopkins. 6 vols. to date. Lexington: University of Kentucky Press, 1959– .

———. *The Private Correspondence of Henry Clay.* Edited by Calvin Colton. New York: A. S. Barnes, 1855.

———. *The Works of Henry Clay.* Edited by Calvin Colton. 6 vols. New York: A. S. Barnes and Burr, 1857.

Floyd, John. *The Life and Diary of John Floyd, Governor of Virginia, An Apostle of Secession, and the Father of the Oregon Country.* Edited by Charles H. Ambler. Richmond: Richmond Press, 1918.

Hale, Salma. "Salma Hale Papers." Edited by Winslow Warren. *Massachusetts Historical Society Proceedings,* 46 (Oct. 1912–June 1913):402–409.

Jefferson, Thomas. *The Papers of Thomas Jefferson.* Edited by Julian P. Boyd. 19 vols. to date. Princeton: Princeton University Press, 1950–.

———. *The Works of Thomas Jefferson.* Edited by Paul Leicester Ford. 12 vols. Federal ed. New York: G. P. Putnam's Sons, 1904–1905.

King, Rufus. *The Life and Correspondence of Rufus King.* Edited by Charles R. King. 6 vols. New York: G. P. Putnam's Sons, 1894–1900.

Lee, Richard Henry. *The Letters of Richard Henry Lee.* Edited by James Curtis Ballagh. 2 vols. New York: Macmillan, 1911–14.

Macon, Nathaniel. "Correspondence." Edited by Charles H. Ambler. *John P. Branch Historical Papers of Randolph-Macon College,* 3 (June 1909):27–93.

Madison, James. *The Papers of James Madison.* Edited by William T. Hutchinson, William M. E. Rachal, Charles F. Hobson, and Robert A. Rutland. 13 vols. to date. Chicago and Charlottesville: University of Chicago and University of Virginia Presses, 1962–.

———. *The Writings of James Madison.* Edited by Gaillard Hunt. 9 vols. New York: G. P. Putnam's Sons, 1900–10.

Mangum, Willie Person. *The Papers of Willie Person Mangum.* Edited by Henry Thomas Shanks. 5 vols. Raleigh: North Carolina Department of Archives and History, 1950–56.

Mason, Armistead Thomas. "Letters of Armistead Thomas Mason, 1813–1818." *WMQ,* 1st ser., 23 (April 1915):228–39.

"Missouri Compromise: Letters to James Barbour, Senator of Virginia in the Congress of the United States." *WMQ,* 1st ser., 10 (July 1901):5–24.

Monroe, James. *The Writings of James Monroe.* Edited by Stanislaus Murray Hamilton. 7 vols. New York: G. P. Putnam's Sons, 1898–1903.

Plumer, William, Jr. *The Missouri Compromises and Presidential Politics, 1820–1825, from the Letters of William Plumer, Jr.* Edited by Everett Somerville Brown. St. Louis: Missouri Historical Society, 1926.

Ritchie, Thomas. "Unpublished Letters of Thomas Ritchie." Edited by Charles H. Ambler. *John P. Branch Historical Papers of Randolph-Macon College,* 3 (June 1911):199–252.

Rives, William C. "Letters of William C. Rives, 1823–1829." *Tyler's Quarterly Historical and Genealogical Magazine,* 5 (1924):223–37; 6 (1925):6–15, 97–106.

Roane, Spencer. "Letters of Spencer Roane, 1788–1822." *Bulletin of the New York Public Library,* 10 (1906):167–80.

———. "Roane Correspondence, 1799–1821." Edited by William E. Dodd. *John P. Branch Historical Papers of Randolph-Macon College,* 2 (June 1905):123–42.

Taylor, John. "John Taylor Correspondence." Edited by William E. Dodd. *John P. Branch Historical Papers of Randolph-Macon College,* 2 (June 1908):253–353.

———. "Letters of John Taylor of Caroline." Edited by Hans Hammond. *VMHB,* 52 (Jan. 1944):1–14, 121–34.

c. Documents

Albemarle Agricultural Society. "Minute Book of the Albemarle (Virginia) Agriculture Society." Edited by Rodney H. True. American Historical Society, *Annual Report for the Year 1918,* 1:261–349. Washington, D.C., 1921.

Commonwealth of Virginia. *Calendar of Virginia State Papers and Other Manuscripts. Preserved in the Capitol at Richmond.* 11 vols. Richmond, 1875–93.

———. *Journals of the House of Delegates of the Commonwealth of Virginia, 1798–1832.* Richmond, 1799–1833.

———. *Proceedings and Debates in the Virginia State Convention of 1829–1830.* Richmond, 1830.

———. *The Virginia Report of 1799–1800 Touching the Alien and Sedition Laws, Together with the Virginia Resolutions of December 21, 1798.* Richmond: J. W. Randolph, 1850.

Kappler, Charles J., ed. and comp. *Indian Affairs, Laws and Treaties.* 3 vols. Washington, D.C., 1892–1913.

Kennedy, John P., and McIlwaine, H. R., eds. *Journals of the House of Burgesses of Virginia, 1619–1776.* 13 vols. Richmond, 1904–15.

Manning, William R., ed. and comp. *Diplomatic Correspondence of the United States: Canadian Relations, 1784–1860.* 4 vols. Washington, D.C., 1940–45.

Richardson, James D., ed. and comp. *A Compilation of the Messages and Papers of the Presidents, 1789–1897.* 10 vols. Washington, D.C., 1896–99.

Statutes at Large of the United States of America, 1789–1873. 17 vols. Washington, D.C., 1850–73.

Swem, Earl G., and Williams, John W., eds. *A Register of the General Assembly of Virginia.* Richmond, 1918.

U.S. Congress. *Annals of Congress: Debates and Proceedings.* 1st Cong., March 3, 1789, to 18th Cong., 1st sess., May 27, 1824. 42 vols. Washington, D.C., 1834–56.

———. *Congressional Directory.* 14th through 17th Cong. Washington, D.C. 1814–23.

———. *Register of Debates in Congress: Debates and Proceedings.* 18th Cong., 2nd sess., Dec. 6, 1824, to 25th Cong., 1st sess., Oct. 16, 1837. 14 vols. Washington, D.C., 1825–37.

———. House. *House Executive Documents.* Docs. 14, 15, 33, 51, 55, 67, 68, 71, 77, 83, 102, 112, 117, 124, 125, 161, 168. 19th Cong., 1st sess., Dec. 1825–April 1826.

———. Docs. 14, 15, 17, 18, 28, 39, 42, 105. 19th Cong., 2nd sess., Dec. 1826–May 1827.

———. Senate. *Senate Documents.* Docs. 14, 45, 90. 19th Cong., 1st sess., Dec. 1825–April 1826.

U.S. Department of State. *American State Papers.* Class 1, *Foreign Relations.* 6 vols. Washington, D.C., 1854–59.

———. Class 2, *Indian Affairs.* 2 vols. Washington, D.C., 1832–60.

———. Class 5, *Military Affairs.* 7 vols. Washington, D.C., 1834–60.

3. Newspapers and Contemporary Periodicals

Alexandria, Va. *Gazette,* 1798–1807, 1811–17.

Baltimore, Md. *American Farmer,* 1819–34, 1839–42.

Baltimore, Md. *Niles' Register,* 1815–42.

Baltimore, Md., *Weekly Register,* 1813.

Charleston, S. C. *Courier,* 1818.
Lynchburg, Va. *Virginian,* 1830–32.
New York City. *Evening Post,* 1828.
Norfolk, Va. *American Beacon,* 1817–25.
Norfolk, Va. *Argus.* 1813, 1855.
Norfolk, Va. *Gazette and Public Ledger,* 1807–16.
Petersburg, Va. *Farmers' Register,* 1833–42.
Philadelphia, Pa. *Aurora,* 1798–1800.
Philadelphia, Pa. *National Gazette and Literary Register,* 1825.
Richmond, Va. *Enquirer,* 1804–42.
Richmond, Va. *Gazette,* 1799–1803.
Richmond, Va. *Observatory,* 1798–1800.
Richmond, Va. *Virginia Argus,* 1798–1807, 1813–15.
Richmond, Va. *Virginia Federalist,* 1798–1800.
Richmond, Va. *Whig,* 1824–42.
Washington, D.C. *National Intelligencer,* 1815–37.
Williamsburg, Va. *Virginia Gazette,* 1765–78.

4. Writings of James Barbour

Address of James Barbour, Esquire, President of the Agricultural Society of Albemarle at Their Meeting of the 8th of November, 1825. Charlottesville: C. P. M'Kennie, 1825.
"Address to the Agricultural Convention of Virginia." *Farmers' Register,* 3 (March 1836):685–89.
"The Cultivation of Wheat." *American Farmer,* 1 (Dec. 17, 1819):301–302.
Eulogium Upon the Life and Character of James Madison. Washington, D.C.: Gales and Seaton, 1836.
"Introduction to the Report of the Board of Agriculture to the General Assembly of Virginia." *Farmers' Register,* 9 (Dec. 31, 1841):688–89.
"On the Improvement of Agriculture and the Importance of Legislative Aid to that Object. Description of the South West Mountain Lands." *Farmers' Register,* 2 (April 1835):703–706.
Remarks on the Bill for Abolishing Imprisonment for Debt. Washington, D.C.: Columbian Office, 1824.
Speech of James Barbour of Virginia on the Restriction of Slavery in Missouri. Delivered in Washington, D.C., 1820. BP UVA.
To the People of Virginia: What Shall be Done for the University? Charlottesville, 1823. BP UVA.

5. Secondary Works

a. Biographies

Alexander, Holmes Moss. *The American Talleyrand: The Career and Contemporaries of Martin Van Buren, Eighth President.* New York: Harper and Brothers, 1935.

Ambler, Charles Henry. *Thomas Ritchie: A Study in Virginia Politics.* Richmond: Bell Book and Stationery, 1913.

Ammon, Harry. *James Monroe: The Quest for National Identity.* New York: McGraw-Hill, 1971.

Anderson, Dice R. *William Branch Giles: A Study in the Politics of Virginia and the Nation from 1790 to 1830.* Menasha, Wisc.: George Banta, 1914.

Balinky, Alexander. *Albert Gallatin: Fiscal Theories and Policies.* New Brunswick, N.J.: Rutgers University Press, 1958.

Bemis, Samuel Flagg. *John Quincy Adams and the Foundations of American Foreign Policy.* New York: A. A. Knopf, 1949.

———. *John Quincy Adams and the Union.* New York: A. A. Knopf, 1956.

Bernhard, Winfred E. A. *Fisher Ames, Federalist and Statesman, 1758–1808.* Chapel Hill: University of North Carolina Press, 1965.

Beveridge, Albert J. *The Life of John Marshall.* 4 vols. Boston: Houghton Mifflin, 1919.

Brant, Irving. *James Madison.* 6 vols. Indianapolis: Bobbs-Merrill, 1941–61.

Bruce, William Cabell. *John Randolph of Roanoke, 1773–1833.* 2 vols. New York: G. P. Putnam's Sons, 1922.

Brugger, Robert J. *Beverly Tucker: Heart over Head in the Old South.* Baltimore: Johns Hopkins University Press, 1978.

Chambers, William Nisbet. *Old Bullion Benton, Senator from the New West.* Boston: Little, Brown, 1956.

Chitwood, Oliver P. *John Tyler, Champion of the Old South.* New York: D. Appleton-Century, 1939.

Clark, Bennett Champ. *John Quincy Adams, "Old Man Eloquent."* Boston: Little, Brown, 1932.

Cleaves, Freeman. *Old Tippecanoe: William Henry Harrison and His Time.* New York: C. Scribner's Sons, 1939.

Coit, Margaret L. *John C. Calhoun: American Portrait.* Boston: Houghton Mifflin, 1950.

Coleman, Mrs. Chapman. *The Life of John J. Crittenden, with Selections from His Correspondence and Speeches.* 2 vols. Philadelphia: J. B. Lippincott, 1871.

Coleman, Mary H. *St. George Tucker, Citizen of No Mean City.* Richmond: Dietz Press, 1938.

Craven, Avery. *Edmund Ruffin, Southerner: A Study in Secession.* New York: D. Appleton, 1932.

Cresson, W. P. *James Monroe.* Chapel Hill: University of North Carolina Press, 1946.

Current, Richard N. *Daniel Webster and the Rise of National Conservatism.* Boston: Little, Brown, 1955.

Curtis, George Ticknor. *Life of Daniel Webster.* 2 vols. New York: D. Appleton, 1870.

Davis, Richard Beale. *Francis Walker Gilmer: Life and Learning in Jefferson's Virginia.* Richmond: Dietz Press, 1939.

Dawidoff, Robert. *The Education of John Randolph.* New York: W. W. Norton, 1979.

Dodd, William E. *Life of Nathaniel Macon.* Raleigh: Edwards and Broughton, 1903.

Eaton, Clement. *Henry Clay and the Art of American Politics.* Boston: Little, Brown, 1957.

Ernst, Robert. *Rufus King, American Federalist.* Chapel Hill: University of North Carolina Press, 1968.

Frary, I. J. *Thomas Jefferson: Architect and Builder.* Richmond: Garrett and Massie, 1950.

Gaines, William H., Jr. *Thomas Mann Randolph, Jefferson's Son-in-Law.* Baton Rouge: Louisiana State University Press, 1966.

Garland, Hugh A. *The Life of John Randolph of Roanoke.* 2 vols. New York: D. Appleton, 1850.

Goebel, Dorothy Burne. *William Henry Harrison: A Political Biography.* Indianapolis: Historical Bureau of the Indiana Library and Historical Department, 1926.

Gordon, Armistead C. *William Fitzhugh Gordon, A Virginian of the Old School: His Life, Times, and Contemporaries, 1787–1858.* New York: Neale, 1909.

Guedalla, Phillip. *Wellington.* New York: Harper and Brothers, 1931.

Harden, Edward J. *The Life of George M. Troup.* Savannah: E. J. Purse, 1859.

Hildrup, Robert Leroy. *The Life and Times of Edmund Pendleton.* Chapel Hill: University of North Carolina Press, 1939.

Kennedy, John Pendleton. *Memoirs of the Life of William Wirt, Attorney General of the United States.* 2 vols. Philadelphia: Lee and Blanchard, 1850.

Ketcham, Ralph. *James Madison, A Biography.* New York: Macmillan, 1971.

Kimball, Fiske. *Thomas Jefferson: Architect.* Boston: Riverside Press, 1916.

Malone, Dumas. *Jefferson and His Time.* 6 vols. Boston: Little, Brown, 1948–81.

Mayo, Bernard. *Henry Clay, Spokesman of the New West.* Boston: Houghton Mifflin, 1937.

Meade, Robert Douthat. *Patrick Henry.* 2 vols. Philadelphia: J. B. Lippincott, 1957–69.

Meigs, William M. *The Life of Thomas Hart Benton.* Philadelphia: J. B. Lippincott, 1904.

Meyer, Leland W. *The Life and Times of Colonel Richard M. Johnson of Kentucky.* Columbia University Studies in History, Economics, and Public Law, 359. New York: Columbia University Press, 1932.

Morison, Samuel Eliot. *The Life and Letters of Harrison Gray Otis, Federalist, 1765–1848.* 2 vols. Boston: Houghton Mifflin, 1913.

Peterson, Merrill D. *Thomas Jefferson and the New Nation: A Biography.* New York: Oxford University Press, 1970.

Poage, George R. *Henry Clay and the Whig Party.* Chapel Hill: University of North Carolina Press, 1936.

Randall, Henry S. *The Life of Thomas Jefferson.* 3 vols. New York: Derby and Jackson, 1858.

Rives, William Cabell. *History of the Life and Times of James Madison.* 3 vols. Boston: Little, Brown, 1859–68.

Shalhope, Robert E. *John Taylor of Caroline, Pastoral Republican.* Columbia: University of South Carolina Press, 1980.

Shepard, Edward M. *Martin Van Buren.* Boston: Houghton Mifflin, 1888.

Shipp, J. E. D. *Giant Days; or, The Life and Times of William H. Crawford.* Americus, Ga.: Southern Printers, 1909.

Silver, James W. *Edmund Pendleton Gaines, Frontier General.* Baton Rouge: Louisiana State University Press, 1949.

Simms, Henry H. *Life of John Taylor.* Richmond: William Byrd Press, 1932.

Smith, Abbott Emerson. *James Madison, Builder.* New York: Wilson-Erickson, 1937.

Tyler, Lyon Gardiner. *The Letters and Times of the Tylers.* 3 vols. Richmond: Whittet and Shepperson, 1884–96.

Van Deusen, Glyndon G. *The Life of Henry Clay.* Boston: Little, Brown, 1937.

Walters, Raymond, Jr. *Albert Gallatin: Jeffersonian Financier and Diplomat.* New York: Macmillan, 1957.

Wayland, Francis Fry. *Andrew Stevenson, Democrat and Diplomat, 1785–1857.* Philadelphia: University of Pennsylvania Press, 1949.

Wiltse, Charles M. *John C. Calhoun, Nationalist, 1782–1828.* Indianapolis: Bobbs-Merrill, 1944.

———. *John C. Calhoun, Nullifier, 1829–1839.* Indianapolis: Bobbs-Merrill, 1949.

Wirt, William. *Sketches of the Life and Character of Patrick Henry.* 10th ed. Hartford, Conn.: S. Andrus, 1848.

b. Other Books

Abernethy, Thomas Perkins. *The Burr Conspiracy.* New York: Oxford University Press, 1954.

———. *The South in the New Nation, 1789–1819.* Baton Rouge: Louisiana State University Press, 1961.

Adams, Henry. *The Degradation of the Democratic Dogma.* New York: Macmillan, 1919.

———. *History of the United States of America during the Administrations of Thomas Jefferson and James Madison.* 9 vols. New York: C. Scribner's Sons, 1889–91.

Allen, Harry C. *Great Britain and the United States: A History of Anglo-American Relations, 1783–1952.* New York: St. Martin's Press, 1955.

Ambler, Charles Henry. *Sectionalism in Virginia from 1776 to 1861.* Chicago: University of Chicago Press, 1910.

Banner, James M., Jr. *To the Hartford Convention: The Federalists and the Origins of Party Politics in Massachusetts, 1789–1815.* New York: A. A. Knopf, 1970.

Banning, Lance. *The Jeffersonian Persuasion: Evolution of a Party Ideology.* Ithaca: Cornell University Press, 1978.

Bassett, John Spencer. *The Southern Plantation Overseer as Revealed in His Letters.* Northampton, Mass.: Smith College, 1925.

Beeman, Richard. *The Old Dominion and the New Nation, 1788–1801.* Lexington: University Press of Kentucky, 1972.

Bemis, Samuel Flagg, ed. *The American Secretaries of State and Their Diplomacy.* 10 vols. New York: A. A. Knopf, 1927–29.

Benns, F. Lee. *The American Struggle for the British West India Carrying-Trade, 1815–1830. Indiana University Studies,* 10:56 (March 1923).

Brock, Robert A. *Virginia and Virginians.* 2 vols. Richmond: H. H. Hardesty, 1888.

Broussard, James H. *The Southern Federalists, 1800–1816.* Baton Rouge: Louisiana State University Press, 1978.

Bruce, Philip Alexander. *History of the University of Virginia, 1819–1919: The Lengthened Shadow of One Man.* 5 vols. New York: Macmillan, 1920.

Buel, Richard, Jr. *Securing the Revolution: Ideology in American Politics, 1789–1815.* Ithaca: Cornell University Press, 1972.

Carpenter, Jesse T. *The South as a Conscious Minority, 1789–1861: A Study in Political Thought.* New York: New York University Press, 1930.

Catterall, Ralph C. H. *The Second Bank of the United States.* Chicago: University of Chicago Press, 1903.

Chandler, Julian A. C. *The History of Suffrage in Virginia.* Baltimore: Johns Hopkins University Press, 1901.

Chase, James S. *Emergence of the Presidential Nominating Convention, 1789–1832.* Urbana: University of Illinois Press, 1973.

Christain, Frances A., and Massie, Susanna W., eds. *Homes and Gardens in Old Virginia.* Richmond: Garrett and Massie, 1950.

Cole, Arthur Charles. *The Whig Party in the South.* Washington, D.C.: American Historical Association, 1914.

Coles, Harry L. *The War of 1812.* Chicago: University of Chicago Press, 1965.

Craven, Avery O. *Soil Exhaustion as a Factor in the Agricultural History of Virginia and Maryland, 1606–1860.* University of Illinois Studies in the Social Sciences, 13:1. Urbana: University of Illinois Press, 1926.

Cunningham, Noble E., Jr. *The Jefferson Republicans: The Formation of Party Organization, 1789–1801.* Chapel Hill: University of North Carolina Press, 1957.

———. *The Jeffersonian Republicans in Power: Party Operations, 1801–1809.* Chapel Hill: University of North Carolina Press, 1963.

———. *The Process of Government under Jefferson.* Princeton: Princeton University Press, 1978.

Dabney, Virginius. *Richmond: The Story of a City.* New York: Doubleday, 1976.

Dangerfield, George. *The Awakening of American Nationalism, 1815–1828.* New York: Harper and Row, 1965.

———. *The Era of Good Feelings.* New York: Harcourt, Brace, 1952.

Dauer, Manning, J. *The Adams Federalists.* Baltimore: Johns Hopkins University Press, 1953.

Davis, Richard Beale. *Intellectual Life of Jefferson's Virginia, 1790–1830.* Chapel Hill: University of North Carolina Press, 1964.

du Bellet, Louis P. *Some Prominent Virginia Families.* 4 vols. Lynchburg, Va.: J. P. Bell, 1907.

Elkins, Stanley M. *Slavery: A Problem in American Institutional and Intellectual Life.* Chicago: University of Chicago Press, 1959.

Ellis, Richard E. *The Jeffersonian Crisis: Courts and Politics in the Young Republic.* New York: Oxford University Press, 1971.

Fischer, David Hackett. *The Revolution of American Conservatism: The Federalist Party in the Era of Jeffersonian Democracy.* New York: Harper and Row, 1965.

Ganoe, William A. *The History of the United States Army.* Rev. ed. New York: D. Appleton-Century, 1943.

Genovese, Eugene D. *The Political Economy of Slavery: Studies in the Economy and Society of the Slave South.* New York: Vantage Books, 1967.

Gray, Lewis C., and Thompson, Esther Katherine. *History of Agriculture in the Southern United States to 1860.* 2 vols. New York: P. Smith, 1941.

Green, Constance McLaughlin. *Washington.* Vol. 1: *Village and Capital, 1800–1878.* Princeton: Princeton University Press, 1962.

Green, Raleigh Travers. *Genealogical and Historical Notes on Culpeper County, Virginia, Embracing a Revised and Enlarged Edition of Dr. Phillip Slaughter's History of St. Mark's Parish.* Culpeper, Va., 1900.

Gwathmey, John H. *Historical Register of Virginians in the Revolution; Soldiers, Sailors, Marines, 1775–1783.* Richmond: Dietz Press, 1938.

Hammond, Bray. *Banks and Politics in America from the Revolution to the Civil War.* Princeton: Princeton University Press, 1957.

Hofstadter, Richard. *The American Political Tradition and the Men Who Made It.* New York: A. A. Knopf, 1948.

Horseman, Reginald. *The Causes of the War of 1812.* Philadelphia: University of Pennsylvania Press, 1962.

Howe, Daniel W. *The Political Culture of the American Whigs.* Chicago: University of Chicago Press, 1979.

Hulbert, Archer B. *The Cumberland Road.* Cleveland: A. H. Clark, 1904.

Ingersoll, L. D. *A History of the War Department of the United States, with Biographical Sketches of the Secretaries.* Washington, D.C.: F. B. Mohun, 1879.

Jordan, Winthrop D. *White over Black: American Attitudes toward the Negro, 1550–1812.* Chapel Hill: University of North Carolina Press, 1968.

Koch, Adrienne. *Jefferson and Madison: The Great Collaboration.* New York: A. A. Knopf, 1950.

Kohn, Hans. *American Nationalism.* New York: Macmillan, 1957.

Lancaster, Robert A., Jr. *Historic Virginia Homes and Churches.* Philadelphia: J. B. Lippincott, 1915.

Little, John P. *Richmond, the Capital of Virginia: Its History.* Richmond: Macfarland and Fergusson, 1851.

Livermore, Shaw, Jr. *The Twilight of Federalism: The Disintegration of the Federalist Party, 1815–1830.* Princeton: University Press, 1962.

McColley, Robert. *Slavery and Jeffersonian Virginia.* Urbana: University of Illinois Press, 1964.

McKee, Thomas H. *National Conventions and Platforms of All Political Parties, 1789–1905: Convention, Popular and Electoral Vote.* 6th ed. Baltimore: Friedenwald, 1906.

Mahan, Alfred T. *Sea Power in Its Relation to the War of 1812.* 2 vols. Boston: Little, Brown, 1905.

Main, Jackson Turner. *The Antifederalists: Critics of the Constitution.* Chapel Hill: University of North Carolina Press, 1961.

McCoy, Drew R. *The Elusive Republic: Political Economy in Jeffersonian America.* Chapel Hill: University of North Carolina Press, 1980.

Mead, Edward C. *Historic Homes of the South-West Mountains of Virginia.* Philadelphia: J. B. Lippincott, 1899.

Meade, Bishop William. *Old Churches, Ministers, and Families of Virginia.* 2 vols. Philadelphia: J. B. Lippincott, 1872.

Meyers, Marvin. *The Jacksonian Persuasion: Politics and Belief.* New York: Vintage Books, 1960.

Miller, John C. *Crisis in Freedom: The Alien and Sedition Acts.* Boston: Little, Brown, 1951.

Moore, Glover. *The Missouri Controversy, 1819–1821.* Lexington: University of Kentucky Press, 1953.

Moore, Joseph West. *Picturesque Washington; Pen and Pencil Sketches . . .* Providence: J. A. and R. A. Reid, 1884.

Mordecai, Samuel. *Virginia, Especially Richmond, in By-Gone Days; With a Glance at the Present; Being Reminiscences and Last Words of an Old Citizen.* Richmond: West and Johnson, 1860.

Morrison, Alfred J. *The Beginnings of Public Education in Virginia, 1776–1860: A Study of Secondary Schools in Relation to the State Literary Fund.* Richmond: D. Bottom, Superintendent of Public Printing, 1917.

Oakes, James. *The Ruling Race: A History of American Slaveholders.* New York: A. A. Knopf, 1982.

Porter, Albert O. *County Government in Virginia: A Legislative History, 1607–1904.* New York: Columbia University Press, 1947.

Proctor, John C., ed. *Washington, Past and Present.* 4 vols. New York: Lewis Historical Publishing, 1930.

Prucha, Francis Paul. *American Indian Policy in the Formative Years: The Indian Trade and Intercourse Acts, 1780–1834.* Cambridge, Mass.: Harvard University Press, 1962.

Randolph, J. W., comp. *History of William and Mary College.* Richmond: J. W. Randolph, 1874.

Remini, Robert V. *The Election of Andrew Jackson.* Philadelphia: J. B. Lippincott, 1963.

Reniers, Perceval. *The Springs of Virginia: Life, Love, and Death at the Waters, 1775–1900.* Chapel Hill: University of North Carolina Press, 1941.

Risjord, Norman K. *Chesapeake Politics, 1781–1800.* New York: Columbia University Press, 1978.

————. *The Old Republicans: Southern Conservatism in the Age of Jefferson.* New York: Columbia University Press, 1965.

Robert, Joseph C. *The Tobacco Kingdom; Plantation, Market, and Factory in Virginia and North Carolina, 1800–1860.* Durham: Duke University Press, 1938.

Robertson, David. *Reports of the Trial of Colonel Aaron Burr for Treason and for a Misdemeanor.* 2 vols. Philadelphia, 1808.

Rothbard, Murray N. *The Panic of 1819: Reactions and Policies.* New York: Columbia University Press, 1962.

Schlesinger, Arthur M., Jr. *The Age of Jackson.* Boston: Little, Brown, 1945.

Scott, W. W. *A History of Orange County, Virginia.* Richmond: E. Waddey, 1907.

Sheehan, Bernard W. *Seeds of Extinction: Jeffersonian Philanthropy and the American Indian.* Chapel Hill: University of North Carolina Press, 1973.

Simms, Henry H. *The Rise of the Whigs in Virginia, 1824–1840.* Richmond: William Byrd Press, 1929.

Slaughter, Philip. *A History of St. Mark's Parish, Culpeper County, Virginia.* Baltimore: Innes, 1877.

Smelser, Marshall. *The Democratic Republic, 1801–1815.* New York: Harper and Row, 1968.

Smith, James Morton. *Freedom's Fetters: The Alien and Sedition Laws and American Civil Liberties.* Ithaca: Cornell University Press, 1956.

Smith, Margaret Vowell. *Virginia, 1492–1892 . . . with a History of the Executives of the Colony and the Commonwealth of Virginia.* Washington, D.C.: W. H. Lowdermilk, 1893.

Stanard, Mary Newton. *Richmond: Its People and Its Story.* Philadelphia: J. B. Lippincott, 1923.

Stanwood, Edward. *American Tariff Controversies in the Nineteenth Century.* 2 vols. Boston: Houghton Mifflin, 1903.

———. *A History of the Presidency, 1788–1916.* 2 vols. Boston: Houghton Mifflin, 1928.

Starnes, George T. *Sixty Years of Branch Banking in Virginia.* New York: Macmillan, 1931.

Strickland, William. *Observations on the Agriculture of the United States of America.* London: W. Bulmer, 1801.

Sydnor, Charles S. *American Revolutionaries in the Making: Political Practices in Washington's Virginia.* New York: Collier Books, 1962.

———. *The Development of Southern Sectionalism, 1819–1848.* Baton Rouge: Louisiana State University Press, 1948.

Taussig, Frank W. *The Tariff History of the United States.* New York: Putnam, 1892.

Tyler, Lyon Gardiner. *History of Virginia.* 6 vols. Chicago: American Historical Society, 1924.

Warren, Charles. *A History of the American Bar.* Boston: Little, Brown, 1911.

Weigley, Russell F. *History of the United States Army.* New York: Macmillan, 1967.

White, Leonard D. *The Jeffersonians: A Study in Administrative History, 1801–1829.* New York: Macmillan, 1951.

Williamson, Chilton. *American Suffrage from Property to Democracy, 1760–1860.* Princeton: Princeton University Press, 1960.

Williston, E. B. *Eloquence of the United States.* 5 vols. Middletown, Conn.: E. and H. Clark, 1827.

Willson, Beckles. *America's Ambassadors to England (1785–1929): A Narrative of Anglo-American Diplomatic Relations.* New York: Frederick A. Stokes, 1929.

Wiltse, Charles Maurice. *The Jeffersonian Tradition in American Democracy.* Chapel Hill: University of North Carolina Press, 1935.

Wise, Jennings C. *The Red Man in the New World Drama: A Politico-Legal Study with a Pageantry of American Indian History.* Edited and revised by Vine Deloria, Jr. New York: Macmillan, 1971.

Woods, Edgar. *Albemarle County in Virginia* . . . Charlottesville: Michie, 1901.

Young, James Sterling. *The Washington Community, 1800–1828.* New York: Columbia University Press, 1966.

Zimmerman, James Fulton. *Impressment of American Seamen.* Columbia University Studies in History, Economics, and Public Law, 262. New York: Columbia University Press, 1925.

c. Articles

Able, Annie H. "The History of Events Resulting in Indian Consolidation West of the Mississippi River." In American Historical Association, *Annual Report for the Year 1906,* 1:233–450. Washington, D.C., 1907.

Ames, Herman V. "The Proposed Amendments to the Constitution of the United States During the First Century of its History." In American Historical Association, *Annual Report for the Year 1896,* 2:395–418. Washington, D.C., 1897.

Ammon, Harry. "Executive Leadership in the Monroe Administration." In *America: The Middle Period; Essays in Honor of Bernard Mayo,* edited by John B. Boles. Charlottesville: University Press of Virginia, 1973.

———. "The Formation of the Republican Party in Virginia, 1789–1796." *Journal of Southern History,* 19 (Aug. 1953):283–310.

———. "James Monroe and the Election of 1808 in Virginia." *WMQ,* 3rd ser., 20 (Jan. 1963):33–56.

———. "James Monroe and the Era of Good Feelings." *VMHB,* 66 (Oct. 1958):387–98.

———. "The Jeffersonian Republicans in Virginia: An Interpretation." *VMHB,* 71 (April 1963):153–67.

———. "The Richmond Junto, 1800–1824." *VMHB,* 61 (Oct. 1953):395–418.

Anderson, Frank Maloy. "Contemporary Opinion of the Virginia and Kentucky Resolutions." *American Historical Review,* 5 (Oct. 1899):45–63; and 5 (Jan. 1900):225–52.

Beach, Rex. "Spencer Roane and the Richmond Party." *WMQ,* 2nd ser., 22 (Jan. 1942):1–17.

Betty, George M. "William Branch Giles." *John P. Branch Papers of Randolph-Macon College,* 3 (June 1911):173–98.

Broussard, James H. "Party and Partisanship in American Legislatures: The South Atlantic States, 1800–1812." *Journal of Southern History,* 43 (Feb. 1977):39–58.

Brown, Everett S. "The Presidential Election of 1824–1825." *Political Science Quarterly,* 40 (Sept. 1925):384–403.

Brown, Ralph M. "Agricultural Science and Education in Virginia before 1860." *WMQ,* 2nd ser., 19 (April 1939):197–213.

Bruce, Kathleen. "Virginia Agricultural Decline to 1860: A Fallacy." *Agricultural History,* 6 (Jan. 1932):3–13.

Burnette, Lawrence, Jr. "Peter V. Daniel: Agrarian Justice." *VMHB,* 62 (Oct. 1954):290–305.

Carroll, Eber M. "Politics during the Administration of John Quincy Adams." *South Atlantic Quarterly,* 23 (April 1924):141–54.

Coleman, Charles Washington. "The County Committees of 1774–1775 in Virginia." *WMQ,* 1st ser., 5 (April 1897):245–53.

Craven, Avery. "John Taylor and Southern Agriculture." *Journal of Southern History,* 4 (May 1938):137–47.

Cunningham, Nobel E., Jr. "Who Were the Quids?" *Mississippi Valley Historical Review,* 50 (Sept. 1963):252–63.

Cynn, P. P. "Philip Pendleton Barbour." *John P. Branch Historical Papers of Randolph-Macon College,* 4 (June 1913):67–77.

Dodd, William E. "John Taylor of Caroline, Prophet of Secession." *John P. Branch Historical Papers of Randolph-Macon College,* 2 (June 1908):214–52.

Drell, Bernard. "John Taylor and the Preservation of an Old Social Order." *VMHB,* 46 (Oct. 1938):285–98.

Eaton, Clement. "Southern Senators and the Right of Instruction, 1798–1860." *Journal of Southern History,* 18 (Aug. 1952):309–19.

Fehrenbacher, Don E. "The Missouri Controversy and the Sources of Southern Separatism." *Southern Review,* 14 (Oct. 1978):653–67.

Fenstermaker, J. Van. "The Statistics of American Commercial Banking, 1782–1818." *Journal of Economic History,* 25 (Sept. 1965):400–13.

Fogel, Robert W., and Engerman, Stanley L. "Explaining the Relative Efficiency of Slave Agriculture in the Antebellum South." *American Economic Review,* 67 (June 1977):275–96.

Gaines, Edwin M. "The Chesapeake Affair: Virginians Mobilize to Defend the National Honor." *VMHB,* 64 (April 1956):131–42.

Gammon, Samuel Rhea, Jr. "The Presidential Campaign of 1832." *Johns Hopkins University Studies in Historical and Political Science,* 40 (1922):11–174.

Good, H. G. "Early Attempts to Teach Agriculture in Old Virginia." *VMHB,* 48 (Oct. 1940):341–51.

Goodrich, Carter. "The Virginia System of Mixed Enterprise: A Study of State Planning of Internal Improvements." *Political Science Quarterly,* 64 (Sept. 1949):355–87.

Govan, Thomas P. "Was Plantation Slavery Profitable?" *Journal of Southern History,* 8 (Nov. 1942):511–35.

Greene, Jack P. "Foundations of Political Power in the Virginia House of Burgesses, 1720–1776." *WMQ,* 3rd ser., 16 (Oct. 1959):485–506.

Grinnan, Bessie. "A Sketch of Colonial Orange, 1734–1776." *Tyler's Quarterly Historical and Genealogical Magazine,* 4 (1923):109–14.

Harrison, Joseph H., Jr. "Martin Van Buren and His Southern Supporters." *Journal of Southern History,* 22 (Nov. 1956):438–58.

———. "Oligarchs and Democrats—The Richmond Junto." *VMHB,* 78 (April 1970):184–98.

Heatwole, C. J. "Origin and Sacredness of the Literary Fund." *Virginia Journal of Education,* 23 (April 1930):329–31.

Hodges, Wiley E. "Pro-Governmentalism in Virginia, 1789–1836: A Pragmatic Liberal Pattern in the Political Heritage." *Journal of Politics,* 25 (May 1963):333–60.

Koch, Adrienne, and Ammon, Harry. "The Virginia and Kentucky Resolutions: An Episode in Jefferson's and Madison's Defense of Civil Liberties." *WMQ,* 3d ser., 5 (April 1948):145–76.

Long, William S. "James Barbour." *John P. Branch Historical Papers of Randolph-Macon College,* 4 (June 1914):3–34.

Low, W. A. "The Farmer in Post-Revolutionary Virginia, 1783–1789." *Agricultural History,* 25 (July 1951):122–27.

Lowery, Charles D. "James Barbour, A Progressive Farmer of Antebellum Virginia." In *America: The Middle Period; Essays in Honor of Bernard Mayo,* edited by John B. Boles. Charlottesville: University Press of Virginia, 1973.

Main, Jackson Turner. "The Distribution of Property in Post-Revolutionary Virginia." *Mississippi Valley Historical Review,* 41 (Sept. 1954):241–58.

———. "The One Hundred." *WMQ,* 3d ser., 11 (July 1954):354–84.

———. "Sections and Politics in Virginia, 1781–1787." *WMQ,* 3d ser., 12 (Jan. 1955):96–112.

Malone, Dumas. "Presidential Leadership and National Unity: The Jefferson Example." *Journal of Southern History,* 35 (Feb. 1969):3–17.

Morgan, William G. "The Congressional Nominating Caucus of 1816: The Struggle against the Virginia Dynasty." *VMHB,* 80 (Oct. 1972):461–75.

Morrison, Alfred J. "Notes on the Organization of Virginia Agriculture." *WMQ,* 1st ser., 26 (July 1917):169–73.

Nagel, Paul C. "The Election of 1824: A Reconsideration Based on Newspaper Opinion." *Journal of Southern History,* 26 (Aug. 1960):315–29.

Pancake, John S. "The Invisibles: A Chapter in the Opposition to President Madison." *Journal of Southern History,* 21 (Feb. 1955):17–37.

Parsons, Lynn Hudson. "'A Perpetual Harrow Upon My Feelings': John Quincy Adams and the American Indian." *New England Quarterly,* 46 (Sept. 1973):339–79.

"Party Violence, 1790–1800." *VMHB,* 19 (April 1921):171–79.

Phillips, Ulrich B. "Georgia and State Rights." In American Historical Association, *Annual Report for the Year 1901,* 2:3–224. Washington, D.C., 1902.

Pole, J. R. "Representation and Authority in Virginia from the Revolution to Reform." *Journal of Southern History,* 24 (Feb. 1958):16–50.

Preyer, Norris W. "Southern Support of the Tariff of 1816—A Reappraisal." *Journal of Southern History,* 25 (Aug. 1959):306–22.

Prufer, Julius F. "The Franchise in Virginia from Jefferson through the Convention of 1829." *WMQ,* 2d ser., 7 (Oct. 1927):255–70.

Remini, Robert V. "New York and the Presidential Election of 1816." *New York History,* 31 (Sept. 1950):308–23.

Reznack, Samuel. "The Depression of 1819–1822: A Social History." *American Historical Review* 39 (Oct. 1933):28–47.

Risjord, Norman K. "1812: Conservatives, War Hawks, and the Nation's Honor." *WMQ,* 3d ser., 18 (April 1961):196–210.

———. "How the 'Common Man' Voted in Jefferson's Virginia." In *America: The Middle Period; Essays in Honor of Bernard Mayo,* edited by John B. Boles. Charlottesville: University Press of Virginia, 1973.

———. "The Virginia Federalists." *Journal of Southern History,* 34 (Nov. 1967):486–517.

———. "Virginians and the Constitution: A Multivariate Analysis." *WMQ,* 3d ser., 31 (Oct. 1974):613–32.

Roberts, Joseph C. "William Wirt, Virginian." *VMHB,* 80 (Oct. 1972):387–441.

Sellers, Charles G., Jr. "Who Were the Southern Whigs?" *American Historical Review,* 59 (Jan. 1954):335–46.

Smith, Carlton B. "John C. Calhoun, Secretary of War, 1817–1825: The Cast-Iron Man as an Administrator." In *America: The Middle Period; Essays in Honor of Bernard Mayo,* edited by John B. Boles. Charlottesville: University Press of Virginia, 1973.

Smith, Edwin James. "Benjamin Watkins Leigh." *John P. Branch Historical Papers of Randolph-Macon College,* 4 (June 1904):286–98.

———. "Spencer Roane." *John P. Branch Historical Papers of Randolph-Macon College,* 2 (June 1905):4–33.

Sutton, Robert P. "Nostalgia, Pessimism, and Malaise: The Doomed Aristocrat in Late-Jeffersonian Virginia." *VMHB,* 76 (Jan. 1968):41–55.

Torrence, Clayton. "War's Wild Alarm." *VMHB,* 49 (July 1941):217–27.

True, Rodney H. "Early Days of the Albemarle Agricultural Society." In American Historical Association, *Annual Report for the Year 1918,* 1:243–59. Washington, D.C., 1921.

———. "The Virginia Board of Agriculture, 1841–1843." *Agricultural History,* 14 (July 1940):97–103.

Turlington, S. Baily. "Richmond during the War of 1812: The Vigilance Committee." *VMHB,* 7 (Jan. 1900):225–41, 406–18.

Turner, Charles W. "Virginia Agricultural Reform, 1815–1860." *Agricultural History,* 26 (July 1952):80–89.

———. "Virginia State Agricultural Societies, 1811–1860." *Agricultural History,* 38 (July 1964):167–77.

Upton, Anthony F. "The Road to Power in Virginia in the Early Nineteenth Century." *VMHB,* 62 (July 1954):259–80.

Van Deusen, Glyndon G. "Some Aspects of Whig Thought and Theory in the Jacksonian Period." *American Historical Review,* 63 (Jan. 1958):305–22.

Wehje, Myron F. "Opposition in Virginia to the War of 1812." *VMHB,* 78 (Jan. 1970):65–86.

d. Theses and Dissertations

Ammon, Harry. "The Republican Party in Virginia, 1789–1824." Ph.D. diss., University of Virginia, 1948.

Andrews, Archie D. "Agriculture in Virginia, 1789–1820." M.A. thesis, University of Virginia, 1950.

Beach, Rex. "Judge Spencer Roane: A Champion of States Rights." M.A. thesis, University of Virginia, 1941.

Coyner, M. Boyd, Jr. "John Hartwell Cocke of Bremo: Agriculture and Slavery in the Ante-Bellum South." Ph.D. diss., University of Virginia, 1961.

Dingledine, Raymond C. "The Political Career of William Cabell Rives." Ph.D. diss., University of Virginia, 1947.

Egerton, Cecil B. "Rufus King and the Missouri Question: A Study in Political Mythology." Ph.D. diss., Claremont Graduate School, 1967.

Harrison, Joseph H., Jr. "The Internal Improvements Issue in the Politics of the Union, 1783–1825." Ph.D. diss., University of Virginia, 1954.

Hickin, Patricia P. "Antislavery in Virginia, 1831–1861." 3 vols. Ph.D. diss., University of Virginia, 1968.

Hutton, Hamilton M. "Southern Nationalism, 1790–1817." M.A. thesis, University of Virginia, 1940.

Jordan, Daniel P., Jr. "Virginia Congressmen, 1801–1825." Ph.D. diss., University of Virginia, 1970.

Nielson, George R. "The Indispensable Institution: The Congressional Party during the Era of Good Feelings." Ph.D. diss., University of Iowa, 1968.

Preyer, Norris W. "The South's Experiment with Protective Tariffs, 1816–1820." Ph.D. diss., University of Virginia, 1954.

Rice, Philip M. "Internal Improvements in Virginia, 1775–1860." Ph.D. diss., University of North Carolina, 1950.

Risjord, Norman Kurt. "The Old Republicans: Southern Conservatives in Congress, 1806–1824." Ph.D. diss., University of Virginia, 1960.

Rosenthal, Herbert Hillel. "James Barbour, Virginia Politician, 1775–1842." M. A. thesis, University of Virginia, 1942.

Russo, David L. "The Southern Republicans and American Political Nationalism, 1815–1825." Ph.D. diss., Yale University, 1966.

Sutton, Robert P. "The Virginia Constitutional Convention of 1829–30: A Profile Analysis of Late-Jeffersonian Virginia." Ph.D. diss., University of Virginia, 1967.

Tanner, Carol. "Joseph C. Cabell, 1778–1856." Ph.D. diss., University of Virginia, 1948.

Index

Wood, James, 67
Wythe, George, 35

XYZ Affair, 18, 21

Yancey, Charles, 119–21
Young, Arthur, 200, 203